THE KOSOVA LIBERATION ARMY

JAMES PETTIFER

The Kosova Liberation Army

Underground War to Balkan Insurgency, 1948–2001

HURST & COMPANY, LONDON

First published in the United Kingdom in 2013 by
C. Hurst & Co. (Publishers) Ltd.,
41 Great Russell Street, London, WC1B 3PL
© James Pettifer, 2013
All rights reserved.
Printed in India

Distributed in the United States, Canada and Latin America by
Oxford University Press, 198 Madison Avenue, New York, NY 10016,
United States of America.

The right of James Pettifer to be identified as the author of this publication is
asserted by him in accordance with the Copyright, Designs and Patents Act,
1988.

A Cataloguing-in-Publication data record for this book is available from the
British Library.

ISBN: 9781849043748

References to Internet Web sites (URLs) were accurate at the time of writing.
Neither the author nor Hurst is responsible for URLs that may have expired
or changed since the manuscript was prepared.

www.hurstpublishers.com

This book is printed using paper from registered sustainable
and managed sources.

The author and publisher thank the following for the use of their photographs
the front cover photograph, and numbers 6 and 7 (Hilmi Asllani), 12 and 13
(Miranda Vickers), and 15 and 16 (Arben Lllalla). Every effort has been made
to trace copyright holders of all photographs, in the event of query contact
michael@hurstpub.co.uk.

For Averil

CONTENTS

Foreword to the Paperback Edition   ix
Maps   xi
Acknowledgements   xv

Introduction   1

 1. The Origins of a Guerrilla Army   11
 2. The Underground War 1950–1990   31
 3. A New Force in a New Balkans 1990–1995   59
 4. Preparation for Battle: A Handgun Army?   81
 5. Autumn 1997: The War is Defined   101
 6. A Liberated Drenica and Milosevic's First Offensive   119
 7. Summer 1998: Golgotha Avoided   143
 8. The Gathering Storm: Autumn 1998   165
 9. Racak to Rambouillet: January–March 1999   185
10. Alliance with NATO and Demobilisation of the KLA   205
11. Preshevo and the Macedonian Sequel 2000–2001   225
12. Epilogue   247

Illustrations   255
Appendix A: Military Organisation in Wartime Kosova,
            March-May 1999   257
Appendix B: Kosova People's Movement (LPK) and Popular
            Front For a Kosova Republic (LPRK)—Chrono-
            logy and Development   261
Appendix C: The Programme of the People's Movement for the
            Republic of Kosova (LPRK)   265

vii

CONTENTS

Appendix D: The Programme of the Kosova Liberation Army
             (KLA)   277
Appendix E: Undertaking of Demilitarisation and
             Transformation of the KLA: 20 June 1999   279

Notes   287
Bibliography   343
Abbreviations and Spelling Conventions   361
Acronyms   363
Index   365

FOREWORD TO THE PAPERBACK EDITION

Since the first edition of this book appeared in summer 2012 there
have been some significant developments in the historiography of the
ex-Yugoslav Wars. The Kosova conflict has been no exception, with
the appearance of further Kosova Albanian personal memoirs of the
period after 1991, and there has also been progress in archive access
and publication in Belgrade and elsewhere. Interest in the role of different Balkan Diasporas and their political and cultural role in the
region has increased. In contemporary politics, debate has continued
about the evolution of the national relationship with Serbia and the
development of relations with Belgrade. There has been public discussion about the possible evolution of the Kosova Security Force into an
army within the NATO framework but at the time of writing it is
unclear what the exact outcome will be. The opening of the new
motorway between Tirana and Prishtina has been a landmark in
regional communications and is likely to have a significant effect on
the future Albania-Kosova relationship.

In terms of regional history in the period covered in this book,
important papers relating to international relations during the Cold
War were presented at the conference organised in November 2012 on
the 100th Anniversary of Albanian Independence by the Institute of
History in Tirana. New work has been published in Russia by Dr
Artyom Ulunyan, in which he has been able to demonstrate on the
basis of newly released documents in Tirana and Moscow and the
memoirs of ex-Minister of Defence Veli Lakaj that the Albanian leadership made plans after 1977 to invade and secure Kosova if the

opportunity presented itself after Tito's death.[1] This new evidence of Enver Hoxha's intentions bears out the general arguments I have made about Albania-Kosova relations in the Cold War period. I have benefited from detailed study of some of the papers presented at the St John's College, Oxford workshop on 'Conspiracy Theories and Histories', organised by my Oxford colleagues Professors Nicholas Purcell and Ritchie Robertson.

I am grateful to correspondents who have explored a number of issues with me since the first edition of this book appeared; a few editorial changes have been made to reflect points made, and minor errors corrected. Insights provided by my translator in Tirana, Aferdita Cesula, and my publisher Bujar Hudri of ONUFRI have been very helpful, particularly on the always complex and debateable issue of the spelling of Albanian and Kosova topographic and personal names.

James Pettifer
St Cross College, Oxford, 2013

LIST OF MAPS

Southern Balkans   xii
Kosova   xiii
Map of KLA Operational Sub-Zones   164

Southern Balkans

Kosova

ACKNOWLEDGEMENTS

I am grateful to the many participants in the war at all levels in Kosova, Serbia, Macedonia and Albania both civilians and soldiers, who have been kind enough to share their recollections with me. I am particularly grateful to Ramush Haradinaj who took me on a tour of Dukagjini battle sites, General Sir Mike Jackson and John Crosland CBE MC for very useful discussions in the United Kingdom, and in Prishtina and Tirana, Valon Murati, Adem Demaci, Xhevdet Shehu and General Agim Ceku. I am also very grateful to many civilians of all ethnic groups who were resident in the conflict zone for part or all of the war for spending time with me discussing the events.

The first seed for this book was planted by the current Kosova Prime Minister Hashim Thaci who tried unsuccessfully some years ago to persuade me to write a biography of the KLA's founding father Adem Jashari. On reflection, this did not seem to be the right way to write the history of the war, but I am nonetheless very grateful for all his time and perceptive advice on this project over the years since we first met. I hope he will feel that the unique contribution of the fighters of the Jashari family to the independence of Kosova has been properly represented.

I have also benefited from reading numerous books of war memoirs by Albanian and Serbian participants, and if I disagree with the content or analysis of a particular work I have nevertheless found study of them very useful and illuminating. In the climate of free publication in Kosova after 1999, many local studies have appeared that include useful material from the post-Tito and wartime periods. The trend towards local studies is also noticeable in the recent historiography of the Greek Civil War. On the Serbian side, I have endeavoured to consult and study as much material, official and unofficial, as has been available, but it should be noted that contemporary history has not been an easy field in the last generation in Belgrade, and this still remains the case after the overthrow of the Milosevic regime. Many of the Serbian accounts of the war and associated matters rest on a denial of many basic realities and contain in my opinion numerous profound errors of fact and interpretation. They will, I hope, soon be superseded by honest personal memoirs based on subjective experience and then sustained professional historical writing. I have in general endeavoured to keep the scholarly apparatus in this book to a functional minimum in order to provide a readable and sustained narrative for the under-graduate and general reader outside the Balkans.

The records of war crimes trials at the ICTY at The Hague have been of importance in establishing a generally agreed chronological sequence of many hitherto controversial events, and I have used them extensively, particularly those from the trial of KLA leader Fatmir Limaj. They do, though—at least in the view expressed in the memoirs of the former ICTY Prosecutor Carla del Ponte—claim an overarching historical authority as a dominant narrative that they do not deserve. They need to be used with care. Most of the ICTY material is focused on the war in Drenica and in my view underestimates or does not even mention many seminal events involving the KLA/VJ conflict else-where.[1] The role of the JNA/VJ in the ICTY Kosova material is often little more than a whitewash depending on ill-understood history.

Local court records from the Yugoslav period in Prishtina have been very helpful and all students of the period are indebted to the diligent labour of Ethem Ceku and Sabile Kecmezi-Basha in making them available in their extensive recent publications of Yugoslav court and secret police archive material and studies of illegal Albanian political and military organisations, and the underground press under Titoism.[2] I am grateful to ex-colleagues at the Defence Academy of the United Kingdom for ideas on some issues, and also helpful staff members in the State Department and Department of Defence in Washington, and most of all the National Intelligence College at USAF Bolling, particu-larly Joe Gordon and Nathan. G. Bein. While working at Princeton University in 2007 I was able to talk to several American-based former participants in the KLA, and like all other students of the war I have learned a great deal from Uk Lushi and Stacey Sullivan's work on the KLA in the United States, Joe Dioguardi and Shirley Cloyes on the

Albanian-American Civic League, and also Riza Sadiku's scholarly (if controversial) writings.[3]

I was fortunate to meet Gani Perolli[4] and Zijadin Qira[5] in New Jersey before the latter's death in 2002. Zijadin was a central figure from the older generation and a sure guide to the complex world of Albanian underground military activity in Kosova in the 1950s.[6] John Phillip's work on the NLA in the 2001 Macedonian conflict has been similarly helpful. The Albanian Diaspora in Switzerland has a unique fund of experience of underground organisation and military fund raising, particularly in Zurich, and many people there have been generous with their time and materials. In particular I am grateful to Professor Nada Boskovska for comment on teaching Hashim Thaci as a Zurich University history student, and for the use of the superb library and facilities at Zurich University, and also the Swiss Federal Institute of Technology (ETH) in that city. I am also indebted to friends and colleagues in Tetovo, particularly Dr Nuri Bexheti in the State University, and Arben Xhaferi, Sadi Bexheti, Vaughan Smith, Tim Judah, Annalisa Rellie, Menduh Thaci and Arsim and Arlindja Sinani, and the library of the School of Slavonic and East European Studies in London. In Prishtina I am grateful to the owners and staff of the Dukagjini organisation, particularly Violetta Bytyci and Murteza Kada, and Hilmi Asllani. I also thank Basil and Steffi Kondis in Thessaloniki and Elias Skoulidas in Ioannina.

I thank Konrad Clewing and colleagues at the Südost Institute in Regensburg for opportunities to explore some of the ideas in this book, also colleagues in Oxford University History faculty, and Bato Tomasovic and His Excellency Igor Jovovic for assistance with documentation from Serbia and Montenegro, Mark Smith for translation from Russian documents, and John Puntis for help with material from Bill Bland's library in Leeds. In Moscow the late Dr Nina Smirnovna was a fund of useful information and research leads.

Bob Churcher, Denny Lane, Shaun Byrnes, Averil Cameron and Miranda Vickers have been ever generous, as was our friend, comrade and mentor the late former Second World War Partisan British Liaison Officer Sir Reginald Hibbert. He was happily able to live long enough to witness the final collapse of Yugoslav rule in Kosova and to visit Prishtina in November 1999 before his death.

James Pettifer, Oxford-Prishtina 2013

'To establish regular secret contact with anyone you please, without ever meeting face to face, you only need set up a chain of regular intermediaries— at least two, but preferably three. Your immediate contact habitually meets twenty people beside yourself, only one of whom is the next link in the chain, and each of these meets twenty others. This gives four hundred possible combinations, and no secret police, no Burtsev, can ever investigate all of them. The ultra-cautious Lenin had several such lines of communication.'

Alexander Solzhenitsyn, *Lenin in Zurich*

INTRODUCTION

Another cause and this is a very powerful one, that makes men conspire against a prince, is the desire to liberate the fatherland of which a prince has seized possession.

Machiavelli, On Conspiracies.[1]

In my earlier books, *Kosova Express* and *The Albanian Question—Reshaping the Balkans* (with Miranda Vickers), I set out the development of the Kosova conflict as it took place after 1990.[2] At that time I envisaged a third volume on the specifically military aspects of the recent war. *Kosova Express* gave a subjective account of the roots of the conflict as I saw it beginning to develop in Kosova after 1991. *The Albanian Question—Reshaping the Balkans* was designed to explore the history of the conflict from the viewpoint of Albania and was developed mainly from local primary source material.

Serbs mostly saw the Kosova Liberation Army as a conspiracy against their country. The question is bound to arise of whether this book is in a certain sense an account of a secretive political conspiracy, as opposed to mainstream historiography, which sees the Kosovan Albanian struggle as an enterprise founded on human rights and the Helsinki Final Act provisions for national self-determination. It is thus in a certain sense a 'parallel structure' in relation to my previous volumes, in the same way as the ancient historian Procopius wrote his 'open' *History of the Wars* as a companion volume to read alongside his *Secret History*.[3] All Kosovan political and military actors, both Serb and Albanian, have been famed for their capacity to work in the 'underground' through secondary structures outside the open state machinery, and this model seemed appropriate.

This is not a recondite academic issue, with its roots in very distant ancient history, as it might first appear to be. Contemporary rulers, Yugoslav or otherwise, easily see conspiracies against them, as Roman emperors did. Contemporary rulers run secret conspiracies themselves, as Richard Nixon did with Watergate. The concept of secret conspiracy is increasingly important in the legal framework for the 'War against Terror', particularly in the United States, and in the new concept of a 'joint criminal enterprise' in politics that is popular at the International Criminal Tribunal at The Hague. Some current popular historical writing about recent wars uses the model of the 'secret history', e.g. Nigel West's *The Secret War for the Falklands*.[4] There is a long tradition in the historiography of the Balkans of works that claim to expose the 'closed' workings of politics, such as Charles Vopicka's *Secrets of the Balkans* (1921) and Sir Reginald Rankin's *The Inner History of the Balkan Wars* (1931). The secret world of the unconscious irrational Balkans is counterpoised to the open and rational world of 'Europe'.

In Donna Tartt's bestselling novel, *The Secret History*, a character observes that history is 'like a long bad dream'.[5] That is how most Kosova Albanian history appears to most Serbs, just as the dangerous gunmen of the Internal Macedonian Revolutionary Organisation (IMRO) seemed an unending nightmare to the previous Serbian generations in the 1920s and 1930s. In many ways Albanian insurgency after 1944 replaced the Macedonian threat of the previous fifty years in the Belgrade political mindset. Serbs, consciously or not, in their thoughts about the Kosova war, have often adopted Orientalist strains of thought where the Kosova Albanian Other is seen emerging from a world of 'background' foreign and secret intrigue, usually financed by criminals, such as Kosova drug barons.[6] In this sense, all responsibly written history is dangerous to undemocratic rulers. This issue has existed for a long time. As Tobias Hill has written of a period long before the times of Livy or Sallust (or Hashim Thaci, or Slobodan Milosevic),

It has been said that history is only written by the victors. The truism is false in this case. The Spartans were once masters of all they surveyed, prevailing over Greece through fear and war, yet did not trust their prevalence to writing. The written word is unselfish. It gives up its secrets readily; it speaks to friend and foe alike. For this reason the Spartans entrusted few things to its care. They were a secretive people.[7]

In the twentieth century in Yugoslavia similar speculations had a fertile climate in which to develop. The Serbs, a small minority, ruled Kosova as the Spartans ruled the vast mass of Messenian helots, largely by military power and their *Krypteia*, the UDBA, the secret police. The helots could never have a history. If they had had a rational, public written history it would have been dangerous to their rulers. As Aaronovitch has shown, conspiracy theories thrive in an intellectual climate where real history is absent.[9] Albanian history is so little known outside the Balkans that Albanian historiography of whatever kind has something of the quality of the unknown for most readers. A 'secret' history is often understood to mean the revelation of a conspiracy, in both ancient and modern historical writing, as a book like Kim Philby's *My Secret War* indicates.[10] Most Serbs had very little real knowledge of Kosova before the war started and fell back upon conspiracy theories to explain what for many of them was an incomprehensible and disturbing event. Equally, before the conflict, most Kosova Albanians knew little about the Kosova Liberation Army and its origins. Many of the memoirs published in the last five years by ex-KLA commanders certainly fall into the category of 'secret histories' as they attempt to explain the closed inner workings of a banned underground military organisation that was often dominated by myth and misinformation when it existed.[11] It is also relevant that the first popular history of the war to appear in English, Henry Perritt's *Kosovo Liberation Army: The Inside Story of an Insurgency*, certainly uses the 'exposure of a conspiracy format' in a Sallustian sense.[12]

All insurgencies are in a sense secret wars, at least in the eyes of security officials and soldiers trying to resist or suppress them. It is often supposed that the insurgents are subject to hidden exterior manipulation by outside agencies or powers. The power of any modern state has come to depend more and more on secret operations, as the 'war on terrorism' shows. There is a very close relationship between secret armies and political conspiracy in the Balkans. For the Serbs, the idea that the KLA was a secret conspiracy in many ways provided a comfort blanket of historical misunderstanding that reinforced Milosevic' proposals to keep the Kosova status quo by—as Aaronovitch puts it—turning a blind eye to the large events and spinning these often contingent moments as the product of 'addled individuals'.[11] This view is not a 'Western' ideological construct, in the Todorovian sense, but a matter of practical political reality in trying to understand what is involved in developing oppositional military and political organisations within long-established police states.[13]

In Kosova, in both the Ottoman Empire and the first and second Yugoslavia, secrecy and underground military planning were essential for rebels throughout the years of Kosovar Albanian resistance to the Ottoman Empire, and then Royalist Yugoslavia and Titoism, long before the KLA military campaign opened after 1993. Secret conspiracy was in the blood of the Albanian majority population as much as growing aubergines or making *fle*. The Milosevic government saw the Kosova Liberation Army as a conspiracy against the legal order in Yugoslavia throughout the conflict, but in doing so it was only continuing a tradition of Serbian political perception of Kosovar Albanian activism that had been long established. Many similar perceptions have also informed scholarly debate about the nature and development of other ex-Yugoslavia wars, as the work of Sabrina P. Ramet has demonstrated.[14]

In the course of research into events since 2000 it soon became clear that it was impossible to understand how the insurgency between 1992 and 2000 had evolved without reference to the extended period of Kosova history under communism after 1945, and the recurrent attempts after 1945 by the ethnic Albanian majority in Kosova in the illegal political underground to form a military or paramilitary organisation that would confront what they saw as the Serbian occupation of their territory. The roots of the Kosova Liberation Army thus lie in the past long before 1992. Historians inevitably ask questions that are conditioned by the preoccupations of the society in which they live. In the case of Kosova, these are now centred on issues of legitimacy, territorial inheritance and state formation. These questions in Kosova, after 1945, were usually defined solely through issues of military and security control of the disputed territory. It was also clear that the fighting in the Preshevo Valley in south-east Serbia in 2000 and the small war in the west of the Republic of Macedonia/FYROM in 2001 were intimately related to these issues in the Kosova conflict and would not have taken place without it.

This book therefore explores the wartime period from a longer and wider perspective than I had originally envisaged. The question inevitably arises of whether this is the right time to attempt a history of the Kosova war. I understand the viewpoint of those who feel it is premature and that a longer period of years should elapse. There are obvious gaps in the written sources which will not be filled until archives in Belgrade, Washington, Rome, Moscow and elsewhere are opened, which is likely to take many years (if it ever happens at all, in some cases), but there is also an element of political and ideological judgement inscribed in this view. In most cases those who argue in favour of delay in Kosova and Serbia are those who did not take part in the conflict, and in some cases have contemporary political interests that benefit from the elision of the war from popular memory. Those who did take part have been in the main generous with their time and reminiscence.

The oral tradition remains very important in Kosova society among all ethnic groups. Many aspects of the Kosova Liberation Army's activity and the conflict in general did not produce written records of any kind, and delaying writing the history will not change that. This source problem is not confined to the guerrilla movement. It is known, for instance, that in the latter stages of his rule Slobodan Milosevic strongly disliked giving written instructions to his political associates and military commanders, and usually used the telephone. It is also true that some aspects of the KLA produced copious records as ICTY trials have demonstrated, but much of the material is of a routine character like the internal records of many armies and casts little light on the wider causes of events. Current oral sources are likely to be of crucial importance.

There is, though, a genuinely hidden history of the Kosova conflict, and this may remain the case for a long time. It is not that important. In the main the type of diplomatic exchange material that is still in closed archives or currently unavailable to historians is unlikely to substantially modify our understanding of the history of the guerrilla war and its origins. However, it is the European and Russian diplomatic history that is in this sense the 'secret history', and given the active collaboration of some governments and their diplomats with the Milosevic regime, this is likely to be the case for some time.[15] This archive material may well have an impact on the understanding of the international aspects of the conflict when (or if) it does eventually become available to historians. It is not likely to influence our understanding of the Kosova Liberation Army itself very much.

In addition, in the past decade there has been a significant amount of other source material becoming available. In the years since the NATO intervention in Kosova in 1999, there has been a growing publication of war memoirs of various kinds, mostly on the Albanian side, and also a partial opening of government archives, court records, police and secret police files in Serbia and elsewhere that have cast much light not only on the 1990s but also on the entire period of Titoist government and its attempts to suppress Albanian nationalism after the Second World War. Material from Moscow archives has been useful in the early part of the story. Many of the Albanian books are biographies and hagiographic accounts of the lives of dead KLA participants, and thus the local Kosova war narrative has started as one of martyrdom.[16] As a result, it has been possible to fill out with firm sources what had hitherto only been vague perceptions of the various attempts to form underground and insurgent military groups in the pre-1992 period. Many observers of the conflict have echoed the comment made some years ago by Mark Mazower, to the effect that it was strange for the Kosova Liberation Army to have attracted outside power support in a way that was denied to previous Balkan insurgencies such as the Internal Macedonian Revolutionary Organisation (IMRO) against the Ottoman Empire and Royalist Yugoslavia.

In trying to explore this question it has been necessary to open up discussion of some of the wider geostrategic and international aspects of the KLA's development. In turn these relationships have a direct and tangible effect on the development of the Kosova insurgencies over the years, as in the early days of Titoism the potential Kosova insurgents' only outside support came from Enver Hoxha's Albania, a severely limiting factor. The development of the later periods of conflict in turn depended on the opening out of the Kosova Albanian world into Europe, as *Gastarbeiter*s and refugees, and finally the development of a new consciousness of the true nature of Titoist Yugoslavia and the successor Milosevic regime in the United Kingdom and the United States. I have not in the main spent very much time on the issue of Milosevic's *modus operandi* as there has already been a great deal of useful and often authoritative material published on this subject.

Successful guerrilla armies generally have a long learning curve, and endure periods of failure and major setbacks before achieving any degree of military efficiency. The Long March of the Chinese Communists is perhaps the strongest twentieth century example, or the Yugoslav Partisans' epic struggles in Durmintor in Montenegro in 1943. There were many local factors for the KLA in Kosova that made this education process particularly protracted, with the ubiquitous secret police, the nature of the landlocked territory, the long experience of the Yugoslav state in controlling Kosova since 1921, and ignorance/indifference on the part of the European powers about what was taking place there.

In the early 1990s there was a failure by most of the international community to understand the centrality of the Kosova issue to the emergence of and survival of Titoist and post-Titoist Yugoslavia. The size of the Belgrade-controlled JNA/VJ military force is sometimes forgotten nowadays. For a long time in the Cold War period the Yugoslav Army was the fourth largest army in Europe. For many Kosovar Albanians, it seemed impossible to imagine creating an oppositional force that would even begin to dent the total control the Yugoslav military seemed to have over most of Kosova for so long. In turn the Kosova Serb minority believed the VJ would always be there to protect them. Ideology is important in many areas: this does not apply only to normal political ideology but also to the specific role of various conceptions of military and paramilitary doctrine that have always permeated Balkan societies since long before the Versailles Treaty period. The Serbian state that emerged in the nineteenth century was based on continual aggressive military expansion and border-creating war like that of nineteenth- and early twentieth-century Greece.

A key issue is the relationship of the KLA to the insurgent military tradition in Kosova. The specifically Communist Partisan tradition was subsequently inscribed deeply in the Balkan armies that developed following the Second World War.[17] In turn this evolution depended on local military traditions that ultimately owe their origins to popular nationalist resistance movements under the Ottoman Empire. The Yugoslav Army in both the Royalist and Communist periods always had a strong internal policing and public order component in its general orientation. Also, under Communism through the militias of the separate component, Republics and the military doctrine of *Mashirovka*, usually translated into English as 'deception' but with a strong overlay of 'total national defence'.[18]

I have seen the Kosova issue as part of the protracted struggle of Serbia throughout the twentieth century to establish a stable southern border. This has yet to be achieved, even after the Kosova independence declaration in 2008. It is also intimately linked, in terms of the southern border crisis, with the re-emergence of the Macedonian Question after 1990 and the short war in the Former Yugoslav Macedonia/ Republic of Macedonia in the spring of 2001.[19] It is possible to see one of the main causes of the collapse of Yugoslavia after Milosevic as a product of over-ambitious attempts to keep Kosova within an overextended southern border. The current debate among Balkans scholars about this resembles that among ancient historians as to whether the decline and fall of the Roman Empire was caused in part by the decision of Hadrian to re-establish the 'old frontiers' of the Empire at its height.[20] The concept of a 'border' was fraught with danger; in antiquity, the boundary was the terrain of the phallus and trade, a place of exchange, sexuality, disorder and danger.[21]

The Yugoslav Communists had come to power after a successful civil war against the Chetnik Royalist forces. From the point of view of regional insurgencies and uprisings at the end of socialist Yugoslavia, this made it much easier for the Milosevic regime to use the army for purposes of internal repression.[22] These mental traces and subconscious inheritances will, I hope, be reflected in my narrative, but in a framework where the explicit hangovers from the Second World War period will be clear. In the same context as in Greek history, where it is impossible to understand much about the 1967–74 dictatorship without understanding the inheritance of the 'secret state' set up by the Right after the Civil War, it is hard to see the reasons for many events in Kosova in the 1998–99 conflict period without reference to the inheritance of socialist Yugoslavia, Tito's treatment of Kosova and the military repression of Albanian nationalism.

It is always hard to define exactly when an insurgency begins and ends. To use the Greek Civil War analogy again, every history book published on the conflict in the English-speaking world tells the reader that the 'Third Round' of fighting 'ended' the conflict in April 1949, but in military reality, the Greek National Army lost 14 officers and 177 men dead in 1950, apart from the numerous Democratic Army and civilian deaths and many more wounded on all sides.[23] A lesser toll continued in Greece in succeeding years, as it did in central Kosova after the Drenica uprising was officially 'ended', in the official view, in the summer of 1945. The prime motivation for this bias in Communist-period historiography in Kosova was to eliminate the anti-communist Balli Kombetar military campaign between 1945 and 1947 from popular memory.[24]

Throughout socialist Yugoslavia there were always areas in central Kosova where Belgrade rule was only maintained by the most draconian threats of force and *de facto* martial law. The Drenica region of Kosova saw itself as the Kosova Sparta where every boy was destined for war against Serbian domination. Some Kosova Albanian historians have argued that an 'insurgency' against Belgrade rule never really ended, it was a forest fire that was impossible to put out and could smoulder into flame again at almost any time. This notion of insurgency to my mind confuses the concept of popular political and civil resistance with military resistance, and neglects the central factor in any insurgency; the arrival on the scene of an effective and functional resistance army, however small, irregular or informal.

A substantial part of this book is taken up with tracing the long winding road the Kosova Albanians had to take before even the first vestiges of such a force existed, let alone a force with the capacity to begin to worry the Serbian military authorities. Yet it was in this time of total obscurity that the fundamental nature of the future KLA was defined. Government uniformed resources were organised in the Prishtina Corps of the Yugoslav People's Army (JNA), between 1945 and 1992, and the Yugoslav National Army (VJ) after that date until the demise of the Serbian-Montenegrin Federation in 2006.[25] The original JNA and VJ doctrine depended not only on their indigenous Partisan-derived traditions, but also on inherited Soviet Red Army conceptions of public order maintenance and 'peacekeeping'. Early military doctrine was thus mainly 'inherited', and inherently conservative. There was little or no doctrinal development in the armed forces in the Communist period and none after Tito's death in 1980. The JNA/VJ always needed allies. In the Milosevic period after the crisis, martial law imposition and turmoil in Kosova in 1989, there was also a steady expansion of the paramilitary police, as well as the introduction of various specialist new units of anti-terrorist and anti-insurgency forces, some of which were responsible for gross human rights violations in the wartime period.

At the onset of NATO's air campaign in 1999, a very complex situation existed on the ground. The NATO air war was fought at a considerable distance from the material reality of Kosova society and the military situation in Kosova towns and villages. This is the main reason why it was so protracted and for such a long time failed to fulfil the expectations of Western political leaders and public opinion.[26] The air campaign was also conducted against Yugoslavia as a whole, and a very high percentage of the chosen targets for NATO bombing were not in Kosova at all, and if they were had often been more or less vacated by the VJ and were not of great military significance.[27] NATO

9

bombing was also conducted at a height that often made operational success rather unlikely.[28]

It was therefore often difficult for the NATO commanders of the original KFOR force that entered Kosova in July 1999 to come to terms with the reality of the Kosova Liberation Army in either its political or military dimensions, and the early formal KLA demobilisation in the late summer of 1999 did not put an end to its influence over later events. It seemed sensible to trace the main outlines of succeeding developments, as the conflicts of 2000 in the Preshevo Valley and in 2001 in Macedonia were intimately linked to the Kosova war and involved many of the same political and military actors. The independence of Kosovo in February 2008 did not resolve the issue of the future Kosova Army, as the Ahtisaari provisions for controlled independence did not allow for the creation of a Kosova military force at the time of the declaration. It is therefore questionable whether Kosova has obtained full independence, and the KLA paramilitary tradition may well reassert itself at some point in the future. The current (spring 2013) discussions within NATO about the designation of the Kosova Security Force (KSF) may result in a recognition of a small Kosova army within the NATO framework, but it is unclear whether (and when) this will take place.

1

THE ORIGINS OF A GUERRILLA ARMY

By dint of the self-sacrificing struggle of our peoples, a struggle waged for a common cause, we have managed largely to unmask the enemies of the new federal, democratic Yugoslavia. And it precisely because these anti-people's elements have resorted to new methods in their reactionary activities, that they are donning sheep's clothing and infiltrating the ranks of the People's Liberation movement that they are becoming a menace; the greatest vigilance is therefore required from all those who hold dear the achievements of this war.

Josef Broz Tito[1]

The Disposition of Forces in Kosova After the Second World War

Guerrilla warfare has taken place for a long time in Europe. For many school pupils, Julius Caesar's descriptions of his battles against the Gauls are an introduction. In British history the Scots and Welsh waged guerrilla campaigns against the invading English monarchs. More recently the Prussian founder of military theory Carl von Clausewitz, while a theorist of formal warfare between state armies, also advocated a guerrilla war against Napoleon to drive the French from Prussia. [2]

In the intervening years there have been many small wars in Europe where guerrilla armies and informal forces played a central role. Many of the conflicts on the fringe of the British Empire in the nineteenth century would also fall into this category, culminating in the first 'modern' example, the Boer War in South Africa between 1899 and 1902.

11

Some of the vocabulary of twentieth century history, like the phrase 'concentration camp', dates from this conflict. In the Balkan Wars of 1912–13 all the emerging Balkan nations used guerrilla formations and tactics against the disintegrating Ottoman army. Most of the techniques of guerrilla warfare go far back to the distant past but have to be rediscovered and adapted to new circumstances by each new generation, while old military techniques are given new names. The mountainous Balkan peninsula is well suited to informal warfare, and it has taken place in all historical periods. Kosova, with its mixed Serbian and Albanian population and with the special status the territory occupies for both communities, has been the scene of this type of warfare throughout its history.

In Kosova Albanian communities there was a living tradition of military memory and an oral tradition handed down through each generation from 1912, if not earlier, to 1945. The origins of the Kosova Liberation Army lie much further back in the distant past of Kosova. The Serbian army conquered Kosova in 1912 as part of its struggle to take as much as possible of the collapsing Ottoman Empire for Serbia, although some Serbs had always lived in Kosova. There was resistance from the Albanian majority and Albanian insurgents fought at different times in the intervening years to reverse that conquest. Family names in prominent roles in the 1992–99 wartime period can be found as rebels or outlaws (in the Serbian view) throughout the twentieth century, and some in the nineteenth. Land ownership and control was the central issue in this history, when agrarian production and subsistence and semi-subsistence agriculture dominated the Yugoslav economy before the arrival of Communism.[3] An archaic mode of production continued in rural Kosova into the modern period, based on sharecropping, and some elements of it in field usage can be seen in a drive across any part of rural Kosova today.[4] Land tenure was deeply insecure, and the struggle for the land continual. The Kosova Albanian rebel or outlaw was often from the family that resisted displacement from their land first by Ottoman *ciflik* landlords and then Serbian and Montenegrin colonisation. In the main, only military methods secured the success of the Yugoslavist colonisation process, particularly in the early twentieth century, and the displaced Albanians found that only rebellion and insurgency warfare were an adequate response to their oppression.

In the early twentieth century, Serbia was as militarised a society as any other European country, except post-Bismarck Germany, with an obligation for military service of all males between the ages of twenty-one and forty-five. This produced what was by local Balkan standards an enormous army of over 200,000 men.[5] It was opposed by random local militias raised by the Albanians at different times. Behind the untidy and often haphazard Kosova Liberation Army stood ghosts of rebellious men and women prepared to endure the most severe hardships, death of their menfolk and periods of exile to fight against overwhelming odds. During the twentieth century, in the ideological and psychological landscape in the Kosova conflict little has changed. For example, a longstanding theme has been the issue of weapons. As the author Ismail Kadare has noted, for the Albanian, the rifle was and is 'an extension of the vertebral column', with the possession of personal weapons an index of the relationship between Serb and Albanian in Kosova, symbolised by the money spent by Albanians on elaborately enamelled and silver-embossed guns, 'an index of force, bravery and pride'.[6] The need for protection from the might of military Serbia was central, as the notion of protection has remained central to Kosova Albanian life ever since. The role of a leader like Ibrahim Rugova was was conceptualised after 1990 in terms of the need to 'protect' the interests of the Albanian majority.

Under Royalist Yugoslavia after the First World War and the Treaty of Versailles Kosova stagnated and remained a very backward agrarian society. Serbian colonists were driven by a vision to recreate a lost and distant past.[7] It was an inevitably doomed enterprise and apart from development of the extractive and mining industries, Kosova made little progress towards modernity under the Royalist state.

In the latter stages of the Second World War, Kosova with its wide and flat central plain ringed by high mountains, was the scene of confused fighting between the retreating Axis occupation forces and various resistance groups. Amid the dwarf oak uplands and marshy plains, Germans, Italians and Bulgarians had occupied Kosova for the last four years. It was a familiar scenario to all the majority Albanian population. An occupying army had ruled them for centuries, whether Byzantine, Ottoman or Royalist Yugoslav, and the disposition of forces on the ground was simply that of the occupying soldiers in their predominantly urban garrisons among the indigenous rural population.[8] Even the military structures were often the same. Some places had been continuous centres of occupation authority for hundreds of years, like Zvecan Castle near Mitrovica that was first built by the Byzantines, then expanded as a regional garrison centre by the Ottomans and finally made into a Royalist Yugoslav police centre and residence for the British engineers developing the nearby Trepca mines in the 1930s.[9]

Most of Kosova was placed under the Italian occupation authorities when Yugoslavia was dismembered in 1941, apart from a small area in the south-east which was given to the Bulgarians, and Mitrovica which remained under direct German control. Axis interest was focused on the protection of the rich mines at Stari Trg, three miles east of Mitrovica. The giant lead, nickel and silver mine was so important that in the wartime period it produced around 17 per cent of the lead needed for German munitions factories. In Royalist Yugoslavia before 1939, Trepca had been the jewel in the crown of the Selection Trust mining combine, and the most important single British investment in the country.[10]

Above the mines and the tall smoking chimneys of the lead reduction plant towered the ruins of Zvecan castle that had guarded the pass up the Ibar river valley into southern Serbia for seven hundred years. Silver from Trepca had decorated the clothes of Byzantine officials, and then their Ottoman successors. Agriculture produced little surplus value by comparison. The continental winter climate made for a much shorter growing season than in more southerly Macedonia and the plains of Bulgaria, which were able to make money selling animal products such as hides for the Ottoman army. Much of the Kosova land was poor soil and remains rough grazing ground interspersed with woodland. Cultivation mostly took place on the boggy central plain. It regularly flooded in the twentieth century winter as it had always done in Ottoman times, and made wheeled traffic useless. The mule and horse were still the main methods of transport in the villages. The single north-south railway ran north to Serbia and south to Skopje and Thessaloniki down the Vardar river valley. To the east vast forests ran into Serbia, where only hunters and woodcutters worked. In the north-west the Serbian Orthodox Church Patriarchate at Pec/Peje stood at the entrance to the Rugova Pass leading to Montenegro. Other ancestral churches and monasteries dating from the medieval empire of the Nemanjas dotted the rural landscape. It was a landscape at once ancient and modern where vital raw materials for the Nazi war machine were mined alongside little family farms with wooden buildings where agricultural methods had not changed for generations.

The landscape was and still is littered with the remnants of numerous past military installations. They have now been joined by functioning and also abandoned NATO/KFOR camps built up after 1999, and numerous KLA monuments to battles and the fallen. The oldest of these ruins are the castle at Novo Berde in the south east and the towering citadel of ancient Theranda on the hill above Prizren. Both had their origins in Illyrian pre-classical antiquity and were in more or less continuous use ever since as guardians of strategic roads and passes leading south to the Vardar Valley and the Mediterranean.[11] The Ottomans who ruled Kosova for five hundred years from the fourteenth century to the twentieth built some new roads, and a series of forts to protect them. Every subsequent government has built new military buildings, from the First World War fortifications visible nowadays at Hani i Elezit on the southern border of Kosova and the FYROM/ Republic of Macedonia to NATO's new airport extension at Prishtina after 1999. The Kosova Liberation Army has left few buildings but many monuments. Monuments sanctify dead heroes. The Kosova Albanian campaigns in the twentieth century were wars of martyrdom. Martyrs create memory. Armies in the Balkans as elsewhere are built on memory, from the essential nature of classical Delphi as a war memorial to the most modest modern plaques on Kosova walls and black granite stones with names and images in windswept fields.[12]

Kosova has for hundreds of years been a strategic frontier land between the northern Balkans and the Mediterranean south, and a place of uncertain boundaries and unending transport difficulties.[13] In 1884 the French traveller and authority on the Balkans, Isambert, observed concerning the journey from Scutari (modern Shkodra) in Albania to Prizren in Kosova, that 'the road is signalled by the authors of Travels in the Slavonic Provinces of Europe as one of the most uncomfortable in Turkey-in-Europe caused by the difficulties and privations of every kind which affect the traveller.'[14]'

The imposition of any kind of civilised order on what for most of its history has been seen by its occupiers as a semi-wilderness has always required military skills. The military road builders of ancient Rome were the first to decisively improve southern Balkan communications, just as NATO after 1999 made the first worthwhile investments in Kosova roads after the Communists. The Byzantines and Ottomans followed in Roman footsteps, quite literally in many cases. The Via Egnatia road running south of Kosova from the Adriatic to Constantinople, remained an artery of empires for over a thousand years.[15] Kosova has a profoundly military landscape. A common thread runs through all Kosova military architecture, past and present; it is designed to safeguard strategic towns, or road passages to those towns, places that under the Axis were always referred to by Tito as 'occupied enemy strongholds'.[16] The towns themselves were the preserve of the occupiers in many different guises, but always drawing tribute from the poverty stricken and potentially rebellious countryside, particularly the mountains. As Zhelyazkova has observed, for Albanians 'the mountain is a refuge of liberty, of democracy and the peasant republic'. [17]

Some towns were linked to the production of particular commodities, like Mitrovica to silver and lead. The medieval castle at Novo Berde was a product of the rich mines nearby and the urban settlement that grew up near them. Only the little chain of forts alongside the Skopje-Mitrovica road built in Ottoman times are the exception, although some of them are little more than guardhouses. All illustrate dangers of disorder coming from the wild and underdeveloped countryside to the 'civilised' towns, whether the bandits of Ottoman times that plagued the roads, or the Albanian *kacak* rebels of the 1920s, or the KLA in rural Drenica after 1991. The political/geographical landscape of Kosova reproduces exactly the Balkan paradigm described by Todorov, where the poor rural areas in the Balkans produce little or none of the income required to permit satisfactory urban development, and such development as does occur during the time of developing capitalist social relations, it does so by imposition of external power and finance.[18]

Military and security criteria have always been at the heart of governing Kosova, and most periods of its history have been marked by conflict between country and town dwellers. Control of the roads has been central to the security perspectives of the rulers in all periods. In the aftermath of the Versailles Treaty the Albanian majority were ruled under martial law from Belgrade, under which movement control by road checkpoints was central to the security system. In the interwar years the Serbs sought to force the Albanians to emigrate along the same roads, mostly to Turkey, and brought in their own colonists. As Bato Tomasovic describes life in the early 1920s, 'The Serbs had an effective monopoly of force and after the defeat of the Kacak rebels in the western hills in the early 1920's, resistance was useless. Many Albanians had weapons hidden at home but there was no concept of unified military or paramilitary resistance and they were most often used in blood feuds.'[19]

When the Axis Powers invaded the Balkans in 1941, the new occu-piers naturally tended to take over the military and police facilities left behind by the Royalist Yugoslavs, just as the incoming United Nations administration in 1999 used Slobodan Milosevic's government build-ings. In the early period of the Nazi occupation, there was little organ-ised opposition to the Occupation authority. The Germans stationed most of their forces in and around Mitrovica, and recruited a local Albanian security force for the mines. Mitrovica became the heart of the German military system, as it had been of Royalist Yugoslavia's. At that time Prishtina was still a sleepy middle-sized town with an Otto-man atmosphere, numerous Ottoman buildings and many street mar-kets. It only became the urban focus of Kosova under communism. Prizren in the south-west was the finest Ottoman town in Kosovo but was in decline as economic activity and trade focused on the newly rich mining areas. By the time the Nazis arrived, Mitrovica was by far the most important town in Kosova, straggling along the main road south in a confusion of industrial buildings servicing the mines, poverty stricken and unhealthy miners' settlements by the Ibar river, and shops, mosques, churches and trading centres. Tuberculosis figures in Mitro-vica were among the highest in Europe before 1939.

In 1941 the Kingdom of Yugoslavia ceased to exist and the collabo-rationist government the Nazis installed in Belgrade had little practical authority of any kind. Hitler and Mussolini decided the future outlines of the southern Balkans. A small part of south-east Kosova, around Gjilan and Kacanik, was given to the Bulgarian allies of the Axis, while swathes of the west and western Macedonia as far south as Struga were placed under Italian control and appended to the central Italian administration in Tirana, and thus formed what Serbs see as the first 'Greater Albania'.

Although this appeared to Berlin and Rome to be an efficient, secure system it had the Achilles Heel that has always haunted rulers of Kos-ova: it depended on military patrols using motor vehicles on the few asphalt roads, and the vast empty forests and inaccessible hill villages were out of day to day contact with the Axis occupation. The near medieval conditions of village life were a shock to the German and Italian soldiers who encountered them without modern military brief-ings or prior indoctrination. The rigid dictates of the Kanun and Mus-lim social tradition towards outsiders discouraged fraternisation and sexual relationships, and a wall of mutual incomprehension divided the rural Albanian majority from their new masters.

At first in 1941–42 this did not seem to be a major problem as the ethnic Albanian majority was pleased to see its position change for the better in terms of cultural and education rights in the Italian-administered areas. Royalist Yugoslavia had banned the use of the Albanian language in education and public life but the Italians were prepared to see it return, and soon many schools were teaching a joint Italian-Albanian curriculum. Muslim religious courts began to revive after many years of suspension in the old Royalist Yugoslavia.

The villages looked for social and political leadership towards the towns which were soon successfully embedded in the Occupation. Every Kosova town of any size had a garrison post, many of them originally Ottoman constructions that the Serbs had taken over after 1921. They were in a real sense the only state that existed. Recent Serbian and Montenegrin settlers from the 60,000 or so who had arrived in Kosova in the interwar period were often victimised and had to leave Kosova to avoid conscription by the Axis authorities into forced labour in the mines. Many did not escape this grim fate. The traditionalist and culturally still Ottomanised Albanian middle class in the towns was in a position to profit from the Occupation through its shops and businesses and certainly did so, and as in occupied Serbia some people carried on working in the same jobs under their new masters, as they had done under the old. The major change took place in the Serbian community where settler families that had come to Kosova in the interwar years began to leave. The Serbian Orthodox churches and their nearby villages were stranded islands in the forested hills without local support from the Serb minority who looked hopelessly towards the exiled monarch in London to rescue them from their oppression.

Kosova had been a land used to violence in the preceding fifty years, from the chaos of the 1912–13 Balkan War period when Ottoman rule collapsed, through to the travails of Serbia in the First World War and the Versailles Treaty period that led to the arrival of Royalist Yugoslavia. It had been subjected to systematic Serbian colonisation for a long time, and this process was to be augmented in the twentieth century by the opening of the rich mines in the Sar mountains on the Kosova-Macedonia borderland and in Kosova itself. The ethnic Albanian majority sought to resist colonisation after the Versailles Treaty had institutionalised Royalist Yugoslavia. This period is known as that of the *kacak* rebellion, and that tradition was central to the foundation of the Kosova Liberation Army seventy years later, but who were the *kacak*s?

In the disorder after the First World War the Kosova Committee sought to organise resistance to the provisions of the Versailles Treaty and the submergence of Kosova within a Yugoslav state, something that was new on the international scene. The *kacak*s were armed bands of irregular soldiers who made hit and run attacks on the new forces of the Yugoslav government. Their origins lie deep in the past, in the *hayduk* rebels against the Ottoman Empire. As Hobsbawm has pointed out, the bandit flourishes in a society based on a peasantry and archaic forms of agrarian production.[20] The *kacak* heartland was the hills of western Kosova adjoining the border with Albania. In western Kosova and poor central areas like Drenica, largely pre-capitalist forms of rural production based on family labour, subsistence and primitive accumulation of money persisted into the late twentieth century. These parts of Kosova did not even enjoy the very limited benefits of the sharecropping system. The efforts of the Royalist Yugoslavs and later Tito's Communists to destroy this world through agricultural modernisation and then collectivisation after 1945 only met with limited success.

The Ottoman landowning and agricultural system as it had developed in Kosova and Macedonia had been focused on great *ciflik* estates in the better-drained parts of the lowlands which had been owned by Muslim landowners. They were the successors to the now defunct *sipahi* system of the post-conquest period.[21] In theory all land belonged to the landlords, but in practice poorer hill land was neglected and cultivated only by the Albanian peasants on an irregular basis. Smuggling and piracy were endemic, as the only reliable sources of money in cash to pay Ottoman state taxes. The bandit tradition developed into the *kacak* movement with a fusion of motives of revenge—against the exploitation of the poor uplands by the newly developing towns, many with a substantial number of Serbian colonists—and political retribution, offering the Albanian peasants a chance to try to settle scores against their new masters. Gradually, from Tirana King Zog imposed order in Albania, and worked with Belgrade against the Kosovars' ambitions. Their campaign died down, with much of the quality of the lonely, anarchic violent protest of the bandit, romantic but ultimately futile. There are some modern resonances of the *kacak* soldiers in the rhetoric of the Kosova Liberation Army, but also many differences. As Althusser points out, 'Marxist political practice is constantly coming up against that reality known as "survivals". There can be no doubt that these survivals exist—they cling tenaciously to life.'[22] In Kosova

they were based on the material base of the continuing archaic economic life and mode of production throwing up, generation after generation, those who looked back to the bandit tradition as their central
revolutionary heritage. They did not seek to achieve replacement, in
the Marxist sense, of this past of a rebellious comfort, the knowledge
that however futile and unproductive their revolt, it was 'good' because
it fell into the tradition of their predecessors, the war of the lonely man
on a cold night with a handgun by the roadside.

The economic grievances of the uplanders against richer lowland
and town dwellers continued down the centuries and erupted again in
the conflicts between the KLA-dominated areas in early 1998 and the
conservative towns with their pro-Rugova outlook. Like the Kosova
Liberation Army in the 1990s, the *kacak*s formed small bands based
on family links and were reviled by their opponents as criminals and
bandits or, in more modern terminology, active in organised crime,
narco-terrorism and the black economy. The KLA social banditry
dimension drew on local 'Robin Hood' traditions and was already
richly immortalised in Kosova song and folklore through figures such
as the 1920s fighting heroine Shote Galicia who allegedly loaded and
fired a black powder pistol faster than any man. The fighting tradition
offered an opportunity for heroism, as the doomed Jashari family were
to discover in March 1998. The historical hero quickly became part of
myth and legend; thus Adem Jashari, the first commander of the Kosova Liberation Army, is always referred to as 'the legendary commander'. They attacked from the countryside the growing urban
institutions and symbols of the imposed and distant Yugoslav state.

Popular relations with the state nonetheless varied considerably
throughout the twentieth century. The Royalist state was essentially
military and soon became, after 1928, openly dictatorial.[23] The state
that the Axis Occupation brought to Kosova was fierce but locally
focused and limited in its objectives, the principal one being the highest possible rate of economic exploitation of the mines. The Communist state did bring some social benefits such as a mediocre but free
medical and educational system and road improvements. Pre-Commu-
nist occupiers had little interest in improving the agricultural economy
and were content to let the traditional Albanian rural culture persist.
In the Axis period, the predominantly Muslim Albanians were a subject people but somewhat better treated than the Orthodox Serbian
minority. Some Albanians joined a local pro-German militia headed by

Xhafer Deva and fought against Tito's forces. Later the SS Skanderbeg Division fought with the Germans against Partisans in Montenegro.[24] The Kosova Serbs were subject to forced labour conscription to work in grim conditions in the mines and quarries for the German war machine. Many escaped back to Serbia proper to avoid this, and were in particular a high proportion of the new settlers who had come to the region in the 1920s and 1930s as privileged colonists. Perhaps 50,000 Serbs left Kosova during the Second World War period. Others took to the hills and joined the nascent Chetnik resistance organisations of the Royalist leader Draza Mihajlovic, while a few committed themselves to the Communist-led groups of Tito.[25] The only official state authority in this beleaguered territory was, as ever, military, whether German, Italian, Bulgarian, Balli Kombetar or Partisan.

The post-war fate of Kosova would clearly be linked with that of Albania, and could embody the long held dream of national reunification. Albanians had been scattered in four different countries as a result of the diplomatic conferences of the First World War period. As the war progressed, resistance grew in both Albania and Kosova to occupation rule. The first serious Partisan-led attacks took place in 1942, and grew in the spring of the following year. There was never much support for Communism in Kosova pre-1939 except among the Mitrovica miners, and as a result the Partisan movement was slow to develop by comparison with Montenegro or Bosnia where Tito saved his forces after the setbacks of 1942. As rule had always been external in Kosova, the collapse of external power meant that for Kosova there was no rule at all. The first major symptom of this followed the collapse and capitulation of Italy. The Albanian anti-Axis movement was weak in northern Albania but after the exit of the Italians was able to gain strength and gradually extend itself northwards towards Kosova. An attempt had been made to unify the different organisations in the Albanian resistance at the village of Mukje near Tirana in August 1943, where the nationalist Balli Kombetar and Enver Hoxha's Communists met to attempt to form a united front to fight the occupation. The Communists had already claimed to have overtaken the Ballists in military terms and saw the People's Liberation Army as a far superior force against the Axis than the Ballist *cheta*s.[26] The basis for these claims was nebulous then, but had more substance after the explosive growth of the Partisans in the winter of 1943–44.[27]

Already, at this early stage in the movement, the classic dilemma had appeared that was later to haunt the mainstream nationalist Kosova

Albanians for two generations: how to form a resistance army to counter their oppressors when the Communists with their Marxist-Leninist
organisation appeared to offer the only model of waging successful
guerrilla warfare. The *ceta* embodied obsolete family based military
traditions. This has always seemed to be a split between 'left' and
'right', the People's Army representing something derived from the
early Red Army model after 1918, while the *ceta* seemed to embody
the Ottoman and pre-Ottoman traditions of clan based rural resistance. A great weakness of the *ceta* system was that it deeply inhibited
the capacity to concentrate overwhelming force on any single point to
disrupt the enemy's forces. This capacity is vital for success in all warfare in all periods, particularly irregular warfare.[28]

In the background was the shadow of another recent war that had
left bloody wounds on European democracy. Several of the commanders of the Partisan units in both Yugoslavia and Albania had fought in
Spain between 1936 and 1938 in the International Brigades, including
Enver Hoxha's alter ego and senior Albanian Partisan commander
Mehmet Shehu.[29] The Spanish experience had hardened all who had
taken part in the conflict and survived, particularly Mehmet Shehu,
and also left them with a fierce determination not to repeat the mistakes of the Spanish Popular Front government through the disunity
and splits on the Republican side of the armed forces. The main legacy
from Spain was a commitment to fierce orthodoxy in political control
of the Albanian and Yugoslav Partisan armies with all-powerful political commissars dealing with any hint of opposition. This made for
various internal efficiencies but also made it very difficult for the army
to work with non-Communists of a different ideological outlook, and
an atmosphere of sectarian righteousness developed. In Albania this
fact, amongst others, laid the basis for the failure of the August 1943
Mukje agreement to unite the Communist and nationalist resistance;
in addition the Albanian Communist party had been formed with
Yugoslav help and had prominent Yugoslavs like Dusan Mugosa in the
leadership. The great asset of the Communist movement was its readily available and superficially coherent belief-system, in a society where
Kosova Albanian leaders had traditionally lacked much capacity to
believe in a better, let alone an independent political future. Their
world in many ways was that of cultural decline from the status of the
Albanians in Ottoman Kosova, and Communism seemed a way to find
a new and positive way of thinking.

Another background factor was religion. The Kosovo Albanians were about 90 per cent Muslim at the time of the outbreak of the Second World War, with a Sunni majority. The Shia-influenced Bektashi sect and other dissident Muslim groups had more influence in western Kosovo. The Sunni Beys were at the heart of Axis collaboration, and with a few exceptions contributed little to the resistance to occupation. The Italian occupation increased the influence and standing of the Roman Catholic minority among the Albanians, and they in turn also provided a ready supply of occupation officials and apologists. The Muslim religion was seen by the Communists as a particular symbol of backwardness and the survival of Ottoman traditions, and with a few notable exceptions the Muslim imams played little part in the Partisan movement or the fight against occupation, in marked contrast to the clergy in many Macedonian, Greek and Serbian Orthodox churches who often worked closely with anti-Axis fighters.[30]

Many elements of Ottoman culture remained in Kosova in 1945. The small openly Turkish minority was concentrated in and around Prizren with a scattering in other towns such as Vushtrri. Ottoman life was well within the living memory of older people when Islam was the official state religion and the Caliphate still existed, and the more faithful believers still felt a sense of loss and disorientation for the remainder of their lives after the old world disappeared. They were the defeated after the First World War and the arrival of Royalist Yugoslavia with its overwhelming Christian majority and processes of Orthodox Serb and Montenegrin colonisation. The south of Yugoslavia was poverty stricken and a territory of the losers in the historical process.

The heartland of socialist power in Yugoslavia was in the north, in Montenegro, eastern Bosnia and the industrialised centre of Serbia. In contrast, the working class in Kosovo was very small and almost entirely concentrated in the extractive industries. The vast rural hinterland was occupied by small and middle sized landowners who held their land in fierce rivalry with their neighbours—in Leninist terms, in a *kulak* or rich peasant world. The minor conflicts over such matters as grazing rights were endemic and were regulated by the ancient rules of the Kanun. This was a law code based on local custom and a code of revenge dating back to the Middle Ages, and embodied a deeply patriarchal and reactionary ideology, but it was all the Albanian majority had in the absence of a respected or democratic state. The imposition of the Ottoman and Royalist Yugoslav systems was to be followed by the imposition of Communism after 1945, with an equally alien ideology. The term 'Marxism' would probably have meant nothing whatsoever to most Kosova rural dwellers in 1939, yet five years later they were to be governed by it. It had been difficult for Tito to organise a functioning or satisfactory Communist party in Macedonia before the Second World War, and these difficulties were much worse in Kosova.[31] There were no large cities or concentrations of working class people apart from Mitrovica. Places such as the former Ottoman *vilayet* capital Skopje were only towns. The vast majority of the people of all ethnic groups lived as semi-subsistence farmers in the countryside. Few roads were capable of taking motor traffic.

From the strictly military point of view, the Kosova central plain was an easy territory to control and pacify. The flat open fields left little scope for guerilla or irregular resistance.[32] The rolling hills of Drenica and the mountainous west were a different matter, as they had been in the 1920s. The deep forests and ravines provided ideal conditions for insurgents and it was in Drenica that the anti-Communist Balli Kombetar made their last stand after 1945. In the chaotic conditions of the collapsing Axis occupation, different armed groups fought for supremacy in different localities. In the official Communist version of this history, the land of Kosova was 'liberated' for the most part by pro-Communist Partisan groups. Noel Malcolm has shown that this was largely a myth. In eastern Kosova the Soviet Red Army and Bulgarian forces took over, while in the west the territory was secured only after the Germans had already left.[33]

In some places Serbian *cetas*, who sought the restoration of the monarchy, held sway, while in much of the west ethnic Albanian Partisan groups were in charge but faced an uncertain future. As Miranda Vickers has pointed out, the key factor for Tito was to keep Kosova within Serbia when the war finished in order to boost support for Communism in Serbia and crush the remaining support in that community for Mihajlovic and the King.[34] Detaching Kosovo from Serbia would have defeated this objective, and as a result the territory was flooded with Partisans from Serbia and Montenegro who saw all Albanian resistants as potential subversives and enemies.

The Drenica revolt had begun in late 1944 when the central Partisan command mobilised all local forces, including many Albanians, to attack the retreating Germans in the north of Yugoslavia. At the same time many prominent Albanians were arrested in Kosova and local weapon stocks collected, on the grounds that they were collaborators with the Axis forces. A prominent Albanian Partisan commander, Shaban Polluzha, refused to accept these orders and within a short time his force of perhaps 5,000 Albanian militants had attacked the Trepca mine complex and other centres of importance. They were joined by up to 20,000 irregulars, drawn from Drenica in the main. Fighting soon spread all over northern and central Kosova and included an attack on Partisan-controlled Ferizaj (Urosevac). It took Tito five divisions to put down the rebellion. The Albanians fought bravely but were no match for the superior numbers and organisation of the battle-hardened Yugoslav Partisans, some of whom had been fighting together for three years and had far superior weapons. The Partisans had benefited considerably from their 'Long March' experience in Montenegro and Bosnia and had destroyed both German and Royalist Chetnik units.[35] The Albanians were no match for them. There was a central problem of strategic focus on the Albanian side, which was to recur time and time again until 1999 in attempts to build a successful Kosova insurgency. The liberation of Drenica was in essence a community defence movement, while what was required to displace the occupiers was a much more ambitious strategy to stage an urban insurrection to challenge for power in the towns and in Prishtina itself. This, of course, involved a considerably higher level of military and political risk. The decision whether to wage a rural war of attrition or risk all on an armed insurrection in the cities is a central dilemma for many insurgent commanders. In the last analysis the militant rural Kosova communities could hardly ever be fully defeated or integrated into Yugoslavia by the security forces, whereas an urban insurrection staked all on one single throw of the dice.

In a general sense the leadership of the revolt was Balli Kombetar, but in many localities there was no clear leadership at all, and the Albanians lacked basic military equipment such as radios, medical supplies and sufficient ammunition. It was a struggle between Communist-led Partisans who had a very specific model of guerrilla warfare based on Soviet training models, in which the Spanish Civil War experience had been particularly important, and disorganised rural combatants.[36] There are many similarities in the campaigns in Albania and Yugoslavia. Mehmet Shehu's Communist forces in Albania had many of the same advantages of clear and efficient centralised command and leadership over the northern nationalist forces they overcame in the Battle of Dibra period in 1994 as Tito had against the Kosovar Albanians.[37] Yet the Titoists had no inhibitions in seeking to absorb their wartime Albanian Partisan allies into a Slav dominated state after the war. As early as December 1946, an officially sponsored Pan-Slav Congress had been held in Belgrade, with prominent Soviet guests such as Marshal Fedor Tolbukhin and Vasil Kolarov, a former Comintern Secretary. The movement towards Slav union in the Balkans, exemplified by the remark of Tito in his conference speech that the Balkan Slavs 'would never again serve alien interests', left little place for minority national-ities, particularly the Albanians. In this period Tito was seeking to absorb the devastated state of Albania into his project for a seventh Yugoslav republic of Albanians, which would have destroyed Albania as an independent state.[38]

By 1947 a substantial proportion of the northern Drenica male pop-ulation were dead, wounded or in exile. Hundreds of villages had been seriously damaged or destroyed. Most farm livestock—the basis of life for every family—was stolen or dead. The end of the rising left the Alba-nian community divided and demoralised. Although there were many villages where the inhabitants were still armed and bitterly opposed to the imposition of Belgrade rule, whether Communist or Royalist, there was little they could do except hide their weapons and attempt to pre-vent the imposition of any meaningful Communist central authority. The Yugoslav security forces, principally the army and Rankovic's secret police, moved to install a military regime and within a few months many of the features of life under Axis occupation had reappeared, with the imposition of martial law, arbitrary arrests, summary trials with little or no access to lawyers, and movement control orders. All political oppo-sition to the League of Yugoslav Communists was banned and so all anti-Communists were forced into illegality, exile, or the political under-ground. Community leadership by educated people was destroyed with the closure of Muslim religious institutions and the rush to exile of those with Balli Kombetar associations. The economic cost to Kosova was very high. The new region was burdened with an expensive and large internal security operation that stifled the development of any normal society, and a cowed, uneducated and embittered workforce. Kosova entered a very dark period of rural poverty and urban stagnation. An early imperative for the Titoist regime was to build up membership of the Communist party and its associated organisations, but the violent suppression of Albanian national rights had made this difficult.[39] Tito saw the Albanians as ripe for colonisation. As he observed in May 1947, to a gathering of Bulgarian journalists:

We know full well that the masses in Bulgaria and Yugoslavia want a closer rapprochement. If that is so, nobody has the right to prevent us from accomplishing this unity, and we must achieve it ... The same applies to Albania. The Albanians are ... not Slavs but have been living with us for centuries. There is an internal social system in Albania which makes it possible for other countries to have the closest relations with the Albanian nation. We must consolidate this union.[40]

Tito was determined to reinforce the old patriarchal structures of village authority and work through them. A characteristic Kosova phenomenon, state and civil society absence, reappeared, with a predominantly Slavic military and security apparatus seeking to rule over a hostile and almost wholly ethnic Albanian society. Foreign travellers were not allowed to visit Kosova, except from Russia and its allies, and few outsiders knew anything of conditions there.[41] After 1948, Tito expected raids to continue from over the border in Albania and they duly did so. Large areas of western and central Kosova remained under siege for many years. The problem of legitimacy was more severe after 1948 because a small but significant minority of Kosovar Albanian Communists took the Moscow side in the split in that year, including the senior Albanian Partisan commander Colonel Quemal Brovina. In some minds, the model of proletarian internationalism seemingly embodied by the Russians might permit greater Albanian freedoms than increasing centralisation of control from Serb-dominated Belgrade. The decision of the Tirana leadership in Albania to take the Russian side was also important, as a matter of what Enver Hoxha saw as national survival. It had become clear by late 1946 that the pattern of joint Yugoslav-Albanian development put forward by Tito had as its final objective the economic and political absorption of Albania into Yugoslavia.[42]

The dialectic of the events of these years illustrates well the recurring problems of organising a successful liberation war for Kosova, which were to reappear in the KLA period two generations later. The habits and local resistance traditions were very strong and there was an almost infinite supply of fighters who were prepared to risk their lives against Slavic supremacy. But they emerged from family structures and inward-looking village environments where community defence was paramount and where the forces of production and the level of daily life were archaic. The types of military skill and organisation needed to challenge a modern army were not merely non-existent in practice, they were hardly even understood. The mechanised troops of the Yugoslav Partisans were modern in that they were organised to achieve total territorial supremacy where they were operating. It was a war of gentlemen against players, and even Albanian civil resistance was doomed. Yet the violent tragedy of these years also enabled the generation of the 1990s to understand the forces they had to overcome. A formal army would be needed that would be capable of confronting the Yugoslav army, not a motley collection of local fighters. It would need a clear and focused political leadership. There would have to be a long period of preparation in conditions of illegality before any front could be opened in Kosova. The force would need modern military equipment, an intelligence service, plenty of money and foreign friends to help it overcome the physical isolation of the Kosova highlands. It was a tall order to meet, and it was never completely accomplished, but enough was eventually achieved to open the way to independence in 2008. But that time was distant sixty years before in 1948 and in an unimaginable future.

After the defeat of the Drenica revolt by 1948–49, the Albanian inhabitants were plainly going to be irreconcilable to Belgrade rule for a long time. It was not long before Tito took a page from the book of Royalist Yugoslavia and began to revive the old policy of forced Albanian emigration to Turkey.[43] This would clear the rural regions of 'difficult' families, it was hoped. At the same time, the party embarked on a policy of urbanisation whereby, as in Bulgaria, semi-coerced movement to the cities would make control of the population much easier.

The Communist showpiece was to be Prishtina. The rambling old Ottoman and 1920s town had seen many vicissitudes in its long history dating back to Roman Ulpiana in antiquity. The panoply of communist administration was planted there and soon after 1945 large concrete administrative buildings began to climb from the Kosovo Polje mud. Urbanisation plays an important part in building communist societies and the pattern adopted can reveal a good deal about the assumptions and *modus operandi* of a ruling elite. The Prishtina elite ultimately depended on the Yugoslav army to secure it, and as had happened under the Ottomans Empire, it was the decline in the army that after 1990 brought their existence to an end. The most prominent motif of Yugoslav Prishtina was insecurity. A military airport was built very nearby so that reinforcements could be brought in if trouble from the Albanians was brewing, and it was only a short drive to Serbia from the north-east Kosova town of Podujeve (modern Besian). Military reinforcements could also be brought in by train from the north, or on the road through the Merdare crossing. Prishtina was also some way from Drenica and 'bad' areas of Kosova like Decani or Junik where militant nationalists were no less committed to their ideas after 1948 than before. In terms of Yugoslavist ideology and historic associations, Prishtina town was not particularly 'Serb' either. It was, though, the headquarters of the Yugoslav martial law administration and housed the headquarters of the secret police (UDBA), the military command and all telephone and telecommunications facilities. It was at one level an 'off the production line' Yugoslavist modern town, but it could hardly be regarded as 'normal'. Kosova was under military rule and would remain so for a long time, and the Yugoslav military saw itself as the final guarantor of Kosova sovereignty for Serbia, as even the official handbook to the 1998–99 war states in its picture of that conflict:

The Yugoslav Army inflicted considerable losses on the enemy and successfully carried out the missions set by the people and the Supreme command. It did not allow the enemy to take an inch of our territory. At the same time, the Army of Yugoslavia in coordination with the forces of the Ministry of Interior disrupted the Shqiptare terrorist bands. Thus it created the conditions for the state leadership to fight by political and diplomatic means for the solutions, which, unlike the Rambouillet plan, and according to the UN Security Council Resolution No 1244, guarantee the sovereignty and territorial integrity of the country and provide only for the forces under UN auspices and flag to come to Kosovo and Metohija. The Yugoslav army ended the war undefeated and as an absolute moral victor, with minimal losses in personnel and weapons.[44]

At one level this is a strange and irrational statement, at odds with any sensible interpretation of the reality of events and in gross denial about the basic outcome of the war, but at another level it echoes far back in Serbian history, with the notion of war as a show, almost a pageant where the forces of Belgrade may lose battles but are never defeated because they are the army of Serbia. Pageantry had been part of the life of many Balkan armies with its degree of conscious archaism, and this was to resurface in the ex-Yugoslav wars where endless pointless shelling of, say, Sarajevo was undertaken and was incomprehensible to outside military observers. Archaism has played a large part in the colourful but often useless armies of the Balkan past in the early twentieth century, of which perhaps the Montenegrin is the best known example. With its secret leadership, high technology communication devices and conspiratorial development, the Kosova Liberation Army was to be the antithesis of this formal tradition of Balkan government armies. It was a tall order for the scattered rural Albanian resistants to meet. When in Serbian eyes the conspiracy against Yugoslavia started to develop on a serious basis, it inevitably did so in cities outside the country, and also outside Kosova. Yet it reached into the heart of Kosova from rooms in the most wealthy, urbane and sophisticated Swiss cities, to *oda* rooms in little Kosova farms where all authority was vested in a paternalistic old man whose family lived by the ancient Kanun code of revenge and where many family members hardly ever went into a town.

2

THE UNDERGROUND WAR 1950–1990

Ambush involves taking up a position in covert in the mountains or plains
of Albania and lying in wait for an enemy in the blood-feud or someone else
who is intended to be killed. (To waylay, set an ambush, to set a trap for
someone).

The Kanun of Lek Dukagjini[1]

In 1950 the most powerful country in the world, the United States, saw
the Tito-Stalin split as final. Policymakers in Washington were preoccupied by the effect of Marshal Tito's decision to break with Stalin as
an issue of Adriatic sea security and Soviet access to the Mediterranean[2] The world of the Kosova highlands and its numerous and serious problems was a very long way away from their thoughts. The
territory in Western eyes would be condemned to deeper and deeper
obscurity for many years. The end of the Drenica rising, its Ballist
aftermath and the establishment of secure Communist government in
Belgrade had left the Kosova Albanian community divided and demoralised. In northern Drenica a substantial proportion of the younger
males were dead or in prison, or had fled to other parts of Kosova,
Croatia, the Sandjak, or over the mountains to Albania. Emigration to
the United States was also increasing. Large-scale massacres of Ballist
fighters like that in Tivat in Montenegro in 1945, involving the death
of over 3,000 people after a forced march from Kosova, terrorised

ordinary Kosova Albanian families and left them in awe of the power
of Tito's military and security machine. The Yugoslav operation against
the Drenica rising had produced perfect conditions for the army to
install martial law, and under Communism many of the features of
government of the Axis Occupation were quickly reproduced. The
security chief Alexander Rankovic and his secret police took a special
responsibility for Kosova. Kosova's industry stagnated to the point of
near collapse.[3] There was a chronic shortage of personnel in the mining industries as Serbian forced labour conscripts were moved out of
Kosova to Serbia. This process was assisted by the expansion in the
1945–50 period of the big copper mines in north-east Serbia at Bor on
the Danube.

It is likely that in his military and security thinking Tito expected a
period of irregular warfare to continue with the ever present possibility of raids from over the border with Albania. In a certain sense he
was right. Large rural areas of central and western Kosova remained
dominated by emotions of hatred and alienation from the government
for years after 1945. The Albanians there were plainly going to be
irreconcilable for a long time. It did not take Tito and the Politburo
long to conclude that the only way for socialism to make progress in
Kosova was by the construction of cities which would hopefully
destroy the radical rural communities, in alliance with the growth of
mining and the extractive industries. This was not a planning priority
elsewhere in Yugoslavia, where many small farmers and peasants were
often strong supporters of Tito and where Communist party membership in the countryside was often significant.[4]

There were isolated pockets of violent resistance to the Titoist settlement for a long time, but these incidents were seen by the regime as
part of a process of rural criminality rather than political or military
opposition. The standard Belgrade 'security' strategy over the years has
always been to depoliticise Albanian opposition by claiming it is 'criminal'. The dilemma facing the Albanian political leadership—insofar as
anything much of it remained—was how to work out a pattern of
struggle that would detach the people from the new system. The government in Belgrade knew that there were significant opposition centres, mostly Ballist, in Italy and the United States and the repressive
measures taken against oppositional individuals and families were
taken in the name of national security. Yugoslavia saw itself as under
siege, despite the post-1948 rapprochement with the West, but unlike

what happened in most East European Communist nations, the political opposition was attacked on the basis of ethnicity rather than class.

In Albania, after the break with Tito and the international Communist movement in 1948, Enver Hoxha had not totally abandoned the Kosovars to their fate, as his critics in the Albanian world have often claimed. The Kosova problem was a way for Hoxha to begin to define the new Albania against Yugoslavia and its slippage back to capitalist theory and practice. Intelligence-led subversion was his preferred tactic, by which most if not all Tirana-sponsored activity was deniable and Hoxha might begin to put at least minor pressure on Belgrade using Albania's very limited resources. It is probable that he received at least some advice from Soviet sources after 1948 in these respects.[5] Hoxha had a close relationship with the Soviet Ambassador to Albania, Dimitri Chuvakin, who was a senior Moscow MFA figure with an intelligence background and direct access to Stalin.[6] Hoxha could please his Russian patrons by obtaining news of Kosova and Yugoslav developments and passing it to the Russians. But this was not the extent of Albanian activity. In 1949 Enver Hoxha and his military commander Mehmet Shehu had been in touch with Stalin about the possibility of forming an armed force to overthrow the Tito government in Belgrade, starting with an armed uprising in Kosova. In his diary for 5 July 1949 Chuvakin notes a discussion he had with Shehu on the military options for dealing with the 'revisionist' regime within southern Yugoslavia, although there was no clear view on strategy in Moscow. He writes:

The question has arisen amongst us of how to organise the struggle against the Titoites in Yugoslavia. We do not know which is better, whether each republic in the Yugoslav federation should conduct the struggle against the Tito clique independently, and in such a case one could allocate the struggle to the autonomous region of Kosovo and Metohije, or whether the struggle against the Yugoslav Trotskyites from the Tito clique should be directed from a single centre.[7]

Understandably the second option did not appeal much to Mehmet Shehu, with his personal experience of the damage Stalinist military command had done to the Republican cause in the Spanish Civil War, and he rebuffed the idea, replying, according to Chuvakin, 'For me personally this question is quite clear in the sense that the Tito clique can only be overthrown by means of an armed struggle against it, and this armed struggle must begin in Kosovo and Metohija, where it is

33

easier to raise the population against the Tito clique.'[8] Chuvakin understood this to mean that Shehu was in favour of uniting Kosova with Albania, noting:

By this MS (Mehmet Shehu) gave me to understand that for the Albanian population of Kosovo and Metohije the question of whether the region should be united with Albania is resolved, that is, K and M should in any case be united with Albania. The only question which arises is when it will be more convenient to engage with this slogan among the Albanian population of K and M: after the end of the struggle with the Tito clique or in the very course of the struggle.[9]

In this atmosphere, Hoxha began to organise infiltration of Kosova of trained militants, who were tasked ostensibly with beginning the formation of underground cells of 'sleepers' to be ready to fight against Belgrade's control in the long-term future and to provide intelligence to Tirana and Moscow in the short term. These often turned out to be contradictory objectives. Secret intelligence gathering is an activity that does not mix well with forming insurgent armies or law enforcement and pacification activity. The Yugoslav military had seen the problem of pacifying Kosova almost entirely as a problem of dealing with rebellious Drenica. Their success there led to complacency. Economic neglect and exploitation of Kosova were already a major issue. Russia was still firmly behind Albania and by 1950 there were thousands of Soviet advisers in the country, mostly working on the major hydroelectric projects in the Black Drin valley in the north, close to the Kosova border.[10] With Russian help, Albania was undergoing an industrial revolution. Apart from the ongoing redevelopment and expansion of the base metal mine at Mitrovica, Kosova by comparison was still in post-conflict disorder and conditions in the villages remained medieval.[11] In view of the later history of Albania it may seem hard to believe today, but in those early years, Soviet-allied Albania was making substantial progress towards urbanism and modernity—albeit at a very high human cost—by comparison with not only Kosova but much of rural southern Yugoslavia.[12] The Tito regime was pouring investment funds into the northern towns in Serbia, the Belgrade region, and Croatia and Slovenia.

The adventurous life of a man such as Zijadin Qira illustrates the Enverist paradigm for Kosova in these years and the attempts by Tirana to start to build a platform within Kosova for a future insurgency. Qira was born in 1932 in the village of Veleshte in Macedonia, eight miles north of Struga and only about five miles from the border with Albania. Veleshte nestles in tidy maize fields nowadays, just below the Quaf e Thanes mountain pass, and has something of a risky reputation as a centre of smuggling and illegal trading. Qira's family had been minor Ottoman officials in Struga and Ohrid and some had fled to Turkey in the interwar period. The hill settlement stands just below the border crossing between the two countries. Veleshte has a history of violence and population displacement dating back long before the Second World War. After the Serbian army took control of Ohrid in the Second Balkan War in 1913 and drove out the Bulgarians, hundreds of Albanians, particularly those of higher rank in the Ottoman system, left Ohrid and Struga to take refuge in the hills and make way for the new Orthodox Yugoslav settlers. Many of these people were Serbian army veterans, moved in by Royalist Belgrade and given land from the old Ottoman *cifliks* north of Ohrid Lake on the ancient Roman model of military colonisation.[13] Muslim Albanians were soon unwelcome in Ohrid, and Veleshte grew from a tiny pastoral community to a large village of Ohrid exiles in those years. These declassed and alienated refugees in their own country, often originally of *Bey* or *Aga* rank, were readily open to radical ideas, whether nationalist or Communist, much as in Greece Asia Minor refugees after 1922 made up a disproportionately large component of the original Greek Communist Party (KKE) leadership. The same process also affected ex-Ottoman officials and landowners in southern Albania, so that prominent Communist leaders from the south, like Adil Carcani, came from these displaced Ottoman landowning roots.

In the time of the disintegrating Axis occupation, Qira was an idealistic young man who wanted to fight for freedom, and he first met Albanian Partisans in the mountains above the village and then went to Tirana as a sixteen-year-old to study in the new military academy the Communists had opened. Albanian Partisan units were operating near the border and were recruiting in the Macedonian Albanian hill villages. Qira had witnessed the savage reprisals against the local Albanian population by the 4th Bulgarian Brigade in 1944, in which over three thousand Albanian people from the Struga area were killed. At first in 1946–47 his radical anti-Serbian and anti-Yugoslavist views brought him into danger in Tirana, and he may only have survived because of his contacts with the family of Liri Bereshova, the senior female Communist in Albania, a Central Committee member and an

Albanian Partisan heroine. But when Yugoslavia's break with Stalin came in 1948, Qira's hitherto radical anti-Yugoslavist views became the conventional wisdom in Tirana and in one of his many zigzags in policy, Hoxha espoused the Kosova cause to a degree, at its darkest hour.

As a trick to provide him with a cover story, Zijadin Qira was one of a group in the Military Academy chosen to be ordered to set up cells to stage a 'revolt' against Enver Hoxha and in favour of Tito's positions. This would be well publicised and exposed in the party press in Tirana. He would then 'flee' to the border with Yugoslavia where he would ask for political asylum. Once in Kosova, he would make every effort to penetrate the security police and become a Tirana secret agent.[14] In the climate of intense repression that existed at the time, and with the efficiency of the Yugoslav security apparatus, the enterprise was inevitably doomed, and in 1951 Qira was arrested and convicted by a military court of spying and sentenced to a long term of imprisonment. It would appear to have been a quixotic, over-ambitious and ill-planned venture. It nevertheless began to set the paradigm for virtually all future work against Yugoslavia organised from Albania right up to the 1990s. In the 1950s Russia was the superpower in the background to Albanian activism, in the 1990s it was the United States. Enver Hoxha could provide useful field intelligence to curry favour with his superpower backers. There was a change of emphasis as the 1950s wore on, with Tirana's espionage priorities on behalf of Moscow driving out all serious attempts to build a resistance army. Yet the ideal of a Kosova army never died. The 1956 espionage trial in Prishtina falls into this paradigm, although it is doubtful whether Noel Malcolm is right in claiming there was little evidence for Hoxhaist activity in this event.[15] In an obvious show trial, the Yugoslav authorities arrested and jailed several prominent Kosovars allegedly for working for the Albanian secret service. They served twelve years in prison as a result. For an unpopular and surrounded nation like Albania espionage was important, similar to the position of some nations in the current world, as the status of Mossad in Israel demonstrates. In his own later activity Qira, as a long-time US resident, remained an Albanian nationalist activist and played a prominent part in the last years of his life in building up the Kosova Liberation Army in New York City. After his release and exile in the United States, Qira wrote that 'the only thing I was attempting to do was to prepare the people for the eventual decay of the Yugoslav Communist regime ... if I could organise the youth and prepare for the time when they could ask for help from the West, we would be a free country.'[16]

His apparently simple statement embodies several key themes in the interrelationship between Albania and Yugoslavia at that time and the nature of the underground struggle for a future insurgent Kosova army. The Yugoslavs could rely on the ultra-conservative patriarchal Kosovar family with its strong dash of Muslim fatalism to inhibit radical action. The old men in the villages had as strong a nationalist sense as any of the young but after the disasters for their cause in the 1943–49 period, had little appetite for direct resistance and less capacity to organise it. Their model of horseback heroics of military resistance based on the nineteenth-century *ceta* had been decisively defeated in Drenica by the mechanised warfare of the Titoist Partisans in 1944–49. The constituency for the Enverist infiltrators like Qira in the late 1940s and early 1950s must involve reliance on the young, just as the Kosova Liberation Army after 1995 mostly relied on the young and fairly young. It would also require a new military model and military doctrine. The latter was in a sense available in the form of the Communist theories of people's war, but it was far from clear how this could be applied in Kosova where there was little Marxist, let alone Marxist-Leninist political consciousness. The key Maoist texts on guerrilla war that were to rewrite the entire doctrine of the subject were unknown outside China until the 1960s. A potential Kosova Albanian insurgent military leader, the ex-Partisan chief Colonel Qamil Brovina, who did have a revolutionary and class conscious outlook was in gaol.[17] The only other Kosovar Partisan of similar standing, Fadil Hoxha, was more a politician in uniform than a revolutionary soldier, and he was a political opportunist who had thrown in his lot with Tito and the Yugoslavs in 1948.

Secondly, Qira and his security service backers had a sense even then that Yugoslav model Communism would not take root in Kosova as a successful government any more than it had as an oppositional focus within post-Axis Yugoslavia, and would in time decay. The revisionist 'reforms' under Tito after 1948 had already released elements of traditional small-scale capitalism. A major event was the decline and eventual collapse of Titoist attempts to collectivise agriculture in the early 1950s. In Kosova this enabled the threatened larger landholding families to hang on to some of their pre-1939 landholdings and some urban property in old Ottoman centres such as Vushtrri. Many of these families were in northern and eastern Kosova and were to form the background of impoverished rural conservatism and petit-bourgeois collaboration with the Titoists that remained a major factor in Kosova for many years. Some had never really lost their local power networks in Royalist Yugoslavia and under Axis occupation. With their status as *beys* and *agas* that the late Ottoman system had given them, they were flexible and adaptable in keeping their supremacy in different social and political systems and benefited from the state absence phenomenon in Kosova.[18] In another illustration of how events around 1948–50 set the pattern of development for many following years, after 1990, many of the same families and districts became the backbone of Ibrahim Rugova's Kosova Democratic League, and their local power networks flourished again.

Thirdly, Qira and his Sigurimi associates came to see many years later that Kosova could not be released from Yugoslavia without external help from the West. Russia and its many satellite states also had long-term strategic interests in Belgrade and the miserable fate of top Kosovar Albanian Partisans like Brovina who had taken the Russian line in 1948 and were 'against the Resolution' to leave the Cominform was no incentive for others to follow them.[19] The Qira mission had a fatal ambiguity, in that it clearly served the priorities of the Hoxha government to obtain secrets from its new antagonistic neighbour and protect Albanian national interests through the Soviet alliance.[20] This was not the same issue as fomenting resistance within Kosova itself. Over the next forty years this contradiction was never satisfactorily resolved, either in Tirana or by the radical Kosovars. Albania was required as a friendly kinship state with a permeable border to act as a base for training, military supply and rest and recreation but the government in Tirana had wider international priorities than Kosova, and this affected its attitude towards illegal political struggle there.[21]

In some periods, the Kosova struggle was at such a low ebb that it seemed essential in Tirana to help develop resistance, if only as a means of stabilising Kosova as it was (however unsatisfactory from the Albanian point of view) and preventing its collapse as an Albanian-majority entity within Yugoslavia, with all the danger that might bring to Albania's own borders. At other times economic cooperation was the priority, as in the 1980s when the LCK was under Albanian control. There was also the issue of what the 'West' consisted of, from the Kosovar Albanian point of view. The 'West' for Albanians meant the

United States, first and foremost. Ever since US President Woodrow Wilson's commitment to the survival of the post-1913 Albanian state in the Versailles treaty period when many European Powers would happily have seen it divided between Greece, Montenegro and Serbia, the United States always had a special role in the Albanian political pantheon, but as the Cold War developed, Tito's Yugoslavia was seen in a positive light in the USA and in the Cold War Albania was within the Russian and later the Chinese orbit. Little could be expected from the United States in 1950 except one thing, the provision of a safe haven for Albanian and Kosovar refugees. This was also the case in Britain where Tito had the additional wartime links with luminaries like William Deakin and Fitzroy Maclean. The attitude of the British Communists to Tito after 1948 was particularly sectarian and dogmatic. The Party expert on southeast Europe, James Klugman, had been in the Special Operations Executive Yugoslav section in the Second World War in Cairo and Bari and was later the subject of various allegations about his supposed role in directing SOE resources to assist Tito's rise to power.[22]

In some of the worst periods, Tirana actively collaborated with Belgrade against the Kosovars, as in the 1980s when militants on the run from the Yugoslav police apparatus were returned to Kosova and long periods of imprisonment. In response, from a very early date, the Kosovars began to form informal networks of sympathy within the Albanian Party of Labour and key organisations in Albania, particularly the security service, the Sigurimi and the military. These were often based on those prominent Albanians with family links in Kosova and northeast border districts like Tropoja, Diber and Has where there was a strong local patriotic tradition of service in the army and police and older inhabitants easily remembered life within the Ottoman *vilayet* system before the 1913 national border dividing the Albanian communities existed.

In another echo of the 1990s wartime period, there were also money-making and smuggling opportunities once the antagonistic post-1948 border had been established. The natural economic hinterland for an important Kosova town like Gjakova included much of these Albanian borderlands, as Prizren was the natural urban centre for the territory west of the Black Drin in Albania. Tirana was not important in these regions; it was a 'new' capital that had been little more than a small market centre and Ottoman garrison town before 1913. The north had been almost totally neglected by the Tirana monarch King Zog in the 1920s and 1930s after his hunting down of Kosova patriots like Bajram Curri and Hasan Prishtina. In comparison, Gjakova had a long record of often wild Albanian resistance to all external rule, Ottoman or Royalist Yugoslav, and Prizren was the fountain head of nineteenth-century Albanian nationalism. Peje citizens were described in the official Austro-Hungarian army guide to the region in 1895 as little more than nationalist wild animals. In another illustration of this long historical memory based on pan-Albanian links affecting the present, officers in the Albanian army from Dibra and Tropoja in 1997–98 were vital in small arms transfer from Albania to Kosova, after the 1997 rising, to the nascent KLA. The most prominent of these was General Kudusi Lama, commander of the Kukes military district.[23]

A new paradigm of resistance was clearly needed and it did not take long for it to emerge. The Yugoslav military was expanding its base rapidly in Kosova in these years, particularly as an infantry training centre. After the 'pacification' of Drenica, the JNA Prishtina Corps had begun in 1946 to consolidate its positions and role all over Kosova. The wartime airstrip at Kosovo Polje was expanded to become Prishtina airport. Large garrison camps were either expanded or built new on greenfield sites, particularly near places where concentrations of the new working class in the extractive industries resided, and above all in Prishtina itself. A massive new artillery and vehicle base was opened just to the west of the city where forces could be quickly deployed all over Kosova in the event of trouble. After 1948 great attention was paid to security on the border with Albania. Deep ditches were dug and concrete posts and minefields placed to mark a 'free fire zone' for the JNA. In the north a closed military zone was established along the Buna river marking the Montenegrin border, cutting off important archaeological sites like Svac for two generations.[24] In the mountains a similar closed zone was attempted, although with less success owing to the difficult terrain. Concrete barriers were built and mines laid along forest roads between the two countries and a border-long system of guard posts set up. The incapacity of the Milosevic government to keep this complex and infantry soldier-intensive border system going in 1998 was one of the first signs that victory for the KLA might be achievable. The military controlled the roads, the telephone system and much else in Kosova life. A major munitions factory was built near the village of Llaushe in the heart of defeated Drenice as a clear message to the local Albanians that not only had they lost their struggle for freedom, but they must also work for their bread in the arms factories of their masters.

Nevertheless some resistance was possible. The villages were still armed, if only with antiquated weapons. They could not be used against the JNA but their existence produced a kind of psychological equilibrium where villages could feel more secure. Yugoslav army conscription meant that soon a generation of young men appeared who had some modern weapons training, although for a long time in the JNA Kosovar conscripts were confined to jobs like drivers and store workers to keep them as far away from weapons as possible. In the towns resistance was more difficult than in the villages, with Rankovic's use of the Soviet 'block supervisor' system of a local party committee in each housing area to report on potential dissidents. Local terror continued. There was nothing the Albanians could do to prevent the mass executions and mass graves of Balli Kombetar families, such at the pogrom in the Cekliku district of Prishtina in 1950. As at other dark times in Kosova history, the cultural struggle was paramount for the Albanians. In some parts of Kosova like Llap, where Balli Kombetar had been strongly supported and still had some underground political organisation and local popular support, civil society associations began to be formed to defend Albanian language use and education against the removal of the rights instituted by the Italian occupiers. Slavic hegemony in education was forced through from Belgrade. Towns like Podujeve, Vushtrri and Mitrovica were again important in this movement. In any more normal or democratic society these would have been only civil society or non-governmental organisations without any security or military aspect, but this was not the case in Titoist Kosova. Titoism with its roots in Stalinist Marxism did not in any case encourage a healthy civil society, even for pro-Yugoslav sections of the population. Throughout Yugoslavia mass organisations such as trade unions were kept deliberately weak while the party and the security services were strong.[25] Churches and mosques were carefully controlled through central religious councils and only politically reliable candidates were accepted at Belgrade university.

From the Belgrade point of view this was vital to develop communism and the Yugoslav man and woman, and to overcome local national and cultural identities. It was necessary for these Albanian cultural and educational organisations to work underground, meeting

41

illegally, usually in remote spots in villages where UDBA informers were few and the police absent. There is a direct link again between this period and the emphasis on cultural nationalism, literary culture and 'parallel structures' education in the Kosova Democratic League after 1990, where a literary critic like Ibrahim Rugova with no political experience whatsoever could seem a natural leader of a major political movement. The challenge for the Albanians was to form a revolutionary nucleus, in the Marxist-Leninist sense, and much of the impetus behind Kosova Albanian underground organisations like the Kosova People's Movement (LPK) in later years involved attempts to solve this problem, for without the revolutionary political and cultural nucleus, a revolutionary army cannot be created.[26] In 1966, for the first time for many years, the crimes and violence of the secret police against the majority population of Kosova were exposed in the international press. After the fall of Rankovic, the Belgrade newspaper *Borba* published details of illegal police executions of Albanians, which were subsequently reported in the London *Times*, *Le Monde* and elsewhere.[27] Many of the victims were education and cultural activists, such as a teachers' leader in western Kosova who had thrown himself under a train to escape police persecution.

The wider issue of political leadership remained in abeyance. The anti-Communist but strongly nationalist Balli Kombetar organisation was illegal and as such had more or less ceased to exist in Kosova by late 1948, and there was a lack of functional leadership and communications with the world outside Kosova.[28] It was to continue an uncertain existence with splits in the membership in the United States and Italy but had little purchase in Kosova. The new leadership was to come from a new direction, and the question of a revolutionary army was firmly put on its agenda. In 1964 the Levizjes Revolucionaire per Bashkimin e Shqiptare (LRBSH) was founded, the Revolutionary League for the Unification of the Albanians. Its most important leader was a novelist and short story writer, Adem Demaci, but it quickly collected a small and committed group of cadres, particularly in Prishtina and north-east Kosova. Demaci was also to become a hardheaded political leader with a deep knowledge of Marxism, and in some senses the intellectual father of the Kosova Liberation Army, but his radical orientation was not typical of all LRBSH members and supporters.[29] Some important figures such as Ahmet Haxhiu came from the 'Right', in the sense that their families were Ballist and based in generally more

Islamic and culturally conservative north-east Kosova.[30] Demaci was a brilliant student in the philosophy faculty while at Belgrade university, where unlike any other previous Kosova leadership generation he had an intensive exposure to Marxism. It did not take him long to conclude that the Hoxhaist criticism of Tito as a renegade from Marxism was correct, and to adopt Albania as an intellectual *pathrithia* rather than his native Kosova. He had been an early visitor there as part of a school Young Pioneers holiday trip in 1946 and noted how far Albania was completely repressed and under Yugoslav control in that year.[31] A small, wiry, bright-eyed urban man with driving energy, he was the antithesis of the ill educated and fatalistic pliss-wearing Bajraktars in the villages. He was a product of the higher education in Belgrade that Communism had brought and in a certain sense was a 'New Man' of the Communist system.

Many of the details of Demaci's early political life are still unclear, although his recent biographer Shkelzen Gashi has cast some light in many hitherto dark places.[32] Adem Demaci was born into a poor family with Podujeve roots which just missed emigrating to Turkey in 1930.[33] They settled in Prishtina and Adem was born in 1935, the youngest of seven children. As a result of bad living conditions and non-existent healthcare only three of the family survived, Demaci and his brother and sister, Maliq and Ajsche. Aspects of his early life were Dickensian in their grinding poverty. His father worked as a Prishtina street cleaner but died when he was eight years old from tuberculosis, a familiar scourge in interwar Kosova towns. Adem got a good education at the Hasan Prishtina school during the Second World War while his mother kept the family from starvation by weaving. She was a fiercely patriotic Kosovar who hated all Serbs. As a little girl she had seen the Serbian army shoot her four uncles in front of the rest of the family in their garden in the First Balkan War in 1912. It was a fitting family background for a man whose life would be dedicated to the Kosova revolution, with all the hardships that involved.

Demaci became involved with a literary periodical, *Drita*, at Belgrade university while on a world literature course. He began to publish poems and stories. The death of his mother ended his studies prematurely. But he had already become politically active from his sixteenth year in 1951, and he was only twenty-three years old when he was first arrested and then imprisoned for political offences in 1959. The years from 1953 to 1958 had been spent establishing his reputa-

THE KOSOVA LIBERATION ARMY

tion as a brilliant young writer. The mass expulsions to Turkey of Kosovar Albanians hung heavily over Prishtina; over three quarters of the population departed from the district where the Demaci family lived. He was sentenced to five years in his first trial but after subsequent trials ended up serving twenty-eight years in Tito's gaols. In his early writing he had called for the unification of Albania and Kosova and for Greek reparations for Cham Albanians dispossessed in the Second World War. It was later claimed that Demaci was first arrested after pressure from the Yugoslav Ambassador in Athens over the latter issue.

However, the real danger of Demaci from the Belgrade viewpoint lay not only in his practical political skills but in his attempt—if not fully achieved—at a reconciliation if not a synthesis of Enverist (Marxist) and Ballist (nationalist) political ideologies and objectives by founding his new secret political organisation, the Levizjes Revolucionare te Bashkimit te Shqiptareve, the Revolutionary League for the Unification of the Albanians, on a new ideological basis. Divide and rule was the central policy for Belgrade against the Kosova Albanians; exploiting the antagonisms between those who had supported Balli Kombetar after 1945 and those who had become Communist collaborators was central to their strategy for rule. Demaci sought to transcend the Ballist-nationalist/Communist-internationalist dichotomy that had dominated the politics of the Kosovar Albanians since 1945. He had a clear fluid style of writing and would clearly develop into a formidable political opponent, and Belgrade had much to fear from him. At the time, the Belgrade government was seeking to remove as many Kosovar Albanians to Turkey as possible, and the second 1964 trial of Demaci involved arms smuggling charges with Istanbul-based accomplices. Other new organisations were forming in Kosova in this period, mostly based in particular localities. An example was the Organizata per Bashkimin e Trojeve Shqiptare that developed in and around Peje (Pec) in 1959 and survived for about five years before it was broken up by the secret police. It had specifically Ballist roots around the Baloku and other prominent Peje families, some of whom were survivors of the 1945 Tivat massacres in Montenegro.[34] The key issue for Belgrade was Albanian disarmament, which was supposed to have been achieved by security chief Rankovic as long ago as 1956. This theme was to continue in Kosova Albanian politics for many years. An armed population was a potentially free population while an unarmed population was at the mercy of a foreign army or security apparatus, as the provision of the right to bear arms in the US Constitution demonstrates. It was only a short distance for revolutionary theorists to extrapolate towards the concept of a popular uprising, as eventually took place in Albania in 1997.

As a result Demaci was imprisoned for many years, although in the trial records it is interesting to note that the allegation that he and his organisation flew nearly forty Albanian flags in Prishtina was as prominent as the arms charges. In his early writing, he emphasised more the possibilities of unification of the nation than the class issues, setting out a programme in three stages, territorial, economic and literary. The emergence of Demaci's Revolutionary League took place at a time of a major new crisis for the Kosovar Albanians. As early as the 1930s there had been a tentative agreement between the Turkish and Yugoslav governments to 'resettle' Muslim Kosovars in Turkey, but it did not really amount to much until 1951.[35] Then a system of forced deportations from Kosova started, using the strong residual element of Ottoman culture, particularly in eastern Kosova, as an identity branding exercise, to reduce the Muslim proportion of the population. At the same time, the security chief Rankovic used the issue as a stick to beat the Albanians generally, and brought in new legislation to impound all personal small arms and weapons held in Kosova communities. Although this was defended as a law and order measure, its real purpose was to reduce the possibility of forcible resistance to the government's deportation plans.

In the Revolutionary League programme, there is a lengthy analysis of the international political situation.[36] The role of the League is not theorised in a fully Marxist way, although Demaci clearly states that the exemplars for the Kosova liberation struggle are in Second and Third World nations freeing themselves from colonialism like Algeria, Cuba and Vietnam. He rejects the Soviet and Chinese Communist models. Demaci's Marxism was always explicitly anti-Stalinist. The radicalism of the 1960s was beginning and a new current in politics were emerging. The Cuban revolution was an inspiration to the young generation of new radicals.[37] Demaci views the division of the world into two blocs critically, but not as critically as he views the traditional leaders of Kosova society, whom he describes as the victims of a feudal world view and petty local quarrels, much as the Italian Marxist theoretician Antonio Gramsci saw the inhabitants of his native Sardinia before the Second World War. Yet the traditional structures included the vast majority of the population. Demaci regards 75 per cent of Kosova Albanians as '*katundarija*', a term which can be translated as 'peasant' but in Albanian culture often also carries derogatory associations like 'hick' in American English. The *katundarija* were ill-educated rurals and often more or less illiterate, particularly the girls and women. They were leaderless and in a state of ideological disorientation after the imposition of Communism and the ejection of the imams from local authority. Demaci sees the working class as small, perhaps 10 per cent of the population, and often relatively socially isolated in a few centres like the mining communities of Mitrovica. The intellectuals only comprised about 1 per cent of the population, and in practice many of them were resident abroad.

It was not an auspicious picture for the aspirant 1960s revolutionary, and one of the factors explaining why Belgrade could move so swiftly and easily against Demaci and the LRBSH, and stage a well-publicised shows trial in 1964, was his isolation. If Demaci was a potential Kosovar Lenin, there was not only no Trotsky but no Radek or Bukharin or even a Stalin to support him. He also utilised the old nineteenth-century Albanian conception of the political League, rather than that of a political party. A long book could be written discussing the exact meaning of an Albanian political league, but in general it has the notion of a voluntary political association of socially and economically prominent citizens; equals but without any very formal internal procedures or hierarchy of authority. In the nineteenth century the nationalist leagues were based on land and family status within the Ottoman administrative system. In the Albanian tradition, late nineteenth-century leagues such as those of Prizren and Peje were good at articulating moderate nationalism and making an effective bourgeois opposition to Ottoman rule, but they were much less useful in organising modern political activity in illegal conditions, let alone being able to start or run a war.

The final crisis of the league concept came with Ibrahim Rugova's Kosova Democratic League and its manifest incapacity to develop effective opposition to the Milosevic regime after 1995. Although the Kosova People's League (LPK) called itself a league, it functioned much more like a Marxist-Leninist political party, at least in the early years after 1982. It had a small clandestine core leadership, a secret membership of whom some were 'sleepers' and a large periphery of supporters who were not invited to join the party but were expected to perform certain open tasks on its behalf.

The modernising currents of intellectual life in Kosova that brought about Demaci's rise to prominence did not cease with his second imprisonment in 1964.[38] Tito knew the Communist system needed modernisation if it was to survive. Pressure for change was coming from the educated young. In 1968 Kosova towns were active partici- pants in the national protest demonstrations centred on Belgrade.[39] In the 27 November demonstration, the demand for a Kosova Republic within Yugoslavia was for the first time shouted on the Prishtina streets by demonstrating young people. This was a major landmark and illus- trates the beginning of the process of breakdown in the hitherto total control Belgrade had exerted over Kosova since the Second World War. Tito and the party leadership knew change was inevitable, although they responded to the 1968 riots at the time with a mixture of waffle and conspiracy theories. Tito blamed 'a group which has incited part of the youth' for the violence, and castigated the media for exaggerat- ing how bad things were in Kosova.[40] The local Kosova party leader Fadil Hoxha blamed 'Ballist and Chetnik enemies' for trying to desta- bilise socialism. In 1974 Yugoslavia gained a new constitution that gave a degree of autonomy to Kosova, although falling far short of republican status with the Federation. The Communist party now had a much larger proportion of Albanian members, and significant advances came their way, particularly in the field of culture and educa- tion, provided that they conformed to the Yugoslavist agenda. The new generation of educated young wanted much greater political advance than mere autonomy and like many other young generations in the 1960s they were very impatient of the assumptions of their elders. Albanian influence in Kosova was increasing, with more intellectual and practical contact and trade deals. An example was the sale of chrome from small mines around Gjakova to the new Albanian smelter at Burrell, and in the reverse direction, beech timber from the Albanian forests to the Yugoslav furniture industry.

The radical educated young had seen television coverage of the 1968 and post-1968 student movements in the USA and Western Europe, and New Left ideas based on rank and file activism, anti-bureaucratic struggle, and confrontation with the capitalist state were becoming more influential throughout Yugoslavia. The father of an important future KLA leader and LPK politician like Bardhyl Mahmuti had been gaoled for his participation in the 1968 demonstrations in Tetovo in Macedonia.[41] As long ago as 1967, student demonstrations in Belgrade occupying the university and the streets had included in their common leadership such disparate people, later to become bitter opponents, as the Serbian Mira Markovic, the future wife of Slobodan Milosevic, and Arben Xhaferi, future leader of the Tetovo Albanian nationalist radicals.[42] In the party itself new faces were beginning to appear, with a very young Montenegrin named Milo Djukanovic becoming leader of the party Youth League in Titograd (Podgoritsa) and a future Milosevic period activist, Tahir Hasanovic, in the same position in Sarajevo.[43] The suppression of the national question under Tito led radicals into nationalist directions, and significant numbers saw Hoxha's Albania in a positive light and so were open to influence from that direction.

Inevitably, given the general climate, a confrontation was inevitable. The demonstrations in Prishtina in favour of a Kosova Republic were organised predominantly by a small revolutionary group, the Organizata Marksiste-Leniniste e Kosoves (OMLK), which had been founded in 1976.[44] This was a direct descendant of Demaci's second revolutionary organisation, the Levizjes per Clirimin Kombetar te Kosoves (LCKK), the League for the National Liberation of Kosova, founded during his second prison term with Jusuf Gervalla.[45] They had a substantial common core of membership. It was very small, perhaps a hundred or so activists, but by precisely focused underground work it had achieved a confrontational mass demonstration. The scale of support for the political demands of what had been seen as only small extremist student groups alarmed Belgrade, and a crackdown was ordered. The demonstrations were the largest against the Serbian regime in Kosova since the Second World War, and called for autonomous Kosova to be made a Republic, equal with the other Republics in Yugoslavia. On 11 March 1981 the army and paramilitary police attacked a demonstration in Prishtina. On 26 March a much larger demonstration called to protest against state violence was also brutally crushed.[46] The Tirana government protested officially against what had happened, and for the first time since 1948 reopening of the national question of the future of Kosova within Yugoslavia seemed possible.[47] Yet Yugoslav force was effective, the sight of tanks on the streets was not in those days covered by the foreign media and no CNN existed. Belgrade was able to retain control by military methods against the Kosovar mass popular action. The chairman of the Central Committee of the Communist Party of Kosova, Mahmut Bakalli, was subsequently sacked by Belgrade.[48] The limited foreign concern was tempered by Western 'realism' and a sense that Titoism was still dominant in Yugoslavia and worth supporting.

On the Kosovar side, 1981 seemed a catastrophic defeat. The limits of mass action in the streets had been reached. In a sense it was a catastrophe, with 1,289 Albanians sentenced over the next four years to prison terms, usually varying from ten to fifteen years. Some Yugoslav gaols after 1981 had a majority of Albanian 'politicals' as inmates for many years. They were to become universities of insurgency development. In a significant break from the Drenica and Dukagjini dominated resistance of the past hundred years, the lists of those arrested and gaoled include many from towns like Gjilan and Ferizaj, which had no radical history and whose growth was almost entirely a product of the Yugoslav Communist years.[49] The newly educated young produced by the Yugoslav education system were rejecting its values, and perhaps part of the explanation for the ferocity of the crackdown on the street demonstrations was the anger the mostly ill-educated and working class Slavic police felt at the newly privileged (in their eyes) Albanian youth who rejected their system. This dialectic was to recur frequently right up to 1999.

Yet a period in prison can prove a good education for revolutionaries, and this proved to be the case with the young Kosovars. 1981 student leaders like Bajram Kosumi and Hydajet Hyseni were to move into leadership positions in the new Kosova after 1999 and after Kosova Liberation Army activity.[50] Bardhyl Mahmuti like many others joined the LPK while in gaol, in his case in 1983.[51] The significance of what happened in 1981 was not lost, its central focus being that military force would ultimately decide the future of Kosova, however strong the political movement might be. Individual actions outside Kosova, like the shooting of a Yugoslav consular official in Brussels in 1981 by Musa Hoti, a member of a tiny leftist *groupuscule*, were good for a headline in Belgrade and Prishtina but not a substitute for facing the central military issues in Kosova itself.[52] There was only one logical response, which was to move to form a new political organisation that could create a Kosova insurgent army. Adem Demaci's close collaborator Jusuf Gervalla was still at liberty, along with some generally older generation militants who had been able to escape the Yugoslav security crackdown after the street demonstrations. Ahmet Haxhiu had been in touch with Gervalla in Germany as long ago as 1974, and had led meetings with Demaci in prison the following year.[53] Gervalla and

Metush Krasniqi had then formed a small revolutionary league while in prison, the Levizja Nacional-Climitare e Kosoves dhe Viseve Shqiptare ne Jugosllavi (LNCKVSJ).[54] A new united organisation dedicated to building towards the Kosova revolution seemed essential. At a meeting in February 1982 the remnants of the OMLK membership joined with the tiny Partia Komuniste Marksiste-Leniniste e Shqiptare nen Yugoslavi (PKMLSHJ) and the equally small Levizja per Republiken Socialiste Shqiptare ne Jugosllavi (LRSSHJ) to form a new organisation, the Levizjen Popullore per Republiken e Kosoves (LPRK), direct antecedent of the LPK.[55] At the same time other very small groups were formed by intellectuals such as Ukshin Hoti, but the LPRK and its direct descendant—the much better known LPK, the Kosova People's League or Kosova People's Movement—exercised a decisive influence on the future and provided a working framework for a whole generation of militants who were to lead the war in the late 1990s.[56] It was, in a real sense, the same organisation, but the 'R' remained in the party name in some contexts until 1991. Almost every significant figure in modern Kosova and Albanian Macedonia activism from Ramush Haradinaj[57] to Hashim Thaci[58] to Adem Jashari,[59] Xharvit Haliti,[60] Ali Ahmeti[61] and Fazli Veliu[62] belonged to the LPRK/LPK or worked with it. For the leadership, there was a single vital decision to take after the killing of the Gervalla brothers in Germany, which was organisational location, and the choice of a Swiss location for the LPK was to be an inspired choice and a great asset in the future. In Jusuf Gervalla's poetry there is a clear sense of the future, of a lonely and difficult struggle, as the manner of his death duly proved.[63] Many Kosovars were moving to work in Switzerland for economic reasons, and Swiss traditions of protecting the human rights of refugees and their right to campaign politically were vital. Without Switzerland and all it could offer through its generous, democratic, and humane society it is unlikely that Kosova would have been able to achieve independence in 2008.[64] The process of Balkan exile in Julia Kristeva's psychoanalytic theory is a rejection of the maternal space and the Oedipal revolt that makes the revolutionary subject possible had to take place outside Kosova.[65] Switzerland, with its democratic traditions and respect for the political exile, constitutes a territory of universal reason in this respect, whereas Kosova was dictatorial, a land without reason. Fazli Veliu,[66] a Macedonian Albanian, moved permanently to Switzerland and took responsibility for producing the *Zeri I Kosoves* newspaper which kept the scattered movement together. He became the central figure in the LPK in Switzerland, and remained so over the years.

What was the ideological and political perspective of the LPRK/LPK that would lead to the successful development of the Kosova Liberation Army?[67] This is a very complex question with many different dimensions. The father-figure of Demaci had not articulated a clear ideological perspective for an insurgent army in his early writings, other than situating the Kosova struggle within a Guevarist Second and Third World framework outside the main Cold War power blocs. He was not working in a well developed theoretical tradition. Yugoslav and Balkan Marxism generally had never produced a major local theoretician of the standing of someone like Gramsci in the Italian workers' movement. Yet like Gramsci, Demaci and almost all the later leadership were of modest origins and were seeking to modernise their country and turn it into a socialist state, at least before 1990. In Fiori's words applied to Gramsci, there was 'a single minded inexorable drive towards modernity' in their thinking.[68] As Mark Mazower has observed, 'during the Cold War a social and economic revolution transformed the Balkans.'[69] Yet that revolution was very incomplete in Kosova, with elements of a new petit-bourgeois bureaucratic class in Prishtina, Djilas's 'new class', ruling over a largely untouched rural hinterland.

Balkan Marxism was itself an undeveloped tradition, as some have also claimed Balkan Islam to be. The writings of the important leaders like Tito, Hoxha and Dimitrov are dominated by short texts about practical military, economic and international relations problems of their time, and only the Bulgarian Comintern chief Georgi Dimitrov could be said to have had a really comprehensive grounding in Marxism.[70] Both Tito's and Hoxha's intellectual formation was imbued with the deformations and limitations of 'Marxism' as promoted by Stalin in Russia, although this was arguably less disastrous than the same process with the Greek Communists of the Civil War period. During Tito's later period in power, fewer and fewer Marxist and Leninist texts were ever published, and publication of them in Hoxha's Albania was equally circumscribed.[71] In comparison, the public were deluged with vast quantities of both leaders' own writings, which were said to be 'Marxist' but in many senses had (at the least) a problematic relationship to the classic Marxist tradition. Enver Hoxha's Albania did however have a commitment to the Marxist ideological struggle, as the official government response to the 1981 Kosova crisis expressed:

the Yugoslav leaders claim that they do not wage the ideological struggle against us. This is not true and never has been. We wage the ideological struggle and we say so, whereas they wage it, but don't say so.[72]

Thus for the new Kosova Albanian radicals a commitment to Albania provided not only practical assistance and a refuge but also intellectual space in which a revolutionary ideology and military praxis could be developed and articulated. The genuinely popular insurgent basis of the Titoist government had been locked within the prison of Yugoslav state capitalism and exploitation by the 'new class'. Albania was still essential if a Kosova army was to be developed. Western Europe was becoming usable dissident Albanian political space, with tens of thousands of *Gastarbeiters* with Yugoslav passports to mingle with, but it was not secure for underground military organisation. A first practical experiment at developing an armed group had been made in Germany by Jusuf and Bardosh Gervalla and Kadri Zeka in the early 1980s but was snuffed out by a combination of Serbian intelligence and the South German police, a security force that always maintained close links with Belgrade.[73] They were murdered in a village near Heilbron called Untergrupenbach.[74] The father of the Gervalla brothers had been in Balli Kombetar in the Second World War.[75] It was important from the point of view of that tradition for the world at large to understand that the Right was as willing to fight for Kosova as the Left.[76] The demise of this group also had important practical results in terms of organising Albanian workers in Germany who left 'Yugoslavist' émigré organisations en bloc and had formed over 200 clubs, often named after Albanian nationalist martyrs like Hasan Prishtina, by 1987. These were to be a central source of funds for the national movements after 1991, as in Switzerland.[77] Thousands of small businesses in catering, transport, travel and associated activities were formed by Kosovar Albanian exiles in this period, and soon began to pay the agreed 3 per cent levy on their profits to LDK funds, and later the KLA Homeland Calling fund.

Over the long period of its existence, from 1982 to 1992 and the formal founding of the Kosova Liberation Army, the LPRK/LPK itself underwent some internal evolution. There is debate among modern Kosova historians as to whether this mainly concerned style or content and revolved around the issue of the nature of its development away from orthodox Marxist-Leninism.[78] Early editions of the *Zeri I Kosoves* newspaper from the mid-1980s are broadly Maoist in style, with drawings of armed Kosova workers marching forward carrying red flags alongside the Albanian national flag (also red). The national movement was specifically seen as conducted on the basis of class and class consciousness, although theorists brought up in the traditions of classical Marxism might see the ideology as populist rather than rigidly class based. Military imagery is common, with armed workers carrying Kalashnikov-type weapons leading the struggle. As late as March 1990, a *Zeri I Kosoves* interview with Demaci referred to him as *shokun* (comrade), but in it the man who was to become the Kosova Mandela makes clear he sees the national struggle as humanist in its content. By 1991 journals were plain and populist, Marxist language had largely disappeared or had been watered down, and they often emphasised rural insurgent images. This can be partly explained by developments in intellectual fashion. In the early 1980s Maoist and Guevarist images of political struggle were still very vibrant, but by 1990, neo-liberal ideas were ascendant. Hashim Thaci was interested in the model of the Cuban revolution for Kosova when he was young.[79]

The always small Kosova working class could never be the whole basis for the new movement. The LPRK had been quite successful after 1984 in spreading its underground organisation into rural areas, after a long time when it had been centred mostly on Prishtina, Ferizaj (Urosevac) and other large towns. It was much easier to protect the underground organisation from the police in the radical nationalist villages and to identify and immediately execute police informers, a draconian but necessary measure in the view of most militants.[80] There was a connection between the student radicals and with the old rebellious Skenderaj area of northern Drenica. Among those who joined the LPRK organisation in this period was a then totally unknown young Skaneraj farmer from a tiny village called Prekaz, Adem Jashari, later to sacrifice his entire family in March 1998 for the Kosova cause. From the mid-1980s onwards, the LPK leadership had observed the decline in the practical efficiency of the Yugoslav security apparatus in some rural areas, and it had been possible to build up small arms capacity in some places, mostly by theft from military barracks or purchase from conscripts.[81] Further evidence, in its way, was provided by the events of 1988 and 1989, in which only a major JNA deployment from outside Kosova was sufficient to crush the street demonstrations and strikes. The absent Kosova state was revealed as just that and only the Yugoslav military and security apparatus fill the vacuum, as had always happened ever since the Treaty of Versailles.[82]

Arming the most militant villages in this period was a decision that was to have far reaching consequences for the later stages of the conflict. When it became known to Yugoslav military intelligence that this was happening it confirmed the view of the Yugoslav army commanders in Nis in south Serbia, where the Prishtina Corps was garrisoned, that only the most ruthless and comprehensive measures would restore their security and control. Kosova Serbs had some genuine grievances under the period of Albanian domination of the League of Communists in Kosova in the 1980s.[83] They suffered some human rights violations in that period generally, and were to be at the forefront of support for Milosevic's 'anti-bureaucratic revolution' at the end of the decade. The rise to power of Slobodan Milosevic was based upon his promise to defend their rights and security.[84] An identity of interest soon arose between the Prishtina Communist leadership and the Yugoslav army leaders in general. It was also familiar territory, practically and ideologically. The entire history of the Serbian and then Yugoslav armies from as far back as the time of the Congress of Berlin in the nineteenth century had been oriented towards colonising ex-Ottoman lands to the south of Belgrade and then securing them for Serbia. Just as Greek nationalist irredentism then had been directed northwards into old geographical Macedonia, Serbian expansionism was an affair of southern territorial security and new border formation.

The Serbian leadership was also aware that Kosova was beginning to rise up the political agenda in Tirana after the death of Enver Hoxha in 1985. His successor, Ramiz Alia, had been a young political commissar in Kosova for a short time in the Second World War, and although he at that point had a poor political record of collaboration with the Yugoslav Partisans, he did at least have some personal first-hand knowledge of and interest in Kosova conditions, unlike many of the Tirana Communist leadership. Developments in the Yugoslav party were being viewed with increasing international concern, although at this stage it is probable that only American intelligence was aware of the threat of a Milosevic takeover of the entire party apparatus. It is clear that certain informal links began to be formed in this period between the Tirana secret intelligence service—which was free to travel to Switzerland because most of Albania's foreign trade finance and payment was conducted there—and the LPK leadership in and around Zurich and Geneva. Much of this business was already in the hands of Sigurimi operatives and in practice it was under Alia's personal control.

As fellow Enverist Marxists, they had a shared political language and were able to explore the developing perspectives for the Kosovars and in particular what practical help could be offered when the next phase of the struggle in the streets started.[85] Alia claims that he foresaw the possibility of a new revolutionary situation in Kosova, and he should certainly be seen as responsible for allowing the first military training of Kosovars in the Tirana Defence Academy in three years' time.[86] It is also definitely clear that Alia saw the Irish Republican Army (IRA) as a possible model for a Kosovar insurgent army, and he obtained publications from Belfast and studied the Provisional IRA's organisation in some detail. He was also able to meet British and Irish Marxist-Leninist visitors to Albania in that period, and discuss the military options with them. There were some organic correspondences with Irish republican military activity in later KLA military planning, in particular the key issue of a shared kinship border which made it more or less impossible for the IRA to be militarily defeated by the British army and security apparatus and ultimately led to the Good Friday Agreements. Tirana was also important for physical communications, as at this stage the LPK leadership in Switzerland had no reliable communications on a regular basis with rural Kosova, but some communications were possible through intermediaries in Tirana and Albania.

Southern border warfare, which the Yugoslav officers thought they knew and understood, was about pacifying rural Kosova. They had been brought up in the military academies on a diet of triumphal history with the crushing of the Drenica Rising in the 1940s. Dealing with the threat from the villages also fitted well with the emerging international doctrines of anti-terrorism, and made the JNA appear a modern and progressive army in seeking to combat it.[87] It also established their legitimacy in the eyes of the Yugoslav public at a time when conscription was increasingly unpopular with the youth and the expense of maintaining what were still the fourth largest armed forces in Europe was a heavy burden.[88] Still, there was no modern peacekeeping or counter-insurgency doctrine available to the JNA or the security police, and the victory in Drenica fifty years before had only been achieved after gross human rights violations and breaches of the laws of war. It was virtually certain that these would be repeated in a modern context, something that duly took place with the destruction of the Jashari family in Prekaz in the first week of March 1998 and in many other places in Kosova afterwards. A modern anti-terrorist strategy would have involved designating 'safe' areas in Kosova and physically isolating the insurgent Drenica and Dukagjini regions, developing 'hearts and minds' campaigns to win over the uncommitted, and corralling KLA soldiers into smaller and smaller areas until they could be overrun by overwhelming military force, breaking their hold over liberated territories. Then a 'peacekeeping' force (in practice a scenario like this was used in NATO planning as late as 1998) would have come in by agreement with Belgrade and subdued the rebellious areas until the last figments of resistance had been broken. Throughout this period, Yugoslav intelligence, both civilian and military, rested on the assumption that crime was the economic motor of the war and that the new radical movement was mostly a front for drug dealing. The political idealism of the young men and women in the LPK and the growing economic strength of the Albanian Diaspora communities in the USA and in German-speaking Europe was not understood at all.

The bitter struggles to protect what was left of Kosovar autonomy from the Yugoslavs in the late 1980s appeared to confirm the analysis of the Enverist militants. The crushing defeat in 1988 of the Trepca miners—the largest section of the organised and highly class conscious working class—when they marched from Mitrovica to Prishtina, left no room for doubt that under Slobodan Milosevic Kosova would once again be placed under military control. This duly took place on 23 March 1989. In December 1989, the Kosova Democratic League was formed under the leadership of Ibrahim Rugova, the chair of the Association of Kosova Writers, and called for Kosova independence. The small revolutionary organisations dedicated to an insurgent army now had a significant rival for popular support. In the new climate post-1990 any form of politics based on Communism seemed to be obsolete and discredited. The West soon swung strongly behind the LDK, insofar as any Kosova Albanian organisation received outside support. A key player was the Vatican, which did not wish to see the emergence of a Muslim-majority state or a Marxist-originated state in the southern Balkans, as the small Roman Catholic minority would then no longer have the special and influential position Tito had given it in the old Yugoslavia.[89] Key external opinion constituencies in the Diaspora rallied behind Rugova, particularly the often wealthy ex-Balli Kombetar families in the United States and the ordinary workers and their families in the Diaspora in Germany and Switzerland who believed, not without justification, that if the support of the West in capitals like

Warsaw, Prague and Berlin had helped popular movements destroy revisionist Communism, the same would soon take place in Yugoslavia.[90] However, they failed to see the powerful hold of the Yugoslav ideal over many Western intellectual and political elites, and the nature of nationalist politics in Serbia that would soon plunge the whole region into ten years of devastating conflict.

3

A NEW FORCE IN A NEW BALKANS 1990–1995

The Nature of Arms decides the composition of armies, their plan of campaign, their marches, positions and engagements, their orders of battle.

Napoleon, *Precis of the Wars of Julius Caesar*[1]

Tom Wintringham, an English veteran of the Spanish Civil War and theorist of irregular warfare, observed in his seminal booklet *How to Reform the Army*, which was published on the brink of the Second World War in 1939, that 'War is not a very certain Business'.[2] The uncertainties facing the tiny group of men seeking to form a Kosova Liberation Army in 1990 were as great as any working within the Partisan insurgent tradition since the time of the defence of the Spanish Republic. As they met in Zurich and in other places in Germany, Switzerland and Belgium, their situation very much resembled that of Lenin and the Russian exiles in the same cities during the First World War. They were, as the novelist Joseph Conrad observed in *Under Western Eyes*, haunted always by a spectre: 'the shadow of autocracy', which 'forever coloured their thoughts, their views, their most intimate feelings, their private life, their public utterances—haunting the secret of their silences'.[3] They knew clearly the threat to the peace of south-east Europe that the Milosevic takeover in Serbia after 1989 represented, but they were isolated in their vision. Although the establishment of a large semi-legal political mass movement like the Kosova Democratic

59

League was a major step forward, Kosova remained under martial law and the continuing harassment of the population, arrests and murders of activists led to a steady flow of recruits to the LPK, often in exile. In January 1990 the Yugoslav police shot dead four Albanians on the streets of Prishtina, bringing the death toll throughout Kosova in the first month of 1990 to fourteen.[4] A curfew was imposed throughout Kosova on 22 January, and tanks and heavy armoured vehicles rumbled through picturesque little wooden villages.[5] One of them was called Prekaz, home of the Jashari family. The Yugoslav air force flew low over towns and urban centres. The Albanian death toll rose to at least twenty-nine by the beginning of the following month.[6] It was clear that from the standpoint of Milosevic and his associates in Belgrade, the war for Kosova had begun.[7] This fact was an embarrassment to the Democratic League leadership and in particular to Ibrahim Rugova himself, who saw the League as the only legitimate representative of the people of Kosova.[8] He used the old Communist party machine ruthlessly against Demaci after his release from prison to stymie any leadership ambitions Demaci may have had then.[9] This perception was also reproduced in the minds of international participants in the crisis. The US Ambassador in Belgrade at that time, Warren Zimmerman, wrote some years later that 'Albanian nationalism as shaped by Rugova was non-violent, but it was determined. It had to be, since it was primarily a reaction to Milosevic's 'aggressive tactics'... It was clear that Milosevic's strong arm approach was pushing the Albanians out onto a path of no return towards complete independence from Serbia.'[10]

In the chaotic new climate in Tirana, the Communist state remained intact at a formal level but was disintegrating from within. The party leader Ramiz Alia was interested in the possibility of freedom in Kosova and had seen the Irish Republican Army as a possible model for a military force against the Yugoslav People's Army.[11] When his interest became known to Western governments via their spies in Tirana, they feared a 'Greater Albania' might soon emerge if the old barriers between Tirana and Prishtina collapsed.[12] Alia saw the secular, class-based 'Official' IRA as a much better model for the KLA than the Provisional IRA with its Catholic nationalist ideology.[13] It is questionable, though, whether Alia and other Albanians really understood that it was the Provisionals who had shown the capacity to bring back guerrilla warfare to the streets of Western Europe for the first time since the

Second World War, and the Official IRA had not.[14] The LPK avoided contacts with radical Eastern bloc countries in this period—insofar as they still existed—and had never had contacts with countries like Cuba or radical Arab and Islamic states. The Albanian link was all-important to them.

The LPK and other radical Kosovars had always had contacts with the Albanian army on the border and the Albanian government through the intelligence service, the Sigurimi. With the end of Communism, the Sigurimi was extensively penetrated by Western agencies. As President of Albania, Ramiz Alia had met the LPK leaders Xhavit Haliti, Xhavit Haziri and Ahmet Haxhiu in Tirana just before he lost power in 1991. This was an open meeting that Western intelligence agents in Tirana would soon have known about. Alia had pledged moral aid to the LPK leaders, but clearly his political opponent Sali Berisha's Western backers may have felt material aid might also follow, and it was yet another nail in Alia's political coffin.[15] It is unclear how far Alia promised to go in support of the Kosovars, and his own comments in interviews and writings on the subject have been somewhat ambiguous. The last months of his rule were characterised by a sense of new foreign policy openings and some initiatives were surprisingly successful, like his visit to the US Diaspora. Contacts with France and Britain and with US officials were increasing. An end to Albania's autarkic isolation would also mean a new opening towards Prishtina. Alia had made a few friends in Washington in his preferred mode of the 'Albanian Gorbachev' who could steer the nation through a peaceful transition. He did not want to be seen as openly encouraging violence in Kosova and impoverished and chaotic Albania was in no position to offer much help in any event. On the other hand, as a political realist he knew that Milosevic would never give way peacefully. At the strategic level, it had been clear for some little time that the small minority of the elite in Tirana who were both interested in Kosova and knowledgeable about the situation on the ground thought the Yugoslav security hold was weakening. There was a definate opportunity for a new guerrilla force. Seen from Tirana, it was difficult to estimate how vigorous Kosova military resistance would be. Although popular faith in the Kosova cause was alive, it had taken some heavy blows in the last generations, from 1945 to 1968, to 1981 and the final imposition of martial law in 1989. The new Kosova warriors had not only to keep their own faith in their cause alive but also revive it among the broad population in Kosova, Albania and western Macedonia. It seemed a time for propaganda by deed, as much as word. The volumes of words of the LDK had achieved very little, and had not found a way of articulating the needs of the citizens.

In the late spring of 1990, with the Tirana government's knowledge and agreement, the Prekaz farmer, Adem Jashari, led a group of the nascent Kosova Liberation Army recruits through the dense forests above the Koshare Pass into Albania to begin training at the Military Academy in Tirana and at local military camps in the Albanian hills. Yugoslav intelligence must have had some idea of what was happening through its informer networks, and on 30 December 1990 his village of Prekaz was surrounded by army and police vehicles, helicopters flying low over the farmhouses.[16] It was to be a rehearsal for the dramatic events eight years later in March 1998, when he died there. The Jashari family had long been fierce opponents of Yugoslav rule in Kosova, and some, including Adem Jashari himself, were in the LPRK. At that time, most of these militants were members of the LPRK—the 'name change' to LPK did not occur until October of that year.[17] As the most specifically 'Enverist' of the small Marxist groups and with a strongly conspiratorial and puritanical ethos, it was natural that LPRK should look towards Tirana for help in the early stages of military development, and that Jashari should seek military training there. They were not alone, though, in their military pilgrimage to Albania. Peje was a centre of paramilitary activity and an illegal group, Besa, was formed which as early as late 1990 had begun importing small arms into Kosova under the leadership of Adrian Krasniqi-Rexha and in the following year had formed an organisation called Aradhen Clirimitare te Pejes, the Liberation Batallion of Peje.[18] The Llap *ceta* in north-east Kosova was also well armed and capable of making successful attacks on Serbian policemen and their barracks. The military struggle for Kosova was beginning. In the Diaspora the Brussels *ceta* was formed, led by Enver Hadri, a young architect whose father had been murdered by Tito's secret police in 1945 when he was an eight-year-old child. It was quickly penetrated by UDBA police informers and Hadri met an early violent demise.

The Albanian Military Academy near the River Lana in central Tirana was dominated by a heavy Enverist ethos and commanded by officers who all had roots in the top Partisan families from the Second World War period. Most were southerners. A general such as Kostas

Karolli was of partly Greek ethnic origin from a Greek Civil War Communist refugee family with roots near Gjirokastra.[19] The main military intellectual theorist and historian Adem Copani was also from the southern Partisan heartlands, and little towns near the Greek border like Erseke were the homes of many top commanders. In one sense they were prisoners of the past and political control over the army, but in another sense they were not. The pro-China period and cultural revolution in Albania after 1967 had led to a weakening of hierarchy and the authority of the party in many spheres of Albanian life, and the army contained many well educated and coherent thinking men and women who could often see the new political openings in the Balkan world for the Albanians post-1990 much better than Tirana politicians. A very high proportion of the officer class were of a nominal but sincere Muslim culture and had no difficulty in helping fellow-Muslim Kosovars. Although only a few had northern links, all would have served there at various times on border duty with Yugoslavia. There is little in detail known about the kind of military training Jashari and his comrades received, but in the conditions of the time it must have been fairly rudimentary. Weapon technology in the army and Academy was low, as almost everything used in the Albanian army was made in Albania at the underground factories around Gramsch and Polican in the south. Doctrine was focused on cheap mass participatory territorial defence where almost the entire population would be armed to fight invaders. It was only just after the period of the *Bunkere* when hundreds of thousands of small concrete bunkers were built all over the country to deter attack.

The AK-47 assault rifle was ubiquitous, and a copy of the basic Yugoslav army pistol, but other more advanced equipment was not made. Looking to the future, the type of specialist training required to handle mines and explosives and military vehicles and technology was simply not available. When Jashari and his group returned to Kosova they had made some vital friends and contacts for the nascent KLA but had learned as much as it was possible to learn in Tirana of practical military science. The Tirana experience seems to have reinforced the mild archaism in the first military models for the KLA—it was to be an army based on extreme egalitarian principles with little difference in practice between the KLA soldier and the armed local civilian. There were no ranks or non-commissioned officers. This was ideal in the political framework at that time for the future war but would have severe military disadvantages, as later events in 1998 were to demonstrate. The return of the Jasharis did not end the military training plans with Tirana, as some have claimed. Under Berisha's government after 1992 other groups (always of ten) followed, like the recruits taken to Albania in 1993 led by Ramiz Qerimi.[20] Although by now the Tirana government had made such training illegal, in practice little or nothing was done to stop it. In this period, the first loyalty oath for the new army was developed, where the new recruit declared:

As a member of the Kosova Liberation Army I swear I will fight for the liberation of the occupied territories of Albania and their unity. I will always be ready to be a disciplined fighter, vigilant and ready to sacrifice even my life for the sacred interests of the Homeland. If I violate this oath I shall be punished with the most severe laws of war. If I betray, I will lose my life. I swear.[21]

In other parts of the complex Diaspora world in 1991 political initiatives were being taken that would have equally far-reaching effects. Adem Jashari met Rugova in Croatia on behalf of the LPK and discussed the military options that seemed to him to be open to the Albanians, but the meeting produced no concrete results.[22] Progress was being made there by Fehmi Lladrovci who had moved to Zagreb in late 1990 after his release from gaol, and he was the main organiser of the nascent KLA in Croatia. Although the general operating environment was safe, the Croats were providing little help and a difficult atmosphere developed. Croatia's President Franjo Tudjman and senior Croatian governing party officials had turned against the Kosovars and in one acrimonious exchange claimed to Lladrovci that the Kosova Albanians 'were not a Catholic people'.[23] Lladrovci was a patient and determined man after his long years in Stara Gradishta prison for political offences in the 1980s. He had belonged to a small Marxist-Leninist organisation in the Prishtina political underground, the Marksiste-Leniste e Kosoves (MLK), and was as early as 1985 put in charge of their military wing. It was not an ideal background for a happy relationship with the clerical nationalist Croats, but he was nevertheless able to recruit some future fighters in Croatia, while his brother Ramiz was organising an arms procurement network in Germany.[24] The KLA framework was being slowly built, an element at a time, that would support the war at the end of the decade. The LPK in Switzerland was working on the 'Union of Albanians in Switzerland' organisation that would be formed the following year. This was the organisational equivalent in the Diaspora of the EAM mass organisation that supported the

Communist-led ELAS resistance army in Occupied Greece. But once again, the LPK and its allies, although central, did not have a monopoly of activity. Kosova Albanian organisation in Zurich region was village-based, and although this (along with impenetrable village dialects even for those who know Albanian) later provided a strong barrier against police and foreign intelligence penetration, it also inhibited centralised direction. The Kosovar émigrés took time to pick up the Swiss efficiency in organisational matters that later served them so well in the wartime period.

In the little town of Stubicka Toplica in Croatia in January 1991 a Pan Albanian assembly of intellectuals met, organised by the Lidhja Demokratike e Shqiptare te Kroacise (LDSHK), the Democratic League of Croatian Albanians. This organisation was loosely modelled on Rugova's Democratic League but in practice was a good deal more effective, democratic and radical. Many Kosovar Albanians, particularly Roman Catholics, had taken refuge in Croatia at various times since the Yugoslav crisis began, and there were many Albanian-owned small businesses dating further back to the opening up of the Adriatic coast tourist industry under Tito.[25] Important later KLA figures who were unknown at the time but emerged into politics after 1999, like Agim Ceku and Naim Maloku, had studied as Yugoslav soldiers at the Zagreb Military Academy and were an important background factor.[26] Participants at the Stublica Toplika gathering included people from Kosova, Macedonia, Preshevo and Montenegro. The purpose of the assembly was to take the strategic decisions to take the national movement forward after the declaration of Kosova independence on 2 June 1990. The question of an army inevitably arose and the assembly laid the foundation for the Forcat e Armatosura te Republikes se Kosoves (FARK), which at the time was simply another nascent and largely virtual armed group, but it was much later to be commandeered by a factional leadership and played a major divisive role in the war in 1998.[27] Croatia was militarily important in this period because Albanian conscripts were deserting in some numbers from the Yugoslav People's Army to fight with Croatian forces in the conflict.[28] They could thus receive the best infantry training of all; participation in battle. The conference also had some initially important practical political results such as the referendum that was held in the Albanian-majority towns in the Preshevo valley in south-east Serbia on 1 March 1992, which produced an overwhelming majority for immediate autonomy of the region within Yugoslavia and the right to join an independent Kosova in the future. Yet it was a time when territorial destiny was being decided by purely military criteria, and without an army or force on the ground, the Preshevo declaration achieved absolutely nothing.[29] There were serious limits to what Albania could offer as the nation was impoverished and about to descend into poverty and intermittent disorder with the end of the one-party state.[30] It was clear, though, that these early soldiers were serious and had a politically modernist approach to their mission, rather than merely being imitative revivers of the 1920s *kacak* tradition as Tim Judah and others have suggested. The LPRK envisaged an underground army on Marxist lines which could gradually clear Kosova of the Serbian security apparatus and culminate in an armed uprising that would take power in a decisive way.

The self-styled Kosova 'government' set up by Rugova after the adoption of the Kacanik Constitution had a Defence Ministry that was under the control of Bujar Bukoshi, Rugova's 'Prime Minister', a kidney specialist who had trained in medicine in Germany.[31] The question quickly arose of whether the government should attempt to form a military force.[32] Bukoshi has claimed that he was in favour of such a policy but was overruled by Rugova who wished to run a wholly peaceful campaign for Kosova.[33] Financing the Kosova army was a very divisive question. In the autumn of 1992 Bukoshi visited Switzerland and held a series of meetings in Zurich and Geneva with the Diaspora leaders. The Zurich Kosova Democratic League passed over a large sum of money from its Kosova Solidarity Fund at a meeting held in Zofingen where a 'Kosova Democratic Association' also was formed.[34] Ramush Tahiti, a close associate of Bukoshi, was appointed the first Minister of Defence of the Kosova Republic, but in fact the title represented very little. On the ground in Kosova the 'Defence Ministry' represented nothing at all. Bukoshi has subsequently claimed that his early efforts to make the Ministry functional and form an army were stymied by Rugova's intense pacifism.[35] The Serbian crackdown in late 1992 and early 1993 resulted in the deaths of at least sixteen Albanians who according to Amnesty International had been shot by the security forces in 'disputed circumstances'.[36] A key figure in Tirana had been Ali Aliu who had been the first Kosova representative in Tirana in the time of Ramiz Alia's government, and was involved in setting up military training schemes at the Albanian Defence Academy for Kosovars.[37] There were a large number of ethnic Albanian army and police officers who had been ejected from their jobs in 1989–90 during the Serbian takeover, but few of them had any clear idea how to proceed towards making any type of Kosova Albanian military or paramilitary force. They required clear and decisive leadership but the LDK did not provide a political perspective that had any military credibility. The Albanian army itself was in rapid decline.[38] Some prominent KLA commanders such as Rrustem Mustafa (Commander Remi) later accused Bukoshi of having been swayed in his view of the development of the struggle by undue contact with the Croatian leader Tudjman in this period.[39] After a year or two, the 'government' abandoned any pretence of having a military component and by early 1993 little was ever heard again of the 'Ministry of Defence', and *de facto* it was replaced by the FARK in the wartime period.[40] A key figure in the development of the LDK in Switzerland, Shaip Latifi, recalls, 'Many times we were in a complicated situation. Rugova did some good things but the LDK came out of Yugoslav communism. We made mistakes.[41]

In this atmosphere, the support of many of the uncommitted in the Swiss Diaspora turned towards the LPK and away from the LDK. This phenomenon was mainly confined to central Switzerland where the LPK was present in sufficient strength to provide a credible alternative and where the LDK leadership was prepared to take more risks. The town of Aarau was important at this time, and it has remained a main centre of Albanian life in Switzerland. With a strong liberal-socialist progressive ethos, prosperous in the 'golden triangle' between Berne, Basel and Zurich, German speaking and majority-Protestant, and the first capital of modern Switzerland in 1798, it did not have the background in Roman Catholic conservatism that often aided the early LDK in Switzerland and elsewhere. On the other side of the political divide patient work continued to build up resources, both people and weapons. The future Kosova Prime Minister Hashim Thaci joined the LPRK in this period.[42] He focused on recruiting 'sleepers' who were to continue in their normal occupations until the appropriate moment to open up the armed struggle.[43] The exact commitment required seemed to vary from place to place but in the main constituted a general dedication to the ideal and strategy of the armed struggle rather than any specific tasks. This was a sophisticated strategy that needed considerable discipline and modern communications among those taking part. The standard expected of recruits was high and there was an ever present fear of infiltration by police or security service informers.

On the ground there was an intense febrile atmosphere, particularly in late 1992 and early 1993 when fear spread in the Serbian community that an uprising in Kosova might be imminent along the lines of those in Croatia and Bosnia. In the West there were also major concerns than an uprising in Kosova might be coming, particularly because reports were reaching NATO governments that the Milosevic security apparatus was losing its iron grip in some areas of Kosova. As a response, the Serbian dictator had moved his criminal henchman Zeljko Raznatovic, nicknamed Arkan, into Kosova to build volunteer militias among the Kosova Serbs. The stage was set for violent conflict. An obvious question that will need to be examined by future historians is why more resistance was not encountered by Milosevic's aggressive crackdown in 1993–94. It is clear that the immediate high tide of Albanian resistance was reached in the winter of 1991–92 when even the Belgrade Communist party newspaper *Politika* was regularly reporting the expansion of areas of northern rural Kosova that were out of control of the Yugoslav security forces. However, the ultra-constitutionalist approach of the Rugova leadership of the Kosova Democratic League did not see this opportunity and did not have the political or military structures in place to begin the challenge for power. There are the obvious factors that the Rugova leadership were not capable of organising armed conflict or any kind of resistance, but the absence of activity by the Marxist militants is less easily explained, unless a political evaluation had been made that with their social revolutionary perspectives mass action was premature and would have met with inevitable defeat. In Prishtina a small group of activists had formally joined to create the National Movement for the Liberation of Kosova (LKCK) in March 1993; they did not agree with the latter view and put their initial energies into preparing the population for mass mobilisation against the Serbs and a popular uprising.[44]

The shock that was felt all over Yugoslavia at the secession of Slovenia and the opening of the war in Croatia nevertheless opened new vistas for Kosova. The seemingly strong and eternal edifice of Yugoslavia was showing cracks. After another period in Tirana, and a visit to Zurich, Adem Jashari and his men returned to Kosova and faded into the background of normal Kosova rural life; the military priority at this stage was to secure basic weapons supplies, a process that carried on throughout the years 1992 to 1996. The KLA was to be, as a senior British soldier later put it who was in Prishtina in 1999, a 'handgun

army'. Switzerland now became the central focus of the military/polit-
ical interface and organisational activity and was to remain that until
the end of the Macedonian war in 2001. Hashim Thaci had been
selected by the LPK leadership as future leadership material and was
financed to attend Zurich University, moving there in the summer of
1991.[45] Thaci's uncle Azim Syla was in charge of KLA practical development and was already in Switzerland at that time. In 1994 Fehmi
Lladrovci finally lost patience in his difficult and intractable dealings
with the Croats and moved his recruitment operation from Zagreb to
Switzerland and Germany, after a meeting with Ali Ahmeti in Zurich
on 9 July.[46] Jashari had first visited Switzerland in the summer of 1990
and met the Swiss-based, mostly LPK-affiliated radicals around the
Macedonian Albanian leader Fazli Veliu, and basic decisions on war
funding and organisation were taken that were to determine the future
developmental model of the Kosova Liberation Army.[47] In essence, an
alliance was formed between the intellectual founding-father Enverists
of LPRK and the slightly broader church of younger militants that later
became LPK and started the formation of the KLA. In traditional
Marxist terms, the critical nucleus had been formed that could enable
the KLA to grow to a serious insurgent military and political force.
The great city of Zurich with its vast wealth, different émigré networks, radical cultural traditions and free atmosphere was a vital element in sustaining the LPK/KLA nucleus in the difficult years of
clandestine struggle that lay ahead. By comparison, the fragmentation
in Albania seemed to rule out much assistance from that direction, and
Democratic Party President Sali Berisha had again been forced to shut
the military training facility for the Kosovars at Labinot military camp,
near Elbasan. The fire of war had to be ignited from Switzerland and
Germany and within Kosova itself.

   In early 1993 a delegate meeting of about 100 people was held in
Drenica where leaders of the LPK and of the very Marxist LKCK,
mainly a student group, joined the LPRK contingent and the orientation and military symbols of the KLA were chosen. Fatmir Humolli
was perhaps the main influence in the LKCK's decision to join with the
older radicals.[48] They were joined early in 1994 by the Geci family
group from Llausche, a militant family who had suffered very badly in
the aftermath of the defeat of Balli Kombetar in Kosova in 1949.
Recruitment grew in the Diaspora, where by now as many as 400,000
people were living and working in nations such as Germany, Switzer-

land, Sweden and Denmark. So far the growth of the nascent revolutionary army was a European phenomena, and there is little evidence of US Diaspora involvement. The arrival of the Geci family on the scene was to be a precursor of future tensions.[49] Although highly motivated and patriotic, they were essentially of a nationalist background and had never been involved in any of the small Marxist and Marxist-Leninist groups that had come together to form the KLA in 1993. The question of leadership structure was central. The early KLA was a horizontal organisation with a strong emphasis on rank and file initiatives and no ranks, officers or non-commissioned officer class. This was in line with Enverist theories of underground military-revolutionary work, but would later pose very serious problems when the KLA 'came out' and engaged in open warfare on a large scale with the Yugoslavs. There was no theoretical model for a command and control system. Here there was a residue of the old *kacak* ethos, where military authority resided with charismatic local family leaders who led their local men into battle, much as happened in eighteenth-century Scotland at Culloden.

Modern guerrilla warfare demands complex patterns of organisation and above all a division of labour between the fighters and those who support them. Technical issues were important. All modern insurgencies including aspects of the Spanish Civil War in Europe and T.E. Lawrence's Middle East campaigns, have included as part of their central strategy the use of explosives and mines by guerrillas to disrupt mechanised army transport and supply lines. The role of roadside bombs in the current Afghan conflict is a contemporary paradigm. The early emphasis in the KLA on the armed individual soldier-citizen was entirely understandable in view of the demolition of the Albanian personal arsenal a generation before and the sudden availability of weapons in 1997, but it was actually an irrelevance compared to the lack of explosives and similar heavier munitions. Joining the KLA was the construction and validation of the military subject through personal weapons possession. Hand grenades were sometimes used if they could be obtained but there is no record of the professional use of explosives in the early period of the Kosova armed struggle.

Most Marxist-Leninist military theory of guerrilla war technical operations derives from the Russian expert Anna Starinov who served in Spain as an adviser to the Spanish Republican forces from 1936 to 1938, and subsequently worked on writing the Red Army partisan warfare manuals in the Second World War. She was not a backroom theorist but had been closely involved in the fighting in Spain and learned a great deal from the defeat of the Republic. Starinov empha-sised the importance of operating with explosives behind enemy lines, on a model derived in her theoretical writings from T.E. Lawrence's struggles in the Middle East against the Ottoman Empire.[50] This would not have been very difficult in Kosova. The Yugoslav army had long and vulnerable supply lines into Kosova from Nis, Vranje and other large barracks in south Serbia. They ran through deep forests with plenty of cover and exposed roads, as from Prokuple in Serbia to Pod-jeve in north-east Kosova. At no stage of the later war were these roads ever threatened or mined by the Albanians. This is particularly ironic in view of the fact that explosives were quite easy to obtain within Kos-ova with its numerous mines and quarries and some Albanian workers had been trained to use them. A possible explanation is the primacy of the Maoist and Guevarist rather than Soviet literature in the Kosova doctrinal formation; Mao says little specifically about explosive muni-tions use in his writings and much more about issues connected with the role of the individual armed subject; the revolutionary soldier.

The nascent KLA was not without organisational acumen, however. An early preoccupation of the leadership was territorial division. With new recruits coming from west of Drenica in the strategic region of Dukagjini adjoining Albania, new operation zones were formed and Luan Haradinaj was appointed coordinator in Gllogjan and Lahi Ibra-himi in Jabllanica village. Luan's brother Ramush Haradinaj had returned to Kosova from Switzerland via Albania and walked across the border. As he noted in a later war memoir, 'I was armed and felt I was a member of the Kosova Liberation Army'.[51] He had constructed himself as a fighting military subject. The reality of the new organisa-tion was advancing to a point where joining it seemed for many recruits a natural act. In the north-east around Podjeve and Vushtrri, Zahir Pajaziti and his group in Llap were developing. Soon similar commands were in existence in Kacanik, a traditionally rebellious val-ley since Ottoman times on the border with Macedonia, and in the remote mountains of Shala. A rough division in the leadership began to form between those who were basically intellectuals exercising staff officer functions, such as the future intelligence chiefs Rexhep Selimi and Kadri Veseli, and those concerned with practical planning and mil-itary activity in the villages and small towns. It was not a rigid division.

The future KLA Political Spokesman Hashim Thaci took part in an attack on a Serbian police post in Drenica in 1993, and in the battle of Rahovec in 1998, as did other future politicians in different war contexts. The level of struggle that was possible nevertheless seemed very small on the wider Balkan canvas. The Croatian and Bosnian wars were raging in this period but were conducted by fragmented formal mechanised armies. The Milosevic regime appeared to have adequate resources to keep urban Kosova under full control. This was not the case in the countryside. The nascent KLA grew most effectively on or near the borders of Kosova, as in Llap and Dukagjini. It had little purchase in the central plain towns and cities. Between 1992 and 1995, about 135 armed attacks were effected against Yugoslav security forces. An important issue is to evaluate the degree of instability this brought to Kosova, compared to the other disintegrative forces of which the most important was hyperinflation in 1993–94.

As I have indicated in my earlier study *Kosova Express*, the degree of Kosova Albanian ignorance and exclusion from the outside world should not be underestimated in this period, nor the degree to which Western collaboration with the Milosevic regime demoralised the Kosova Albanian population. This exclusion and displacement also applied within Serbia itself. The nation was exhausted by the Croatian and Bosnian wars. In 1995 the Dayton Accord excluded Kosova from the peace agreements to end the Bosnian war and the Kosova Democratic League policy under Rugova finally collapsed as a credible strategy. In the Belgrade liberal press in these (and preceding) years, Kosova is both absent and invisible. The educated middle class in Serbia simply did not wish to think or know about the simmering crisis in the south. Many took the view that Kosova was always 'going wrong' in some form, it was a doomed and benighted land and the less one had to do with it or knew about the details, the better. This meant that the 'Kosova discourse' in the media and life elsewhere was still dominated by the outlook of nationalist extremist publications like Arkan's magazine *Sebsko Jednistovo* or the ultra-nationalist Vojislav Seselj's weekly *Velika Serbija*. If a Serb wished to read news reporting from Kosova, on the whole it was only these and similar extremist publications that printed any. In Albania there was a similar problem of invisibility.[52]

The new Albanian defence policy document published in 1995 with an introduction by Sali Berisha himself bent over backwards to make conciliatory gestures to the Yugoslavs and called for 'stability' with the neighbours.[53] There was at this point a vast distance between the official army rhetoric in Albania and the Kosova fighters in the Drenica forests. In 1995 and 1996 the pace of attacks against the Serbian apparatus had accelerated but they were still within the same hit and run framework that marks the early stages of an insurgency. Accounts of the process of weapons acquisition illustrate the problems in KLA development.[54] In his biographical study of the Llap military hero Zahir Pajaziti, Driton Sejdiu explains very well how slowly weapons supplies were built up, the long dangerous walk to and from Albania and then the possibility of conflict with Milosevic's police leading to violence and/or loss of precious weapons.[55] This limited potential activity. In the autumn of 1995 there were probably only about three hundred soldiers in the KLA and the majority were in two relatively small areas in Drenica and Dukagjini. In the spring of 1996, the KLA became more ambitious and successful frontal attacks to destroy police posts were undertaken, but in terms of the world outside Kosova the KLA was still a largely unknown and mythical organisation. By the summer of 1996 this was beginning to change. An attack on the houses of Serbian refugees from Croatia marked the first assault on Serbian civilians which was primarily conducted by LKCK-affiliated soldiers, and for the first time a communiqué was issued to the press afterwards about what had happened. This was a major step forward. Kosovar Albanian inhibitions about a front against the Serbs in Kosova were disappearing, with attacks on police taking place in urban settings in Prizren, Vushtrri and Mitrovica. The first successful recorded use of explosives was not until January 1997 when the Rector of Prishtina university, Radovan Papovic, was blown up in his car in Prishtina.

In Albania the government of Sali Berisha approached collapse in early 1997 when faced with an armed uprising led from the south. The Albanian armouries contained tens of thousands of weapons which were soon released to the people.[56] This was a seminal event in the region, and immediately appeared to offer the Kosovars an opportunity to solve the weapons and ammunition supply issues of a new people's army. There is no doubt that the uprising had a major psychological effect on the KLA leadership from the Marxist wing, as it clearly showed an armed insurgency was a practical possibility in modern Europe. They could plan to spread it to Kosova. Leaders like Rexhep Selimi and Xharvit Haliti already had good Tirana connections and realised that Tirana offered a route to external assistance for their struggle. The Sigurimi's interest in helping the freedom of Kosova had survived since the times of Qira in the 1950s. According to the new, post-communist perspectives, there was a great deal of money to be made out of the collapse of Yugoslav Kosova. On the other hand most Kosovars admired Berisha. They regretted his departure in May 1997 and the collapse of his government and had little in common with the southern Albanian Communists and recent ex-Communists who were active in the uprising. In this situation of inter-Albanian political fracture and international detachment, the role of the Albanian army became important. They were a bridge between the two communities and the bitter ideological divisions in the Kosovar scene. [57] They had suffered a devastating series of blows between 1991 and 1996 and many disaffected ex-officers were local leaders of the 1997 rising. Many were able to start trading arms towards Kosova within days of the fall of Gjirokastra to the uprising in March 1997. The Albanian army had always discussed plans about how to deal with a future Kosova crisis. It had been mobilised to the north east border as long ago as 1985, in expectation of a Kosova rising.[58]

The conventional picture of a flood of weapons moving towards Kosova from Albania is far from the truth. As Ramush Haradinaj shows in his interviews in *A Narrative of War and Freedom*, there were many difficulties in distributing the weapons throughout Kosova and even greater difficulties in obtaining and distributing ammunition.[59] Ammunition is heavy to transport and requires mechanised transport capacity which the KLA did not have. A mule or donkey can carry a considerable number of AK-47 Kalashnikovs but is soon burdened by heavy ammunition boxes. In this sense the Albanian uprising was something of a mixed blessing for the Kosovar insurgents. At one level it was intoxicating, it provided a successful model to follow; but it was also unique, *sui generis*, and in Kosova, Albanian fighters had to face and overcome an experienced and still quite well organised police, army and security apparatus rather than Berisha's discredited and disintegrating forces. In Albania, the pyramid bank crisis meant that the vast majority of the population had major grievances against the Democratic Party and Berisha, and were angry and ready for mass mobilisation, whereas in Kosova in the mid-1990s many of the people were nervous and timid and had little confidence in their political leaders to bring change. By late 1995 only about ten per cent of the Kosova population lived in places where there was any practical possibility of KLA protection from the JNA and security apparatus.

The dramatic events of 1997 lay two years in the future in 1995. The period of Dayton was difficult for all Kosova Albanians, whatever their location or political loyalties. It appeared to most that the United States had abandoned their cause and would wish to see Kosova always part of Serbia. It strengthened the hand, though, of the most politically radical who saw the IRA insurgent model as relevant and the Sinn Fein 'we ourselves' philosophy as the most useful model in contemporary Europe for Kosova. Rugova's faith in external help bringing independence had been defeated by events. The initiative was passing to those in the Diaspora who favoured the armed struggle. The construction of the new Kosova would begin with the construction of the Kosova military subject taking revenge on the Serbs, gun in hand.

An informal council of war was established by the LPK in Switzerland in 1996, based in the Perparimi (Progress) club in Zurich, a LPK creation. The main task would be fundraising for the KLA, and a fund called 'Homeland Calling' was established to channel the money from the Diaspora that had hitherto gone to Rugova's Democratic League.[60] The issue of identity of donors to this new fund was sensitive. It was clear to Thaci and the political leadership that all practical contact with Islamic nations needed to be avoided. In 1994 and 1995 the Berisha government has begun to develop a 'special relationship' with many Islamic countries, guided by the SHIK Intelligence chief Bashkim Gazidede who was a devout Muslim and chairman of the Islamic Intellectuals Association of Albania. Increasing American concern at the growth of radical Islamic influences eventually culminated in the arrests in August 1997 of alleged Egyptian jihadists in Tirana.[61] It has been claimed that this event was a key element in the development of the CIA's anti-Al Qaeda strategy, but this seems extremely doubtful; the Americans had been operating against Egyptian radicals to protect their key Egyptian ally for many years, and the speculations of those in the neo-conservatism orbit give Albania a significance in this area that events and evidence do not justify. That said, Haliti, Selimi and Thaci were very astute in protecting the little army from the danger of 'guilt by association' with major Islamic nations at this early stage, over five years before 9/11. To many Kosovars, it must have appeared that 1994 and 1995 were years of defeat and inertia, but in fact decisions on strategy and organisation were being taken in the Swiss underground organisations by the LPK that were in almost every case correct and perceptive and would lay the foundations for the public emergence of the KLA in 1997 and its rapid growth during the difficult military struggle in 1998.

The question inevitably arises of how far these decisions were taken autonomously, or how far there was any foreign guiding hand from abroad. 'Abroad' in real terms meant only one country, the United States. It is always difficult to establish concrete evidence for secret intelligence relationships but there does not appear to be any direct evidence for US involvement in advising the nascent KLA in this period, indeed right into the wartime period, of the type that came into being in 1999. Virtually all Americans had been evacuated from Albania in the violence in the spring and summer of 1997, including the CIA mission in the US Embassy. Foreign missions were very Tirana-centric in those days, and there were few of the non-governmental organisations that came to proliferate in the late 1990s in the Balkans and offered the CIA and other Western agencies useful data conduits from the provinces.[62] Churches, missionaries and NGOs were the only Western presence in most places and were bound up with their own work and priorities and not involved in politics. In any case they too had been evacuated in 1997, in the vast majority of cases. The main source of information would have been in Switzerland but the Kosovars themselves had little wish for contact with unknown outsiders, particularly tough ex-prisoners who knew the extent of the Serbian intelligence apparatus and the possibility of data leakage in that direction if they spoke to any foreign agency. The Swiss authorities also have famously strong principles against foreign spies dealing with legitimate political exiles who reside in Switzerland.[63] It is also hard to see what could have been achieved.

There were nonetheless very well informed people in the USA. The close links that had existed between the CIA and prominent US-based émigrés go right back to the late 1940s and early 1950s and attempts to overthrow the Hoxha regime. Many had some knowledge of events inside Kosova and Albania as a result of family links and they were important to US intelligence during the Cold War. When the crisis began they had privileged access. Most were of a generally Right-wing background like the Bardha family in Michigan, but there were always people in the US diaspora who communicated with Tirana, particularly in the Massachusetts community of mostly very long established and generally Orthodox southerners.[64]

It was necessary at this stage for the KLA to grow from a tiny group of politically conscious militants to an army and this meant the core of perhaps thirty senior leaders that formed in 1992–93 had to make a structure that would allow a base leadership cadre of several hundred people to develop all over Kosova. This was never an orderly or easy process. Once a popular resistance movement starts it is almost impossible to control who joins it and how they behave. Propaganda by deed was the key to successful recruitment. This is most clearly demonstrated in the war memoirs of the Llap leader Remi who explains that in 1991 and 1993 little was achieved because although there were young men ready to fight in the villages, nobody was keen to take the first steps against the Serbs for fear of reprisals. When paramilitary activity got under way more successfully through the Llap *ceta* in 1993, the KLA grew apace. Llap had been a militant region for a long time and as early as 1979 an organisation called the 'Kosova Red Front' had been formed in Podujeve. Hasan Ramadani had joined the LPRK in prison in 1982 and throughout the 1980s a majority of the Llap membership were in gaol.[65] When they emerged they were a serious and battle-hardened cadre group with deep personal grievances in human rights terms against the Serbian police. They would have no reservations about killing as many of them as was necessary to achieve Kosova's liberation. This background of political training in conditions of incarceration and real hardship was never understood by the internationals who governed Kosova after 1999, except for some of the more informed sections of the British, German and American military and intelligence services. The majority of internationals believed the moral ideal of the Kosova Liberation Army could quickly be discredited. This was not to turn out to be the case.

In classical Maoist and Enverist terms, the development of the KLA as an army (as in the Long March period in the Chinese revolution) started to replace the LPK (the party) as the focus of all cadre efforts.[66] As a typical recruit in Llap, Ramadani was a clever and dedicated young man who fell under the influence of Adem Demaci at an early age. Born in 1948, he had seen a vision of socialist social justice and freedom in Yugoslavia dashed by the policies of Tito and the return of capitalism. He circulated handwritten copies of Demaci's programme for a Revolutionary League for the Unification of the Albanians in his school. In a typical militant personal narrative trajectory Ramadani had been caught up in the 1981 student demonstrations. He entered illegal work for the KLA as soon as it was formed and was shot dead by the Serbian secret police (UDBA) in a field near his house in 1994.

In this period, to destroy the Llap *ceta* was a top priority for Belgrade. His biographer and local people believe, probably correctly, that his death was caused by a police informer for the Serbs.

Some future political leaders like Ramush Haradinaj had, according to their own accounts, started to drift out of the LPK in this period. They were, unlike Thaci, men without formal university education and with little in-depth interest in ideology that did not serve the needs of the moment. The LPK was for a young man or woman a way to contact 'the action', but once in a militant social and political network, the LPK outside the main Swiss cities did not always offer very much. The KLA thus became not only an asymmetrical army but also an asymmetrical party. The LPK, in one of its major achievements, avoided the classic problem of revolutionary exiles, fissiparous splits over personalities, but it had cultural limits. Once a local leader became immersed in developing the military organisation in Kosova, most politics seemed to become irrelevant and the timeless problems of all guerrilla warfare took over: securing civilian support, recruitment of fighters, making weapon and ammunition dumps, securing food supplies and so on. Foreign intelligence or military contractors of the postmodern SAIC or MPRI type could have contributed little to this process. In any case the leadership around Haliti and Thaci itself had major communication problems with its soldiers. A commander like Rustem Mustafa (Remi) has demonstrated in his post-war writings and memoirs that individual KLA commanders in different districts had major practical problems in communicating outside their own areas.[67] They received few or no commands from an external leadership. Information about the new army was nevertheless reaching the West, much of it from Serbian and Greek intelligence, and painted a picture of a drug-financed narco-terrorist army which depended on the profits of organised crime in Western Europe. This analysis fitted into longstanding Serbian theories that all that Kosova required was effective policing and crime busting to obtain social tranquillity and economic progress, a recurrent theme in Kosova politics over the years that was repeated with dreary regularity in the international community administrations after 1999.[68]

This shallow and inaccurate perspective depended on an almost total absence of understanding of the forces that drove young men and women into the KLA in the first place. It also neglected the comprehensive research undertaken by the Swiss federal police on the drug trade in Zurich and elsewhere, which showed the more prominent role of

West Africans, Turks, Kurds and other émigré groups. It is also worth bearing in mind the numerous legitimate Albanian businesses in Switzerland (over 10,000 in Mittelland alone) which became the backbone of KLA financial support. Few foreign observers saw this, or knew anything of the émigré community, and the Serbs established a dominant narrative in INTERPOL, and later, EUROPOL. This was reinforced by the employment in INTERPOL's Lyons headquarters of prominent ex-Milosevic Serbian police as consultants in the immediate post-2000 period. Unemployed, poor and with no social position, the young Kosovan rural or urban workers needed not only an army but a social revolution to liberate them. The key leadership cadres had been through twenty years of violent oppression, gaols and secret police shootings. The idea of martyrdom—not for Islam but displaced into simple Kosova patriotism—was never far away.[66] Remi is honest enough to point out that many of his soldiers were recruited in the local *madrese*, but there is no suggestion that they were anything other than mainstream nationalists once in uniform.[70] The songs and poems of the war often tell this story better than official or unofficial analytical and historical writing. In his collected poems praising the American volunteers who came to fight for the KLA a few years later, in 1999, Nexhat Imeraj writes:

> *Thoughts drying up*
> *Like autumn fountains*
> *Souls burning with fire*
> *In a foreign land*
> *Heart comes to you*
> *My beloved country*

In this popular literature derived from the war timeless Kosova Albanian themes emerge and re-emerge time and again, as songs describing battles against the Turks transmute into songs about fighting and killing the Serbs,[71] but any mention of God, let alone Islam, is almost totally absent. The theme of martyrdom is common but in an entirely national, not a religious context.[72]

The psychological makeup of the typical UCK/KLA recruit certainly included the possibility of a violent death, but so many families had experienced this in previous generations of struggle against Serbian external rule that it seemed almost an inevitability, particularly for those from traditionally militant villages and regions. There was a population waiting and ready for the new army, and many willing and potential recruits who were willing to risk their lives for Kosova. There was a new leadership who wanted to organise such an army but were sometimes distant from the masses. In between was the Kosova Democratic League with a commitment to avoiding war, and much international support from supporters of continuing Serbian hegemony over Kosova who saw Ibrahim Rugova as their best hope. The story of the insurgency in the years between 1995 and 1997 is the story of how the LPK, as by now the overwhelmingly dominant radical political organisation, decided to try to bridge that gap. Should it be done on the prime basis of class, or of nationalism? This was the ideological dilemma that had yet to be resolved.

4

PREPARATION FOR BATTLE: A HANDGUN ARMY?

Conditions for armed struggle were more unfavourable in Kosovo and Meto-hija than in any other area of Yugoslavia. The terrain was flat, surrounded by high mountains, which made manoeuvring more difficult.

Svetozar Vukmanovic, *General Tempo*[1]

In their influential book on Balkan revolutions, the American histori-ans Djordjevic and Fischer-Galati observed in 1981 that the time of Balkan social upheavals may not have ended with the establishment of Communist governments in most Balkan countries:

The story of Balkan revolutions is thus not completed by this study since the 'objective conditions' which have led to revolutionary activities in the past have not been eliminated. The Pax Sovietica has devised more effective means of control over the peoples of the Balkans than had either the Romans or the Ottoman Turkish but it has been unable to eradicate the dissatisfaction and disaffection of the inhabitants of the Peninsular with conditions which cannot be described as fulfilling of their historic hopes and aspirations.[2]

It is possible that they had in mind the student uprising in Prishtina that year, which but for the collaborationist policies of the Kosova Communist party leadership could have led to a link with the working class and a much more viable political movement. In the view of the Albanian Communists in Tirana, the 'objective conditions' were 'the economic situation, bad living conditions, the discrimination which they suffer in comparison with other students at Yugoslav universities.'³ The central demand of the demonstrators for a Kosova Republic was carefully downgraded to a secondary issue.

Much had changed in Tirana between 1981 and 1996 but certain constants remained. The Berisha leadership in Tirana, like their Enverist precursors, wished to see a better Kosova but after late 1993 were not pressing the issue internationally. The usual line of the Belgrade leadership was to blame Tirana for stirring up discontent in Kosova. The issue of full independence was rarely raised in reality, and like the Rugova leadership of the LDK Berisha had expected it to be dealt with by the Dayton peace agreement for Bosnia as part of a wider regional settlement. Sali Berisha was alarmed by the turmoil in Yugoslavia and well aware of the bitter divisions and potential for conflict in his own country. He saw the socialist opposition in Albania as having some links with Yugoslavia and feared contagion. His fears were to be entirely borne out the following year. His Prime Minister Alexander Meksi had a more activist policy and frequently called for better human rights in Kosova and the end of Serbian hegemony, but the word 'independence' was hardly ever used in Tirana. In this period Kosova played no central part in either Richard Holbrooke's highly personal diplomacy or State Department policy generally.⁴ It was in this difficult climate that the leaders of the Kosova Liberation Army had to plan their emergence onto the international stage and how to begin the war. Yet there was also a window of opportunity opening. Kosova was ripe not only for military resistance to Serbian rule but also for social revolution. The Communist elite and the docile lower middle class of the towns were living both figuratively and literally on the capital of the old Yugoslavia, but it was fast running out. Dayton had provided constitutionalist and pacifist Kosovars with nothing but it had also opened up political and ideological space for new politics. Theoretical perspectives were important.

In the Enverist orthodoxy the Albanian national movement expressed through the socialist revolution had been circumscribed after 1945 by the unfavourable international context, in which the Albanian people in the Balkans had been held back by a framework of hostile alliances and international control mechanisms in the Balkans. This process accentuated after 1948–50 with collapse of resistance in Drenica, the establishment of a West-leaning Yugoslavia and the defeat of the Left in the Greek Civil War.⁵ Many years later the end of communism had brought chaos to Albania and Milosevic to Kosova, but it had also brought the end of the Cold War international relations factors in the region. The younger generation of Kosova militants who were drifting into the LPK and KLA orbit were largely free of the dependent political mentalities that were a product of the position of Albania in the world during the Cold War. They accepted the reductionist and in some ways self-serving explanation of what had gone wrong that emanated from Tirana, but they were also beginning to find a new faith in themselves and in what they might achieve politically on their own. For that reason they were hard for the older diplomats and foreign intelligence officers to understand, and the fact that the great majority came from peasant or working class backgrounds made them easy to dismiss. The Kosova militants felt uncertain and on edge themselves in 1995 and 1996. They knew that after the Dayton fiasco they would be forced back on their own resources and the armed struggle was the only way forward, but they knew the magnitude of the tasks ahead before they could change history. A young KLA recruit at that time, Ajvaz Berisha, later wrote, 'In the years 1995/6/7 the situation in Kosova was very delicate ... our priority was to rebuild our historic small arms arsenal.'[6]

The development of the little liberation army in 1996 followed many of the textbook guides to guerrilla warfare. Memory of Second World War activity played a significant part in many older militants' thinking.[7] This did not extend to prioritising supply of explosives and establishing ammunition and arms dumps, either in Kosova itself, or in Albania as near to the Kosova border as possible. Supply of handguns and bullets for them was the overwhelming priority, a rhetoric of personal weapons possession. By the beginning of the following year, the political leadership clearly felt that at least part of the Kosova population was ready for armed conflict—something that must have been influenced, as Tim Garton Ash later pointed out, by the armed insurrection in Albania,[8] but even before that began, the influential LKCK journal *Climiri* observed in an attack on Rugova's policy in January 1997:

The pacifists tell the people that one must not on any account dare to attack the fortress, because we are unarmed, while the fortress's defenders are equipped with the most modern weapons, and if we attack them we will soon be totally defeated! Since 1990 this propaganda has had total success ... however, now, as events have run their course, people have become disappointed at this approach, and there has been disillusionment among the pacifists themselves.[9]

The LKCK analysis is also important as it sets out very clearly the debate within the KLA leadership about the true nature of the Marxist tradition of informal warfare. The journal went on to describe those who

advocate an immediate attack on the fortress, regardless of the current opinion prevailing among the broad masses or the organisation of those who would
wage the war. The other camp considered the people to be the decisive factor,
and said that the fortress must be attacked without fail but that the people
must first be organised and the enemy's fortress must be besieged in an organised manner. Both currents of thought considered the people to be the decisive
factor, but differed in their positions on how the people should be
organised.[10]

At one level the summer 1996 military struggle was unspectacular after the major events of the spring, but it was an essential period of work. Important future leaders joined armed groups, like Syleman Selimi, future intelligence chief and KLA commander. Arms dumps, usually in remote rural surroundings, were gradually established, and training areas, usually in deep forest and scrub. There is no evidence at this stage of KLA access to explosives, although many of Kosova's aged and badly built concrete bridges dating from early Communist days would have been vulnerable to attack, as the British General and first KFOR commander Mike Jackson later observed in his autobiog-raphy.[11] Groups of fighters began to be formed on an informal basis and began detailed surveys of territory and the deployment of Serbian forces. A series of attacks in early July brought comment in parts of the international press.[12] There was a particular focus of activity in north-ern and north-east Kosova, which until 1996 had been an easy region for the Serbs to control. This was also part of the process of the emer-gence of new commanders of local standing who were not part of the original Drenica-based KLA leadership group, or from Macedonian Albanian LPK cells like Fazli Veliu and Bardhyl Mahmuti. It is a sign of the ICTY's narrowness of focus in the Limaj trial material that none of this activity is mentioned, even in the historical narrative section of the trial judgement.

The dominant figure in this regional development was Zahir Pajaziti, a tall and urbane young man who had been through the familiar polit-ical learning curve of the 1980s student demonstrations, a visit to the Albanian Military Academy in Tirana for training in 1991, and disap-pearance into the Kosova political underground afterwards. In that year he had been heavily influenced by reading the military writings of Dr Fehmi Pushkolli and had concluded it was necessary to form a Kosova guerrilla army.[13] The organisational model used by the LPK enabled him and others like him to act on their own outside a central command structure to set up armed groups in different localities, in Pajaziti's case the Llap borderlands in and around Podujevo. The command system was rudimentary—something for which later the KLA was criticised—but they were in fact following the traditional methods described by Levy in a standard British handbook for Second World War Resistance fighters, where aspirant guerrillas were advised:

Every guerrilla leader worth his salt encourages initiatives amongst his men. Before executing a coup of some kind—an attack on an enemy patrol, an ambush on an enemy convoy, or whatever it may be, the leader will explain clearly to the group the job ahead of them; he will outline the tactics to be used, and will ask for criticism and alternative suggestions. Thus every man will have a part in planning the forthcoming action. Through such discussion the members of the band have a full understanding of what is required of them, and also confidence in their leader and ability to do the job. This method is genuinely democratic, and it also happens to be the most effective, as democratic methods often are.[14]

Regular attacks on a small scale on police posts were continuing, but these would never be sufficient to move the Belgrade regime. This situation began to change in the spring of 1996. The Exterior organisation of the LPK, meeting in Geneva in January 1996, had taken the decision to accelerate the armed struggle in response to the Dayton failure, and in February Kosova Liberation Army FX communications had also begun to appear in newspaper offices, although at that stage many journalists were unconvinced a real organisation was behind them.[15] In late April and May a series of coordinated attacks on Serb police posts and Serbian refugee colonies took place in and around Decani and Peja in western Kosova. Five Serbian officers were killed and for the first time armed insurgent resistance in Kosova made the news headlines in the international press.[16] The choice of targets was intelligent as the newly arriving Serbian settlers from the north of Yugoslavia were bitterly resented by all the Albanian population.[17] The nascent army and inevitable war were emerging into the public domain, a fact emphasised by the arrival in media offices of yet more press releases sent from Switzerland by fax on behalf of the Kosova Liberation Army.[18] The early involvement of the media showed some intellectual sophistication in LPK Exterior. The war for Kosova would be fought in the media as much as on the ground and Western perceptions of the new army were crucial. The early FXs and most later ones were clear, accurate, professional and gave Western journalists leads into the main stories, and turned out to be invaluable by comparison with later material from the Yugoslav army which was often hectoring, inaccurate and full of stereotypical terminology.

In essence the early 1996 military strategy that the LPK adopted was more of the same recipe, but more of it and better organised. Although they found it hard to admit, the LPK and KLA leadership were working already well within the inherited Yugoslav Partisan problematic of guerrilla warfare. This was the inherited subconscious knowledge that all Yugoslavs had to learn at school about the origins of their nation before 1945, and then had drummed into them during national service as conscripts. As a commentator on Tito's doctrinal writings has written, the central issue in developing a Balkan insurgency in Tito's view was not only

the organisation of the armed force but also its methods of warfare needed to be developed before the insurrection could assume the character of a permanent offensive war. Tito's experience from Serbia, Montenegro and elsewhere was again highly significant. It warned him that he should avoid formal fights, even at the cost of abandoning free territories. Tito knew very well that in the initial period of the war, the consequences would be much worse for the movement as a whole if he stubbornly defended the free territories.[19]

In order to reach the point of establishing free territories, of which the most obvious was rural western Drenica, the insurgents had to reduce and if possible stop VJ use of the asphalt roads. In turn this meant the destruction of the MUP police posts that controlled important road junctions. This had also been the stock in trade of Balkan insurgencies against the scattered garrison posts and forts of the declining Ottoman military security system. Structures of inherited military knowledge, often in oral tradition, had a long history in popular mentalities. Attacks using hand grenades and Kalashnikovs had been the staple fare of the KLA since 1993, all that had changed was the degree of ambition and greater coordination with the aim of introducing the population to the idea of clearing territory of Serbian security forces in defined locations. The targets were almost always police stations within hostile Albanian-dominated rural environments, and often those, as at Klina in May 1996, that controlled strategic road junctions. Both sides realised early on that much of the battle for Kosova would be about control of the asphalt roads which were essential conduits for Yugoslav army and MUP heavy vehicles and armour. The marshy plain and its dirt roads could quickly turn into a winter quagmire for non-tracked vehicles. It is worth noting that although many of the staples of guerrilla warfare had remained the same since the time of T.E. Lawrence, the Spanish Civil War and Second World War Partisan movements, others had evolved.

In all guerrilla army operations from the Boer War onwards, attacks on trains and railway lines had played an important part, in fact it could be said they were the central part of Lawrence's theories and practice against the Ottoman forces in the Middle East, but trains and the rail lines in Kosova had been built primarily for mineral ore transport and played little part in Yugoslav military structures. Virtually all supply was by road. Blowing the railways up would have been easy but equally would have achieved nothing militarily against Belgrade.[20] The KLA focused almost exclusively on the MUP uniformed police. There was particular animus between the majority population and the police who were seen as a specific Milosevic force that had terrorised the villages for years, as opposed to the army in which many older Kosovar Albanians had served and which still attempted to preserve a veneer of the old ethos of multi-cultural Yugoslavism. There was also, in Albanian culture, the issue of revenge. Almost everybody in the Albanian population knew someone who had been maltreated or killed at the hands of the police. To kill a policeman was to draw blood in the revenge process, an attractive opportunity to regain honour under the dictates of the Kanun code which is the ethical basis of the Albanian family.[21] It provided a status of instant honour to the revenging Albanian and elevation to a leadership position in the local community. In many of the founding KLA families such as the Geci family in Llaushe, KLA adherence provided an opportunity to avenge the oppression endured in previous generations, which in their case had suddenly been repeated under Slobodan Milosevic.[22] Or, as the poet Nexhat Imeraj wrote a little later during the war:

> *Dua te shkruaj*
> *Me gjakun e Serbit:*
> *'Kosova e Lire'*

> *Using Serb blood instead of ink,*
> *I want to write the following:*
> *'Free Kosova'*[23]

There were also practical issues. The army was in large and heavily fortified urban garrison barracks and was usually immune from frontal attack. The troops patrolled the countryside in heavy armour plated vehicles that could only have been attacked by mining of the roads followed by assault with armour-penetrating weapons, which at this stage the KLA did not have. The army was also a declining force. As a result of the demands of the lengthy Bosnian conflict VJ barracks had been denuded of munitions, equipment and supplies and the conscription system was breaking down all over Yugoslavia. Weapons sales by disaffected soldiers were an important early source of KLA munitions supply. Milosevic was forced to rely more and more on the police for the security system, and also on vicious anti-terrorist units who were to be guilty of many gross human rights violations at different stages in the conflict.[24]

The shootings contributed to a rise in political tension in Kosova, but after the first flurry of activity in May-June 1996 the whole situation became more and more overshadowed by the looming banking collapse and the subsequent anarchy and violence in Albania, eclipsing Kosova in the international media and Western diplomatic deliberations. In the spring of 1996 there was nevertheless a useful trial run for the LPK leaders in working out how to propel the new KLA force to the centre of public-dimension events. It was also a time when new leaders and potential new leaders were starting to emerge.[25] The dead Serbs were almost all local boys in the police, such as Milos Nikolic from Podejeve, along with a sprinkling of non-Kosova Serbs from traditional Serbian centres of police and army recruitment outside Kosova like the garrison city of Nis, home of the Prishtina Corps of the army.[26] The militia leader Zeljko Raznatovic, Arkan, visited Kosova shortly after further attacks on police stations in the first week of August and commented that they were 'the work of amateurs' but called for 'Podujeve to be reinforced with police special forces which will discourage local terrorists and bring peace and security to both the Albanians and Serbs who are equally endangered.'[27]

Arkan rarely moved without Milosevic's personal sanction, and his visit can be seen as a sign of the Belgrade leadership's recognition of the success of the Llap group of the KLA in clearing Serbian security forces from many places in and around Podujevo and Vushtrri. Arkan added that his paramilitary formation, the Serb Volunteer Guard, 'is prepared to help' in these processes, a grim warning of the local terror that was to follow in the next year.[28] In mid-September the KLA campaign flared up again, with explosions and shootings around several Kosova police stations such as at Izniq, Junik and Luzhan near Podujeve, and in Klina the Town Hall was attacked.

It did not take very long for the new military developments on the ground to be understood in Belgrade and in Europe. Albanian attention was temporarily distracted from the growing crisis by the death of Mother Teresa on 8 September.[29] In the Serbian capital Milosevic expanded the security police presence all over Kosova, particularly in the west, and the end of the Bosnian war had released military forces from that theatre. Visas for foreign journalists were difficult to obtain, although this did not stop Milosevic *apparatchik*s complaining about the lack of foreign coverage of the Serbian elections. Troops were moved south to the main Prishtina Corps headquarters at Nis and arrests of Albanian suspects took place all over Kosova. Numerous Albanians were convicted of 'association for purposes of hostile activity' under Article 136 of the criminal code, repeating the crackdowns of the previous decade, while others fled abroad. This was not the case with Ibrahim Rugova and his circle.

As late in that year as November, 'Prime Minister' Bujar Bukoshi was reported in Belgrade as saying that his government had no information on the existence of any Kosova army or Kosova Liberation Army.[30] His doubts were echoed by Rugova himself in Prishtina. In a local climate dominated by petty arguments between the Serbian parties about the degree of Milosevic's manipulation of the Kosova votes in favour of his Socialist Party of Serbia/JUL electoral coalition, the remarks of the old LDK leadership were as lost as leaves in the wind. In a contrarian outburst, that same week Adem Demaci attacked current trends in US and German policy which saw the future of Kosova within Serbia, and he began to assume the role in the international media that Rugova had vacated and abandoned. A new reality of conflict on the ground was developing with a Serb official and a policeman assassinated by the KLA near Podujeve on 1 November. Demaci had the unique capacity among the older Kosovar leaders of being able to ignite and renew faith in the Kosova cause, something that was often desperately needed in the long years of repression and LDK leadership incompetence. Kosova Albanians often have a strong 'rank and file' instinct, in the Marxist sense a trade union consciousness born of the long struggles in the mines, but they find faith in a political leader more difficult.

What was the doctrinal basis of Serbian military operations at this stage of the conflict? In essence, the Yugoslav army command did not welcome involvement in the details of the Kosova security system. They saw themselves as responsible for border security and patrolling the roads in heavy vehicles. The more intelligent senior officers were well aware of the practical difficulties they would face once any serious encounters with the Albanian majority began. Plans for a Kosova crisis had been made for many years, as part of the stock-in-trade of military planners' activities, and they were very old fashioned in character. They depended ultimately on the psychology of the 1936 Cubrilovic memorandum where driving out as many Albanians as possible was the desired objective. These reflexes were further developed as the Albanian armed uprising developed at the end of 1996 and in the spring of 1997, when it was suddenly clear that large quantities of arms were held by the population in Albania and many might find their way to Kosova. The arid disputes among some Western commentators about whether the plan for ethnic cleansing of Kosova, 'Operation Horseshoe', actually existed miss the point. Removing Albanians from Kosova had been central to all Serbian colonisation plans throughout the twentieth century.

In early 1997 a new factor entered the situation. After the killing of Zahir Pajarziti and his group in Llap, in the words of Ramush Haradinaj, 'the KLA suffered a huge setback'. But as later when the Jashari massacre inspired Hashim Thaci, Fatmir Limaj and their group to return to Kosova, the Llap killings brought the Haradinaj brothers, Fehmi Lladrovci and their group fully onto the scene. They were all living in Albania but resolved to return to Kosova to open up the armed struggle until death. Haradinaj observes in an interview:

Following the killings of Edmondo, Zahir and Akifi, we wanted revenge and we wanted to attack through a large scale operation, to make Serbia understood we could fight back.[31]

They opened up fighting in the first week of May 1997, and it is significant that the Haradinaj-Lladrovci group had already started to receive financial and practical help from the LPK network in Albania. Haradinaj also had significant financial backers of a Ballist family background. Ali Ahmeti had prepared them organisationally, and the longtime Marxist-nationalist revolutionary Emrush Xhemali went with them into Kosova.[32] Xhemali was a founder of the LPK in 1982–83 and ideologically was still in many ways a contemporary Enverist with connections with old Sigurimi networks in Albania. He was a born and hardened underground organiser and conspirator. They crossed into Kosova led by Luan Haradinaj through a very obscure route in the Has region, and initially avoided Serbian surveillance. Then disaster struck. They were seen and attacked by a sizeable Serbian infantry force and Luan Haradinaj was killed. This caused a crisis for the whole family and Ramush Haradinaj was withdrawn from Kosova and spent the next months working in munitions supply in Albania, principally with Ilir Konushevsci (Commander Mergimit) and Ardian Krasniqi.[33] Both were killed later in the war, Krasniqi soon afterwards during a Serbian ambush while the group were attacking Klicina police post, and Konushevski in a targeted assassination in the Albanian mountains.[34]

As these bloody encounters in the remote western Kosova mountains in late 1996 did not find their way into the Western media, their significance was not immediately understood. Young Albanian fighters were killing their first Serbs, taking the life of 'The Other' and in doing so removing whatever little remained of the heritage of Yugoslavia from within themselves. In their schools they had spoken nothing but Serbian until the age of 17 and they never wished to speak it again. Their guns would speak in Albanian discourse.

In Belgrade these events formed a key part of the mosaic of often improvised decision making in and around the Milosevic circle that accelerated the tide flowing towards all-out war and, above all, the determination of Milosevic to find a 'final solution' to the Kosova problem. His initial perspective for the conflict was essentially that of a rerun of the Drenica counter-insurgency operation at the time of the foundation of socialist Yugoslavia. It seemed easy to destroy by military means the Albanian 'liberated space', as it had been to flatten the sacred free space of a Tekke by a single shell. But 1997 was not 1945. To lose control of the border with Albania was entirely a different matter, in terms of both practical military issues and also political psychology. As Ramush Haradinaj himself observed:

Throughout the war there were two schools of thought in the army. The first was that the war should turn into a national uprising, and the second was that the war should turn into an organised guerrilla war.[35]

In the time of the uprising in Albania that was beginning, Milosevic may have felt that the rational course of action was to implement the long held objective of all Serbian nationalists to ethnically cleanse as many Albanians from Kosova as possible. This would pre-empt the risk of an uprising in Kosova where he could not be sure his forces would win against the Kosova Albanian masses. This plan was indeed known as 'Operation Horseshoe'. At a military conference held early that year, a senior military academic, Radovan Radinovic declared:

Kosovo and Metahije are the chief objectives of any armed aggression against the Federal Republic of Yugoslavia, regardless of whether the attack would come from the southern Balkan mountains, or the Adriatic strategic direction or whether the aggression would be triggered by a 'civil war' coming from an armed rebellion of the Albanians attempting to secede. In addition, Kosovo and Metahije are an important airdrop location which can receive invasion forces of strategic proportions ... the FRY should opt for a strategic concept of an aggressive defence which implies a swift and decisive military action which aims at defeating the forces of armed secession, and, if necessary, rapidly transferring military activities into the territory of any neighbouring state which is militarily aiding an ethnic Albanian armed revolt.[36]

With this thinking dominating the government and the military in Belgrade, and a rising guerrilla movement, it was inevitable that the conflict would rapidly intensify. The threat of an invasion of Albania was clear, in addition to the onslaught on the Kosova Albanian population if the Berisha government did anything concrete to help the Kosova insurgency. This awakened memories in Albania of the two occasions when Serbian forces had previously invaded Albania in the twentieth century.[37] Slobodan Milosevic's own instincts as chairman of the National Defence Council were very close to those of his military leaders and the only issue to be decided was that of timing of the offensive. Milosevic had high hopes of returning to the mainstream of the international community after the Dayton Accords the previous year and was seen in the West as someone who could be relied upon to deliver agreed deals. He did not wish at this stage to have a full blown Kosova insurgent war on his hands, and seems to have been unaware of what a second rate army the VJ had become.[38] But his military and police leaders were receiving disturbing intelligence reports about the growing strength and support for the nascent KLA and were anxious to snuff it out as soon as possible. In August 1996 a series of explosions had taken place at police stations in Prishtina and Podujeve in the north-east of Kosova. This marked a further development in the military technology available to the KLA, as until now bombs had played no role in the campaign. Hundreds of Albanians were detained in response. The rural guerrilla movement which the Serbs had been struggling to understand had threatened to turn into an urban insurgency, which had not been seen in Kosova before.

A particular concern for Belgrade was the arrival of the KLA in localities like the strategically vital Kacanik Gorge leading from Ferizaj south to Macedonia, and the north-east town of of Vushtrri, well away from the militant Drenica heartland where the Serbs were used to oppositional movements.[39] In the Serbian police mentality the towns and cities were thought to be safe ground, as opposed to the potentially dissident and violent countryside, and the attacks were a gauntlet thrown down to the Milosevic regime, showing that the new enemy was serious about a full-scale confrontation with the regime in the future. The LPK also took political initiatives within the Albanian community to broaden their base of support.

Although later in the conflict the KLA leadership was criticised for its military errors, of which the most obvious was the attempt to take towns and urban centres too early in the campaign in the spring of 1998, at this stage there was in the 1993–96 development phase a remarkable avoidance of the main errors made by twentieth-century Balkan guerrilla movements. There is no sense of the nascent KLA relating to the Internal Macedonian Revolutionary Organisation (IMRO) or Serbian 'Black Hand' traditions of random assassination as a main weapon of the struggle, or their shadowy links with the criminal underworld. The emphasis was always on military confrontation with the Serbs in the open field of battle against the institutions of the security apparatus. A central success was the integration of the 'party', the LPK, with the 'movement', the people of Kosova, and with the nascent KLA army. By comparison with the Greek Civil War and the Greek Communist Party (KKE) the insurgency gave room for individual commitment and initiatives outside the party, but the LPK remained a guiding force in the background. There was no formal structure of political commissars within KLA guerrilla groups. The Kosova struggle did not suffer from being guided politically by a stultifying rigid Stalinist party. However, the LPK did, in many senses, follow a Leninist policy, obeying the dictates of the Russian leader that an insurgency should not call easily or lightly for an armed uprising when there was a well organised army, state machine and police apparatus to defeat.[40] The question of the final struggle for power in an insurgency can from the insurgent's standpoint always be postponed. The central issue was not that the revolutionary force was initially capable of defeating the state forces but that a pattern of work and development should be established so that it could achieve military superiority in the extended course of the struggle.

The influential Montenegrin theorist of twentieth-century Balkan revolutionary war, Svetozar Vukmanovic (General Tempo), who was Tito's emissary to the Greek insurgents, saw this equally clearly. In the Greek conflict he blamed the KKE for seeing the main centre of struggle as being in the towns using traditional tools of struggle like workers' demonstrations with armed detachments of workers as the core of the insurgency. He blamed the KKE leaders in Athens for failing to make clear to the party membership in the towns that they should do everything in their power to supply and reinforce the rural and mountain guerrillas. He also saw the KKE as at fault for failing to use explosives and sabotage to disrupt the enemy supply lines and destroy industrial capacity.[41] In reality, there was little scope for early KLA development in the towns of Kosova, least of all in the capital Prishtina. The sociology, recent history and class structure of the new towns that had developed in Kosova under Communism did not lend themselves much to radicalism, quite apart from the fact that the 'Drenica' traditions of armed resistance to Belgrade rule were based in the countryside.

Yugoslav revisionist Communism had created a nervous and insecure lower middle class of Kosova administrators, urban shopkeepers, and petty officialdom of all kinds. They were a poor shadow of the 'New Class' of rich and privileged party collaborators Djilas described in northern Yugoslavia, but many were still wedded psychologically to the old system and had minor privileges, however small, to protect. Although many had lost their jobs in the Milosevic purges of the early 1990s, they were mostly still deferential, confused, terrified of Milosevic's police, and the more political were under the spell of Ibrahim Rugova's leadership of the Kosova Democratic League.[42] Many of Rugova's urban party members were ex-Communist party members. In the most conservative northern districts of Prishtina there was also still a residue of Muslim fatalism and passivity derived from the arrival there a generation before of penniless refugees after the defeat of Mullah Gjilane's Ballist revolt in Preshevo in the late 1940s.[43] It was a bad mixture for any form of militancy or resistance, and the continuation of some aspects of it after 1999 was the basis for the dysfunctional UNMIK international administration which between 1999 and 2004 sought to turn the clock back to the Yugoslavist past. That administration was unaware, or did not wish to be aware, of the social upheavals the events of the conflict between 1996 and 2000 was bringing to Kosova.

In this atmosphere where the inevitability of conflict seemed to be dominating all Kosova political calculations, the Vatican moved to quell Kosova militancy and bring what it saw as peace to the region, although its highly conservative perspectives actually strengthened the hand of Milosevic and Belgrade. The Sant'Egidio conflict resolution organisation began to become very active in Kosova. It was an apparently independent organisation in the eyes of many Kosovar Albanians, with head offices in Munich and in Rome, but in reality it was under the close control of the Vatican diplomatic service, an often-underestimated organisation in world affairs. It attempted to stage conferences where 'moderate' Kosova Albanians and Serbs would meet and interact to find new solutions to problems, but in reality all active support came from Roman Catholic Kosovars from the Catholic minority, and had it not been for an one chance factor, it would have little historical importance. The random factor was the British Ambassador in Belgrade, Ivor Roberts, who was a Catholic of part-Italian descent and had become a close and respected confidant of Slobodan Milosevic. A key objective of Robert's diplomacy was to draw Milosevic into the Sant'Egidio processes.

The British 'special relationship' with Serbia acquired rekindled energy in 1996 and the strongly anti-Islamic basis of Vatican diplomacy played very directly into Milosevic's hands, as did the fact that the only international non-governmental organisation allowed to operate in Kosova in this period was the Mother Teresa charitable organisation.[44] The British Conservative government's thinking was still dominated by figures like Douglas Hurd and Christopher Patten who had been through the Bosnian war and supported the many compromises made with Milosevic in that period. They hoped a similar deal could be struck between Milosevic and Rugova that would keep Kosova within Serbia. It chimed well with thinking in Belgrade, with Milosevic wishing to appear to be reasonable over Kosova in order to try to rehabilitate Serbia in the international community and get United Nations sanctions lifted. This was part of the traditional Serbian strategy, going back many years, of strengthening Kosova Catholics to reduce as far as possible the political leverage of the Muslim majority. The LDK leader Ibrahim Rugova's response was to refuse to be drawn on a compromise solution for Kosova that would fall short of independence, and Vatican diplomacy did not accomplish much. The Sant'Egidio initiatives are also important in indicating the near-collapse of European Union diplomacy in Kosova. The Dayton Accords only emerged as a result of American and NATO commitment to the region, and the Vatican was the only player with a specifically 'European' alternative that might prevent another potentially violent NATO intervention in the region. Vatican policy was sophisticated, being happy to see NATO in action to bring a new Roman Catholic majority state like Croatia into being but being unwilling to see a new Albanian-Muslim majority state emerge in Kosova.

The Yugoslav army mobilisation was unaffected by these diplomatic and conflict resolution initiatives. Roads in western Kosova were more and more heavily patrolled by the ugly diesel-spewing dark green armour plated vehicles that had been brought down from the Prishtina Corps headquarters in Nis in the spring of the year. Any attempt to keep a vestige of normal life in western towns like Peje and Gjakova was abandoned. As autumn approached and the nights were dark earlier, an informal curfew was introduced, so civilians did not dare venture out at night and the remaining elements of the rule of law vanished. The saturation strategy seemed designed to intimidate the armed groups and deny them that freedom of movement across the countryside that was needed to set up ambushes of police posts and move guns and munitions around. Little of this was seen by the international community. Milosevic did not allow the Organisation for Security and Cooperation in Europe (OSCE) into Kosova, and visas for journalists were severely restricted. There were almost no telephones at all in rural areas except in government-controlled post offices and mobile phones were in their infancy without Kosova network coverage. As autumn and winter approached, the always isolated Albanian communities were plunged into deeper and deeper obscurity and isolation.

As the year drew to a close, news began to drift across the mountains that there were problems with the banks in Albania and a financial crisis was in the offing. It meant little to most Kosovars who knew little of what went on in Tirana except how difficult material life was there in the aftermath of Communism. Unknown to them, within three or four months the country would be awash with weapons and a new factor would enter the Kosova equation. In the far south of the country small groups of men with the same Enverist roots in their political philosophy as the LPK leadership were looking to mobilise the population against the near-dictatorial government in Tirana, and although no evidence has ever been produced to prove formal organisational links, there was a common thread between their thinking and the more radical wing of the Kosova leadership.

The struggle for power in Albania was complex and had complex consequences for the Kosova leaderships. It was not a simple equation of weapons meaning Kosova liberation was possible. As the KLA commander Ramush Haradinaj pointed out in his observations on the origins of the war, *A Narrative about War and Freedom*, there were many difficulties in actually shipping weapons into Kosova during the whole wartime period. The key issue with the downfall of the Berisha government in ruins by June 1997 was that it symbolised the final collapse of the international relations and Cold War alliance control mechanisms over the Albanian Question. The Berisha government had taken a principled stand over some aspects of the national question after it was first elected in 1991–92 but had steadily retreated afterwards. The political vacuum in Albania and lack of government in the summer and autumn of 1997 provided an ideal platform for the Kosovars to launch their campaign as a new factor in the regional equations. An armed people was certainly important at the symbolic level but a disarmed and impotent central government in Tirana was equally important for the insurgency.[45]

There were new political factors entering the Kosova Liberation Army development from elsewhere, particularly the town of Tetovo in western Macedonia where there was a long tradition of general political radicalism and nationalism.[46] Tetovo had a strong Balli Kombetar tradition dating back to the Second World War, and an educated, often radical middle class that had been radicalised by the neo-Communist anti-Albanian post-1991 regime run by Kiro Gligorov.[47] Adem Demaci in particular was very influential in Tetovo and the more radical of the ethnic Albanian political parties led by Arben Xhaferi and Menduh Thaci had many links with the KLA leadership.[48] Demaci spent a good deal of time in Tetovo in the summer of 1996, in between meeting various international delegations led by Javier Solana, Elizabeth Renn and other international and European Union functionaries. By the end of

May the better informed American newspapers had begun to report on the possibility of a Kosova crisis fundamentally destabilising the Balkans once again.[49] The arrival on the scene of Demaci as a Kosova spokesman of equal standing to Rugova was a great asset to the KLA, and may have helped precipitate the decision to 'go public' as a military force within Kosova in the autumn of 1997. The media dimension of the future conflict had been intensively analysed in LPK Exterior in Switzerland and the role of Demaci was critical. Although not a formal member of the LPK, Demaci shared the same political roots and used the same political language. His vibrant witty personality was a marked contrast to the inertia and moralising absolutism diplomats saw in Rugova, and he created vital political space for the emergence of the KLA with the internationals.

In his 1996 visits to London and Brussels for talks with the British Foreign Office and the European Union, Demaci concentrated on making clear that the pacifist strategy of Rugova and the Kosova Democratic League had failed and that the armed conflict option was a real option for the ethnic Albanian majority. His realism was a great asset with his emphasis on the idea that unlike the LDK, the LPK was not a party intending to take power, but a political movement for the liberation of Kosova. This was not strictly true. The LPK in its origins had a rigid Leninist-derived internal structure based on small cells that police informers would find hard to penetrate, and it also turned out to contain many with political ambitions who later became politicians. It had by 1996 moved far enough away from its Marxist-Leninist and anti-revisionist origins to convince the uncommitted to join the war effort on a purely national and not an exclusively socialist or communist basis. The meetings with NATO leader Javier Solana were particularly difficult for Demaci. The urbane, profoundly Spanish diplomat occupied a different political and ideological universe from Demaci and they were soon at loggerheads on whether the international community, the Europeans in particular, had turned their backs on the terms of the Helsinki Final Act which provided for the right to self-determination in ex-Communist nations. Demaci returned to Prishtina convinced that nothing could be expected from Brussels, in either the EU or NATO, against Milosevic, and armed struggle was the only way forward.

The standing of Rugova in Kosova was further undermined when he attended meetings with Milosevic brokered by the Sant'Egidio representatives on 2 July. Demaci and the leading Kosova author Rexhep

Qosja accused Rugova later that week in the Tetovo and Prishtina press of having a policy 'of capitulation and defensiveness' towards Milosevic and the Serbs,[50] and personal 'despotism and arrogance'. The next months at the diplomatic level this would be taken up with increasingly frantic diplomatic attempts to boost Rugova and find a way out of the labyrinth that the Sant'Egidio negotiations and Ivor Roberts had unintentionally or intentionally created for him. These initiatives made little difference to the military situation on the ground. Rugova was like a blind man in a dark room when faced with the developing conflict.

In December 1996 the Serbian authorities became seriously concerned about totally losing control of parts of the important Llap district in the north-east bordering Serbia, and ordered a crackdown. Newly emerging local KLA leaders like Edmond Hoxha were targeted and he was duly shot down with others near Pestove on 31 January 1997. A native of Junik, Hoxha had been brought up in a patriotic family with a tradition of Kanun expertise. He had formed an informal armed group in 1994 after living in Durres in Albania for two years. Durres was an important—if generally little known—centre for nascent KLA organisation in the 1994–97 period, and prominent later leaders like the Macedonian Ali Ahmeti and the influential LPK figures Xhavit Haliti, Emrush Xhemali, Garfurr Elshani, Homeland Calling chief Jashar Salihu, Bardhyl Mahmuti and Luan Haradinaj had all lived there for periods of time. The free and easy atmosphere of the old Adriatic port with its sprawling Byzantine walls and grand Roman amphitheatre was an ideal environment for clandestine activity. Durres had labyrinthine international smuggling links and many local residents with Kosova family origins.[51] Sometimes important political meetings took place at nearby Lezhe, where the young militant recruits could be inspired by the grave of the Albanian national hero Skanderbeg. Some took their oath to join the KLA in the Skanderbeg grave enclosure.

Unlike Tirana, there were few foreigners in Durres and virtually none at all after March 1997, and most importantly, little effective presence of the Albanian secret police, the SHIK, which contained elements of dubious patriotism and links with the Greek intelligence service, rapidly expanding its activity in Albania in this period. Edmond Hoxha's funeral at Junik on 3 February 1997 was attended by hundreds of people and was the first mass public gathering of its kind in support of a dead KLA soldier. It was a precursor for the media-promoted Geci funeral in November 1997 where the KLA emerged on the public stage in the Western press, and similar events involving the Jashari family at Prekaz the following spring.[52]

In the intervening months the spreading disorder in Albania would develop into the first successful armed uprising in mainland Europe since the Second World War, and would fundamentally transform the political and military perspectives of all Kosova political actors and later international actors. The limits to Albanian political action in advancement of the national question that had remained frozen by the international relationships of the Cold War period would decisively break down and provide a new political space for the KLA to begin accelerating its military campaign. In the meantime, the local arm of the KLA was beginning to lengthen with the killing of a prominent Albanian collaborator with the Socialist Party of Serbia, Maliq She-holli, who was executed in the street in Podujevo on 9 January. 1997 was to prove to be a year of rapidly spreading violence on all sides and in many new localities in Kosova.[53]

5

AUTUMN 1997: THE WAR IS DEFINED

Join!—Or Die!

Benjamin Franklin, 1774

When the Kosova Liberation Army emerged in public at the funeral of Halit Geci in Llausche, Drenica on 28 November 1997, it seemed to most observers of the Balkans that a long overdue event had occurred.[1] Three days earlier, a MUP police patrol had been attacked in a small village called Vojnik nearby, caught unawares by the KLA. A firefight started which lasted several hours. On 26 November the MUP returned in a convoy of heavily armoured vehicles to find the road blocked by a bulldozer and the convoy was pinned down so that it had to be rescued by two helicopter gunships called in from Prishtina airport. The wily old LDK vice-chairman Fehmi Agani observed in Prishtina, 'It would be a great mistake to either ignore the existence of the UCK or see their appearance with euphoria.'[2]

This was a rebuke to the bankrupt policy of Rugova, but also a statement of what most Kosovars knew in their hearts, that war was inevitable but many people dreaded it. Almost all knowledgeable people in Kosova knew that such an Albanian guerrilla force existed and that the KLA had been in military action for three or more years. The Geci funeral in the windswept and exposed Llausche village with its many wooden cowsheds and small farmhouses was in many ways as

101

symbolic and ritual-based an event for the Albanians as the visits to the monument at Kosova Polje to commemorate the 1389 battle each year were for the Kosova Serb population.

The tempo of the insurgency on the ground had been accelerating sharply during the late summer and early autumn period but had mostly been obscured from international view by the continuing instability in Albania after the spring armed uprising. Within Kosova, the real date of emergence of the KLA can be seen as seven weeks earlier, when a spectacular series of attacks on police barracks on the night of 10–11 September set buildings alight as far as 150km apart, and destroyed several MUP vehicles.[3] Local people who knew of the overall Serb system of police checkpoints along main roads and the very poor and heavily tapped phone system were aware of the existence of a force capable of executing complex and planned military actions. On 16 October another military landmark was reached, with the first use of anti-tank weapons in the conflict in a village near Decani.

The Prishtina Corps commanders in their Yugoslav army barracks in Nis had been studying the pattern of violence for some time, and were ready to put into operation long-made plans to end it. They were concerned, understandably, about the problems that lay ahead and there is every sign that the Serbian army commanders had a much clearer perception of the risks of a Kosova war than Milosevic had. This applied in particular to the overall commander, General Momcilo Perisic, whose lack of enthusiasm for major engagement in Kosova eventually led to his removal from this post late in 1998 by Milosevic. Many of them may also have expected the violence in Albania to spread to Kosova. This was an awesome and disturbing prospect for them. Berisha's army had proved impotent to control Albanian disorder on the streets and it was unlikely the VJ would fare any better.[4] There was also, in their own military and security cultural world, as professional army officers, an even more uncomfortable contemporary example. Over the same period of years as the Kosova conflict had developed, the major counterinsurgency conflict on the international scene was in the Caucasus, in Chechnya, between 1994 and 2000. The Chechen war had shown the difficulties of a modern counterinsurgency operation against a determined enemy and above all the risks for formal armies in urban combat.[5] Combat in modern urban contexts demands thousands of well trained and ruthless infantry, the absence of the foreign media and the willingness to take high casualties and to see overwhelming destruction of local infrastructure. All this took place in Grozny, where in most respects the Russian forces demonstrated that little had changed since in these matters since Tacitus wrote of making a desert and calling it peace. The Yugoslav army did not have the infantry resources for a prolonged urban subjugation of Kosova against a more or less universally hostile population. The only substantial advantages the VJ had were its airpower and monopoly on heavy weapons and heavy armoured vehicles. These existed not only as a result of the JNA and VJ's natural status as a long-established government army but as a result of the United Nations international arms embargo in the earlier stages of the ex-Yugoslav wars, for as Susan Woodward has pointed out,

The UN embargo thus reproduced the effects of economic reform and westernisation and the EC decisions on recognition and aid. In its early days the embargo largely affected the Bosnian army, Muslim paramilitaries, and special forces created by the Albanians in Kosovo. Able to purchase or receive from foreign patrons, émigrés and arms markets abroad substantial imports of light arms and ammunition, they could not overcome their disadvantage in access to heavy weapons (artillery, tanks) and aircraft of the Slovenes, Croats and Serbs, because the supply routes were commanded by their potential or real enemy.[6]

The Serbian man in the street was nevertheless tired of endless conflict under Milosevic's rule and there was little appetite outside hardline nationalist circles for another debilitating conflict. Most Serbs had believed—or at least hoped—that the 1995 Dayton Accords would bring some version of normality back to the lives of the peoples of the region. They knew the background of international intervention in the Bosnian war had brought human rights and law of war issues to the minds of Western leaders. A scorched earth campaign on a mass scale was not politically possible in modern Europe, albeit in the Balkans, even if it was possible in the Caucasus in a country few Western television viewers knew. Islam was also becoming a key issue. The Chechens were seen as having elements of Islamic extremism and 'terrorist' supporters among the population which the Kosova Albanians did not, despite some limp attempts by journalists close to the Belgrade propaganda machine to suggest they did. There is reason to think major international players were willing to allow the Russians a clear run against the Grozny insurgency for this reason. Pogroms of the Kosova Albanian population would bring international military action against Serbia, as duly happened in 1999. But the critical issue was military decline in the VJ itself. Some KLA leaders such as Ramush Haradinaj and Rexhep Selimi who had served as conscripts in the JNA or VJ knew how poor an army it had become, top heavy, over-officered, irregularly and poorly paid, short of trained men, and with antiquated doctrine and many technical problems such as shortages of spare parts for vehicles. This accounts for what seemed at the time to many older Kosovars, who had served in their youth in the JNA in a better era, as overconfidence among young KLA leaders about the possibility of military victory. Armies do not prosper by inactivity and for over forty years the great Partisan force of 1945 had slowly ossified and decayed within Titoist Yugoslav society.[7] It had not fought any kind of war since 1945, nor taken part in international peacekeeping activities. For Milosevic, it was inevitable that local and focused terror would be required to overcome these large-scale structural handicaps. Hence the various anti-terrorist units were thrown into the conflict at an early stage and became a substitute for adequate regular forces.

Earlier in the year KLA actions had been undertaken on a wider and wider field of operations throughout Kosova, including the vicinity of the symbolically important cities of Mitrovica, Vushtrri and Prizren. The pattern of KLA activity was almost always the same, with night attacks and ambushes of police vehicles, often near railway crossings or bridges where heavy vehicles had to slow down and the police had no local cover. Isolated police posts in remote areas were common targets for attack; they were often empty and unguarded at night and could be destroyed by simply throwing hand grenades through a window. In Belgrade alarm spread through the more complacent sections of the Milosevic leadership as they believed that much of the KLA activity was synchronised from Albania and that the breakdown in government and plethora of weapons from the summer events would enable the insurgency to spread rapidly.[8] The current strength of about 13,000 police armed with paramilitary equipment could not control an urban uprising of the type just seen in southern and central Albania. The 6,500 Yugoslav Army (VJ) soldiers permanently based in Kosovo were only a notional strength, divided between the border areas and four main garrisons. Traditional plans made many years before provided for a rapid reinforcement force of about 10,000 more troops from Nis, Leskovac and elsewhere in southern Serbia.

It was only a matter of time before the inevitable Yugoslav military response took place. In the mentality of the Belgrade leadership, little had changed over the last two generations and all rebellious activity in Kosova was seen as originating in Albania. Milosevic and his army commanders were still stuck in the Enverist paradigm of analysis of the KLA as an Albanian-origin and Albanian-based insurgency, when in reality the KLA was becoming a much wider based movement whose most important lines of support were abroad, in Switzerland above all at this point, and then a little later in the United States and other nations. The problems of the Nis command would in many ways have been recognised in the times of Tacitus and the Roman struggle against 'barbarians' in Germania. Like the Roman officers, the Serbian officers were commanded by a tyrannical leader in a distant capital city who knew little in detail about what was happening on the ground. The army was ordered to repress a mobile and ever-changing threat. The southern border of Serbia, like the northern border of Greece and the upper Danube border with Germania in the Roman Empire, was always fluid. Fixing Serbia's southern border was a national military preoccupation throughout the twentieth century, and the issue remains open in some of its aspects to this day. The Serbs had invaded Albania twice during the twentieth century and there seemed to be every possibility—as seen from Nis—that the army might be required to do so again.

In a further sign of the war of symbolic structures inherited from the past, the Yugoslav military response was most severe in the Drenica heartland. The Yugoslav security forces were not as strong as they had been in the winter of 1991–92 when they faced a similar challenge in Prishtina. The army was in decline after the long Croatian and Bosnian conflicts and although Arkan still had his Tiger paramilitary units in formal existence, many of them were shadows of their former selves and the political initiative on the ultra-nationalist Serbian right in Kosova had passed to Vojislav Seseli's Radical Party. Seselj's party had taken over part of the Prishtina secret police complex as its headquarters. In contrast, the photogenic Arkan with his prominent football team and glamorous folk singer wife seemed to be more and more becoming part of the Belgrade-New Rich entertainment industry for the Serbs. The glamour of 'volunteering' to defend Serbia had much less glamour after the losses and bloodshed of the Bosnian war period. The paramilitary leader was a Kosova Member of Parliament in the Belgrade Assembly, but hardly ever visited Kosova except for when his FK Obilic soccer team was playing there. Arkan's Tigers could be deadly in local contexts, as the Dubrava prison massacre later in the Kosova war showed, but they then operated under the umbrella of the main Yugo-slav forces in a way they had not done in the early 1990s in Kosova.[9]

The response to the KLA would have to be made through the offi-cial Yugoslav armed and security forces, and tactical and operational details were going to be important. Milosevic could have ordered his forces to pick off the KLA selectively and fairly quietly using covert operations in its newest and weakest areas, but there is no indication he chose to do so. He chose an early showdown in Drenica. This was his first major strategic mistake of the wartime period, to opt for fron-tal military confrontation in Kosova using a combination of over-whelming force derived from the combination of anti-terrorist special units and the regular military. The effect of this on the majority popu-lation does not seem to have been thought through, maybe it was not even considered. Milosevic's speeches about Kosova at the time echo the rhetoric of the War on Terror ten years later, where a threatened state mobilises against a terrorist threat. He told a US negotiator a lit-tle later in the conflict that the security of Kosova in 1945 had been achieved by crushing the Second World War rising in Drenica and he intended to do the same.

The Serbian dictator did not seem to understand the difficulties of warfare in what in the intervening sixty years had become a much more urban and complex society. It was a very unwise decision. It will be an interesting question for future historians to consider how far this approach was a product of the dark and atavistic side of the Milosevic psyche where his defence of socialist Yugoslavia was dominated by inherited past, or whether the same collective psychology also domi-nated the minds of his army commanders.[10] The whole issue of the reawakening of a 'lost' Balkan past after 1990 will be a preoccupation in future historiography.[11] At a practical level what mattered was that the Yugoslav security forces were not what they once had been and a frontal attack on the KLA in Drenica risked rallying the ever-restive population behind the insurgents, as it duly did that winter. It also seems clear that between about the end of January 1998 and the end of February, Milosevic's thinking evolved. In January he was content for the MUP Special Forces to spearhead the assault on the KLA, but by a month or two later, it is believed, he met the security chief Jovan Stanisic and Serbian Police Minister Radovan Stojicic in February in Belgrade and decided on a full implementation of the 'Operation Horseshoe' plan which involved an assault on the Kosova Albania population as a whole.[12]

The preparation of the Western media by the LPK in Switzerland for the information and media war had been efficient, and within days reporters from many major Western newspapers were working in Kosova. The irregular little FXs from the Aarau supermarket in central Switzerland had done their work well. Many international reporters were instinctively sympathetic to the KLA after being fed so much pro-Serbian propaganda by French and British military and diplomatic press officials in the Bosnian conflict.[13] The events in Kosova were seen as an extension of the uprising in Albania earlier in the year. The funeral of Halit Geci in Llaushe was attended by over 20,000 people who covered the little hillside above the village like a human carpet. Among the masked KLA soldiers at the event who fired AK-47s over the grave were future senior KLA leaders like Daut Haradinaj and the intelligence chief Rexhep Selimi. In the years between 1994 and 1997, when according to Serbian statistics 136 attacks were mounted by the KLA against security forces and installations, the organisation of the KLA was horizontal, where every soldier could be a leader in his own locality. Now there was a new leadership cadre emerging into the public domain. Few people knew who they were and as they wore balaclava helmets and dark glasses that hid their faces, it would be some time before anyone, Kosovar or foreign, could find out.

The KLA had thus arrived not only with a programme but also an image vocabulary. The FXs from Switzerland had placed the organisation firmly within the Balkan insurgent tradition of mysterious clandestine revolutionary organisations, and the dress style and behaviour at the Geci funeral borrowed the messages of the Special Forces units of top armies like the British SAS. It was a paramilitary theatre designed to play on the Serbs' deepest subconscious fears of an externally-assisted Kosova Albanian conspiracy against them, and it duly did so. Yet there was also a local postmodern-style vocabulary which was mainly established by the Jashari example. KLA men could be clean shaven and neat but local commanders tended not to be, and many grew beards and flourished moustaches and sported a variety of local symbolic objects. The style embodied the spirit of rebellion from the past. The new underground force wanted to be seen as serious, dangerous, clandestine and capable of inspiring fear, and it did so. The tone and content of the verbal messages at the graveside were quite different from the threatening visual imagery and were only addressed to the local Kosova Albanian audience. The simple address emphasised that the KLA was a movement for the liberation of Kosova and a *de facto* invitation for anyone sympathetic to join, irrespective of political views.[14] The image from the Geci graveside was also meant to convey to the Albanian people of Kosova that there was a serious, modern, effective and ruthless leadership in place that would be capable of fighting the Serbs over a prolonged period. The dominant image and leadership model of Rugova's Kosova Democratic League had been quite different, with conservative figures with a personal style that could have been taken from British academia in the 1950s 'handing down' policy to the people and no sense of a leadership that could inspire the people to independent political initiatives, let alone prolonged military struggle.

There does not seem to have been any ostensible influence in this development from previous Balkan revolutionary models within the Communist tradition outside Kosova. This is not merely a matter of arcane historical comparison but also goes to the heart of what the KLA was and what it became. Insurgent armies draw on tradition and popular memory as much as formal armies. There was a specific Communist organisational and practical model of warfare current throughout the Balkans after 1945. The Second World War had involved hundreds of thousands of people in anti-Axis Partisan warfare throughout the region. The Greek, Albanian and Yugoslav popular resistance movements in the Second World War should have provided the most obvious organisational models for the KLA. The long agony of the Greek conflict had assisted the development of almost every possible feature of Balkan insurgent organisational praxis in the mountains, from the picturesque *neo-klepht*s of the very early days in 1941–42, to the mass membership of ELAS and EAM, to the monadic and Stalinist-led force that the Democratic Army became by 1949. The Greek insurgency had a bifocal nature, with a mass political movement, EAM, and the people's army, ELAS. The most obvious comparison with the appearance of the KLA in November 1997 was with the dramatic appearance of the Greek Communist resistance movement ELAS. ELAS was born, in public terms, when the future commander Aris Velouchiotis marched with a group of men behind Greek and red flags through the little village of Domnitsa in remote Karpenisi in central northern Greece in June 1942.[15] The Geci funeral was a similar moment of sudden and defiant public visibility for the KLA. Some of the LPK leaders like Xhavit Haliti were steeped in the Balkan Marxist historical and political tradition and knew Greek history very well, and there seems to have been discussion of the possibilities of forming an EAM-type support organisation for the KLA in early days in Kosova and Switzerland.[16]

Yet there was a major obstacle in the way of this strategic option. In a sense, an 'EAM' already existed, in the form of the Kosova Democratic League, the LDK, even if its leadership from the point of view of the militants was most unsatisfactory. This overarching mass-membership political organisation was most unwelcome in the eyes of the LPK and KLA leadership and had inhibited the national movement. The LDK leadership belonged to the old revisionist Communist tradition of Titoist Yugoslavia. The political basis of the LPK and LPRK was in origin Enverist, rank and fileist and further to the left, but it did not have a single coherent theorised ideology by the year 1997, and this was to be a recurrent problem throughout the KLA's entire existence. Political organisational models represent the mediation between political theory and political practice. The thinking behind the original KLA organisation was in some respects narrow and rigid.

A clear military doctrinal model for a Kosova insurgent force did not exist in 1997, any more than it had done for Zijdajin Qira and the lonely pioneers of underground work in Kosova in the 1950s. Yet the practical similarities with the Greek insurgency after 1943 are inescapable. Both the Greeks and the Kosovars had to face Right-wing diversionary movements, in the Greek case Napoleon Zervas's EDES movement in north-west Greece, in Kosova the FARK militia in Dukagjini commanded by Tahir Zemaj.[17] There was also the issue of the Partisan name itself. The Partisan military tradition in socialist Kosova had been firmly associated in the popular mind with Yugoslav Communism and as an agent of what the Albanians saw as Slavo-Communist government imposition on the majority people of Kosova. Even if a form of Partisan structured warfare was inevitable against the Yugoslav forces, the KLA leadership operating in the Kosova Albanian context had to be careful to avoid undue overt association with local military traditions derived from the Communist movements in the Second World War.

Another issue that had to be considered was that of geographical factors affecting war planning, which in turn affected the security of the political and military leadership. Although Kosova has many remote and mountainous areas, in the main their physical inaccessibility is only serious in the far west in Dukagjini and on the borders with Macedonia and Montenegro. The Kosova landscape elsewhere is certainly (apart from the central plain) hilly and deeply forested but does not have the vast and wild mountain massifs of northern Greece, southern Albania and western and southern Macedonia that provided impenetrable natural fortresses and base camps for the Greek, Macedonian and Albanian wartime Partisan fighters. These countries also have a plethora of caves in the mostly limestone mountains, which the Kosova hills generally do not, an important resource as munitions stores and for shelter if guerrillas have problems with enemy airpower. Road communications had improved considerably since 1945. The Yugoslav Communist regime had prioritised road building and many places in Kosova were much more accessible to the Serbian forces than they had been in the fighting there during and after the Second World War. It was not really possible for the KLA to have a safe 'mountain' area of retreat and regrouping at any stage of the war in the sense that other earlier Balkan insurgent movements had, or the Macedonian NLA had on Mount Korabi in the 2001 conflict.[18] The thick woods in the Berisha area of Drenica and similar upland locations were the only serious equivalents. The Yugoslav forces still had total command of air space, although in practice their practical ability to mobilise helicopter support for their troops was much more limited than outside military analysts realised.[19] The geographic organisational model of the KLA areas of operation was derived from those of formal state armed forces and did not envisage the possibility of breaking down the large battalions of fighters into more flexible smaller units that could evade Serbian armoured attacks.

The political leadership after November 1997 was not any more physically secure than before then, in fact it was less so. Key figures like Thaci and Haliti had long been used to living with a Serbian price on their heads, whether in Switzerland or in the Balkans, and the significant minority of collaborators and police informers within the Kosova Albanian community was a major deterrent to open activity. It is significant that in this period and also later in the spring of 1998, executions of collaborators were a priority for the KLA, particularly of those Albanians who had joined Milosevic's Socialist Party of Serbia and taken up seats in the Belgrade parliamentary assembly. This latter ethnic recruitment by Milosevic was a development that had been encouraged by foreign embassies in Belgrade, but in the end it con-

demned many of those involved to death.[20] Much political activity had
to be undertaken in Tirana or elsewhere in Albania, which was in a
state of near anarchy and where it was easy for foreign intelligence
agencies to operate 'hit squads'.[21] The murder of the 'Ministry of
Defence' leader Ahmet Krasniqi in the summer of 1998 in Tirana, and
the narrow escape from assassination of Hashim Thaci soon afterwards in the same city, clearly demonstrate this.[22]

It was a short autumn that year, and as it happened a long and severe
winter soon followed and the sunny wooded hillsides of dwarf oak
were covered first in thick fog and then in deep snow. There was no
rapid follow-up action by the KLA and the Yugoslav forces retreated
to barracks and normal road patrolling. Western reporters mostly went
home while intelligence officers traced various violent but essentially
random and minor incidents across Kosova. By early December there
was very heavy snow and Kosova entered its usual winter condition of
frozen immobility. The new army was not idle, however, and in the
Drenica heartland around Prekaz village and the Jashari farm, a small
'liberated zone' developed where Yugoslav forces could not go.

The LPK newspaper *Zeri I Kosoves* for 11 December reported rapidly rising tensions throughout Kosova, and a week later referred to
the existence of a 'Republic of Skenderaj' coming into existence. On 24
December long sentences were announced in Prishtina (some *in absentia*) on a group of nineteen Albanian fighters who were accused of KLA
membership, including prominent figures such as Nait Hasani and
Agron Tolaj. The sentences totalled 186 years in prison. Various diplomatic efforts began, mostly from Germany and Austria, to persuade
Milosevic to begin talks on a solution to Kosova's problems, but they
were far from the reality of the accelerating conflict on the ground. It
was clear developments were moving towards a major confrontation
when the snow melted in the spring. In neighbouring Montenegro
social and political tensions were also rising rapidly, in a sign of the
often little-noticed practical linkage between the anti-Milosevic movement in both lands. The pro-Milosevic stooge government of Montenegrin President Momir Bulatovic was besieged in Podgorica by
thousands of often violent demonstrators during and after the Orthodox Christmas, in a further sign of developing resistance to Belgrade
political control.[23] In Kosova the KLA attacked the ferronickel plant at
Gllogoc, the first major effort by the insurgents against a significant
infrastructure target. It was only a partial success as the KLA did not

have explosives to sabotage the plant itself, and Serbian security forces were able to return to it soon after the battle. In Switzerland this event was seen by the LPK with concern. Haliti believed that a new and improved arms supply system was vital and the 'handgun army' concept must be abandoned. It became a main priority for Veliu and the LPK innercircle to develop the 'Homeland Fund' as quickly as possible into an effective fundraising arm for the new army and capitalise on Diaspora sympathy for what was happening on the ground in Kosova. This would enable the purchase of a major new arsenal.

Events moved faster than the political and military plans of either side. Small groups of KLA fighters had been beginning to spread through the Drenica heartland of insurgent support for some time. The landscape of small farms, dirt track roads and beech and oak woodland had a long history of conflict. In the manner of many wars, a random and largely unprovoked incident triggered the beginning of the wider war. At little Likoshane on 28 February, four KLA fighters ambushed a Serbian police vehicle, and in the ensuing firefight a Serbian policeman was killed and a KLA fighter wounded.[24] The KLA fighters escaped into the woods, taking their wounded comrade with them. They left a famous group of six oak trees in the village growing from a single root, which had always embodied local self-confidence and legend. The next day hundreds of Serbian forces arrived in the village by road and in helicopter gunships. They beat ten local Albanian residents to death in front of their families in a classic reprisal action. By the end of the day another fifteen residents had also died in the fighting between the tough Serbian counterinsurgency troops, newly arrived KLA in the hills nearby, and the largely unarmed villagers.[25] It was, in its way, an equally important encounter as the massacre of the Jashari family a week later, but it has never had the same resonance of martyrdom.

Serbian security efforts then focused on the Jashari family in Prekaz, thirty miles north, and destroying the 'liberated area' that stretched for some miles around the village.[26] On 22 January the family farm complex was attacked for the first time, but to little effect as most family members had left and were hiding in nearby woodland. In a sinister development that was to be a precursor of many later events in the war, the paramilitary leader Arkan's 'White Tigers' militia was involved, acting under the wing of the mainstream military. British military observers at a later stage in the conflict felt this was in grotesque imitation of the role of the Special Forces in British military doctrine.[27]

In actions designed to take the pressure off Prekaz and liberated Skenderaj, shootings of Serbian police and officials took place in the next two weeks in Podujeve, Malishevo, Kline and Ferizaj, but they did little to prevent the Serbian build-up around Prekaz. It is unclear if Adem Jashari intended to become the central martyr of the conflict, or if Ireland in Easter 1916 was in the minds of any of the KLA leadership, but events evolved in exactly that direction. The self-sacrifice of Jashari and his family on 5 March when the war began in earnest was a very similar catalytic event to that in Dublin in the Easter Rising. In each case the violent death of a few idealistic revolutionaries fighting overwhelming odds inspired thousands to join their cause and eventually ended foreign military occupation.

On 4 March, Serbian troops and paramilitaries flooded into Prekaz and the Jashari farmhouse was destroyed with the death of fifty-one members of the family. The fighting lasted on and off for three days and by the end of it the farmhouse and its surrounding buildings were a smoking ruin and nearly every member of the family was dead. The question obviously arises as to whether this was a planned sacrifice, a martyrdom for the Jasharis that would inspire the nation, or simply a random event where particularly violent and ruthless Serbian forces created martyrs for the Albanian cause without intending to do so. In all the voluminous Albanian literature published on the Jashari family since the war ended, the family is often portrayed as passive victims of events. This was not the case. It is perhaps more germane to recall the provisions of the Kanun where the owner of the house should die fighting in it if it is attacked. The Jasharis behaved throughout exactly as the Kanun dictated. At an international political level, the Jashari massacre brought in various sanctions against Yugoslavia from the Contact Group. There can be no sure answer to the martyrdom question, other than to note that the horizontal organisation of the struggle in this period would have made it impossible for any political leader to order the Jasharis to sacrifice themselves. Martyrdom is at its most effective in mobilising support for a cause when it happens to a committed individual acting on the basis of deeply held personal beliefs against repressive external state forces, as the early Christian martyrs in Rome demonstrate. The national struggle was always seen in terms of martyrdom, even in Communist Albania. The first documentary response to the 1981 student riots in Prishtina published in Tirana speaks of the fact that 'Three times this century you (Serbia) have inflicted heavy bloodshed on the martyred Albanian people living in Yugoslavia ... you shed their blood in 1945, in 1968 and again covered them in blood in 1981.'[28]

The beauty of the Jashari sacrifice from the Albanian point of view, and the nightmare from the Serbs', was that it was both contingent and random. It was, in rhetorical terms of popular culture, Custer's Last Stand, but it was, in military terms of the typology of the war, also his First. But unlike so many of the previous national martyrs, the Jasharis actually resisted and died fighting with guns at the hip. The 'legendary commander', as Jashari has now become always known, acquired this standing not merely through physical sacrifice but through military struggle while it was taking place. Unlike what happened in the days of December 1991, Prekaz had fought back. The sacrifice could thus inspire others to action in a unique way. The massacre also involved the destruction of almost a whole family, including many women and children, thereby grossly violating the regulations of warfare and revenge in the Kanun.[29] It broke all the Geneva Conventions, just as the Russians had done in Chechnya. It seemed to ordinary Kosovars, if not to much of the diplomatic community for a long time (with some honourable exceptions), that Milosevic was running a vicious anti-Albanian counter-insurgency operation not only against the KLA but also against the Albanian population as a whole, and memories were reawakening of old Serbian nationalist plans to ethnically cleanse all of Kosova. It was also the final protest of the poor and oppressed against tyranny. The Serbian armed forces were agents of Milosevic's apparatus against the people of Kosova and were in their way as much under the domination of a tyrant at Tacitus's Roman political actors in the *Annals* when an emperor such as Domitian forced them to consider their ultimate loyalties, to human values or to the imperial state. They were, perhaps inevitably given Serbian history and their own traditions, loyal to the orders of the tyrant, Milosevic.

The Jashari funeral brought out huge crowds and passed off peacefully, with the Serbian security forces staying away. Funerals play an important part in the development of many insurgent movements. They provide an opportunity for popular mobilisation and political participation that even the most tyrannical regimes find they cannot easily control. In the act of venerating the dead, a sense of collective strength and solidarity can be born. Funerals also break government movement control regulations and permit distribution of illegal propaganda. For the ordinary villagers the Jashari family also provided an opportunity for them to see that the internationalisation of their struggle might be possible, thanks to the presence of the first reporters with television cameras. British crews such as Frontline Television had been able to get access to Kosova, although with considerable risk.[30] The Milosevic system of repression in Kosova depended to a significant extent on maintaining the cultural and physical isolation of the Kosova Albanians from the outside world and trying to keep them nervous and lacking confidence in their own cause. After the time of the Prekaz massacre the option of secret terror that had been so useful for so long to the Serbian police apparatus began to become less and less viable, although it revived in the early weeks of the NATO bombing campaign with numerous serious human rights violations involving rapes, massacres and extra-judicial executions.[31] In turn many of these incidents laid the foundations for the Albanian revenge attacks on Kosova Serbs in the summer and autumn of 1999.[32] This pattern of events has been recurrent in Kosova history.

This event provided a significant boost for the KLA, but it also precipitated the most severe Serbian repression throughout Kosova. Some KLA 'sleepers' were told to leave and go to Albania. The political leadership also scattered. Hashim Thaci and Fatmir Limaj returned to Kosova as a consequence but then spent a good deal of time underground in Albania and Slovenia in this period. The Swiss-based LPK leader Ali Ahmeti, a Macedonian Albanian, was moved to a safe house in Tirana in Albania to take charge of KLA mobilisation there. Political dealings with the Tirana government of Fatos Nano were left to the experienced and worldly-wise Xhavit Haliti. Gradually the old LPK inner core who in some cases (Ahmeti and Haliti for example) had been working together for twenty years or more in the political underground or in prison were becoming a flexible and reasonably coherent internationally-based leadership. Veliu remained in Switzerland at the coordinating political centre.[33] Refuge in Albania and movement between the two countries were becoming increasingly difficult with more and more patrols and shoot-to-kill squads operating in border areas, and this in turn brought to a head an issue that had long been discussed in the top LPK leadership, that of opening a secure route across the Kosova border to Albania for munitions and personnel movement. There were still very serious shortages of weapons in Drenica, let alone elsewhere, and even more severe shortages of ammunition. Many people in Kosova and a trickle from the Diaspora were coming forward and expressing a willingness to fight, but they had no means of doing so and held drills in villages with only staves and pitchforks for weapons. Outside Kosova there was considerable pressure on the Swiss government to close down the Homeland Fund and cut off the supply of funds for the KLA.

In a seminal decision that was to alter the course of Balkan history, the Swiss government in Berne resisted these intense international pressures, principally from Britain and France, to close down LPK/KLA Homeland Fund fundraising operations.[34] It is believed the LPK leadership was told privately in Lausanne that only pro-KLA fundraising in Switzerland would be allowed and arms trading on Swiss soil was not permitted.[35] It is in any case unclear how much munitions supply actually took place in Switzerland by this stage. According to Ramush Haradinaj, Lahi Ibrahimi had been coordinating military equipment purchases in Switzerland for the KLA from 1994, including quite advanced weapons such as Heckler and Koch semi-automatic rifles and long barrelled weapons.[36] By a stroke of luck, the Macedonian Ambassador in Berne, Alajdin Demiri, was an Albanian and a former Mayor of Tetovo with some KLA links through the Mahmuti family in Tetovo to the LPK leadership, and he was able to deflect some international pressures on the LPK within Switzerland quite successfully. The Swiss defence model of a locally armed and mobilised population was an important early influence on KLA doctrinal thinking, another facet of the vital Swiss background and determinant cultural influence in creating the new Kosova insurgent army that has not been very widely understood.[37] Another background factor was the counterproductive nature of the Serbian and Interpol claims that the KLA was mainly criminal financed. Many in the Swiss governing elite considered this a slur on the Swiss federal police who had been keeping a close watch on the development of KLA fundraising and where all the evidence pointed to widespread donations from members of the the the Swiss-Albanian Diaspora engaged in normal employment.

The onset of war caused a major crisis within the Kosova Democratic League leadership, particularly for Ibrahim Rugova himself. While he stubbornly stuck to his line that the new Army did not exist as a legitimate organisation but was a diversionary creation of the Serbian secret police, events on the ground made his positions seem irrelevant, even ridiculous, to ordinary Kosovars. There were many LDK leaders with strong private disagreements with the Rugova position with its pacifist focus on diplomatic activity alone, and some such as Fehmi Agani who had had private contacts with KLA leaders for some time.[38] Others at more local level had contacts with the militia leader Tahir Zemaj who sought to create an LDK-controlled force as an alternative to what he saw as the left-wing political leadership of the KLA.[39] As recruits to the war came to congregate in Albania, the birth and slow growth of the FARK came to be a new factor on the scene. There were many questions about the character of Zemaj and his suitability for military leadership. Some details of his biography are controversial, but he served in the Yugoslav army and then for the police before leaving and becoming embroiled in allegations of drug dealing. He had been a close associate of some prominent LDK leaders in the late 1980s and early 1990s. In this period of the war, his role is inextricably mixed with the militia irregulars who continued to support Berisha and the Albanian Right against the new Tirana government established in June 1999, and who later became the core soldiers in FARK.[40] It has never really been clear who the shadowy backers of these forces really were; the most important point is that the FARK never amounted to very much militarily by comparison with the KLA, a few hundred FARK men against a KLA force that eventually grew to about 18,000 soldiers.

In the meantime, in the depths of winter increasing numbers of Yugoslav army tanks and heavy armour lumbered slowly southwards from the sprawling VJ bases in and around Nis into Kosova through the Merdare crossing. It was an army that was eventually to prove incapable of adapting to the challenges of irregular warfare, but that did not mean that it was incapable of inflicting very serious damage on the KLA. The setbacks to the KLA and the Kosova Albanian national cause in the next spring and summer would demonstrate this. Long-standing ambiguities about the nature of the KLA and how it could operate as a modern insurgency, which could be contained while it was a small and struggling force, could not be hidden once it had the capacity to take and secure ground and so face the dilemmas of all infantry forces in both ancient and modern warfare.

6

A LIBERATED DRENICA AND MILOSEVIC'S FIRST OFFENSIVE

What is basic guerilla strategy? Guerilla strategy must be based primarily on alertness, mobility, and attack. It must be adjusted to the enemy situation, the terrain, the existing lines of communication, the relative strengths, the weather, and the situation of the people.

In guerilla warfare, select the tactic of seeming to come from the east and attacking from the west; avoid the solid target, attack the hollow, withdraw, deliver a lightning blow...

Mao Tse-tung[1]

As the Yugoslav VJ heavy armour and infantry moved south from Nis into Kosova and prepared for what they saw as the inevitable intensi-fication of the conflict, the Kosova Liberation Army insurgents as well as the VJ were faced with a number of pressing practical problems. It is unclear whether anything like the massacre of the Jashari family had been anticipated by the KLA or LPK leadership, but it is most unlikely. It was also a surprise to the better informed parts of the Belgrade dip-lomatic community who knew that the family had been 'under siege' for some time but did not anticipate the bloody outcome.[2] The VJ had the advantage of knowing that a violent outcome to the Prekaz siege was virtually inevitable but did not anticipate the political conse-quences correctly. When it did take place it was accompanied by an

119

outburst of anger and nationalist feeling among the entire Kosova Albanian majority community. A mass demonstration of students organised by the political parties in Prishtina on 7 March turned into an enormous march of over 100,000 people that filled all the central area streets. If the LPK had determined to try to overthrow Serbian rule by mass action, this vast and angry demonstration was arguably a missed opportunity as the limited Serbian forces then deployed in Prishtina would have been incapable of defending the VJ and police command and control buildings in the centre of the city, but there was no functional insurgent political leadership in Prishtina with such a perspective for mass action. Once again the absence of practical explosive munitions capacity was a telling factor, as it would have been necessary to blast their way into the VJ command buildings.

The clear spontaneous direction and slogans carried on the march were calling for international intervention, with many placards calling for it in English, and in a certain sense this was a continuation of the traditional Rugova-ist LDK ethos of seeking a rescue of Kosova from Serbia through international action. It was after all a Prishtina demonstration, in the most conformist and docile city that Titoist Kosova had created. In the background was the conscious decision of the political leadership to prioritise creating a rural-based army and avoid the risks of an urban insurrection, particularly in Prishtina. Some of the key members of the LPK leadership in Switzerland had not set foot in Prishtina for fifteen years and had no detailed knowledge of the exact state of feeling on the ground, particularly the angry radicalisation of the young. Even those most in contact with Kosova life like Hashim Thaci could only make brief visits, once they had left for exile. These visits were to safe houses in Drenica and occasionally Prishtina and there was little information reaching Veliu and his comrades from elsewhere in Kosova. It is arguable that this was a poor decision by the LPK on the insurrection issue, as the Jashari massacre had electrified and angered Albanian Kosova and the Serbs were on the back foot with only limited forces actually in Prishtina. It is doubtful if they would have been capable of holding the central command buildings for more than a day or two against a determined assault by trained units. A substantial part of the VJ's electronic and radio communications could have quickly been destroyed.

Underlying the problems surrounding this decision is the wider issue of the intellectual makeup and ideological formation of the 'new generation' of younger leaders as against those of the older men of Rugo-va's Kosova Democratic League. In one sense, in espousing the Enverist revolutionary tradition the young were espousing what most after 1989 in Europe would have regarded as backward and obsolete ideas. Yet it was through working out their own intellectual development in the Enverist framework that they were able to make progress with the national question, and face key issues, such as the issue of a Kosova army, that others managed to avoid. There is always a subterranean tension between new and old in Kosova. This became augmented by determination drawn from loss of comrades in the struggle in cruel and often violent deaths and hatred of the Serbs and their government. This is sometimes stereotyped in abstract terms by the 'eternal hatreds' school of Balkan historical interpretation, but in actual fact, for young men and women of Thaci's generation, it was local and specific.

As a boy and young man Thaci had been educated in an Albanian-majority culture hegemonic system; by the time he was 21, it had been destroyed by Milosevic. The rescue of a denied legitimate identity is a recurrent theme in modern Kosova Albanian history, and understand-ably so for Thaci and Haradinaj and those like them in their genera-tion in the LPK and KLA leadership. Yet within this identity there was a dualism, between the set and almost timeless world of the poverty-stricken Kosova village, heavily patriarchal and with the severe rules of the Kanun very much in use, and the imperative for modernity, in terms of Thaci's life developed through his higher education in perhaps the most opulent and seductive city in modern western Europe, Zurich. Yet Zurich has its own dualisms, between Swiss exceptionalism and neutrality and the vitality of its great universities and their interna-tional and globalised intellectual life.

Elsewhere the people were innovative and moving to make up for the deficiencies of the political leadership. In the villages near Prekaz, the inhabitants began to dig trenches and make local defensive fortifica-tions after the Serbian heavy armour withdrew. This was a rank and file reaction to the crisis and one based on the instinct for the 'weight of numbers' factor in modern warfare, where as in the Korean war, tens of thousands digging trenches can slow and disrupt an advancing mech-anised force. At this stage the size of the KLA was only about 500–600 organised fighters who were soon surrounded not by the Yugoslav army but by hundreds of willing new recruits. The KLA had no weap-ons to give them, and in many places no administrative framework for training and orientation into which they could be fitted. At the same time Serbian forces were built up quickly, with what was described in the official Yugoslav press as a massive build-up in and around Gjakova. This appears to be have been based on the incorrect intelligence assessment in Belgrade that the insurgency originated in and was controlled from Albania. Milosevic does not appear to have had much intelligence capacity in Switzerland at this time. The Kosova border was most vulnerable over the hills between Bajram Curri in Tropoja in northern Albania and the cities of Gjakova and Peje. In the Serbian villages there had been a major arms build-up for many years, and all citizens of Serbian background could hold weapons legally.[3] These were being augmented from official VJ munitions stores. The Serbs also appear to have thought that the KLA at this stage of the war was much larger than it really was. A March 1998 document produced by the VJ General Pavkovic to brief the 3rd Army command speaks of a

terrorist organisation of 3500 to 4000 men armed and trained for armed raids and guerilla operations ... the basic aim of Siptar terrorists in this phase is to take control of extensive territory in Kosovo and Metohija, and to create a Liberation Army, which for the international community would represent a legitimate popular army, not a terrorist organisation ... by their manner of operation and application of intelligence and security, engineering and logistics support measures, the terrorist forces are increasingly taking on the attributes of a military organisation and are setting up units from platoon to company size ... The terrorist organisation's members morale and resolve for armed resistance has lately been on the rise, due to the inefficiency of the MUP and its poorly executed operations aimed at destroying terrorist nuclei.[4]

The VJ commanders were now taking over *de facto* control of operations from the police. This was understandable at the time but in a wider context it illustrated the divided and unsatisfactory nature of the Belgrade command structure. In practice it would not be long before the VJ was seen as incapable of solving the security problem, and the 'police' in the form of the anti-terrorist units would be back at the centre of events.

In the meantime, the VJ heavy armour moved to secure the villages on the Albanian border above Gjakova, Junik and Decani, Morina, Molliq, Nivikaz, Batusche and Koshare. These occupied the high uplands and traditional mule track trade routes dating back to medieval and ancient times on the border with Tropoja district in Albania.[5] The priority the VJ gave to these little isolated places illustrates the fear of the contagion of political chaos from Albania into Kosova, and the firm dogmatically held view that the aim of the KLA was to create a 'Greater Albania' rather than simply liberate Kosova.[6] Junik had been a particular target of Serbian opprobrium throughout the twentieth century. It was a centre of the *kacak* movement in the 1920s and of Balli Kombetar during and after the Second World War. As early as 1992 Junik had been recommended for 'military action' by the warlord Arkan in his publications in Belgrade.[7] On this issue the VJ was a victim of its own propaganda, and it led to a shift in the centre of gravity of the conflict towards the border that in retrospect the VJ would have been wise to avoid. Settlements such as Junik paid a heavy price for the VJ presence but in a wider strategic sense the focus helped the KLA as the fighting destroyed any vestige of remaining 'normal' society on the western border and encouraged local people to join the KLA. It allowed time for Drenica to rebuild confidence and try to integrate new recruits into the KLA in the aftermath of the Prekaz massacre, and for the KLA to recruit and train elsewhere in central and eastern Kosova districts with little or no military attention from the VJ. In reality in Tirana the preparations for war being made by the government were entirely defensive, with Defence Minister Sabet Brokaj announcing plans on 9 March for the establishment of reception centres for refugees. The Tirana OSCE director Daan Everts toured the border the following week and appealed for calm and for both sides to avoid provocations.[8]

Elsewhere in Kosova the army moved to secure the major strategic north-south roads, and the KLA countered by trying to disrupt it. The only modern hotel in central Gjakova was taken over as a barracks for VJ army officers, *de facto* martial law was established and roadblocks were set up to check every vehicle entering or leaving the town. It is probable that the emphasis on border security had been decided in early February when the Yugoslav Chief of Staff Momcilo Perisic had visited units of the Prishtina Corps of the Third army in Kosova, and had gone to Gjakova as well as Urosevac (Ferizaj) and Mitrovica. At this time many people in central and eastern Kosova may never have heard of a tiny border village near Decani called Koshare, but it was to become the scene of the longest and most important military confrontation of the entire ground war. Koshare was chosen by the KLA as the valley to establish a corridor to move arms from Albania to Kosova, and in the spring of 1999 it was where the KLA massed as a force under the direction of NATO country military advisers to take a full part in the last stage of the ground war.[9]

In many ways the last weeks of February and early March 1998 laid down the nature of the ground war in a way that would not materially change very much until the start of the NATO bombing campaign the following spring. Belgrade had to try to restore control over large internal areas of Kosova that had been lost in previous years.[10] The statement of the KLA issued on 3 April encapsulates their view, with a call for 'multiple vengeance' for the Jashari massacre and other similar recent events.[11] The Milosevic authorities claimed that the troops build-up was only part of the normal increase in force levels in Kosova for the spring training programmes, but it was clear this was not the case. As well as the VJ activity, large-scale police manoeuvres were taking place, particularly around Peje. Some army commanders including General Perisic did not share Milosevic's enthusiasm for a new conflict. At a news conference in Nis, Perisic's underling General Samardzic had already said in early January 1998 that the army 'would not meddle in the resolution of political questions in any part of Yugoslavia, including Kosovo'. In practice, the likely deficiencies in the army would cause Milosevic to rely more and more heavily on the police.[12]

On 12 March a small group of young men assembled in Switzerland, said goodbye to the parts of their families resident in the Swiss and Austrian Diaspora and set off for Tirana on the Swissair flight. They were Hashim Thaci, Agim Bajrami, Shukri Buja, Fatmir Limaj and Ismet Jashari, who were to become the nucleus of the KLA General Staff in Kosova.[13] They were moving to Kosova to open up the war on all possible fronts as part of a long discussed political and military strategy but also on an immediate mission of personal revenge for the Jashari massacre. The intellectual and ideological worlds of the austere Marxist debates within LPRK/LPK and the medieval dictates of the Kanun of Lek Dukagjini converged in their minds. The 'old commander' was gone and the young men suddenly had heavy responsibilities thrust upon them, even if in some cases they had been preparing themselves for this war to the death for many years. Adem Jashari had been particularly close to Hashim Thaci and had identified his leadership potential at a young age, they had carried weapons together in various early KLA military activities. They moved the next day up to Tropoja in north-east Albania and crossed through the forests into Kosovo carrying bags full of ammunition. Intermittent, sporadic fighting was going on all over Drenica and they made their way over there the following day.

As in a mass strike against a government, spreading the area of struggle in a guerrilla war is always the key to success.[14] The first priority for the KLA would be to establish itself all over Kosova and to spread the conflict out of Drenica and hopefully out of Serbian capacity to control it. It is clear that the Swiss-based LPK Exterior had taken a decision to set up a fairly formal army structure, and those favouring this course had won the argument against those who favoured trying to foment an immediate popular uprising. This decision was kept top secret at the time, to avoid the sense in the rank and file that there might be splits in the leadership. It is arguable how far this change of perspective was shared by all involved, or even known by rank and file KLA soldiers. The senior commander Luan Haxhiu, who was one of the first KLA figures to meet the US Balkan envoy Richard Holbrooke in February, was calling for a 'a march on Prishtina' as late in the summer as 22 July 1998, although in the same interview he admitted that the Rahavec defeat had brought a change in tactics.[15]

About a week later the new leadership group, augmented by some emerging local leaders, met at Tica village and began to plan the new internal Kosova organisation of the KLA. Shukri Buja was allocated the Lipjan and Shtime municipalities, Agim Bajrami moved to Kacanik and Fatmir Limaj to Maleshevo. Ismet Jashari (Commander Kumanovo) was allocated Suva Reka. Imri Llazi began to form a KLA unit in Ferizaj (Urosevac) municipality. Some of these units became functional much more quickly than others, and their capacity was affected by the tough terrain in many places, residual Serbian security activity and weapons and ammunition shortages. Skukri Buja was put in charge of organising weapons supply from Albania to Kosova to the Kacanik, Lipjan, Ferizaj and Shtimle municipalities.[16] At the same time very small groups of fighters began to appear in other places, as the LKCK and other very small groups began to militarise their membership. The nascent army had its continuing strong presence in the Llap region north of Vushtrri in the north-east.[17] The Western media, which were beginning to move in significantly on the Kosova story, knew little or nothing of these developments and in the aftermath of the war media figures have commented on how suspicious of them many KLA soldiers were and how little those soldiers understood how a sensible approach to the media might help them.[18]

From the point of view of Serbian intellectuals of a nationalist bent, a final and decisive struggle was approaching in what they saw as a long campaign that had been carried on throughout the 1990s against their state. A typical analyst wrote:

Kosovo and Metohija are a manipulative element in the policy of the only surviving superpower. Its strategic value in relation to this region of Serbia was announced as early as 1991 by the then secretary of state for foreign affairs, James Baker, who said that Serbia should be 'reduced to the size it used to have before the Kumanovo Treaty'. In regard to the role played by the international community concerning the question of Kosovo and Metohija we need to disperse all our doubts and become aware of the dangers awaiting us. Our efforts should be aimed at formulating a consistently Serbian—that is Yugoslav—policy, and finally stop being the losers in a game which has been imposed on us.[19]

The relationship between the scattered and novice fighters on the ground in KLA uniforms in the Dukagjini forests and these geopolitics was as yet totally unclear in Belgrade, except that Milosevic and his ministers and army chiefs saw that under Sali Berisha, Albania had cultivated over-close relationships with the United States and NATO. It seemed inconceivable to Milosevic that the US or NATO would collaborate with a Marxist-led insurgent force in Kosova, and their collaboration with Berisha's Albania was in ruins after the 1997 uprising. Berisha's government had collapsed and more socialist circles in Serbia were aware of the very different ideology of the new government in Tirana under Fatos Nano. Most American military and civilians had been evacuated in the chaos of the early spring and summer and it seemed to some in Belgrade that a new beginning with Tirana might be possible and the Kosova insurgency might be controlled from within Albania. Greece was a key factor in the uprising and the dominant background political factor in the new Tirana government. It was not long before Milosevic made a visit to Athens to stay in the villa at nearby Vouliagmeni owned by his son to meet sympathetic political and business leaders, particularly from the Cretan New Democracy orbit around Prime Minister Constantine Mitsotakis and his daughter Dora Bakoyannis.[20] The traditional Greek New Democracy position had been to oppose all international intervention in the Balkans and Milosevic wanted this to continue during the looming Kosova conflict as during the Bosnian war. In less coded terms this meant the United States and NATO should not involve themselves in the problems of the Balkans, which in turn reflected an Athens viewpoint based on the desire for continued Serbian hegemony in the central Balkan region.[21]

In the Belgrade elite view this was once again the case of an Albanian-inspired insurgency against the border with Kosova that must be quickly faced and defeated. It is unclear how much of this viewpoint was really understood in the European Union and the capitals of Europe, where the whole problem of Kosova was seen almost entirely in terms of ethnic relationships rather than national self-determination of the kind sanctioned by the Helsinki Final Act. Rugova's political ineptitude allowed these illusions to continue much longer than was necessary, with his proclivity to speak of the national question in terms of ethnic relations within Yugoslavia, however much this was tempered with calls for formal independence. In the United States a much clearer understanding of the developing war was present. Three KLA soldiers had spoken at a packed meeting in Brooklyn to a Diaspora audience in February. The International Crisis Group research organisation with its close US links published a report on 20 March, *Kosovo Spring*, detailing the rapidly growing support for the KLA in the US and the close links pro-KLA organisations were forming with other anti-Serb Balkan nationalities, particularly Bosnians.[22] The huge all-party rally that had been held in Tirana in support of Kosova freedom had also been widely reported in the US media, but completely neglected by the BBC and most European newspaper media.[23]

Milosevic seems also to have been ill-informed about the details of many of these developments. The VJ suffered a setback on 22 March when the KLA ambushed a military column at Smolica, near Ponishovac. The MUP assault on the Haradinaj family house near Gllogjan had been repulsed on 24 March and another Prekaz-type liquidation of a leading Albanian family had been avoided. In the Diaspora Serbian intelligence in the USA was much weaker than in earlier days. There was no Serbian diplomatic presence in Tirana. In the past, as far as Albanian opponents of Yugoslavia were concerned the Serbs had used the Royalist networks supporting King Leka as a front for UDBA activity, with some success over the years. Published documents indicate that many Royalist émigrés were prepared to work with the Belgrade regime in the hope of overthrowing the Communist government in Tirana and seeing the return of the Zogist monarchy there.[24] It was much more difficult for the Serbs to have good information on the post-1990 modern Diaspora activity in the USA, with its greater numbers and constant augmentation by new immigrants from Kosova and the Albanian world in general.

The problems of intelligence were mirrored by the wider issue of whether, on the evidence of the first weeks of the war, the VJ was actually capable of transforming itself into a modern and functional armed force. The scorched earth pattern of random shelling and village destruction that was being followed by the VJ suggested it would not be. This question was also relevant for the police. The MUP operation against Gllogjan and the prominent Haradinaj family had been botched. Abroad, the perception was different. Foreign commentators on the Kosova crisis often failed to notice that it was only as recently as 1996 that the old Milicija with its roots in the militia of early Communist days had been transformed into the Policija, a supposedly modern police force. As events showed during the crisis, it had actually changed very little in content, whatever changes there may have been in uniforms and vehicles. The army was faced with the same opportunity for transformation, when the old JNA became the VJ, and it also failed the test. In the earlier days of the Milosevic regime the army was meant to be used for the strategic defence of Yugoslavia's borders and not for internal security issues connected with ethnic relations. This was the inherited Yugoslav tradition.

Although Milosevic had no scruples against using the VJ for whatever purposes he required, this was not the view of many army commanders where the Yugoslav mindset and a notion of internal military legality were at least sometimes present in their minds: the internal security of the government itself in their opinion should be a police matter. It was clear in Belgrade by the end of 1997 that this distinction would not be supportable for very long in the event of the Kosova crisis developing into an open war spread all over the territory. By March 1998 the concept was irrelevant. It nevertheless led to much local demoralisation and confusion and, most important for the KLA, constant leakage of weapons and ammunition through cash sale by deserting or disillusioned soldiers to Kosovar Albanians.[25] The recurrent financial crises of the Milosevic regime also meant that the soldiers and policemen were paid irregularly and often very late. Albanian money prised open many barracks arms store doors in these circumstances.

The first definite outcome of the KLA organisational impetus provided by the arrival of Hashim Thaci and his comrades on the scene was the extension of violence to areas of Kosova that had hitherto been peaceful. This was achieved surprisingly quickly and efficiently and is one of the sources of Thaci's high post-war reputation and subsequent political career. A large police station in the Vranjevac suburb of Prishtina was attacked and the building substantially damaged by a bomb on 13 April. Attacks on numerous police posts followed, all over Kosova. As a result widespread harassment of Albanians by the secret police followed. In a tit for tat situation, ethnic Serbs were forced out of their homes in most towns in western Kosova.[26] Activity on the border also intensified, with the interception of an arms convoy of several horses and a mule train carrying weapons and ammunition from Tropoja in Albania into Kosova. This was part of what was soon seen by observers of the war as a major turn in VJ and police attention towards the Decani region and away from Drenica. Already, within weeks of the outbreak of serious combat, the centre of gravity of the conflict had moved towards the Albanian border. The VJ commanders had prioritised the security of four main roads from Prishtina to the border with Albania, and it was already clear that, in the words of one officer, there was a 'sieve-like quality' to the landscape and the Albanian fighters would be able to slip through gaps in their security walls.[27] The tough VJ 63rd Parachute regiment soldiers who had been brought in from Vranje to reinforce the 3rd Army soldiers from Nis were simply not numerous enough, given the nature of the Kosova terrain, to make much difference to the basic situation. The VJ commanders in this early stage of the conflict do not seem to have clearly thought through the problem of how to apply their superior numbers and material assets against the KLA in a focused way. Milosevic was clearly well informed about these military weaknesses and in the week leading up to 23 April began a major reinforcement of the VJ with Ministry of the Interior (MUP) troops. The ease with which the KLA was able to cross the border was to become a thorn in the side of the Yugoslavs.

At the same time, the KLA was being enlarged by new arrivals, mostly from abroad. The work of Ali Ahmeti and his logistics and recruitment team based in Durres in Albania was beginning to bear fruit. A deal was secretly negotiated with the Tirana government to allow KLA training at a small number of Albanian army facilities, like the obscure little camp at Mulleti, near Petrela castle. The Drin Gorge ferry was the most popular way for these soldiers to reach Kosova, via Fierza in Tropoja. About 200 KLA fighters attempted to cross the border on 22 April near Gjakova and although about sixteen were killed in a firefight, most of them made it into Kosova and Junik village. Ahmeti also moved key aides into Kukes in northeast Albania, and in close collaboration with regional Albanian army commander General Kudusi Lama effectively took control of this remote mountain town near the big hydroelectric dams.[28] An open air small arms market quickly developed where recruits could buy a weapon before trying to enter Kosova.[29] This was also the case in Bajram Curri, to the south, but here anarchy prevailed and there was little or no Albanian army presence to try to stabilise the situation. As a result the local state authority (such as it was) collapsed and anarchy prevailed as in a Wild West town in the USA in the nineteenth century. It was generally believed in this week that about 1,000 potential KLA fighters were waiting to cross the border from Tropoja at this point.[30]

In these early crossing marches, the KLA suffered unnecessary casualties due to inexperience; by walking up main tracks usable by VJ vehicles, fighters often walked straight into ambushes, with deadly results. The thick dwarf oak and thorn scrub on either side of the tracks appeared to provide good cover but in these early days the Serbs still had some intelligence from Albania and were able to intercept groups on the march. These operations were much more successful than the VJ use of artillery which was loosely positioned and used to fire fairly indiscriminately against border areas. Truck mounted guns were also used to shell and burn out villages but had little effect on the people as they had already left to hide in the forests. Armed citizen militias were beginning to appear in Albanian villages in Dukagjini in response. In most cases these initiatives had no connection with the new KLA General Staff. Serbian villages were already mobilised and were well armed and able to defend themselves against attack.[31] Long distance gun battles soon began between villages across the ethnic divide and the whole process illustrates the well-known dictum of military historians that Balkan wars usually start over possession of towns or frontiers but soon become wars between rural communities. The lack of enough KLA uniforms for potential recruits would turn out to be a significant media gain for the Albanians, as it appeared to outside observers that it was primarily an informal village defence force, far from the narcoterrorist/Islamic stereotypes the Serbs were promoting in the international radio and TV networks.

In Belgrade, General Nebosja Dimitrejevic gave a briefing in which he claimed the KLA had a training camp in the north-eastern Albanian district of Tropoja with as many as 2,500 men waiting to enter Kosova. Although this figure seems (and was) very exaggerated, it indicated a panic response to the crisis and was a sign that the Serbs did not appear to have realised how effectively the Albanian Diaspora could begin to affect events and mobilise new fighters to take part in the developing conflict. In a burst of self-confidence, the KLA issued a nine-point statement to the media via LPK Exterior in Switzerland and the *Bujku* newspaper in Prishtina, saying that 'the nation was in a state of war and the KLA was fighting to liberate and unify the nation's occupied territories.'[32] These weeks were perhaps, from the point of view of the KLA leadership, the blessed verdant spring of the war. The VJ was reeling under unprecedented local insurgent pressure in previously quiet areas of Kosova and quite large numbers of fighters were able to enter the fray from Albania. When they came into action, they soon found they were able to move almost at will over the whole territory at night, when the VJ and MUP stayed holed up in their barracks.

In Belgrade, Milosevic's response to these setbacks was very simple. He moved towards local terror against the majority population, with four units of the feared JSO special anti-terrorist units being deployed in Kosova, under central coordination from the Peje (Pec) military barracks.[33] In an equally predictable reaction, refugee movements mainly from the more isolated Albanian villages began on an appreciable scale, with over 5,000 people arriving in Montenegro alone by the third week of the month. Inhabitants knew the KLA could not defend them from this Belgrade terror in any effective way. Those with intelligent and well informed village leaders knew exactly what was coming and were not going to wait around to experience it. In line with time honoured Balkan traditions, the men would go to the hills to fight and families had to be moved to safety elsewhere. Villages with soldiers in KLA units began to move their women and children in any possible direction out of Kosova. The isolation of a village was no protection. The JSO, unlike the army and mainstream MUP, had top quality modern 4x4 SUV vehicles and could reach almost any rural location and kill the citizens on an industrial scale in a short period of time. It was not long before they were in action, as Milosevic sought to prevent the ultimate Serbian nightmare of a collapse of security on a major border crossing with Albania. At local level, the war for Koshare had begun.

A savage local encounter also developed in and around the little settlement of Ponoshec (Ponosevac) on the edge of the hills near the Quaf e Morines pass linking Gjakova in Kosova with the minor road down to Bajram Curri in Albania. This was becoming an important KLA transit route. The Ponoshec inhabitants were driven out and their houses raked with gunfire and then burnt down. Girls as young as ten were raped systematically in front of their families. In an equally ominous development, the VJ began to lay anti-personnel mines along tracks that crossed the border, which soon began to take their toll on local people, farm livestock and KLA soldiers. In a society where the entire domestic economy depended on family owned animals, and the death of the family cow could be a major financial disaster, it seemed total war in Balkan terms was beckoning. Louis MacNeice wrote of the Spanish Civil War that 'death stalked the olive groves picking his men, his leaden finger beckoned, again and again'. In Kosova he stalked the hill tracks above little wooden cowsheds and the outhouses hung with sheepskins. The emptying of Kosova had begun, an agonising and protracted process that did not end until the June the following year. For those who had been involved in or followed the Bosnian war, it was all drearily familiar.[34]

The area of most focus was almost inevitably around Decani and Junik. The pretty little town of Upper Junik with its Ottoman grey stone *kulla* tower houses held the key to the Koshare arms transfer corridor above it. Junik had been a stronghold of Albanian rebellion and nationalism in all periods and also a key transit point en route over the hills to Albania. Thousands of people from outlying villages had crowded into Junik and they were soon being shelled from truck mounted artillery on the Peje-Decani road. Many houses were set on fire and the whole area was swathed in dense black smoke while the dead and wounded casualties lay unattended in the streets. The Decani military base fifteen miles north was still safe for the VJ and patrols in armoured cars ventured out along the Peje-Decani main road into the largely deserted countryside, machine-gunning livestock and burning down barns and hayricks. The scorched earth policy for Kosova had begun. These heavy handed terror tactics did however indicate a kind of success for the KLA as they indicated the fear of loss of control from Belgrade and the breakdown of 'normal' (in Milosevic-regime terms) police methods of security. Police had withdrawn from local police posts over a wide area of central Kosova. Yet the Serbian cause was not lost. The KLA had tried to fight from formal positions to defend Junik, and this had been a total failure. It was to be a paradigm for the much more important loss of Rahavec on 19 July later in the war, which was to be a turning point and open the way for the VJ 'Summer Offensive'.

As May wore on, more and more VJ assets were gradually moved into Kosova. They were met with serious resistance which they do not seem to have expected. The KLA commander Fatmir Limaj made his military name on 9 May in a successful attack on a Serb armoured convoy along the Peje-Prishtina road, blowing up a Pinzgauer vehicle with spectacular results. The political leadership of the KLA had to determine what a clear response should be. Hashim Thaci left Kosova on the last day of April and went to Albania until the middle of May, spending a good deal of time with Ali Ahmeti and Xhavit Haliti on organisational and recruitment issues. He returned on 15 May for a few days of meetings in Kosova and then was away for another month, until 20 June. He again left after a few days and spent all of July in foreign countries, particularly in Vienna, Zurich, Germany and, for the first time, London.[35] Already, at such an early stage of the war, Thaci's role was becoming largely diplomatic and later on, in the winter of 1998–99, more and more of his time was spent outside Kosova. This was to have serious long-term implications for Kosova politics after 1999, but at the time his life was dominated by the random, improvised nature of the conflict and its arbitrary demands. While he was out of Kosova, a joint meeting was held on 11 May at which after some negotiations, the LKCK leadership signed an agreement with the KLA General Staff whereby the military capacity of the LKCK would be merged with the KLA under a single command, but the LKCK would continue to preserve its separate political identity. It was also decided to set up a joint organisation for the political and propaganda war, but few practical consequences came from this decision.[36]

On 26 May, eleven MUP coaches, thirty heavy trucks and other JSO special forces vehicles were moving from Prishtina barracks to Peje, an increasingly regular occurrence as the violence spread over a wider and wider area from its epicentre near Junik and Decani. It is a moot point what would have happened to the KLA if this scale of force build-up had happened three months earlier. Ramush Haradinaj has expressed the view that the Serbs underestimated the KLA in the narrow military sense at this stage, and the evidence is on his side.[37] Milosevic appears to have felt for a time that the majority loyalty of the Kosova villagers to Rugova and the Democratic League would isolate the militants and allow the 'anti-terrorist' operation to succeed.[38] Available VJ airpower, particularly helicopters, was not being used much; a sign of complacency. The political atmosphere in Belgrade was aiding those who sought a rapid military solution, with Milosevic moving towards alliances with the most radical and nationalist forces on the political scene. The security command structure was confused between the different departments and agencies. Milosevic's response was to try to unify the government behind him as a prelude to dealing with the security weaknesses the advances of the KLA in the spring had demonstrated. On 24 March a coalition government had been formed to run the war between Milosevic's Socialist Party of Serbia (SPS) and Vojislav Sesejl's ultra-nationalist Radical Party (SRP).[39]

In a sign of the changing atmosphere in the Diaspora, 70,000 Albanians demonstrated in Bonn while the Contact Group meeting on the Kosova crisis was held there. The Albanian Diaspora in Germany was the main stronghold of monolithic LDK/Rugova adherence in Europe and it was a sign of the changing times that the rally was addressed not only by the LDK 'Prime Minister' Bujar Bukoshi but also by a relative of the Jashari family.[40] The seriousness with which the situation was seen in Washington is indicated by the reactivation of Richard Holbrooke as the US Balkan peace envoy, repeating his Bosnian role. On the other hand, as Haradinaj also points out, the Albanian war effort also had many problems. The KLA General Staff was in his view 'in crisis', with none of the new Zone Commanders represented on the KLA General Staff, and the sense of a General Staff presence in and direction from Tirana that were getting increasingly distant from the rapidly changing realities on the ground in Kosova. The senior and respected, but far from universally popular General Staff figure of Xhavit Haliti was in Tirana almost all the time and was conscious of the need to professionalise the army leadership.[41] His personality did not appeal to everyone and he had a reputation for clandestine dealing and intrigue. His defenders argued that these qualities might exist but they were vital to all he had been able to do for Kosova and his survival in the political underground for so many years.[42] He did, though, have a vital attribute, in local Albanian operational terms, of a good relationship with the Durres KLA logistics chief Ali Ahmeti with whom he had worked since both were members of Ahmet Haxhiu's Llap based group of LPRK revolutionaries in the 1980s. Then Ahmeti was only a teenager, and Haliti a veteran and highly ideological Enverist-Marxist and former political prisoner from Peje.[43] There was a paternal element in their relationship of a very Albanian type.

Their importance, and that of the Albanian operation generally, are linked to the fact that significant numbers of ex-Yugoslav army soldiers were beginning to appear in Durres and Tirana as potential recruits who had, in theory at least, valuable military skills. But dealing with these people was not to be easy or straightforward. Some might be (and indeed were) UDBA spies and deviationists with Belgrade links, others might have command aspirations based on old JNA rank rather than relevant current military utility. They were not instinctively likely to acknowledge the authority of the General Army Council, Thaci as Political Spokesman, or new field commanders such as Haradinaj and Mustafa (Commander Remi) who were having considerable success in their localities and had become very important regional leaders. Some of them still envisaged the war ending in a popular armed uprising where traditional military authority structures would have little importance.[44]

International dimensions to the war as April 1998 wore on were also not encouraging for the Albanians. On 29 April the political directors of the Contact Group met again in Rome but played down the Kosova violence, and at the same time NATO sources said there was 'little appetite' for intervention. The Contact Group foreign ministers meeting also produced proposals for deployment against 'spillover' of the conflict into Albania and Macedonia that offered no encouragement to the Kosova Albanians, with the suggestion that NATO might guard the Albanian border, something that would have been a blessing for Milosevic had it ever been practically possible.[45] The NATO plan would have done nothing at all to protect Albanian civilians who were already subjected to occasional VJ shelling from Kosova in border regions. The Contact Group split along deeply predictable lines with Britain and Germany backing the tough US stance but Russia, France and Italy opposing it.

In Kosova these deliberations were closely followed by the Albanians who concluded that in the absence of international intervention and with a certainty of intensification of the war, a move into the woods for the summer was the best option. More and more villages emptied and tent and plastic sheet settlements began to develop all over central and southern Kosova, resembling a vast scale reproduction of the British Greenham Common Peace camp of the 1980s. Young men left for Albania to train for the KLA while families retreated to the wooded fastnesses of the hills. The VJ saw the empty villages as easy risk-free targets and systematically laid them waste, poisoning the wells with dead animals and levelling farm buildings.

Serb shelling was particularly severe around Klina, north of the main Prishtina-Peje road, and hundreds of families left there en masse to try to find safety in the woods. A new pattern of the war was developing, with neither side in control of large areas but the Serbs controlling the perimeters of the contested areas through their heavy armour. The elite groups of JSO special forces went into inhabited villages to 'clean up' after shelling but could not stay there to hold them. Ibrahim Rugova was left with less and less credibility as a national leader after agreeing to attend talks with Milosevic in Geneva. The weight of numbers on the Albanian side was beginning to tell, with hundreds of men starting to dig trenches to stop the Serbs controlling the Prishtina-Peje road.

Peje itself entered the war for the first time on 29 May with fighting spreading from the villages of Zajm, Dollova and Grabanica on the border of the Klina-Peje local government *opstina* demarcation boundary. Dollova had to all intents and purposes been destroyed and was a smoking ruin with no inhabitants. Peje itself was shelled on its northern outskirts where KLA fighters were beginning to establish a presence on the road leading up from Peje to the border with Montenegro. This was another critical strategic objective for both sides. While the exact political stance of the Montenegrins was as yet unclear, with elections due there on 31 May, the exceptionally wild and remote terrain near Kosova was potentially a valuable respite base and source of resupply for the KLA. Peje itself was coming under considerable pressure in these weeks from other directions, as food began to run short as a result of the VJ blockade, and the local hospital that was taking casualties from the fighting in the villages was put under full Serbian military/police control. Refugee flows were also starting away from Peje, mostly moving directly into Albania around Bajram Curri. Human rights officials claimed there were now between 15,000 and 20,000 refugees from Kosova in Albania.[46] The government in Tirana had sensibly decided to try to relocate them away from this anarchic and dangerous town and in collaboration with UNHCR began to construct large tented camps at nearby Kukes. Serbian villages in central and southern Kosova were becoming increasingly isolated by these processes. A village like Gorazdovac south of Peje became an improvised little fortress with access roads blocked by piles of burnt out cars. Although most inhabitants remained, heavily armed and well dug in, some nearby majority Albanian areas were under KLA pressure and it was not long before some Serbian refugee movements began northwards towards Serbia itself.

Another developing focus of the war was through the southward spread of fighting in Drenica, which led to more and more villages around Malisheva and Rahavec coming under KLA control. While Decan and Junik remained under intense pressure from Yugoslav air attack, heavy VJ forces moved into the Malisheva area and began shelling Drenoc, Grabancia, Kepuze and other nearby settlements. Around Klina, in the first signs of specific 'Operation Horseshoe' tactics, villagers were not allowed to return to their ruined villages after shelling had ceased but were told to leave and go to Albania. The process of ethnic cleansing at a formal level was well under way by early June and accelerated throughout the month, although it had been taking place *de facto* since March. In Peje the feared JSO paramilitary anti-terrorist units commanded by Frenki Simatovic had appeared on the scene. In Tirana Foreign Minister Pascal Milo spoke of an openly 'genocidal policy' from Belgrade, and under pressure of events the LDK leadership broke off the talks that were supposed to be held under international supervision on 4 June.

The international community was forced to begin to rewrite decisions that had only been taken a month earlier under the pressure of events, particularly in the light of the threat to fragile Albanian governmental and social stability caused by the increasing refugee flows. Intelligence officials with genuine insurgency experience could easily see that the KLA had broken through the informal but widely accepted criteria for early success of an insurgent movement and formed a secure platform for long-term activity. In Northern Ireland British officials used to define this as the active support of five to ten per cent of the population and the passive support of at least twenty-five per cent. By early June the KLA had the strong support of the vast majority of Kosovar Albanians under thirty-five and some support in all age groups. The LDK leadership cabal around Rugova and his Italian- and Vatican-influenced advisers had less and less contact with most Kosovars. On 5 June a Rugova aide, Fehmi Agani, stated that the Serbian-Albanian dialogue was 'over', and the LDK delegation refused to attend the talks proposed by Milosevic in Prishtina the following day. In reality the dialogue had never started. By the second week in June the war had formed three main front lines, in Drenica at Lapusnik and Komoran along the Prishtina-Peje main road, across the triangle between the municipalities of Klina, Decani and Peje, and along almost the entire length of the Kosova-Albanian border.

All intelligence estimates made by NATO suggested that a long war was in the offing.[47] Internal intelligence reports suggested that although the Serbian police were successfully terrorising the population, poor coordination with the military meant that aircraft and helicopter backup resources were not being well used and there were insufficient troops available to crush the KLA. Some Serbian soldiers were alleged to be unwilling to engage in close infantry combat with the KLA because of their lack of knowledge of the terrain. Public pressure for action was growing on NATO and a show of force seemed to be required. A NATO Defence Ministers' meeting in Brussels in June authorised planning procedures for future air strikes and a joint NATO-Albanian air force-FYROM/Republic of Macedonia air force operation duly took place afterwards on 11 June, although to little practical effect.[48] On the ground it was clear that the next target for the VJ and MUP would be the little southern Drenica town of Malisheva. Relatively untouched so far in the conflict, it had evolved into a main KLA supply and operations centre, and seemed to be the model for the way a town in Kosova could come under KLA control. This turned out to be a dangerous illusion, but it was nevertheless a good week for the insurgents.

The KLA moved closer to the possibility of cutting the main Prishtina-Prizren road after blowing up a Serbian hotel in nearby Suva Reka, with positions as little as half a mile away from the road. Yet these advances that would have been hard to imagine only two months ago for most Albanians were to lead to overconfidence and a rapid reversal of fortune. By the third week of June, Kosova was awash with rumours that a major KLA assault on a large town was imminent. This marked a major change in tactics and strategy, away from the classic and hitherto successful rural guerrilla hit and run campaign. Whether by design or, more probably accident, the KLA had fallen into the trap set for them by the VJ and had been drawn onto the terrain of formal warfare. It is unclear how this decision was arrived at but a significant factor was the arrival in KLA ranks of more and more soldiers who had been in the Yugoslav army and an accompanying high degree of military conservatism and orthodox thinking. It also seemed on the KLA side the right time to strike for a main symbolic target to demonstrate to their people how Serbian control was crumbling. This was a miscalculation. After the underestimation of the political and military potential for an Albanian seizure of power in

April 1998, by the early summer there was an overestimation. It was nevertheless understandable. On the ground KLA forces were steadily moving east out of central Drenica and taking and holding ground. They were moving much nearer to Prishtina and if not halted within a week or two would be on the outskirts of the city. KLA snipers had appeared in the conflict for the first time and were operating from mosque minarets and industrial building roofs in Fushe Kosova (Kosova Polje) and terrorising the numerous Serb villages to the east of Prishtina and the little town of Fushe Kosova itself. Local Serb mayors demanded protection from the centre.

In Belgrade it was clear that a major counteroffensive was needed. Ethnic cleansing of Prishtina was accelerated with the population massing by the railway station and being herded onto trains to the Kosova border with Macedonia south of Kacanik. Random shootings by JSO-controlled gangs of Serbian volunteers emptied the streets and made a journey to a local shop a risky experience. On 24 June KLA fighters attacked the Belacevac coal mine, less than ten miles from the Kosova capital, after kidnapping groups of Serb workers at a roadblock. As this was the main supplier of coal to Obiliq power station nearby, the assault threatened the Kosova power supply. Elsewhere in Kosova endless small skirmishes and random encounters between the VJ and KLA dominated the next two weeks, but even the least informed in Prishtina knew that the centre of gravity of the conflict was moving southwards and eastwards and would focus on control of the Prizren-Prishtina road. The capture of Rahavec by the KLA would open the way towards Suva Reka where there was strong support for the KLA in a traditionally radical town, and here the main east-west highway could be cut.[49] Then Prizren itself might fall to the growing numbers of fighters on Mount Pashtrik above the town on the Albanian border.

Although the KLA attack on Rahavec has been much criticised in post-war Kosova, and it appears to have taken place at least in part in the absence of a real top level decision and as a result of random choices by low level commanders in the locality, it nevertheless had strategic logic. The town of about 17,000 Albanians and 3,000 Serbs was a prosperous wine producing centre and the key to control of a large area. The entire Serbian security strategy had been based on maintaining control of the four main arterial roads in Kosova since the beginning of the war, and a major reversal in such a key strategic area bordering Albania would have been a KLA victory indeed. It could have almost doubled the area of Kosova under effective KLA control at a stroke and could next have given the Albanians control of the symbolically important town of Prizren, birthplace of the nineteenth-century Prizren League and modern Albanian nationalism. The easy advances through the Rahavec regional villages had given the KLA commanders a false sense of security, with the VJ largely absent from the field of battle.[50] As KLA soldiers assembled about three miles away from Rahavec between 10 and 13 July, their intentions were clear to the Serbs and the Nis command decreed that the town should be defended at all costs. A large force of heavily armed infantry was sent from Prishtina to the area and in the three days of heavy fighting that began on 16 July, the KLA suffered severe reverses and was forced to retreat in a rout into the countryside. The inhabitants suffered three days of local terror with many homes burnt to the ground after hand grenades had been thrown into underground wine cellars where people were hiding.

The Albanians correctly saw Malisheva as the VJ's next target and thousands of people began to flee from the town into the woods in the week starting 20 July. At last, after three months, from the point of view of Belgrade the scorched earth policy seemed to be working and the KLA was losing control of large areas that it had dominated only three weeks before. If this was to be a war of positional advantage and disadvantage, as it duly turned out to be, the KLA had a baptism of fire that week and discovered how quickly the fortunes of war could change. The war was not going to be a matter of simple Albanian territorial advance and Serbian retreat, culminating in some liberation of Prishtina like the liberation of Berlin in 1945. Kosova was actually a highly complex operating environment that demanded local military leadership with a clear final vision of victory but an almost infinite tactical flexibility in achieving it. Underlying the Rahavec disaster was a mechanical approach to the campaign and a residual element of very traditional doctrinal thinking. There was also the element of a predominantly rural KLA force of offspring of impoverished rural families who were happy to attack the privileged in the towns. However understandable from a psychological and sociological viewpoint, it was not going to be a recipe for success in Kosova.

The very successful first three months of the ground war for the KLA had obscured underlying weaknesses, and the Yugoslav forces were for the first time able to concentrate overwhelming firepower and military strength on small localities in a way that had not occurred at earlier stages in the conflict. The KLA strategy of taking and holding small towns played into Belgrade's hands in this matter. For the people, the only choice was to leave their homes and become refugees. A similar exodus to that in Maleshevo took place from Suva Reka on the main Prishtina-Prizren road, which the *Daily Telegraph* journalist Julian Strauss reported as 'largely empty with dozens of newly brought in Serb soldiers bunkered down behind sandbags.'[51] The KLA had fought strongly and had been able to knock out two Serbian tanks, but in the end had no option but to retreat to the forests.[52] 'Manpower losses were increasing and by early July were bringing a deeper involvement of the Albanian army in the conflict, although this was largely unknown to the international community. Albanian army helicopters were deployed to bring the KLA wounded for treatment in Tirana hospitals. Within the liberated area of Drenica, Albanian fighters blew up most roads leading to central Drenica; a very long overdue use of explosives on their part. The failure to use local explosives resources by the KLA will be seen, given the size of the mining and quarrying industry in Kosova and availability of trained personnel, as one of the most serious and irrational weaknesses of the early KLA campaign strategy.

The war was seen as a matter of personal revenge for aggression of the Serbs which focused KLA fighters' attentions on obtaining a high kill rate for Serbian police and soldiers. The role of sabotage to undermine the Serbian war effort by taking out vital infrastructure such as bridges, stores and petroleum installations that might not involve direct kills does not seem to have been considered by the General Staff at any stage of the war for which records are so far available.[53] In this atmosphere of individual commitment to resistance but overall serious tactical and organisational weaknesses, the KLA faced a long and difficult summer. The Serbs still securely held Mitrovica, historically the centre of all previous urban insurgency in Kosova and the key to security in the north. Observers of the war were sometimes puzzled at the importance of Vushtrri for the KLA given its relative obscurity as a place, but the reality was that it was the nearest town to Mitrovica in which the KLA could easily operate.[54] There is little or no literature extant about the KLA in Mitrovica, for the simple reason that at this stage of the war it hardly existed there, or elsewhere north of the Ibar river. It only began to grow near the town when KLA fighters from the hills west of Podujeve moved across to threaten Mitrovica and take over the Stari Trg mine complex in the late spring of 1999. Conspiracy theorists have seen this development and its accompanying certainty of mass bloodshed between the large Serbian community north of the Ibar and the Albanian majority south of it as one of the 'secret war' triggers NATO had set in the period between the winter 1998 and spring 1999 that led to the NATO intervention in Kosova in late March 1999, and the internationalisation of the war. The NATO leadership had seen the wars in northern ex-Yugoslavia as wars over the possession of valuable infrastructure, and believed the same forces were at the root of the Kosova conflict. This is an interesting speculative theory but until supporting evidence emerges it will remain no more than that. Elsewhere, the scene was set for intensification of the war in the next months while the international community dithered and remained confused in its approach to dealing with Slobodan Milosevic. A major factor was the absence of much United States intelligence presence on the ground, which led to a high NATO reliance on British and European material, which in turn involved a degree of active contact, if not collaboration with Belgrade in terms of the wider assumptions about what was happening.

7

SUMMER 1998: GOLGOTHA AVOIDED

Evil times came to the Albanians—Again

Ismet Jonuzi-Krosi[1]

We spent 62 days isolated in the forest living off dry dough, beans, water, salt and grass plants. In the forest on all sides we were surrounded by Serb army and police. They had dogs with them. Fortunately, it seemed they did not dare enter the forest because they feared the KLA, they often passed near us but we were never spotted. The first three days they were sometimes only two or three metres from us.

Hatmane Musliaj, from Shapteji, Decani[2]

The defeat of the Kosova Liberation Army at Rahavec after 19 July 1998 was not only a military landmark and a belated success for Milosevic's First Offensive but a political disaster for the Kosova Albanians in general. It ended the myth of KLA invincibility. In terms of guerrilla warfare doctrine, they had lost the vital aspect of positional advantage. At the same time intensified fighting on different parts of the Albania-Kosova border had, according to Belgrade military statements, left over 90 Albanians dead, although this is likely to be an exaggerated figure.[3] Important weapons supply channels had been closed near Loges village, although never to the extent the Serbs claimed at the time.[4] The loss of Rahavec had happened as much as a result of ran-

143

dom chance as of calculation on either side, although there is no doubt that the increasing pressure of VJ heavy armour on southern Drenica would have brought Belgrade results at some point. In reality the catalyst for the Rahavec battle was a chance event. In Rahavec, a group of KLA soldiers had left their lines south of Rahavec without permission to go visit their families in the town and had been seen by Serbian forces, which had moved to arrest them.[5] Fighting broke out in the centre of the town in a chaotic encounter with the KLA men attempting to defend their control of the police station. The resident population was immediately exposed to serious danger and so more KLA forces were sent into the town to try to protect them. This had the immediately opposite effect, of precipitating a full scale assault on Rahavec from VJ heavy armour. The KLA General Staff commanders for the area, Rexhep Selimi and Bismil Zurapi, knew nothing about what was happening and hurried there the following morning, but although fighting in and around the town continued for three days, it was too late for the KLA to recover what had been lost.[6] Fatmir Limaj was almost killed by a random shell. The KLA Political Spokesman Hashim Thaci (who also took part in the battle) later went so far as to allege that some of those involved may not even have been true KLA members and were misusing KLA uniforms.[7] Parts of Rahavec were soon left a smoking ruin and the population joined the lengthening columns of refugees trudging along the roads or riding in farm carts to seek safety over the mountains in Albania. MUP units moved in to shoot any Albanian stragglers and their livestock and poison the drinking water wells.

In the media the episode was eagerly seized on by journalists such as Tom Walker of the London *Sunday Times* who were of a pro-Serb inclination, to predict the demise of the KLA.[8] The entire sequence of events seemed to conform to the stereotype of the Albanians critics who claimed the KLA were a rabble incapable of military organisation or discipline.[9] In reality it was a serious setback but of the type that is very common in Partisan warfare. Partisan soldiers are encouraged to take individual initiatives and decision making is devolved right down the authority chain in all successful guerrilla armies. Sometimes these decisions will go wrong and produce unexpected and negative results. Given that it was a Balkan war, there was also an additional element of chance and disorganisation to factor in. At Rahavec the process of military improvisation had been taken too far by the local KLA at an unfortunate time, but it was not out of kilter with informal warfare doctrine. It nevertheless strengthened the hand of orthodox and establishment military analysts in nations like the USA and the UK which were closely watching the development of the KLA as a potential anti-Milosevic force, and some of whom advocated working with the KLA to form a more formal army.[10] In the United Kingdom the government proceeded with setting up the planning framework for the top secret 'Operation Horn'; an undercover assistance and military advice operation for the KLA.[11] The British saw themselves as having a unique understanding and expertise in guerrilla and counterinsurgency warfare. The British forces were almost the only NATO army in the twentieth century to have successfully resisted and overcome guerrilla opponents, in Malaya, Kenya and Cyprus.[12] There was also private concern in London that the Americans were being seduced by KLA propaganda to see the war as an anti-colonial conflict, deserving of full American support.[13] This could lead to the destabilisation of the Milosevic regime in Belgrade, which at this stage the mainstream of military and diplomatic opinion in London did not want.[14]

In response to the Rahavec crisis, Adem Demaci announced his long-awaited return to active politics. He stated that he did not recognise Rugova's 'Parliament in Kosova', a clear sign of his imminent re-entry to the political area as spokesman in Kosova for the KLA. This took place on 16 August. A British aid worker, Sally Becker, was jailed for thirty days by Belgrade for allegedly helping the KLA. 19 and 20 July were days in the timescale of the war on which all local observers felt the parameters of moderation were collapsing, but little or none of this perception affected the deliberations of the international community.[15] Many Western diplomats in Belgrade attended the eighth anniversary celebrations of the foundation of Milosevic's Socialist Party of Serbia that same night.

In terms of inner-Belgrade security politics, Rahavec was a victory for General Nebosja Pavkovic who was an advocate of VJ commitment of heavy armour to the internal operations against General Momilo Perisic, the Chief of General Staff of the VJ, who at least in public maintained the official 'Yugoslavist' line that the role of the army was to defend the nation's borders. Until then the Belgrade Ministry of Defence spin doctor and official spokesman Dragi Ojdanic had been briefing the diplomatic community to the effect that the army was not involved in internal security operations.[16] Although it was not appar-

ent at the time, this was the beginning of the end for Perisic, and Milosevic replaced him as Chief of General Staff in October 1998. Pavkovic
became the field commander for the Kosova operations until the end
of the war. Thus, Rahavec was a turning point for the Serbs as well as
the KLA. It marked a turn towards total war and strengthened the grip
of extreme fundamentalist nationalists in the VJ leadership. For the
KLA it marked the effective end of the Partisan-derived principle that
the army was a collection of semi-independent units, with minimal
communication between them for security reasons.[17] The Enverist-
derived horizontal structure was not capable of dealing with the strains
imposed by a modern conflict. It was, in any case, a theoretical construct, which the theorists in the LKCK and LPK perhaps took too literally. In the Partisan war as it actually developed in Albania in
1943–44, strong central control was maintained over the Albanian
guerrilla force by Hoxha, Mehmet Shehu and their close associates
through the political commissar system.[18] This never developed in the
KLA, a sign of its distance from Marxist roots.

It was only a month since the major change of US policy developed
by the State Department Balkan envoy Richard Holbrooke and Secretary of State Madeleine Albright, which set a new direction for a Kosova war settlement. Albright had decided that any final conclusion to
the war that did not involve the KLA would not work and that the policy position of most of the Europeans and the Contact group, viewing
the KLA as a terrorist organisation, was obsolete and mistaken. This
change of policy was in part determined by Holbrooke's meetings with
the KLA in various western Kosova locations around 24 June, when he
saw the breath of popular support for the KLA and how it was primarily a local defence force, not a terrorist conspiracy. He also met the
wide variety of local people involved in the community support for the
war effort. It was reinforced by a meeting a week later in Switzerland
with the KLA's local Political Spokesman, Bardhyl Mahmuti.[19] The
urbane French-speaking Mahmuti, as a serious and well educated
young man with the Swiss sophistication that many prominent Albanian exiles seem able to rapidly acquire, made a good impression on
Holbrooke and his staff and belied the 'narcoterrorist' image that Belgrade was promoting.[20]

As a result of the new turn in US policy, Xhavit Haliti started moves
to remove the last traces of Partisan habits and Communist-type military symbols from the KLA in Tirana. It was a sign of the postmodern

capacity of the KLA leadership to see the war in terms of changing visual images. Even KLA saluting was modified to look more 'Western'. The international media war had begun in earnest, as Haliti well knew.[21] The Serbs opened a Media Centre in the gloomy and cavernous Grand Hotel in Prishtina.[22] The paraphernalia of yet another Balkan war was smoothly dropping into place with many old hands of all professions meeting again in unfamiliar new Kosova surroundings. In the international community, quiet recruitment began of mostly ex-military staff for a future international observer mission that might watch over some hypothetical future negotiated ceasefire. This would become KDOM, the Kosovo Diplomatic Observer Mission, a small fixture on the wooded landscape in the next few weeks. In October it would metamorphose into the Kosova Verification Mission (KVM), after the Holbrooke-Milosevic October ceasefire agreement. Many of the KDOM staff came straight from the Bosnian conflict.

The military advances the KLA had made were also important in changing US policy. From January to June 1998 the KLA had seemed an inexorable and growing force. The setbacks to the insurgents north of Suva Reka and the battles for the Prishtina-Prizren road were a gift for Milosevic. They strengthened the hand of the doubters over the new policy in Washington, who were mostly (but not all) in the military and among Pentagon staff. They still believed it was unnecessary to deal with the KLA as a political actor because Milosevic would destroy it in anti-terrorist operations. It is an open question how far at this stage the Serbian leader was aware of the change in the US line and whether clear orders were given to the VJ generals to intensify the conflict. There is every likelihood that this was the case. The almost accidental and contingent Serbian success at Rahavec was quickly followed by a similar onslaught against the KLA at Lapusnik on 25 and 26 July and at Carraleve on 25 July. Although the fighting in these villages was less conclusive for Belgrade than at Rahavec, as it was basically about control of the Peje-Prishtina road, it had the immediate effect of producing another mass population movement, so that in a tiny village like Kishna Reke on the edge of the Drenica massif near Prizren, almost twelve thousand people had taken refuge.[23] Food supplies in many places were running low. By comparison with two months before, enormous Serbian armoured forces were now deployed. About 140 tanks were involved in the battle for Lapusnik and the little village was bombarded with Katyusha rockets and 220m cannon for several hours and reduced to rubble. By comparison the KLA only had 82mm and 150mm mortars.[24] Fear spread throughout Kosova when these facts were known. The US-based monitor Human Rights Watch estimated that as many as 300,000 people were on the move or fully displaced by this week of the war.[25] In reality the situation was less critical for the KLA than it appeared, particularly in the media where it was widely reported that Milosevic now had the upper hand in the conflict. Although Serbian armour could overwhelm the KLA in particular battles, the Serbs did not have the size of infantry resources available to effectively occupy and pacify the territory they had 'gained' and often the KLA moved back into it when the heavy armour withdrew.

In this period of crisis for the nascent Kosova army, a new and more coherent pattern of organisation was clearly needed. The priority was to avoid rash and ill-thought-through local actions such as had resulted in the difficulties at Rahovec. Commanders like Sylejman Selimi ('the Sultan') were told to establish a brigade structure for Drenica, and he became KLA Chief of Staff. This started with the 111th Brigade at Likofc, within the seven KLA military command zones covering the whole of Kosova. Another important brigade established now was the 121 Brigade on Mount Pashtrik on the border with Albania above Prizren. At this stage these brigade names were largely nominal and the strength was not that of a brigade in a normal modern army. This activity was sensible and rational but it did not really face up to the central dilemma of the KLA at this stage of the war, that of satisfactory base areas. In all guerrilla wars bases are of critical importance. As I have already indicated, Kosova did not have very remote mountainous refuges for the new army and in their absence, the KLA drifted into the creation of bases in what were in effect towns, like Malisheva, or very large villages. These were vulnerable to aerial attack and the kind of frontal assault using overwhelming force of VJ heavy armour that occurred at Rahavec after 18 July.

At a deeper level, the Rahavec events inevitably raise the question of how far the LPK/KLA leadership had actually thought through how the war might evolve before it started. The dominant school of thought, predominantly 'Enverist' in and around the older figures in LPK and also shared by the young Marxist-Leninist radicals in LKCK, believed that the war would lead to a rapid popular uprising along the lines of the 1997 model in Albania; the Serbian occupiers' power would be replaced by Albanian-majority people power and the KLA army would mainly be a catalyst. In terms of traditional Marxist insurgency theory this was not an unreasonable assumption, as on the key issue of breaking the coercive mechanisms of the capitalist state, it could be argued that the Serbian state in Kosova was terminally weak by 1998. There were extensive debates in the pages on the LPK newspaper *Zeri i Kosoves* between 1994 and 1996 about how a war might evolve but they are almost always focused on what kind of army was needed to start an uprising rather than what a KLA force should actually do in a protracted conventional conflict and how such a conflict might be won. This is not the serious criticism of the LPK Albanian leadership that it might appear to be. NATO is also frequently criticised for failing to anticipate the length of time the Milosevic regime might resist in the 1999 bombing campaign, but much the same criticism could be applied to the KLA leaders in some aspects of the guerrilla war in 1998.

It is unclear when the KLA leadership began to realise that in a prolonged guerrilla war it would be hard to defeat the Serbs, but eventually thoughts turned to international intervention and NATO, following the Bosnian war model. It is probable that the 27 July advance of the VJ out of its Prishtina central bases to retake the main Peje-Prishtina highway was a major event in this direction. In the same month the VJ officially extended the border exclusion zone to 5km, which allowed the army to shell to ruins a string of villages between Gjakova and Prizren, many of which were strong pro-KLA supporters.[26] The KLA centre at Likovac was taken and occupied by 8 August.[27]

In a sense this did not matter very much because elements in the international community were already thinking along these lines. The American change of policy led to a similar change in London, and in turn military advisers from both countries were in touch with each other and with the KLA. This was eventually symbolised by the arrival of Agim Ceku from Croatia to take over as KLA commander in the following year, but the British and others had been talking to Ceku and other ex-JNA officers of Croatian army experience and Albanian ethnicity much earlier than that. Ceku did not actually leave the Croatian army until February 1999 and saw little of the critical earlier stages of the war in the summer and autumn of 1998 from first hand observation. A tall, serious ex-JNA officer who had changed sides early in the ex-Yugoslav war and fought with the Croats in 'Operation Storm' against the Yugoslav forces, he was a British and US protégé and a

totally conventional[28] postmodern soldier with no strong Kosova political affiliations.[29]

It should be emphasised that the British plans were significantly different from the American, at least as they evolved over time, and this
was duly reflected in some political developments in the post-1999
period in Prishtina when military actors like Ceku began to play a
political role. The future appointment of a figure like Ceku was in normal line with British counter-insurgency doctrine under which senior
figures are appointed to an insurgent movement London wishes to
both control and support, perhaps linked to promises of munitions
supply and political backing. The person concerned is expected to steer
the movement in a direction London approves of, and prevent political problems. The priority in London was to avoid a popular uprising
in Kosova on the Albanian model where leadership might fall into the
hands of what were regarded as far-left groups like the LKCK.[30] Fear
of the 'Communist' element in the KLA background was strong in the
British military, but much less important in Foreign Office and MI6
thinking and hardly present at all among their allies in the US forces
and in advanced nations in Europe such as Germany. The appointment
of Ceku was in essence a device to weaken the hold of the political radicals on the orientation of the KLA and hold it hostage to the future. It
is unclear how far Ceku was aware of his future role. He was a tough
and credible soldier and many of the KLA rank and file who were often
confused by their novice General Staff leaders welcomed his arrival on
the scene. In Kosova, surprise has often been expressed at the speed
and efficiency of the installation of Ceku the following spring. The
answer to this question is simpler than it may appear in that the British military had been working with Ceku since 1998 and had a close
organisational model to follow, that of Fitzroy Maclean's sponsorship
of Tito in the Second World War, and had been following it for several
months before most actors in the conflict were aware of it. The Yugoslav Partisans had in Winston Churchill's and Maclean's view gone
through a period of initial military success and then serious defeat and
disorganisation after Axis assaults. As Maclean recalls in his memoirs,
which were still a stock in trade of British military academy reading in
the 1960s and 1970s when later generals such as Mike Jackson and
John Reith were cadets,

Undeterred by their misfortunes, the Partisans set about reorganising themselves on a more orderly basis. Larger, better organised units were formed and

a proper chain of command instituted. The operations which they now undertook, though less ambitious in scope, formed part of a well thought out plan.
During the winter of 1941, encouraged by the news of Tito's arrival in eastern
Bosnia, they succeeded in fighting their way back into many of the areas from
which they had been expelled and regaining much of the ground which they
had lost. But if the Montenegrin Partisans had learned by their military mistakes, they showed no sign of mending their ways politically. With typical
Montenegrin exuberance and with little regard for the more moderate line laid
down by Tito, they established in the areas under their control a Communist
regime of the most extreme kind.[31]

Most of Maclean's remarks about the Yugoslav situation in 1941
could be directly transposed to Kosova in 1998 in the minds of the
British military. The KLA needed to be guided by a strong leader into
military effectiveness and political moderation. The later American
policy was quite different and involved the use of the military contrac-
tor Military and Professional Resources Inc. (MPRI), a very large private warfare organisation run mostly by ex-US military figures and
ex-Pentagon staff where the political ethos was much more focused in
building up a movement to use Kosova as a catalyst for the rapid overthrow of Milosevic. At this stage that was not part of mainstream British defence or Foreign Office thinking at all. The British were thinking
ahead to Kosova's social stabilisation within a reformed democratic
Yugoslavia and had no perspective for Kosova independence, still less
for a Kosova army. Intelligence material produced by the Defence Intelligence Service (DIS) in London embodied profoundly old-fashioned
Yugoslavist assumptions, in marked contrast to that of the US Defence
Intelligence Agency (DIA) which with its strong USAF orientation had
been centrally involved in the NATO air strikes against Milosevic in
Bosnia. The British were the most influential Western nation in Belgrade under Milosevic and wished to protect that traditional 'special
relationship' influence that had reached its apogee in the period when
Ivor Roberts was Ambassador between 1993 and 1996. Thus, the British moved faster than their opposite numbers in Washington; Ceku
was in place by spring 1999 while MPRI did not become fully involved
until much later on. Ceku soon became the main point person for
NATO in the KLA. This gave Tony Blair a particularly influential position in international deliberations. Until Christmas 1998 Blair had
been content to let Foreign Secretary Robin Cook 'make the running'
in Kosova matters, as a student of his military campaigns has described
it.[32] When war became inevitable, after Racak, Blair wished to be the

commanding influence within NATO. In the spring and summer of 1998 in the KLA, command issues were of little importance and a stable structure did not exist. In the short term, the organisational reforms Selimi proposed were quite uncontroversial and accepted as necessary by most in the KLA after the setback at Rahavec and in southern Drenica. Later on, soldiers did not see the wider implications of Ceku's appointment. In the longer term his presence was a less positive factor, as it exacerbated the divisions in the insurgent force between those who had received formal military training in the JNA and VJ and those who had not.[33]

The Belgrade authorities tried to build quickly on the post-Rahavec advances. The 15 June NATO 'fly over' of Kosova was an abject failure as a deterrent to Milosevic and VJ ground forces were still pouring into the region.[34] The July events at Rahavec and the absence of most Western media in August led to an acceleration in the pace of selected attacks on villages and ethnic cleansing. The VJ did not overplay its hand in one sense, although even official Belgrade spokesmen admitted to local diplomatic observers that they had entered the area of humanitarian law violations and in practice local terror was being employed.[35] But it was on a carefully limited scale. In Milosevic's famous if apocryphal words, 'a village a day keeps NATO away'. This was to be a war where spectacular large-scale episodes like the levelling of Vukovar or the siege of Sarajevo would be avoided by the VJ. The generals wished to show Milosevic that they had learned from their traumatic experiences in Bosnia, and had gained a somewhat clearer understanding of the likely role of the Western media in the Kosova campaign than they had in 1991–95.

A slow, measured war suited Milosevic at this stage. Nature also seemed to be favouring the Serbs. The hot and dry August weather spread the raging fires caused by sustained shelling and rocket fire, and on some days most of Drenica lived under a dense cloud of choking smoke. Many events were still being determined by the aftermath of the setback at Rahavec in late July. The height of Serbian success was perhaps reached about 20 August after Junik had been retaken by the MUP on 16 August. The *Financial Times* speculated the same day on the possibility of the imminent collapse of the KLA.[36] Official Belgrade media claimed that 'the police control all of Kosovo and border area at peace'.[37] In an equally familiar tone, Belgrade clamed to have arrested a gang of 'international criminals of Albanian origin' who were guilty of various attacks on Serbian police. In reality the battle to recapture Glodjane for the KLA had already started and the Prizren-Peje road was still closed. Ramush Haradinaj would establish his future reputation as an outstanding field commander in these weeks. In an omen for the future with the massacre of January 1999, the name of little Racak village near Shtime is heard in the war for the first time, as fighting spread there from the north near the Prishtina to Macedonia main road. It was also clear that little could be expected in terms of immediate action from NATO or the United States, with the US Ambassador to Macedonia, Christopher Hill, echoing Slobodan Milosevic's call for the Albanians to join talks.[38] This type of diplomacy was a great encouragement to Milosevic's generals. On 7 September heavy VJ armour moved towards Ponerac south-west of Malishevo and pounded it and other nearby villages with heavy guns leaving thousands of people fleeing along the roads and homeless into the forest. Characteristic horse-drawn Kosova timber wagons were now containing terrified refugees. The London *Times* correspondent Antony Loyd noted:

ghost town dusted by recent shellfire whose streets were only occupied by wandering dogs and abandoned livestock. Outside the southern end of the town, two Serbian anti-terrorist police, the grim augers of misinformation, stopped us, while on the slopes beside them, soldiers moved forward.

'Go back', they warned us, placated by a familiar routine of raised hands and fixed smiles. 'There is no problem at the moment but there is going to be a big problem soon. Terrorists are operating in the area.'[39]

This was happening all over Kosova. The KLA leadership faced a difficult dilemma. New recruits were pouring into Albania, where the very large German Diaspora was at last throwing off the heritage of LDK loyalty and matching Swiss Albanian energy and commitment. Money and arms flows over the border were increasing in scale and regularity and the Kosova 'Minister of Defence' office in Tirana under Ahmet Krasniqi was negotiating with local commanders about shipments of bread and food to the growing army.[40] International elite support was increasing, if slowly, with British politician Paddy Ashdown calling for NATO air strikes against the Serbs.[41] The setback in Rahavec was not paralleled elsewhere and in Dukagjini the area of territory under effective KLA control was expanding, not contracting. Ramush Haradinaj's forces were able to threaten the Serbian positions on the hill north of Glodjane. KLA soldiers were retaking land lost to the Serbs in the spring around Suva Reka and Prizren, although in the village of Zhur on the border with Albania, senior KLA commander and founder Remzi Ademaj was killed. The more advantageous terrain was playing a large part in this advance for the Albanians, with Serbian forces on the ground insufficiently motivated, mobile or numerous to pursue KLA soldiers into woodland and upland retreats, or over the border into Montenegro. Although they and their commanders, except perhaps Ceku and other ex-VJ soldiers, were no doubt ignorant of the text, the KLA soldiers were following instinctively the exact dictates of the Red Army Partisan operations manual:

Never fight foolhardily or obstinately: do not become stereotyped or remain immobile in the same place. When your troops take up combat positions find out routes of access and quick and easy retreat ... When the fight is over you must withdraw quickly and try to fight the enemy again and prevent his possible return. Without this speed we may be deprived of favourable opportunities, lose men and ammunition, and ourselves be encircled by the enemy.[42]

At the same time another model of KLA warfare was developing spontaneously. The characterisation of all Albanians as supporters of 'terrorism' in much of the Belgrade media frightened the Albanian villagers. They knew the entire future of their communities in Kosova was at stake. In countless cafes, barns and house *oda*s all over western and central Kosova meetings were held to decide what to do. Local people were proving the truth of the old dictum that improvisation is the heart of guerrilla warfare. The ordinary Albanians felt it was now time to contribute what they could to support the war, after decades in which they had dreamed of independence and escape from Yugoslavia. This did not mean always taking on the uniform of the full KLA soldier. There were many villages and small towns where significant if often small numbers of local leaders were coming forward who were not formally connected to the KLA General Staff or other local leadership structures. Many of these localities were off the beaten track, and in some places settlements had had a strongly pro-Rugova and pro-LDK population with few LPK, LKCK or Diaspora radical political links. A typical example was little Isniq, an obscure settlement on the Dukagjini Plain.[43] Within weeks of the crisis developing in the region after March 1998, some young men had gone to the mountains to join the KLA and those remaining in the village had raised a 'Home Guard' type force, and dug a web of complex trenches so that the inhabitants could defend themselves against infantry attack.[44] The activity seemed purely defensive and also exclusively led and organised by local people seeking to defend their communities from the VJ. It was brave and quixotic and against the Serbs, inevitably doomed in the short term. But in the Western media it looked quite different. It was a particularly sympathetic image of the 'KLA' for the world's media, a world away from the sophisticated Marxist intellectuals of the Swiss Albanian Diaspora. In a way such fortified villages became primitive base areas, contradicting the usual dictum of guerrilla warfare doctrine that bases for the guerrillas are only vital if the resident population is not fully behind the war.

The Isniq population and that of hundreds of villages like it certainly was fully behind the war, but in their exposed situation on the plain and vulnerability to VJ reprisal attacks, the village itself had to become the guerrilla base, even if it had limitations. Above them, in the hills, the Koshare corridor and other supply and escape routes had to be kept open at all costs. The apparently unnecessary savagery and wanton violence of much of the VJ shelling of villages can be understood in this context; if the village seemed to have become a base, it could only cease being one if it was completely physically destroyed. Killing or driving out the inhabitants and poisoning the water supply were insufficient from the VJ viewpoint. On their side, the KLA did not have to hold villages, but could use them according to need. It was never imperative that they were held, once the static model of warfare that had come to disaster at Rahavec had been abandoned, and the insurgents could benefit from the severity of reprisals against the population that would quickly bring new recruits.

The KLA also avoided the mistake of the Greek Communist Democratic Army in 1948–49, who believed they had to hold the Mount Vitsi/Mount Grammos triangle area in northern Macedonia to survive, a fact which (amongst others such as the closure of the Yugoslav border) led to their final military defeat in April 1949. The local defence forces that became part of the KLA in this period illustrate the fact that by this stage of the war, there were in fact several 'KLA's', not 'the KLA'; the mantle of the army being shared between those in different districts with sometimes very different subjective histories and military conceptions. A KLA war identity was a subject that could be constructed quite easily. It was not even necessary to have a military uniform to do it. Above all, the village self-defence concept gave people something to do to join the war and try to destroy Serbian practical

155

power if the KLA could not supply them with weapons or ammunition, which was a very common problem. Village self-defence also meant women, the elderly and the very young could make a contribution.

The KLA did not discourage women recruits and by the end of the conflict there were many women fighters in different localities, particularly in and around Prizren and in Shala, but the KLA military culture and sub-structures and the conservative traditions of the Kosova family and self-image did not always make it easy for women to come forward.[45] The average low marriage age in Kosova households meant that many women of military age were already responsible for children in the refugee and family preservation process by March 1998 and were unable to join the KLA. By August-September 1998 the reality of the war had moved far from the LPK ideal of an open urban worker- and peasant-led urban insurrection against Belgrade rule. The Kosova war truly becoming a 'people's war', but the indigenous traditions of informal rural resistance were reasserting themselves in the conflict. There is some evidence to suggest that the most rapid time for female recruitment and KLA activity was in the last stage of the war, during the winter of 1998–99 and in the March-June 1999 bombing campaign, as the interesting memoir by Drita Simnica of her time in the KLA in Shala illustrates.[46] There is no fixed distinction in most guerrilla armies between combat and support roles, but as Simnica shows, even a deeply committed and active female fighter like herself seems to have been more employed in support roles (the camp kitchen and munitions transport) than in direct combat, although she did learn how to use a high powered assault rifle quite successfully. A significant proportion of the women fighters in the KLA had lived for a period in the Diaspora; an indicator of the role of foreign Diaspora life in Kosova female progress and emancipation. This experience would correspond to much of that of women in the Greek mountain warfare in the Second World War, exemplified by the well known heroic images of the women of Epirus carrying heavy ammunition boxes on their backs up the mountain paths to the male soldiers thousands of feet above them.[47]

As the summer of 1998 neared its end, the tide of refugees did not diminish and humanitarian agencies started to put intense pressure on governments about their likely fate in the cold Kosova winter that was approaching.[48] Refugees showed a surprising if instinctive knowledge of how to deal with the Western media and provide the kind of stories

that would help the Albanian cause.[49] Atrocity stories filled the newspapers and NATO seemed marooned and outwitted by Milosevic.
Prominent British Conservative figures like the Shadow Foreign Secretary, Michael Howard, berated the Blair government for inaction in the
face of mass murder.[50] The spread of KLA fighters into hitherto quiet
parts of Kosova like Kamenitsa and Gjilan in the south-east and a
much wider area around Prizren also rang a warning bell for governments and NATO. The Quaf e Morina pass into Albania south-west of
Prizren was one of the best land routes into northern Albania and its
loss would be a major setback for the VJ. Elsewhere fighting intensified, and the political temperature in the Albanian world rose with the
dramatic assassination of the FARK/'Ministry of Defence' leader
Ahmet Krasniqi in Tirana on 22 September. This had little effect on the
ground in Kosova, but the subsequent street fighting in Tirana and
armed confrontations between different political groups there effectively destroyed the FARK and the remnants of Bukoshi's 'Defence
Ministry' as a force in the Albanian capital. This was consolidated by
the departure of Fatos Nano as Albanian Prime Minister and the
arrival of Pandeli Majko's government.[51] The FARK continued to be a
force in Tropoja, though, for some time to come.

In terms of classic guerrilla war doctrinal theory, the KLA was
changing the agenda by trying to establish positional advantage in theatres of the war where the VJ was not numerous or well deployed.
After Rahavec the VJ had achieved positional advantage in the central
south area, but it never achieved as much elsewhere. In practice, for
the KLA this meant the decisive areas were north-east Kosova and
Pashtrik in the south-west. In Llap on 15 September the KLA had won
a pitched battle with the VJ after an ambush on a convoy in Kacanoll
gully and destroyed eight vehicles. The always shaky theory that Milosevic might be able to destroy the KLA by the end of the summer was
clearly fallacious and in the classic model of all insurgencies, the KLA
was winning by simply surviving.[52] The prospect of a spring uprising
was once again on the minds of diplomats and intelligence officers, and
the likelihood of a major bloodbath with it. In response, the US State
Department under Madeleine Albright reactivated the Holbrooke mission and talks with Milosevic began that led to the October agreement
for the deployment of an international observer mission. At this stage
the American leadership was vital for the Albanians; in London Robin
Cook and Tony Blair were still under the spell of the prospect of a

Dayton-type negotiation along Bosnian lines that would end the entire conflict and allow a peaceful entry of a NATO force into Kosova.[53] The British Foreign Office does not seem to have realised the isolation of Rugova and the LDK leadership group from the realities of Kosova, and persisted in believing they could deliver the Albanians in a Bosnian-type negotiated deal. Probably the angling of information by the British embassy in Belgrade with its dependence on 'spun' UDBA intelligence sources and the army-background KDOM observers also contributed to these illusions. On 24 September Milosevic had been warned that NATO air strikes were in the offing if the violence on the ground did not stop.

The political leadership in Kosova began to take new initiatives. Adem Demaci held a press event on 6 October under the banner of his new post as 'General Political Representative of the Kosova Liberation Army'. His appointment was a breakthrough for the KLA in terms of some parts of the media and it took some of the intense pressure off Thaci and Syla on the General Staff, and the loyal and principled but somewhat weak Jakup Krasniqi as press spokesman. It also delayed their appearance in the public domain, a masterly tactic for maintaining the atmosphere of mystery and conspiracy on which the KLA thrived in the Western newspapers and television stations. The ageing conspirator relished his new role and Demaci made a strong statement to the press demanding that the 1991 Kosova Constitution be reinstituted as a way to open the road to independence, emphasising that the KLA was making 'hits' on the Yugoslav military-industrial complex, not the Serbian civilians. In his way, and in a context that NATO did not understand, Demaci as a master politician was setting an agenda that NATO would later be forced to follow to defeat Milosevic and his political/military machine.

It is not clear what the reactions of the disparate KLA leadership were to Demaci's new position.[54] Hashim Thaci and most Drenica colleagues saw Demaci as a revered nationalist father figure but their view was not universal in the KLA. Demaci could be dogmatic and not always an easy colleague. He brought little new political support with him, and did bring the disapproval of the old Right who saw him as trying to challenge their revered Rugova for the general leadership of the Kosova Albanians. His only important young follower was the radical student leader Albin Kurti.[55] He was a very talented student politician and youth leader but was very young at that time and had no military dimension, although he had an impeccable record of resistance to Serbian rule. Although there was universal respect and admiration for all Demaci had done for Kosova in the past, his willingness to talk to Serbs at some earlier points in his political trajectory and his old campaign position for a Kosova Republic within a new Yugoslav Federation had alienated some of the more fundamentalist nationalist opinion-groups within the Albanian orbit. He was nevertheless indispensable and he also had the additional political asset of excellent contacts within the new Socialist government orbit in Tirana.

During all these complex diplomatic processes the rank and file KLA soldier on the ground could relax—up to a point—and wait for positive developments, local circumstances permitting. Munitions supplies had improved considerably in many places in the last two months. Weapons purchased by and transported from the Diaspora in the United States had begun to arrive in Kosova via Albania as early as August 1998, but initially numbers were small.[56] The flow increased considerably in the late autumn of 1998 and dramatically after the Racak massacre, and involved very high-technology equipment such as Florin Krasniqi's imports of American Barratt Light 50 sniper rifles, a legendary weapon that can kill someone over two miles away from the fire point, penetrate armour plate and bring down helicopters.[57] Krasniqi's network had been threatened by FBI action early in 1998, but vigorous lobbying by Joe and Shirley Dioguardi and the Albanian-American Civic League had defeated attempts to have it banned in the US as a terrorist organisation.[58] News of the 'superweapons' arrival spread rapidly, and the Light 50 was a useful psychological weapon against the nervous VJ conscripts. Numbers of KLA recruits were also rising considerably as volunteers from the Diaspora arrived who had felt compelled to take part after the reverses of July and August. Exact data is absent but by the beginning of October perhaps five thousand KLA soldiers were in the field, although not all were properly armed. The international community and the media were once more fully engaged in the crisis, if not always in ideal ways from the KLA viewpoint. The KLA received a considerable boost from the German Defence Minister, Volker Ruehe, on 18 September when he called for new air strikes on Yugoslavia.[59] Two days earlier the KLA recaptured its old headquarters village of Likovac which had been lost in late July. The agony of the mid-summer KLA defeats had been survived, and the flow of new recruits and energy from Albania was reviving some largely defunct units. The departure of Demaci from his spokesman post on 21 September was on health grounds, contrary to much speculation in Kosova.[60] Weapons and ammunition supply was rapidly improving as the Koshare corridor stayed intermittently functional, and more and more munitions were starting to come in over the Sar Mountains from Tetovo in the FYROM/Republic of Macedonia.[61]

The qualities the old Ottoman army recruiters liked when they sought Albanians for the Sultan's forces were much in evidence in the summer of 1998: stoicism, indifference to hardship, pain, food shortages and physical discomfort. The mass of the population remained firmly behind the war and was willing to put up with severe physical conditions in the forests. For those who preferred to leave, a new way of life was developing in the camp tent city outside Kukes in Albania, which had defeated the international community's attempts to disperse the refugees well away from Kosova. The young could join the KLA as easily in Kukes camps as in Kosova itself.[62] It is likely that recruitment and training in and near Kukes in the late summer played a large part in the takeover by the KLA of Mount Pashtrik above Prizren in September. This was a considerable step forward for the KLA as it broadened the front the VJ had to cover and exposed the VJ infantry shortages. In another landmark for the insurgents, the Stari Trg mine at Trepca was attacked for the first time in September and production had stopped by the end of the month.[63] As many as 15,000 refugees from the Salja Bajgorske hill villages east of the mines had left home and most of the hills thereabouts were soon KLA controlled. The refugees were prevented by the VJ from entering Mitrovica and so fled into the forests north of Vushtrri.

On 9 October, Holbrooke met Milosevic in Belgrade and delivered an ultimatum that unless he immediately ceased the ethnic cleansing processes, NATO would unleash major air strikes on Yugoslavia. Most of the Western diplomatic community left Belgrade in a series of road convoys as fears grew of reprisals against them. On the local battlefield, fighting flared up again as reorganised KLA guerrillas opened a new front around the beleaguered little southern Drenica town of Maleshevo, seeking to recover ground lost in August. The evacuation was unnecessary. On 13 October NATO withdrew the threat of air strikes as Milosevic made some minor concessions to NATO in terms of promised troop withdrawals and allowing the deployment of a 2,000-strong international monitoring/ceasefire verification team, the

Kosova Verification Mission (KVM). It did not take long for the media to expose the ineffective nature of the 'verification' deal. Only a few days later, in the London *Evening Standard*, the veteran British war reporter Robert Fox noted that Milosevic was using the removal of the air strike threat to reinforce his troops, rather than withdraw them.[64] A few days later, a reporter for *The Economist* noted that few refugees were returning to their homes, and most of the 250,000 displaced people remained so.[65] One refugee remarked, 'We have been on the move for months', as the reporter noted that the KLA had returned to nearby Jablanica, formerly a KLA stronghold but burnt out twice in the last six months where the only woman to be seen was a female KLA soldier carrying a rifle.

On the ground, the people did not believe the war was over or that the Serbian dictator would keep his word. Basic supplies of maize and potatoes were hidden in dumps all over the combat area and the KLA was beginning to learn the skills of long-term guerrilla survival in the forests. Butane stoves were being used to avoid smoke from fires revealing the location of hideouts. Water was plentiful but often suspect if the Serbs had poisoned the wells. Beans were another staple, but meat and fish were largely absent from the soldiers' and refugees' diet. Eggs were important, as in the Korean war. Vegetables could be found in abandoned plots in many villages but fruit was largely unknown once the autumn blackberries had been eaten. In practice, the war was winding down for the winter, as Balkan wars usually do, and in that light the achievement of the Kosovo Verification Mission (KVM) was even emptier than it seemed to many observers at the time.[66] The KVM observers were slow to arrive, their briefing was often poor, and many of them were almost immediately in daily contact with a designated VJ officer who supplied them with a mixture of information and mostly misinformation; in a short time the majority were taken in by what they were told.[67] In response the KLA increased attacks against the MUP and the VJ, and within a few days of the ceasefire violence was as endemic in most of Kosova as it had been before it. The stage was set for the final intensification of the conflict. The international community was to pay a high price for bitter heritage of collaboration with Belgrade and Rugova for so long; the research organisation International Crisis Group pointed out in late August that 'Even though it is clear that as currently structured the Rugova-led negotiations will fail to lead to any breakthrough, Western capitals are placing an excessive

161

degree of hope in the talks.'[68] The same psychology was applied to the KVM mission which was rapidly overtaken by events and doomed by the Racak massacre in early January 1999.

The KVM mission did nevertheless have some positive value for the KLA. In many localities, particularly those where the insurgency was weak or only recently established, the ceasefire, however notional, did take some pressure off the men and women on the ground and allow for resupply and reorganisation. It was more difficult for VJ and MUP armour to retaliate against attacks with human rights violations. There would have been obstacles to the Serb forces and opportunities for the KLA in the winter snows in any event, but it was much easier to achieve results when VJ heavy armour was constrained by the ceasefire. It was possible to partially reopen the Koshare corridor and other new supply routes to Kosova from Albania and Montenegro and train many new recruits in the realities of the war. The Kosova liberation radio station Radio Free Kosova was fully established in the Drenica woodlands, in Berisha village, a significant milestone.[69] In another mission that was obscure at the time but was later to have important long-term consequences, the New York-based Human Rights Watch began research into the ground events in Drenica since the end of June, and in due course produced an influential volume that substantially assisted the arguments of those in favour of military intervention against Milosevic.[70]

Meanwhile the fighting intensified in many localities throughout Kosova, including some that had been quiet throughout the war. A small KLA unit was able to start attacks on the Prishtina-Gjilan road from a base near the Novo Brdo medieval fortress. The KLA sought to outmanoeuvre the VJ in Drenica by drawing vehicles and tanks into local ambushes, and to stretch VJ infantry resources by opening up new fronts in hitherto quiet areas, particularly those where the KVM was either absent or thin on the ground. Fighting spread around the Lake Batllaves vicinity in the eastern hills near Podujeve and towards the border with Serbia itself. This remote and backward area was a problem for the VJ, with few asphalt roads capable of taking their armoured vehicles and many places where a mule or horse was more useful as a means of transport than wheeled vehicles. Within a few weeks, the KLA controlled all the land east of the Mitrovica-Prishtina road to the border with Serbia, and threatened the key Merdare corridor leading down from the VJ headquarters at Nis into Kosova.

On the western border, some VJ shells fell on Albanian territory while fighting for the Koshare corridor intensified, with a VJ soldier killed on the border itself. Many international observers feared it was only a matter of time before violence spilled over into the Albanian border district of Tropoja.[71] Diplomatic concern about regional desta-bilisation also grew as a result of the renewal of violent turmoil in Albania after a group of mostly Kosova soldiers loyal to the FARK attacked Prime Minister Nano's offices in Tirana on 14 September in an attempted coup d'état.[72] Although the Prime Minister escaped through a window, his government was doomed and after days of street violence he resigned before the end of the month.[73]

After an assault on the village of Glodjane, near the home of the Haradinaj family, the VJ claimed to have opened up the Peje-Prizren road to normal traffic. In reality these claims were exaggerated; the VJ's base on a hilltop at Dashinovic was largely impregnable but it did not control the territory south of it in any meaningful sense. The Yugoslavs had more success at Junik, where the village was sur-rounded by a VJ anti-personnel minefield and KLA control of the nearby hills was under threat. At this time United Nations estimates stated that Milosevic had about 29,000 army troops active in Kosova, which (at least officially) would draw down to about 14,000 after the October ceasefire and KVM deployment agreement.[74] Although the extent of the drawdown was in all probability exaggerated by the UN, there is a clear picture of a theatre in which KLA operations could be rebuilt. The often cruel and bitter Kosova winter was ahead. In an ominous time for the Albanians, the Clinton administration in Wash-ington was becoming distracted from Kosova and many other interna-tional problems with the preparations for the President's impeachment in the House of Representatives in December 1998 over the Monica Lewinsky affair, and the launch of Operation Desert Fox against the Iraqi dictator Saddam Hussein. A difficult winter for the Kosova Lib-eration Army, in every sense, lay ahead, but in circumstances where the basic strategy was bearing fruit and the battle for physical survival could be won.

Map of KLA Operational Sub-Zones

8

THE GATHERING STORM: AUTUMN 1998

For the KLA to win, it would need to lure Serb forces into committing another massacre and disgracing themselves before the world so that NATO would have to intervene. It was the sneakier force that was going to win this round, and history had shown that the Albanians were a step above the Serbs on that level. 'We had to be sneaky our whole lives', Florin had once said, 'In our culture, breaking the law was always considered a good thing because the laws were evil.'

Stacy Sullivan[1]

A week before the Holbrooke-Milosevic aerial verification agreement was signed in the third week of October, new clashes broke out as the Serbs moved a large force of about seventy-five tanks and other heavy vehicles into the low hills north of Vushtrri. The village of Dobratin was shelled and burnt out, with about forty-five Albanian deaths. The efforts of diplomats were having little effect on the ground war, with the KLA having opened a safe movement corridor between Vushtrri and Mitrovica that the VJ was desperate to close.[2] KLA control of this area would not only threaten VJ control of Mitrovica as a city but also could bring the war into the strategic Merdare crossing and thus very near the border with Serbia itself.[3] This was a much greater factor in Belgrade decision making than the international community realised at the time. It would have been a catastrophe for Milosevic if violence from the KLA had spread anywhere near the Kosova-Serbia border, and into Serbia. Although there had been a wartime press crackdown in Belgrade, there were still relatively independent journalists working there and it would have been impossible to conceal violence within Serbia from the media. The official discourse of the Milosevic leadership was now in any case losing contact with reality. The Serbian Prime Minister, Mirko Marjanovic, addressed the Belgrade Parliament on 6 October and claimed that Serbian security forces would be withdrawn to bases as 'the terrorist groups in Kosovo had been defeated'. In reality, real control of the ground was being slowly but steadily eroded by the KLA and local defence forces over a larger and larger area and it was advantageous for Milosevic as well as the KLA to have a pause in the war.

It is not clear if Holbrooke and the Americans in general realised the real situation. The US had very limited human intelligence capacity on the ground when the conflict started and there were only a few Americans among the KDOM verifiers, albeit they were often people of high quality. An American verifier had run foul of both the MUP and the KLA near Malishevo in the early days of the mission and had narrowly escaped kidnap. Some American verifiers did not leave their bases very much. The technological mastery of the US satellite and telephone intercept technology intelligence system told the National Security Council little about the advances of the KLA in rural eastern Kosova. A pause in the war did not materialise in any case for more than a few days. Most American and hence NATO 'hard' intelligence came from intercepts of Serbian military transmissions and it was only from this material that NATO learned of the growing revival and success of the KLA in the north-east. A new KLA field regional HQ was set up in an old hotel in a remote area near Batllaves lake and functioned without disturbance for much of the rest of the war. Once again the Llap KLA proved superior in both the doctrine of guerrilla warfare and practical organisational skills to most other units elsewhere in Kosova.

Although heavy armour was supposed to be confined to barracks under the Holbrooke-Milosevic agreement, the agreement did not stop the VJ counter-terrorist campaign, as Belgrade defined it.[4] The hopes of US President Bill Clinton expressed on 13 October, that Milosevic would comply with UN Resolution 1199 and implement a ceasefire, were being defied in many different districts. Milosevic was caught in the conceptual bind of most anti-insurgency warfare; war for the KLA insurgents was absolute and total, but the Serbs could in practice only deploy a portion of their military force against them. This did not stop them trying to do more. If shelling from truck mounted artillery was going to be ruled out through a ceasefire, there were other methods of continuing the ethnic cleansing of Kosova. On 17 October large VJ forces left their base in the Kutllovc district of Mitrovica and attacked the villages of Mazhiq, Rrashan and Medenic with heavy machine gun fire. These attacks did not destroy buildings as shelling did but they certainly terrorised the inhabitants, who fled into the nearby woods. The VJ had camouflaged a massive arsenal near the base and was content to use it.[5] In other clashes near the Prishtina-Malishevo road, three Serb policemen were killed and several others wounded in an attack on a MUP convoy. Tanks moved into positions near the Klina district village of Sferk. The KLA responded with a mobilisation of fighters all over western and central Kosova, no doubt linked to the formal rejection of the Milosevic-Holbrooke deal by the KLA political leadership.[6] A week before, the KLA political spokesman Bardhyl Mahmuti had rejected any agreement that fell short of full independence, although a three-year transition period was offered to the Serbs.[7] His views were reinforced by a stronger statement critical of Holbrooke by the KLA senior commander Shaban Shala the following week, who said that Holbrooke had been 'duped' by Milosevic.[8]

These differing political responses by different people in the KLA leadership were a reflection of the changing realities on the ground. By this stage of the war the background control influence of LPK Exterior in Switzerland had been engulfed by the scale and complexity of wartime events, the practical difficulties of Switzerland-Kosova communications, the wide variety of new commanders who were emerging everywhere—most of whom had no connection with the LPK—and the impossibility of external control of a popular partisan movement from a foreign country. It would be wrong to suggest, though, that the LPK was unimportant. The majority of war finance funds raised for the Homeland Calling Fund were raised in Switzerland and predominantly through the LPK and LPK-influenced channels. Perritt estimates that 'the vast majority of contributions to Homeland Calls came from Switzerland. Swiss Albanian expatriates paid membership dues to the LPRK, even before it transferred itself into the LPK. The rate of contributions from a broader class of contributors began to accelerate only in 1996 and 1997, and mushroomed in 1998 and 1999'.[9] The 'Tetovo connection' was a reflection of Macedonian Albanian acumen and organisational skills and the fact that most of the remaining senior

LPK Exterior leadership in Switzerland came from Macedonia, like Fazli Veliu.[10] Veliu had built up a successful business in Switzerland while he was in exile there, and along with Xhavit Haliti had perhaps the most mature organisational skills and general common sense acumen of any of the LPK leadership. Although the Koshare corridor was still under intense pressure and as well as other parts of the border, which may account in part for Haradinaj's approval of the KVM deal, elsewhere in Kosova the KLA was taking root in places where hitherto it had only a minor presence and, above all, where the hitherto intractable problems of weapons and ammunition supply were beginning to be solved. The key to this change was the city of Tetovo in the Albanian-minority area of the north-western FYROM/Republic of Macedonia, and to a lesser extent, small arms transfers from Turkish-based KLA supporters in the Istanbul Kosova exile community via the Preshevo Valley.[11] The Kosovar Albanian exiles in Istanbul were, and some still are, a cautious and conservative community. Most exile organisations in the 'Arnaut-Turkish' world supported ex-President Berisha in Albania and were very disoriented for a time with the overthrow of Berisha in the spring of 1997.[12] By late 1998 and early 1999 this caution had disappeared and there had been a much more activist policy.[13] There had been important figures from Tetovo in the KLA since its earliest days, but in the mid-1990s they were not typical and the city was culturally conservative and very divided politically between the different Albanian parties. The prospect of the defeat of the KLA in Kosova in the summer of 1998 had galvanised rank and file political opinion, particularly in the PDSH party of Arben Xhaferi and Menduh Thaci, then the largest of the Albanian parties.[14]

A sophisticated and well-funded arms supply channel was set up from Tetovo over the Sar Mountains via Kodra Diell to Prizren and Ferizaj and then into Drenica, involving large weapons and ammunition consignments in trucks, also on mules, and the sophisticated use of public transport and public transport couriers. In Tirana the departure of the Nano government and the arrival of Pandeli Majko as Prime Minister two months before had emboldened the Albanian army to find more weapons for the KLA and both the KLA representative in Tirana, Xhavit Haliti, and the logistics chief Ali Ahmeti had a more favourable operating environment for the clandestine small arms procurement network.[15] Swisscom coded mobile phones were used for communications.[16] The appearance of large numbers of Kosova refugees also helped transform the atmosphere in Tetovo. Arben Xhaferi[17] was the intellectual doyen of all the Albanian political leaders and a man of strategic vision with strong family roots in Kosova, and good connections in Turkey. He saw that without the full backing of the Macedonian Albanians, Kosova might suffer a humiliating defeat that would set the cause of independence back for generations. The stakes were high and also rising. But the PDSH party in Tetovo and Gostivar had considerable capacity, Ali Ahmeti in Albania was in a position to initiate activity in his more southern home vicinity around Kicevo, and there was also the Islamic thread in Macedonian Albanian life, greater than in Kosova, which sought to see the Kosova conflict as a potential holy war. This thread was very minor but it did exist in a few parts of the community and could in time risk the involvement of extremists in the Islamic world in a way that would be very harmful for the Albanians. Xhaferi wished to avoid this at all costs. Menduh Thaci was the organisational heart of the PDSH party with numerous contacts in all spheres of Tetovo life. A brilliant young politician who had taken over the old PDP party with Xhaferi when he was only 33 in 1993, he was anxious in 1998 to make his mark in the intensely competitive world of rival reputation and prestige of the leaders of the different Albanian communities.[18] The Kosova war was a perfect opportunity and he took it. He was a natural foil to Xhaferi's philosophical depth and ease of communication with international figures.

Tetovo was also rich, at least by comparison with most northern Albanian and Kosova towns, and the kind of money needed to bribe customs officers and policemen was not a problem for the Tetovo munitions smugglers. A set procedure was developed, particularly at Blace checkpoint, where the customs officers were notified that a munitions convoy was coming through a day or two before, and a set sum agreed for safe passage. This would be paid in advance to the police and border officials from Tetovo and the weapons would pass in the night without disturbance. Mule track routes were set up involving the horse breeding communities of Lura in northern Albania and their counterparts just over the Kosova border in the Dragash (Gora) region of far south-west Kosova. The Gorani and Torbesh ethnic groups of Slav-speaking Muslims who lived there were not natural friends of the KLA, as the destruction of Zhur village had shown in summer 1998, but money talks volubly in the small arms trading world and it overcame politics.[19] These routes, and also the opening up of other new channels through the Rugova Pass between Plav in Montenegro and Peje in Kosova, were far superior to the chaos and danger of Bajram Curri, the Koshare corridor and other Tropoja routes. The notion of Kosova as an entity with a fixed and functional modern and secure border was being rapidly eroded in the autumn of 1998; small arms transfers eroded it like water might erode a sandcastle wall on a beach. The same process had happened on the border between 'Republika Srbska' and Serbia in the Bosnian war.

Arms smuggling from Macedonia also avoided the threat of interference from the numerous cohorts of foreign police who were beginning to be deployed in Albania as part of post-1997 conflict stabilisation deals between the EU and Tirana.[20] But for the smugglers the absence of an easily manipulated local police in northern Albania could be as much a problem as zealous foreigners. There were problems for KLA arms dealers in the still anarchic areas of the northern Albania where there was no law and order at all. This anarchy was not the advantage for the Albanian war machine that foreign journalists often painted in their colourful dispatches picturing gun-toting anarchy in these regions. News of arms movements was hard to conceal in Bajram Curri and Kukes and it was always possible a consignment might be hijacked and seized by gangsters. There was intense and sometimes violent competition for the lucrative small arms trade between networks loosely linked to the two big political parties, independent smugglers and the FARK militia.[21] The best system for smuggling by an insurgency is with a pliable and poorly paid local police and customs who can patrol the trade, to their own profit and that of the smugglers. They perform a function of market regulation, akin to any other trade or financial regulator. Macedonian Albanian smugglers were ideally placed in this respect. There is also the question of the viewpoint of the Slav government and its bureaucrats in Skopje to consider. It was clear to many in the FYROM/Republic of Macedonia official Slav world in Skopje that the Albanians might win in Kosova, or at least could eventually do so, and it was wise, in the Balkan tradition, to be helping the winning side. The Skopje government was afraid of a possible Albanian uprising in western Macedonia along the 1997 model in Albania, as a result of the Kosova conflict. It did not seem to be very well informed about the substantial Macedonian content in the KLA, and its policy towards the Albanian power centre in Tetovo had to tread a difficult balance between intervention and benign neglect.

The VJ had reacted to the arrival of American U-2 spy planes over Kosova under the verification agreement with the movement of a battalion of soldiers to central Kosova to guard newly deployed anti-aircraft artillery. In a quiet sense the air 'phoney war' had already begun by December 1998 as a prelude to the NATO bombing campaign of spring and early summer of 1999. The USAF and Milosevic's air force and air defence troops were already silent adversaries by November 1998. The KVM deal gave the Serbs time to relocate anti-aircraft artillery and other air defences.[22] Serbs were encouraged by the tacit support they appeared to be receiving in Washington from the diplomatic *éminence grise* Henry Kissinger who said that week that a 'A fight between the Christian and Islamic culture is being carried out in Kosovo', and by the view of National Security Advisor Sandy that the ceasefire was holding.[23] The Clinton administration was sinking into the miasma of the Lewinsky scandal. The view of the agreement and its effects in the main Western media began to diverge considerably between the USA and Europe, with the BBC reporting on 27 October that 'Kosovo air strike threat recedes' as a result of Milosevic's 'compliance' with the agreement, while the more realistic CNN had reported the previous day that air strikes had become more likely as Milosevic was withdrawing more troops in a sudden panic move to try to prevent imminent air strikes.[24] In reality little was changing on the ground, with the Media Centre in Prishtina claiming that 'The Yugoslav army started the withdrawal of its troops into their garrisons today morning hours. Three huge army vehicle convoys withdrew from the regions of Komorane, Volujak and Stimlje into their original military bases.'[25] Unusually for this news organisation, that bulletin was quite accurate, but what was happening was not in compliance with the KVM agreement under which heavy armour was supposed to be removed from Kosova completely. As so often in the ex-Yugoslav wars, agreements with Belgrade meant very little.

This cat and mouse game in the diplomatic sphere also meant very little to the ordinary KLA soldier, and some intelligent senior KLA commanders like Remi still did not expect NATO to get involved.[26] Their priority was to rebuild their army and on a better basis than it had existed before. As Tim Judah has pointed out, 'the fact was that the Holbrooke agreement was with Milosevic and the Serbs. The KLA were not party to it, and as far as they were concerned, not bound by it either. As the Serbs pulled back, the KLA followed in their wake, reoccupying the positions they had left during the summer.'[27] Ramush Haradinaj went as far as to say the agreement was 'lifesaving' for the KLA. This was not simply a matter of weapons supply, or the outcome of a particular battle or firefight:

After September's offensive, our population lost faith in the army, they started to think we will not be able to finish our duty, because after every fall we did not rise stronger as we were supposed to, but naturally we faced harder situations of organisations and transportation of technical equipment. In the meantime, the Serbs sent big forces in the border strip, seizing ammunition in big amounts, apart from small groups, which could only bring ammunition to make the war alive, not to make it stronger ... conversations held with the international verifiers were a big power for us ... when it was seen that the internationals are appreciating, accepting and respecting the KLA, then also, our population did the same.[28]

Ramush Haradinaj's views have become the received wisdom in much of Kosova about the KVM deal but need critical evaluation. It is likely that Haradinaj's military problems in this period were more acute than those of many senior KLA commanders elsewhere, and his view of some of the KLA's difficulties may be a little exaggerated. His own base vicinity around Decani and Junik had arguably had the worst time of any district of Kosova in the war, with Junik a particular target for the Serbs' artillery bombardment since the early days of the conflict. The local people had borne six months of violent displacement, most of their homes were in total ruins and every family knew someone who had died. Junik people had little or no information about the progress of the war elsewhere in Kosova or the possibility of growing international support for their cause. They also knew that the KLA could not protect them from the VJ if the latter was able to concentrate enough heavy armour in one place against them. Winter was coming, and there was little cause for optimism in their lives.

In addition, Haradinaj had the problem of the role of Tahir Zemaj and the FARK paramilitaries concentrated in his region, unlike the central Drenica, Sar or Pashtrik KLA commanders where the FARK was wholly absent. There were also political difficulties that affected the military campaign. In local political terms in Dukagjini towns, there was then a particularly Rugova-ist and inward-looking regional leadership of the Kosova Democratic League. Unlike the LDK in most other places by this stage of the war they found it hard to overcome old prejudices and family quarrels in favour of a united effort behind the KLA. Many young people from LDK backgrounds did indeed get very involved in the war effort by the spring of 1999, as in Gjakova where the youth wing of Rugova's party in November 1998 decided to join the KLA *en bloc*, but far fewer of their fathers did.[29] In these communities the issue of the potential social revolution that a KLA victory might mean was posed in acute form. An independent Kosova under a KLA-originated government would mean a transfer of assets from Yugoslavia, which the town middle class might not welcome: as collaborators and operators in the old system, they might not own them or be in charge of them. This drama played out across all of Eastern Europe in different forms after 1989, with the elite in some countries like Romania and Bulgaria managing to hang on to power quite successfully and asset-strip the old Communist economic system, while in others like Albania there had been major changes.

It was not simply an issue of economics. The ex-Yugoslavia wars had brought a serious depression in the standard of living in all towns, with the collapse of reliable public transport, dysfunctional schools and hospitals, irregular payment of state employees' salaries and rapidly rising food prices. The countryside villages, with much of their food often coming from local plots, were much less severely affected. Without assistance from émigré remittances, many urban families could not survive. In this atmosphere, social nostalgia for the securities of the old Yugoslavia in its better days before Milosevic and the spell of Rugova's pacifism were hard to dispel, particularly in the more prosperous urban households in towns like Prizren and Gjakova which had done better out of Communism than the villagers. There was also the minor issue of religion. In Gjakova, with the largest concentration of Roman Catholics in Kosova, the LDK was 'their' party and the fact that all the KLA leadership came from a different political tradition created difficulties for the older and middle-aged urban elites from the old society in involvement in the war. Every town had different war experiences. North of Haradinaj's immediate territory, the town of Peje was already beginning to receive the MUP attention that would make it the most bitterly contested town by July 1999.[30] It is also worth bearing in mind that Haradinaj's views were also expressed in his interviews in 2000 retrospectively at a time when he was seeking to put his new political party, the Alliance for Kosova, on a firm footing and where the backing of international opinion was important. In that context, he was likely to express his support for the KVM as strongly as he could. He was on safe political ground as the absence of an enforcement mechanism for the KVM deal meant the Albanians could not be unilaterally blamed for the reopening of the fighting.

As November opened with its usual descent into thick fog and flooded fields, much of lowland Kosova turned into a quagmire. As many of the KLA General Staff as could attend, plus one or two other independent figures, met in Zurich on 19 November to assess the political and military situation.[31] KVM enforcement based on field observation became difficult, which meant that the verifiers became more and more dependent on their VJ contact officer for information, or more often, misinformation. Many of the verifiers, particularly the British, spoke Serbo-Croat from their Bosnian wartime experiences, but few spoke any Albanian at all. This affected the intelligence process. They found communications much easier with the Serbs and the VJ than with the Albanians. With British verifiers there was also the well known fact of the traditional conscious and often also subconscious leanings of British army officers towards the Serbs in most Balkan crises.[32] It did not take long before the VJ officers realised it would be easy to steer the KVM mission along anti-Albanian lines.[33] In practice the KVM staff depended for their security, as unarmed observers, on a stable relationship with the VJ.[34] It was similar in structural problems to military missions in Bosnia which turned out afterwards to have been wining and dining with war criminals.[35] The Serb police reactivated heavy armour patrols on the asphalt roads, but could do little elsewhere. Both sides played the verifiers along with misinformation, knowing many of them were military intelligence officers in very thin disguise who would be sending back intelligence reports to their capitals.[36] NATO senior figures knew what was happening and knew the ceasefire would not amount to very much. Quiet early preparations for a future air campaign went ahead, with the Supreme Allied Commander Wesley Clark concentrating on getting enforcement of the little-noticed 25km free-flying zone for NATO over the border area that had been agreed for all NATO observation flights. The Serbs were supposed to be withdrawing all SAM missiles and air defence weapons including radar, radio controlled guns and hand launched missiles from this zone. As in earlier months, the impetus of the US planning effort was coming primarily from the United States Air Force, the CIA and the Defence Intelligence Agency, who did not expect anything but very short-term compliance by Milosevic with the terms of the agreement.

British and European official perceptions were much more permeated by wishful thinking.

By 11 November, as sporadic fighting was going on in many different Kosova locations, even this degree of compliance was in doubt. Parts of western Drenica were again as much (or as little) controlled by the KLA as in the early summer. In some cases the fighting was serious and resulted in injuries and fatalities, as in Negrovac on 10 November where a well-known KLA commander, Abedin Bujapi, was killed, while in other places the firefights were short and often only symbolic statements of military intent. On that same day two Serbian policemen were abducted and killed near Malisheva. The town was still almost empty after the population left en masse in late summer for refugee camp life in Kukes in Albania.[37] NATO urged restraint on both sides but within a few days the area of fighting had expanded and the KLA claimed an extension of control over a much larger area. Whatever the views of the more dogmatic and militant commanders about the KVM deal, in practice the reduction in VJ infantry numbers was aiding the insurgents considerably. More and more international community bodies were demanding compliance with the ceasefire, such as the Contact Group, but there was little or no connection between this diplomacy and the parties on the ground, and above all no enforcement mechanism for the deal at all.

Balkan leaders were gloomy about Milosevic's prospects, with the Montenegrin Parliament Speaker Svetozar Marovic saying that 'President Milosevic's policy in Kosova would cause the Serbs the greatest defeat of the Serbian nation this century.' He and others in the region, like the Skopje leadership, with detailed knowledge of the terrain and the changing munitions supply situation knew that if the KLA could survive the winter and recruit and gently expand the territory under their influence or control, they would be well placed for a spring offensive, when the weather improved, against the stretched MUP and VJ forces. The Montenegrins were also (as always) well informed about Belgrade developments and already rumours were sweeping the Dedinje diplomatic district that General Momcilo Perisic might be replaced by Milosevic as supreme commander, which would have been an unlikely development if the war was going well for the Serbs.[38] In central Drenica the KLA senior commander Sami Lushtaku was reorganising the force along lines that some Serbian intelligence read as preparation for an all-out assault on Prishtina in the spring.[39] The neighbouring Balkan leaders also knew how much Milosevic's power depended on satisfactory relationships with the army. As Branka Magas has pointed out, looking back to the time when Milosevic's power was greatest,

At the beginning of 1991, Milosevic appeared at the height of his powers. Although the dissolution of the Yugoslav Communist Party had scuppered his earlier plan to use the party machine to win for Serbia the hegemony it had enjoyed in pre-war Yugoslavia, the illusion that this could be achieved per-sisted, because of the Army's evident hostility to the new regimes in Slovenia and Croatia ... He entered Yugoslav history as the first republican head of state to ask the Army to intervene in a domestic dispute. Indeed, Milosevic pressed the Army to introduce a state of emergency throughout Yugoslavia.[40]

The problems in his dealings with the VJ leadership eight years later over Kosova policy limited the Serbian dictator's political options. In these circumstances the regime had only the most draconian methods of population control to fall back on. The severe weather was aiding the KLA as thick fog made many local movements invisible to the VJ and the KVM monitors. The spreading but still scattered violent inci-dents of November were rapidly intensified in the first week of Decem-ber with fighting all over Mount Pashtrik near Prizren as the VJ attempted to stop a large group of KLA fighters coming from Albania. They were unsuccessful and the KLA recruits disappeared into the for-ests near the city. The war was spreading into urban centres like Prishtina and Prizren that had hitherto been largely peaceful. The area of influence/control of the KLA in southern Llap was within a day's march of Prishtina and the northern suburbs of the city had many fam-ily links with Vushtrri and Podujeve people, who unlike Drenica fam-ilies had been more easily able to establish a presence there under Titoism. In the south-west the war was developing most rapidly. A major firefight on the Quaf e Morines border pass east of Prizren on 4 December produced eight Albanian fatalities, and in other separate incidents twelve Albanians were killed in less than 24 hours. It was becoming more and more difficult for the KLA General Staff headquar-ters near Glogovac, at Prekaz I Eperme (Gornja Obrinje), to follow, let alone control the rapid train of military developments on the KLA side.[41] In the towns, the MUP secret police units were using the dark nights to liquidate targeted opponents. In parallel, in Belgrade hardlin-ers were increasingly taking control of the war, with the sacking of Per-isic by Milosevic, and his replacement by ex-VJ press spokesman

Dragoljub Ojdanic now confirmed. Odjanic stated in his first press conference that political interference in the operations of the army would no longer be tolerated. As always in VJ leadership crises, the Belgrade government was seeking to legitimise its divisive policies through changes in the army leadership, a grotesque distortion of the original Tito-Partisan relationship.

In the Bosnian war it had been a coherent strategy through pliable hardline nationalist Bosnian Serb Generals like Ratko Mladic, but there were no equivalent and capable figures in the VJ army officer corps coming from the Kosova Serb community. The crisis in the legitimacy of the military and its role continued.[42] It is perhaps significant that Milosevic chose to replace an experienced and generally professional soldier of Yugoslavist inclinations like Perisic with a hardline military spin doctor. It was a triumph of the politics of appearance over the politics of reality. In between days of serious violence in Kosova there were days of calm with few incidents, which the proponents of the KVM attributed to the mission's presence but was much more the result of the normal development pattern of small Balkan wars. 'General Winter' was dominating the field of battle. Behind the VJ's late spring and summer assault was the shadow of the Ottoman armies laying waste the harvests of rebellious areas after quelling a revolt and then returning to Constantinople to avoid the Balkan winter. As in Skanderbeg's conflicts in the fifteenth century, there was a time to fight in the spring and summer, and also a time to return to barracks when deep snow and ice covered the forests and the mountain passes were closed.

The crisis in the VJ leadership developed further in the first week in December when Momcilo Perisic in Belgrade claimed that he had been illegally dismissed from his post by Milosevic. Political observers felt that one of the main reasons for his exit from the Chief of Staff post was his very bad relationship with the Radical Party leader Vojislav Seselj, who defended his removal by saying it was constitutional. The affair had little effect in the short term on Milosevic but was an indication that months into the Kosova conflict there were opinion constituencies in the army that were unhappy with the ultra-confrontational policies of the dictator, knowing these would sooner or later bring NATO into war with Serbia. Here the Milosevic ideological construct of the KLA as a purely 'terrorist' force was unhelpful to the successful prosecution of the war from Belgrade's viewpoint. Milosevic's *idée fixe* on this issue meant that the central VJ military problem could not be faced: lack of sufficient VJ infantry numbers prevented them from really subduing and effectively occupying the rural hinterlands. Milosevic persisted in seeing the KLA as a tiny extremist minority which could be separated from what in his old fashioned way he saw as the passive sheep-like Kosova Albanian majority. In military terms this was a wholly obsolete perspective. Perisic was a classic infantry soldier in the Yugoslavist tradition, and he knew how hard it is to defeat an insurgency that has wide popular support and an adjoining kinship state with porous borders. The Belgrade leadership's view of the Albanians and their capacity was dominated by out of date myths and belief in the superiority of their heavy armour. Press censorship also played a role in Belgrade's self-imposed problems. It was difficult for the limited number of Serbian independent journalists to investigate and report on the problem of declining VJ morale. If the KLA did not harass them, which often occurred, there was no guarantee that editors in awe of Milosevic would print anything in their newspapers that seemed unpatriotic. On the ground, many VJ soldiers felt little incentive to push themselves to the limit and risk their lives in dangerous forest infantry encounters with the KLA. As a result patrols were frequently of a superficial nature and did not unduly restrict the rebuilding of the KLA.

The growing violence in Kosova and the atmosphere of instability in Belgrade led the NATO foreign ministers to meet on 16 December in Brussels. The NATO group leaned heavily towards the Serbs in the final communiqué from the meeting, which called on the KLA to effectively disarm while the Serbs were only expected to 'reduce the number of Serbian security force members in the southern province' and to 'refrain from further acts of intimidation'. The meeting produced a highly adverse reaction in Prishtina, with Adem Demaci completely rejecting the proposals for a political solution to the Kosova crisis by the US envoy Christopher Hill, a view that was also echoed by the LDK-dominated Kosova negotiating team. Demaci pointed out in his statement that 'there was not one word about who will guarantee the right of the Albanians to self-determination.' In Belgrade *VIP News* said the KLA was now 'arming itself quickly in Kosova.'[43] As Christmas approached the attempt by the international community to impose a control mechanism through the Milosevic-Holbrooke deal and the KVM observation mission was visibly disintegrating. Verifiers were living lonely and isolated lives in the deteriorating weather conditions, and what was supposed to be a 2,000-strong mission still only numbered a few hundred people. A substantial minority took Christmas leave and left Kosova altogether. By far the largest contingent was British but with a sense of realism that was often absent from other national contingents, plans were already being made in London for a possible future evacuation of the mission to Macedonia if conditions continued to deteriorate. In a final nail in the Hill plan's coffin, the Serbian government also rejected the plan, despite its many advantages for them. American diplomacy in this period was as marooned and ineffectual as a stranded whale on a dry beach. [44]

The failure of the whole process with its antiquarian emphasis on the restoration of the autonomy of Kosova under the 1974 Yugoslav constitution model illustrated that now there was a straightforward war for the final destiny of the land underway and compromise 'Yugoslavist' solutions had no future. For a diplomat so profoundly steeped in the Yugoslavist tradition in his wing of the State Department, this was a major catastrophe for Christopher Hill. Demaci knew how vulnerable the US diplomatic position was and called immediately for the removal of Hill and Holbrooke from their posts. Although this did not occur, the significance of the situation was not lost on Secretary of State Madeleine Albright, who from now on took increasingly personal control of Kosova policy. This continued until the Rambouillet conference in the spring. A new version of the settlement plan was produced but Hill found himself talking to fewer and fewer Albanians, as more astute members of the LDK team like Fehmi Agani knew the whole course of this diplomacy was over, even though they had said they held high hopes for it only a few weeks before.[45] With Demaci's acute grasp of Washington politics, he knew that outside the State Department other agencies, principally the CIA with much more radical agendas for the region, were waiting to become the guides of events. Although different CIA officials obviously had different views on Balkan issues, like staff of any other US government organisation, the collective ethos of the Agency was always willing to consider radical solutions against the Yugoslavist status quo in a way other officials often were not. CIA intelligence assessments on the poor future of Yugoslavia had been on the whole borne out by events ever since 1991.[46]

The Pentagon remained firmly non-interventionist over the next six months, as the end of Wesley Clark's career ultimately demonstrated.[47] It is likely that the same views as Demaci received were reaching

Hashim Thaci in the field in Kosova from Xhavit Haliti in Tirana. Neither Thaci or Haliti had any personal experience of the United States or the complexities of Washington agency politics, but in the cosmopolitan atmosphere of Zurich some time before they had made their first contacts with US CIA agents and had a sense of how Washington worked.[48] Once again, in a way that was invisible in Belgrade, the Zurich and Swiss connection in Kosova Albanian politics was central to the development of events.

At a local level the KLA did enough to keep the war moving without over-extending their resources in the difficult winter conditions. The toll of dead and wounded still grew steadily each day.[49] After a fairly quiet week between the 8 and 15 of December, apart from a Serbian ambush on a group of more than 140 KLA fighters moving into Kosova near Kukes, a string of attacks and counterattacks developed throughout the month in Drenica. Fighting also broke out along a long stretch of the border with Albania and in Peje itself. In the deteriorating weather conditions some KLA soldiers were withdrawn to Kukes hospital for treatment for frostbite. It is likely that Serbian intelligence had reported to Milosevic the growing number of NATO-member army secret or semi-secret training missions attached to the KLA in north-west Albania. The British army mission, part of 'Operation Horn', was located north of Kukes, in a remote and thoroughly depressing oak-scrub border area with heavy rainfall, near the Kruma chrome mine. Missions of varying size, from a few men up to over fifty, were elsewhere in Tropoja from Holland, Germany, Italy and other NATO nations. Although all were supposed to be secret, in practice their existence was quite widely known. The British operation was organised from the SAS headquarters barracks in Hereford.[50]

In the Balkan mountains secrets are not kept easily and the need to go into towns like Bajram Curri from time to time meant local discovery was inevitable. The most the secret soldiers could hope for was to keep journalists away, which the British did quite successfully. 'Operation Horn' is still top secret in Britain but anecdotal evidence and reporting such as that of Christian Jennings indicate that the foreign experts found many of the Kosovar recruits intractable and difficult to train and often suspicious of outsiders.[51] General Mike Jackson, as head of Kosova planning in London, was already looking ahead to the time when ground forces intervention might be necessary and he wanted advance SAS teams in Kosova, well dug in with the KLA, before any invasion started. Jackson and his team had been closely monitoring the situation since the summer of 1998 from the BAOR base at Rheindahlen, and many of those involved felt a NATO stand against Milosevic was inevitable in the future and had almost no confidence in the KVM mission objectives, international diplomacy or the capacity of the KVM monitors to achieve much.[52] They did nevertheless soon teach the KLA some soldiering skills in the meantime, and the OSCE Albanian mission head, the Dutch diplomat Daan Everts, noted on 23 December that, 'The romantic rag-tag KLA seems to have given way to more serious professional military leadership. The holiday fighters have gone home.'[53]

It is hard to say what difference the foreign missions made, but appearances are important in infantry soldiering, in all armies, and they certainly made the KLA look more like a conventional force, with neat new uniforms and effective winter footwear. The KLA claimed over Christmas that the December border ambush was an aberration and most new soldiers were able to enter Kosova from Albania without incident. Within Kosova the conflict ground on along predictable and familiar channels, dominated by the seemingly interminable and inconclusive struggles for control of the main roads. A Serbian MUP patrol was massacred near Klina on 15 December, a signal to the MUP command that it could not hope to restore safe passage along the contested Peje-Prishtina road without serious opposition. The border fighting had started after a MUP patrol opened fire on a large group of new KLA soldiers who were entering Kosova from Albania east of Prizren, itself an indication that the importance of the Koshare Corridor as a crossing point was declining as the KLA used the Has region of Albania, Macedonia and Mount Pashtrik more and more for movement of new soldiers from Albania.

As Christmas approached, the war continued its familiar on-off pattern with the ceasefire holding on some days but not on others. The severe early winter weather and dense fog combined to make most military operations virtually impossible in the central lowlands and on the waterlogged plain. The violence was focused mostly in Llap and around Podujeve where the KLA had expanded considerably in the previous three months. By now the American component of the KVM had increased in strength around there and reports were reaching the Pentagon of the rapidly increasing numbers and capacity of the KLA in this area.[54] The American verifiers prioritised persuading the VJ and the KLA to wind down their 'contentious' positions in this area, but with little success. The VJ saw the KLA as threatening the main road to Serbia where the border lay only fifteen miles north-east, and they had no intention of giving ground.

Fighting intensified over Christmas, so that after Christmas Eve more than 15 people were killed in the snowy hills to the north of the town. The KLA had started to attack some of the few ethnic Serb villages in the vicinity. Rumours swept the area that the KLA were planning an assault on Podujeve so that by holding the town they would control the main highway from Prishtina into Serbia. The insurgents were digging trenches within twenty yards of the main road. Rising concern at the crisis in the north-east led the KVM mission chiefs to rush 100 additional monitors into the area, but there was little they could do to reduce the intensity of the conflict, with unarmed and often ill-briefed foreigners in vehicles that could not use many of the narrow mule tracks in the forests. By now the KLA's numerical strength had grown to about 6,000 men and women across Kosova, with no less than a minimum of 2,000 in and around Podujeve. The insurgency here had reached a new point, of the *de facto* merger of the people with the army on a scale that was absent elsewhere in most of Kosova. Nearly all these north-eastern villages were deserted except for uniformed KLA soldiers, with headquarters in the village of Lapastica, a mile south-west of Podujeve. The KLA had matured as a force since the crisis at Rahavec and made no attempt at a final assault. They wisely left the town to its own devices so that even a small Serb population hung on there throughout the war. In Rustem Mustafa (Remi) the Llap KLA had perhaps the most effective and underestimated figure on the KLA side in the conflict, a small unpretentious man and a superb field officer.[55] On the border the long-term standoff between the VJ and the Albanian army continued in appalling winter weather conditions in the more open areas of the highlands. The Reuters correspondent Kurt Schork, observing the Morina crossing near Prizren, noted that the border had been officially closed since May, but that

dozens of Yugoslav troops in battle gear are dug in along a football pitch a few hundred metres away ... on the Albanian side there are a few battered Kalishnikovs and one museum-worthy wheel-mounted heavy machine gun. The gun appears not to have been fired in decades and has no ammunition ... at least one of the Albanian border guards, most of whom wear civilian clothes, rides to his post on a bicycle.[56]

On the border there was an increasingly rooted and timeless confrontation, with KLA soldiers slipping in and out of Kosova to safe houses in the Has region to the north. The town of Kukes and the sprawling tent city of refugees were under effective KLA control and there was a bustling market for munitions and food supplies. After the violence and dramas of the spring 1998 period, much of what was happening in western Kosova had an empty ritualistic quality, while the real dynamic of the war was in Llap and the north-east and moving towards Mitrovica and Serbia itself. The Milosevic regime knew its central priority was to stop the rot and prevent the north-western violence from spreading.

On 24 December the Llap KLA commander Remi had a difficult meeting with American KVM mission chief William Walker in which Remi had demanded that the mission should order non-compliant Serb forces out of Kosova, and told him that he was planning to reopen the war full-scale in that region. Demaci intervened afterwards but the military die had been cast, and Demaci eventually accepted that Remi had the full support of his soldiers in wishing to open a new front in the north-east. In Remi's version of events, Walker stormed out of the meeting, prophesying that the KLA would lose the war.[57] After intensive mediation by the verifiers, the VJ and KLA commanders reached a ceasefire agreement on 29 December, but few observers believed it would hold for very long. The OSCE negotiators themselves said the situation, and their mission, were near breaking point then.[58] In support of them, NATO Secretary General Javier Solana issued a statement calling for both sides to support the two-month ceasefire agreement. His words seem to have had some effect, as the days and nights over the New Year were relatively peaceful, although the Serbian media reported alleged murders of suspected Albanian collaborators in Prizren and other cities. According to LDK sources five Albanians and two Serbs were killed over the holidays. On 30 December Milosevic's senior official in Kosova, Veljko Odalovic, accused the KLA of acting to threaten the truce with collapse, and called for the United Nations to designate the KLA as a terrorist organisation and close down their financial networks abroad. By now the KVM mission numbered about 700 people after staff returned from the holiday period, and it was clear their skills would soon be needed in the coming year. The Yugoslav Foreign Minister Zivadin Jovanovic claimed on the same day that the KLA had broken the October ceasefire agreement 470 times and that the Serbs' patience was running out.[59] The first week of the New Year of 1999 was also relatively peaceful. But the Kosova citizens' world would have been destroyed by the New Year of 2000. By the end of 1999 they would have been subject to a 76-day bombing campaign and seen the results of NATO's first war and the collapse of Serbian rule in Kosova, but before that the ground war would enter its final phase. The KLA soldiers and their leadership would have to face the question of whether having turned themselves from farmers and shopkeepers into soldiers, they would then transform themselves into social revolutionaries, following the model Konni Zilliacus described the Titoist Partisans taking after 1945.[60]

9

RACAK TO RAMBOUILLET: JANUARY–MARCH 1999

The strategy, the entire strategy of the KLA was adopted to the specific conditions of the territory in which we were in and the specifics of our military organisation. Our guerilla activity was never out of the daily agenda, if I can put it that way, it always existed. But the conduct of a frontal war, we did this in places we were forced to, and where it suited us. There were cases in which we were—we had to fight a formal war to defend the civilian population.

Fatmir Limaj[1]

In the second week of January the nature of the Kosova war fundamentally changed as a result of the Racak massacre and its aftermath. The war once again became an international issue as the news of the atrocity allegations reached the world, and Racak set in train a course of events that made NATO intervention inevitable. The post-Racak crisis, in addition, soon started to end the autonomy of the KLA as a military force, as they became drawn more and more into the negotiations in France as a political factor and more and more foreign special forces advisers arrived to work with them. The decisions taken in this period were to have very long-term consequences for Kosova Albanian politics, with the then unknown Rambouillet delegation leader Hashim Thaci, now twelve years later, Prime Minister in Prishtina, and many of the same group of LPK-background Rambouillet delegation members also in powerful positions in the new Kosova.

Racak was an aberration in one sense, a departure from a hitherto fairly successful doctrinal practice for the Serbs. To the world at large it appeared to be a sudden and violent breakdown of the KVM-brokered ceasefire. In the early stage of the war Milosevic and his security and military apparatus had stayed intelligently with the doctrine of 'one village a day keeps NATO away', but Racak broke with this problematic conclusively. The killing of forty-five people including many old people and a twelve-year-old girl was not the largest or worst massacre in the ethnic cleansing process in the Kosova war by comparison with the massacre at Krusche near Prizren or that of the Berisha extended family near Suva Reka on 26 March 1999, but it was the most newsworthy.[2] In a war of symbols it became the most resonant symbol, with various Balkan antecedents. Like the Batak Massacre in nineteenth-century Bulgaria which brought Gladstone to his crusade for the freedom of the Christian nations of the Balkans, Racak had a cataclysmic effect. It was so beneficial for the Albanians that the US diplomat William G. Walker, who was head of the OSCE/KVM mission when it occurred, was accused of fabricating the event.[3] This was plainly untrue, as all independent verification of the facts has revealed, although it was not always easy to tell exactly how many of the dead were civilians and how many were KLA soldiers; some KLA fighters wore uniforms, others did not. Like many atrocities in wars it seemed a random event but in fact it was a product of the changing nature of the conflict as the KVM mission became steadily less effective with the onset of winter. If the KVM mission had been totally successful and the ceasefire had been observed, Racak would not have occurred.

The main background factor to Racak was that as time wore on after the October ceasefire, the situation of the Albanian civilian population had become more and more difficult. The Serbian military leadership considered Milosevic hoodwinked by Holbrooke then, and were faced with mounting difficulties in control of the territory. As Jha points out, 'No sooner did Serb forces vacate an area, than the KLA would move in. And the inflow of arms continued unabated. When, after weeks of mounting provocation, the Serbs opened their December offensive, the KLA had won.'[4]

But winning in field conditions was a conditional concept. The long months of field experience in difficult conditions in small 'battle groups' had improved the quality of the VJ's dispersed and combined arms operations, something that made later air attacks largely ineffective.[5] This was particularly the case in one of the most contested areas, around Shtime. On the south-east fringe of the Drenica hills and standing above the valley and lowlands just west of the main north-south road in Kosova between Prishtina and Macedonia, Shtime is poor and ekes out a living from forestry and sheep rearing and as a minor market town. Three kilometres north-east of it lies tiny Racak village. As in all wars, places that nobody in the outside world has ever previously heard of can suddenly achieve prominence, like Vimy Ridge in the First World War or Auschwitz in Poland in the Nazi period. In little Shtime the social structure with its mixture of very poor farmers and slightly less poor traders would, and did, naturally lead to Kosova Liberation Army support and activity, but after the disaster at Rahovec the KLA had concentrated on the surrounding woods and villages and was not yet strong enough to challenge for control of the key Prishtina highway. Yet as the 1998–99 winter wore on, unseen forces were moving again in the KLA's direction. As the town was not a priority area for the VJ, not having a history of major violence in the spring offensives, there was only a modest army presence there. In the relative tranquillity after the Holbrooke-Milosevic agreement in October, some of the VJ withdrew to secure more difficult and contested areas, like Shala and the Llap hills near Mitrovica.

It was a perfect opportunity for the KLA to move into Shtime, and they did so. A Serb policeman was abducted in early December 1998; in the Serbian view this was one of the main catalysts for the violence in mid-January in Racak.[6] The food supplies in the town were quite good as it was near the main road, and soon heavily loaded mules were plodding off through the woods into southern Drenica and supplying the KLA units there. Grain and flour were in very short supply by now in many small places, after the violent chaos and widespread fires in Kosova at harvest time three months before. Food was becoming a weapon in the war. In practice the KLA had 'taken' the town without a fight and produced exactly the kind of situation the Serbs were most anxious to avoid, where a safe supply base could be established for the guerrillas before the predicted spring offensives.

The Serbian MUP special police unit first arrived in Shtime in numbers around 10 January, on what appears to have been a reconnaissance mission to ascertain the strength of the KLA in the area. They then disappeared to barracks in Ferizaj (Urosevac), the big industrial town on the plain, but it did not take long for them to reappear. The days from the 8–11 January had seen several initiatives on the KLA side which had been very provocative to the Serbs. On the 8th a group of Albanians had kidnapped and killed employees of the Kosova electricity company, and afterwards armed Serbs had blocked all roads leading to Prishtina. In response, on 9 January the VJ and MUP moved heavy armour into an offensive against the Podujeve villages held by the KLA with heavy shelling of Bradash and Peran.[7] On the 10th a KLA group captured seven VJ soldiers and one officer in humiliating circumstances near Mitrovica; the day before the KLA had killed three MUP police near Suva Reka.[8] The large numbers of MUP in Kosova had been deployed in what an observer of the war has described as 'Penny Packets' which were often isolated from one another with poor communications and vulnerable to KLA raids. Many of the MUP special police were very young, only half trained and unsure of what they were supposed to be doing in the ceasefire situation. It appeared to the VJ provincial command centre in Prishtina that the KLA was breaking the ceasefire without international hindrance and could operate with increasing military sophistication all over Kosova. It was unclear how they could stop it without violating the rules agreed with the KVM observers.

Tension was also rising among remaining local Kosova Serb minority villagers who felt more and more uncertain and threatened, and felt the KLA would be making a major spring offensive soon.[9] The KLA knew the Serbs had themselves grossly violated the ceasefire on numerous occasions, and they needed to take military initiatives that would keep their opponents on the back foot. On 12 January a Serb police vehicle was blown up by an anti-tank mine near Decani. The nightmare spectre of a Kosova-wide spring armed uprising and fighting spreading all over the territory seemed more and more a possibility. Above all, in the short term, the VJ wanted to prevent the KLA from cutting the Prishtina-Blace road with its strategic and practical importance.

The US diplomat Christopher Hill returned to Kosova in the emergency atmosphere and condemned the violence and deteriorating situation of the last two weeks. The KVM mission was in serious crisis by this point in time. The prisoner exchange deal negotiated between the Serbs, the KLA and the Mission in January almost failed because of acrimonious arguments between Walker and the KLA representative, Jakup Krasniqi, and internal difficulties in the KVM leadership cadre. In the KVM, characterised by one senior ex-KVM figure as 'a huge dysfunctional bureaucracy virtually from the beginning', very serious strains were beginning to show by early January.[10] The OSCE staff from Vienna who had set up the KVM had little interest in drawing on the experience of the predecessor KDOM organisation. The US mission head William Walker presided over a leadership crisis and protracted organisational infighting. According to senior international officials present at the time, Walker had failed to establish his authority over the Mission in its early months by spending much of his time outside Kosova involved in personal diplomacy and conference attendance. Many day to day decisions were taken by his deputy, a French diplomat who was sympathetic to Serbia.[11] They disliked each other and were never able to work together satisfactorily. Most operational management was in the hands of the British General John Drewienkiewicz, whose staff of mainly British army observers were primarily interested in intelligence collection with an eye to future conflict rather than conflict resolution. Although highly professional officers, many of the verifiers had a degree of the anti-Americanism that can be common in some sections of British army officer elites and they did not communicate much with Walker. The crisis at Racak presented Walker with a perfect opportunity to project his uncertain authority both within the Mission and in the world at large and to make a reputation at international level in the process.

Shtime and Racak were only a few miles from the main road and it was in an area where the MUP command hoped the KLA could be rooted out before it had time to grow. KLA units had attacked the MUP in Suva Reka and Ferizaj south of Shtime in the preceding days, and Shtime was alleged to be the base of the KLA unit responsible. If it went for a major security response in some parts of rural Kosova the VJ would have to fight its way in against KLA opposition, but that did not apply on the minor road leading from Racak to Lipjan town. A short surgical anti-terrorist operation seemed an ideal option. It duly took place. Alleged KLA members and sympathisers were rounded up and executed at Racak. The MUP anti-terrorist commanding officer Goran Radosaljevic and the police made one major strategic error in leaving a gully on the outskirts of Racak cluttered with the dead bodies.[12] They left a smoking gun. Racak was easy for the MUP to enter and leave near the main road, and the same applied to the KVM verifiers. The KVM chief William Walker was there very quickly indeed, and pronounced the event an atrocity, and it was widely covered in the international press as such. In the climate of the time this took real courage on Walker's part, something which his critics in the mission did not respect. He observed in the press conference on 16 January, the next day, that 'as a layman, it looks to me like executions'.[13] His views were collaborated by the BBC journalist Jackie Rowland who noted that the dead 'were all ordinary men; farmers, labourers, villagers. They had all been shot in the head.'[14] The *Daily Telegraph* reporter Julian Strauss speculated that Serbs wearing black balaclava helmets, the majority according to the surviving Racak inhabitants, had been members of the elite anti-terrorist unit, the Specijalna Antiterroristika Jedinica (SAJ) under the command of Frengi Simatovic.[15]

Disputes with the French element in the KVM who sought to cast doubt on Walker's conclusions did not alter the general media perception very much. The Serbs put out their version of events, that the police had been attacked by KLA units and the deaths had resulted from the ensuing pitched battle, but the forensic evidence was clear that that was not the case.[16] In response to the crisis, NATO SACEUR General Wesley Clark and the German General Klaus Neumann met Milosevic on 19 January and told him that an air war against Serbia was in preparation. In fact, in some senses, this had already been happening for some months, as Milosevic undoubtedly knew, but it had not been reported widely in the press. In Britain, the Cabinet discussed Kosova and according to Alistair Campbell, 'TB (Tony Blair) said the situation was serious, RC (Robin Cook) that it was very grave. War crimes were being committed. There was a humanitarian crisis.'[17] It is doubtful if such a discussion could have taken place without the Racak events, as the absence of any substantial mention of Kosova whatsoever before January 1999 in Tony Blair's memoirs indicates.[18]

Within a week the KVM mission began to disintegrate as Milosevic declared William Walker *persona non grata* in Yugoslavia and he and other American members of the Mission started to plan to leave. Details leaked into the press of the planned evacuation of the entire mission to Macedonia.[19] In many localities what remained of the cease-fire collapsed, and verifiers were left marooned in their orange vehicles with nobody taking any notice of them. At the same time, the KLA began to reappear as a serious force on the ground in international perceptions as a result of Racak, in a way that had not occurred since the end of the previous summer. The old summer 1998 political scenario that Milosevic would be allowed to defeat the KLA and then a Dayton-type imposition of Kosova autonomy would follow was now totally dead in the water. The military establishment in much of Europe had assumed either that Milosevic's anti-terrorist campaign would succeed, and the KLA would be snuffed out, or that the winter would destroy their ambitions. Neither had occurred.

The mainstream American and European security establishments began to see that a new Balkan war involving NATO was probably near. In an important series of articles for *Jane's Intelligence Review* the Montenegrin analyst Zoran Kusovac presented what was known about the development of the guerrillas for an expert military and security audience, and pointed out that 'another Balkan bloodbath' might be in the offing.[20] In anticipation of a scenario that would resemble the Bosnian interventions, where a peacekeeping force would enter Kosova after a negotiated deal between the Serbs and Albanians, NATO began to plan in detail for a new post-KVM force with an armed military content.[21] The scene for the negotiations was to be Rambouillet, a château town on the fringes of Paris.

The story of the Rambouillet negotiations is well known. The conference was loosely modelled on the Dayton, Ohio conference that led to the Accords in 1995, but it was held in different circumstances. At Dayton the Bosnian participants were war weary and a Pentagon plan had been already implemented to help the Croatian military force Milosevic to the negotiating table. All sides were ready for a deal and the atmosphere was highly coercive.[22] At Rambouillet, international help for the KLA was in its infancy and many on either side wanted to fight on. The Serbs did not take the first week of talks very seriously and international opinion was galvanised by the shock election of Hashim Thaci as head of the Kosova Albanian delegation. The young man from Buroje village had arrived at the centre of events and with him came the Enverist-derived LPK and LKCK political tradition in the Kosova Albanian world, an alternative to that of Ibrahim Rugova and the LDK. In her memoirs US Secretary of State Madeleine Albright reflects on how little the US leaders knew about Hashim Thaci, or the KLA in general. He was 'a student with a brilliant potential but a penchant for turning in his assignments late,' she felt. Albright consistently pressured the Albanians to drop their demand for a quick independence referendum and Italian Foreign Minister Dini, always a bitter opponent of the KLA and Albanian national aspirations in general, tried to force the Albanians to give up the objective of independence altogether. Thaci's clarity and resolve under these pressures left him isolated in the delegation and it was only the firm backing of Adem Demaci for what Albright and Hill regarded as an intransigent position that prevented a debacle for the Albanians. Thaci knew that the Albanians would eventually have to sign, but time was on their side. It was widely rumoured in Tirana that the Pentagon and NATO had set war activation plans in motion as early as 19 January, and Haliti would probably have known this and told Thaci about it, but there is no evidence that it was conveyed to the KLA General Staff. From the Albanian point of view the longer the war machine was in motion, the more difficult it would be for NATO to wind it down and stop it. There were also genuine problems for Thaci in getting the agreement of the key KLA commanders for the deal. The role of Demaci was critical. It was a tribute to the power of the *plak*, the oldest man, in Kosova Albanian culture in conferring political sanction on the actions of the younger man. Thaci was fortunate to have Demaci available to speak to Albright at this time, and so was Kosova. In another little noticed public debut that was to be a sign of the times, Demaci's assistant, the student leader Albin Kurti, held a press conference in Prishtina on 2 February on the situation in the aftermath of the Racak massacre, which set out firm and principled positions on the kidnapping of over 700 Albanians by the Serbian forces in the conflict to date and called on the entire Kosova population to join and support the KLA and become completely identified with it.[23]

The key priority on the Albanian side was to draw NATO clearly and openly into the conflict. The KLA leaders (with the possible exception of Haliti in Tirana) probably knew little or nothing at this stage about the actual details of the degree of USAF and RAF advance planning, particularly the build-up at Aviano air base in Italy. American intelligence reports indicated that the Prishtina Corps of the army was already moving substantial forces from the Corps HQ in Nis down towards Kosova, and an all-out assault on the KLA was clearly planned. It is not clear how far Thaci or any of the other KLA leaders was aware of the extent of this but it is probable they had some knowledge, simply because it had been going on for such a long period. The first plan which was known as 'Operation Nimble Lion' was conceived as long ago as June 1998; this would have sent about 250 NATO aircraft to bomb targets throughout Yugoslavia.[24] This plan was an exclusively USAF document developed within 32nd Air Operations group at Ramstein base in Germany. A separate plan, called Concept of

Operations Plan (CONOPLAN) 10601, was written by NATO. Although the second plan was based on the first, in Lambeth's view, 'the thrust of each was different. Nimble Lion would have hit the Serbs hard at the beginning' but Plan 10601 called for 'a gradual, incremental, and phased approach. The latter ultimately became the base for Operation Allied Force.'[25] It was conceived in its final form as a plan without the projected use of ground forces, partly for practical logistical reasons but much more because of the reluctance of the Clinton administration to authorise use of such forces. Clinton felt that neither Congress nor the European partners in NATO would accept this as a military option.[26] However unpalatable to the Albanians, this was a realistic evaluation of the situation, as the difficulties in getting effective and rapid action in the later bombing campaign showed.

At this stage there was no intention to carry on the offensive to overthrow Milosevic, despite the views on this of SACEUR Wesley Clark and many others, mostly in the United States.[27] It was, as Lambeth has pointed out, 'a coercive operation only, with the implied goal of inflicting merely enough pain to persuade Milosevic to capitulate.'[28] Clark had called for immediate air strikes against Milosevic as soon as he had heard about the Racak massacre, but his views were overruled within the upper echelons of NATO, which gave the Serbian leader time to prepare for the air campaign and removed any element of surprise for NATO.[29] If surprise is the key element in successful warfare, NATO had lost it by February 1999. Clark knew that Milosevic would attempt to operate with the maximum tactical flexibility until the last possible moment and that it was important for NATO to move quickly to close down as many options for him as quickly as possible in order to get the situation under control. At the time this merely seemed to be part of Milosevic's personal *modus operandi*, but in fact it had been at the heart of the Yugoslav Communists' survival strategy for two generations. As the CIA observed as long ago as 1979, 'The LCY's main strength over the years has been its tactical flexibility.'[30] The divisions between the US and the UK, on one hand, and nations such as Spain and Germany within NATO at this time had the practical effect of keeping many tactics open for Milosevic, giving him, in the colloquial phrase, 'wriggle room'.

The world of NATO planning meant little to the average KLA soldier on the ground. The spring was coming and conditions of life were improving somewhat, particularly with better food supplies if they were based near the Prizren or Gjilan supply routes. The main bakery in Prishtina was baking mostly for the KLA and supplies were driven out of the town at night northwards towards KLA-held areas. It was an indicator of how a creeping KLA presence was developing in parts of the capital for the first time. LKCK members like the Humolli family were important in this process. Coming from Llap and the flourishing KLA units there, they had a confidence in the ability of the Albanians to fight on that was based on a real military achievement in the north-east and a strong political distrust of what NATO might eventually bring in it wake. To the LKCK, NATO was an imperialist organisation and the KLA was still an agent for a social revolution in a way not seen in many other Kosova political orbits. The Enverist heritage in the organisation was still alive in the LKCK, perhaps more than in the LPK by this stage of the war, and the simplicities of the war for its mostly young cadres were a means of overcoming the political ambiguities in that heritage in terms of internal Kosova politics. The accelerating rate of shootings and grenade attacks in Prishtina and in other towns was bringing a spring security crisis nearer. This fact among others was noted by the International Crisis Group in a bulletin issued from Brussels on 22 January, which had clearly been in preparation for some time but had been rewritten in some haste after Racak. It noted the unpalatable options now facing the international community after the massacre and observed that

despite the hard learned lessons of the past decade, US and European policymakers are repeating in Kosovo many of the same mistakes that they made before during and after the wars in Croatia and Bosnia ... the US only intervened in a serious way in Bosnia when faced with the even less pleasant prospect of having to send troops to evacuate UN peacekeepers in an election year. After neglecting the Kosovo issue for nearly a decade, US and European policymakers only began considering it when large numbers of dead Albanians began appearing on their television screens.[31]

Nevertheless, the campaign for military intervention always had the key drawback and weakness that none of the NATO nations had a vital national interest at stake in Kosova, at least on the surface. The long-term thinking of the Pentagon involving the role of the US Navy in dominating the Adriatic coast as a means of power projection towards Turkey and the Middle East was not generally in the public domain at this stage, outside very specialised strategic planning circles. It is ironic that some of the nations most opposed to outside intervention were those like Greece, which would be mostly directly affected by the spread of war across the region. NATO had always been concerned about the stability of the FYROM/Republic of Macedonia ever since the independence referendum there in 1991; with its large Albanian minority in the west it was the prime candidate for destabilisation. The doubts of various figures in the Clinton administration about war had been well aired in the media and many in Kosova, on both sides of the ethnic divide, found it hard to believe it would ever take place. There was still an opinion constituency among orthodox military analysts and commentators that instinctively sought to downplay the degree of Albanian opposition to any prospect of long-term Serbian rule in Kosova and often made a simultaneous over-estimation of the capacity of the VJ and MUP.[32]

It was nevertheless clear to most KLA soldiers and definitely to the General Staff that there was a real prospect of NATO intervention. News was beginning to leak into parts of the Italian press about new deployments of NATO air assets at the massive high-technology Aviano air force base north of Venice and elsewhere in Italy. By mid-February the KLA could be more or less certain that NATO would join the fray within a few weeks. The impact of Racak in the propaganda war, however, posed a dilemma for the KLA General Staff. The Albanians, through Racak, had resumed their cherished position of victims in Balkan conflicts, which indeed they usually were in history. The Racak images had played a large part in the international change of policy. It was important that the KLA should not now appear on television screens as an aggressive and highly motivated people's army, still less in a context where they could add substance to Serbian allegations of terrorism. The spread of the violence into central Prishtina would undoubtedly have run this risk and anecdotal evidence suggests that the American secret soldiers with Remi played a part in discouraging this.

There was much to be said from the KLA's viewpoint for an extension of the KVM mission to calm the conflict down while the talks were taking place. The internationals had varying degrees of influence in different localities. American military aides had been operating with Commander Remi in Llap since June 1998, first largely in secret and then openly through KDOM and finally the KVM.[33] The Llap KLA organisation was poised to begin much more serious military action in the towns, particularly Prishtina itself, but this would inevitably raise the perennial question of whether it was a terrorist organisation. The arrival of reasonable quantities of land mines and hand grenades gave the KLA the capacity to create urban mayhem but there was no doubt Serbian reprisals would follow and the outcome of such encounters would be at best unpredictable. The question became more acute for the KLA in Prishtina after a Serbian bomb attack on a restaurant on 1 February that killed two Albanian youths in revenge for KLA activity in northern Prishtina.[34]

Diplomatic activity increased that week with meetings between Robin Cook, the LDK and KLA leaders, in preparation for the Rambouillet conference that was planned. On the Albanian side the LDK in the form of Fehmi Agani promised he could deliver the KLA to attend the talks but his view was quickly countered by the KLA Political Spokesman Adem Demaci, who said that in his view the KLA should not attend, as the preconditions for talks had not been met. Indications of this were the continued killing of Albanian civilians, such as the machine gunning of a family on a tractor near Peje a few days before, the defiance of the Holbrooke-Milosevic agreements on heavy armour withdrawal, and many other matters. On 8 February the atmosphere worsened with news in Prishtina that the VJ had shelled several villages near Decani and Gjakova, and others in the KLA-held area around Podujeve. There is no doubt that there were serious splits in the KLA at this point, and the General Staff faced many difficulties. The Hill-Holbrooke mission was still in a kind of formal existence, but it was only necessary to read the international press to see that in practice all main policy decisions were being taken by Secretary of State Madeleine Albright and SACEUR Wesley Clark, who both favoured military action. At this stage nobody knew what form this action might take, and memories of the failed NATO 'fly over' in June 1998 were still fresh. Some in the KLA secondary hierarchy, like Shaban Shala, feared that any talks would be protracted and could make it difficult to continue prosecuting the war.[35] There was an important strand of opinion represented by Remi in the north-east that NATO would not in the final analysis take action.

In the end diplomatic events had a momentum of their own and the following day the composition of the three Albanian negotiating groups was announced. The KLA team was in essence a transplant of the LPK-origin and Drenica-based General Staff, and included Azem Syla, Hashim Thaci, Rame Buja, Jakup Krasniqi and Xhavit Haliti. It

was a final irony that after the many years' struggle to build and mobilise the KLA, its final fate and that of Kosova might be decided by the
same group of then totally unknown and mostly young men who had
set it in motion from a LPRK and LPK background in obscurity in
Switzerland a few years before.

In practice the influence of the KLA was wider in the talks than this
group would indicate. The LBD coalition group of the intellectual
leader and author Rexhep Qosja also included figures such as Hydajet Hyseni and Bajram Kosumi who had been imprisoned for a long
period after the 1981 student demonstrations and had been LPRK or
LPK members. Hyseni was actually a founder member of the LPRK in
1983. It is unlikely that the international diplomats like British operative David Slinn could have known this, or they might not have given
them such an influential role in the delegation. Perhaps Slinn was seeing Hyseni in his preferred later identity as a LDK 'dissident' who had
broken with Rugova at the famously acrimonious LDK gathering at
the Restaurant Dora in Prishtina in 1996.

There were in practice three tiers of authority within the Albanian
military scene. The first and most important was that of the KLA field
commanders who had often only a formal and uncertain relationship
with their KLA Operative Zone commanders, then there was the General Staff in Drenica, and finally the negotiating team. There were also
some influences coming from the government in Tirana and others
from powerful Diaspora nations such as Switzerland, Germany and the
USA. Given the fissiparous nature of the Kosova Albanian political
world, this was not likely to be a mechanism for making quick or efficient decisions, and much international community thought was
focused on this problem. The American Diaspora, in particular, comprised over 350,000 people and included many wealthy families who
after initial suspicion of the KLA, in many quarters, as a 'Communist'
type army were now moving in with substantial financial support.[36]
The political background of most of them was Balli Kombetar or
Zogist and the war opened for them a revival of perspectives on an ethnic Albania and national reunification, and in their hearts many Alba-
nian-Americans did not want the war to stop at the borders of
Kosova.[37] This may explain the prioritisation the Pentagon gave to
relations with the Llap KLA as a good unit on the border with Serbia,
with the potential capacity to cause trouble within Serbia itself at some
point. However, as the Rambouillet conference turned out, the Serbian

side was where the most difficulties in coming to a signed deal would be found. In a symbol of the problems to come, very heavy snow started to fall over almost all of Serbia and Kosova on the night of Sunday 7 February, just as the talks opened at Rambouillet château outside Paris the following morning.

The Rambouillet conference was opened by the French President, Jacques Chirac, and called for a peaceful solution to the conflict. On the ground in Kosova, events were inauspicious, with the Serbian airport authorities refusing to allow most of the Albanian delegation apart from Rugova and his staff access to the French aircraft that had arrived to bring them to the talks.[38] Only intense pressure from the OSCE on the Serbs allowed Syla, Buja and Krasniqi to board. Adem Demaci, as the KLA political representative and member of the delegation, accused the Serbs of undermining the peace talks before they had started. It was a violent day in Prishtina with three Albanians dead from a bomb blast when a hand grenade was thrown into a shop and a retaliation attack dynamited a Serb shop later in the day. VJ artillery shelled Racak village and Shtime and the KLA said this was also trying to destabilise the talks. Progress in the talks was limited, with both sides playing to the world media gallery, the KLA to emphasise it would not accept the territorial integrity of the FRY or disarmament, and the Serbian delegation emphasising that border change was not on the agenda, foreign troops were not going to be allowed to enter Yugoslav territory, and Serbian sovereignty would be maintained. After a very difficult first week, the LKCK issued a statement calling for the KLA section of the delegation to walk out, an indication of the difficulty Thaci and the delegation would have in selling a deal to the KLA rank and file.

The conference deadline was extended on 17 February after Madeleine Albright blamed the Serbs for most of the delays and unresolved issues. But with the two sides still far apart and the Contact Group document containing many proposals that one side or the other would find unacceptable, a final agreement was slipping further and further into the infinite distance. The NATO military clock was ticking satisfactorily fast for the Albanians. Hashim Thaci had consolidated his position within the delegation, and Ibrahim Rugova seemed uneasy but accepted his position as Thaci's deputy. It was an extraordinary reversal of fortune for these two men, who so recently had been radical opponents in the world of Prishtina politics in the early 1990s when Thaci was a student leader in the university and secret member of LPRK and Rugova was virtually a monopolist of Albanian international political credibility.[39] Two days later the British and French foreign ministers, Robin Cook and Hubert Védrine, agreed that the talks had made some headway, but time was running out. In Kosova there were many quiet days that week, with no incidents at all reported on 17 February. Both sides were nevertheless active, with the Serbs bringing in new heavy armour to reinforce positions near the Serbian border north of Podujeve, and 'numerous' movements of the VJ and MUP being reported to KVM verifiers.

February wore into March with the talks almost at a standstill, and increasingly the focus moved to NATO issues. The British, Canadian and some other Belgrade embassies had already started evacuating some staff and closing visa sections in anticipation of the forthcoming bombing campaign. The Belgrade press speculated on the position of the VJ if war broke out, the air force in particular. The VJ generals would face problems of national mobilisation, when it was clear that significant sections of opinion were keen to avoid yet another conflict with NATO. Many reservists might not respond to mobilisation directives, and the VJ would have to move with only its currently active soldiers. The air force had 16 MiG-29 fighter planes, which were fairly up to date and effective, and also some elderly MiG-21's, which would be easily overcome in a conflict. The anti-aircraft missile defence system was based on the Russian stationary SA-3 Neva and mobile SA-6 Kub systems. The latter had a good performance record in the Bosnian war, and in Belgrade analysts' opinion might cause NATO problems for a time.

It was clear to all observers that the VJ could not defend its assets in a prolonged heavy air assault from NATO and according to an editorial in *Nin* magazine, that would be inevitable and final. In fact the exact opposite was to occur. The VJ general commanding the 3rd Army in Prishtina, General Nebojsa Pavkovic, seemed to have little doubt what was coming on 3 March, when he issued a statement to all the Prishtina Corps troops calling on the army to 'fight like heroes' in the coming conflict, and 'if need be, go bravely to war'. In fact the ground war was continuing much as usual with fierce fighting between the KLA and MUP around the village of Bukosaj near Vushtrri, with several Serbian deaths, both villagers and police, and a KVM protest against a MUP attack on a verifiers orange-pained vehicle. The following day the Rambouillet talks were officially adjourned with resumption fixed for 15 March. Thaci and the rest of the delegation returned home to face their own people, as did the Serbs. The pressure on the delegation was lifted the following day with a carefully orchestrated statement from the KLA General Staff calling on the Albanian people to consider the proposed document about an interim three year autonomy period before an independence referendum 'in a spirit of tolerance and unity'. The post of prime minister of an interim government was to come from within the KLA ranks. This meant that the political option proposed the previous week by KLA spokesman Adem Demaci had been abandoned. Demaci was opposed to the creation of an interim Kosova government, and felt it was time for the Albanians to withdraw from Rambouillet. In turn Rugova proposed its acceptance, with the reappearance of familiar Kosova Albanian political divisions within the delegation. Fehmi Agani stated that the delegation had agreed to accept FRY sovereignty during the interim period, something that was bound to make the deal hard to sell to the KLA commanders on the ground, as duly proved to be the case.[40]

The international response to this problem was the arrival in Prishtina on 6 March of US Ambassador Chris Hill and the EU Special Envoy, the Austrian Wolfgang Petritsch, to meet the Albanians, Demaci and some dissident KLA commanders in particular. Speaking in Vienna over the weekend, Petritsch emphasised that the threat of air strikes was real and implied that the KLA should trust the EU not to go against US and NATO initiatives to get the air campaign moving. In Belgrade, Milosevic had again ruled out a foreign troop presence in Kosova in talks with the Norwegian OSCE head Kurt Volleback, while in Prishtina it was announced that Hashim Thaci would appoint the Kosovo Provisional Government. This was a KLA General Staff decision taken at the American's behest, with a sweetening of the pill for the more militant commanders in the shape of Suleyman Selimi's appointment as KLA commander-in-chief. In an ironic addition, in view of later events, Krasniqi complemented the delegation, saying none of them 'was ever prepared to sign an agreement envisaging the disarmament and dismemberment of the KLA'.[41] Yet this was exactly what was to take place with the agreement of Thaci's Provisional Government only six months or so later, in radically different circumstances.

Many KLA soldiers found the situation confusing. Rumours were beginning to circulate in the north-east and then all over Kosova about major new Serbian troop deployments near the border in the Merdare crossing corridor. Most Serbs found the situation simpler to understand, with Glas Javnosti declaring in a headline that day, 'Serbs are getting ready for war with the Western Powers'.[42] People had started to lay in extra stocks of food; a population with what seemed endless experience of war and economic sanctions in the past ten years did not wait for the government to instruct them in what to do to survive. The Serbian government, as always thinking in traditional terms on this subject, widened the border exclusion zone with Albania to ten kilometres in the expectation that the crisis was being used by radicals to unify Albania with Kosova. The following day, 5 March, the tempo of violence within Kosova increased dramatically, with fighting breaking out in numerous different locations. According to the KVM verifiers, the number of VJ troops within Kosova was now over five times the limit set by the Milosevic-Holbrooke October deal, with 15 VJ units in the field rather than the permitted three.[43] Most KLA soldiers, at whatever level, were trying to think ahead to what a bombing campaign by NATO would mean in their locality. It would clearly mean the end of the KVM mission or any other international restraint on the VJ and MUP and fighting would intensify considerably. Reprisals against the remaining Albanian civilian population would be certain. The usual contests for control of the roads would continue and be even more crucial. The KLA could hope that the equipment shortages, low morale of soldiers and spare parts problems would hinder or even cripple the VJ and MUP, but there was no doubt that the old and flagging army still had considerable material resources it could put into theatre against them.

Conceptualising the development of the war in advance had always been a KLA weakness, and to some extent this continued, with many feeling that the overwhelming power of NATO would soon prevail and they would be spared the worst scenarios. There was no knowledge or expertise at all in the KLA leadership about the limits of bombing and air power, and the average soldier saw it as something that would quickly ensure a KLA victory, as if by magic. In reality a debate was already taking place within the international military community that would have disturbed the KLA if they had been aware of it. The initial plans by Clark to use graphite air weapons to attack the Serbian electricity supply were ruled out on humanitarian grounds, and there was a steady reduction in non-strategic target planning in these weeks.[44]

Intelligent diplomacy with the international community was the priority of the General Staff, and on 11 March the KLA team agreed the terms for signature of the Rambouillet deal. Realists, they had rejected Demaci's principled rejection as absolutist and utopian and saw that a signature was necessary in order to tie their fate completely to NATO. The one essential provision was that there would be an independence referendum within three years.[45] The State Department spokesman James Rubin called the development 'significant', but remained somewhat sceptical about it leading to a final deal.[46] Holbrooke was meeting Milosevic the same day but the meeting produced nothing new; Holbrooke emerged after eight hours saying that the Serbian leader 'had not altered his position'.[47] In Prishtina, Pavkovic reiterated his view that there were 'eight to ten thousand terrorists in Kosova', who would be dealt with whatever NATO did. Opinion polls indicated that most Serbs, almost 70 per cent, thought that the VJ would face NATO in a new conflict, and only 12 per cent thought they would not.[48] Thaci had left Paris and returned to Kosova for four days to meet Haradinaj and other key KLA commanders in Glogjan village, where he was able to get their agreement to signing the document.[49]

The remaining days between the Albanian's signature of the agreement on 11 March and the start of the bombing campaign on 26 March had much of the character of other phoney wars, with daily life in progress, laying in of ammunition, digging of trenches and other routine preparations. But as in earlier stages of the war, the KLA still did not have the capacity to mine or booby trap the northern access VJ supply routes into Serbia along the main roads, something that could have transformed and shortened the conflict. The American and British special forces assistance to the new army had many limitations and this was one which was to have important long-term consequences. Effective action to blockade Serbian military supplies and destroy local infrastructure could have quickly crippled the VJ and MUP in Kosova after 26 March and the onset of bombing and saved many lives, both Albanian and Serbian. Yet the political imperatives coming to commanders from London and Washington were in general angled towards doing nothing more than keeping an eye on the KLA and preventing it from becoming too dominant in its localities, with a view to the postwar settlement.[50] In her account of the Rambouillet negotiations, Madeleine Albright recalls a conversation with Milan Milutinovic, the President of Serbia, in which she notes:

I began by sitting down in Paris with Milan Milutinovic, the president of Serbia. Milutinovic had slicked-back silver hair, a beautifully tailored suit and polished English. I told him the political settlement we put forward would be good for his country. It would disarm the KLA, maintain Kosova within Yugoslavia, and allow the army to continue patrolling the border. The presence of the NATO-led peacekeeping force would help, not hurt, by safeguarding the human rights of Kosovo's ethnic Serb minority.[51]

These terms were rejected by the Serbs but in practice, after the bombing campaign, they once again became the core of American policy, and it was a long nine year struggle to independence in 2008. The Kosova Albanian majority had to overcome the heavy burden of Yugoslavist thinking and assumptions even in Washington. In the meantime the KLA had to survive and fight in the most difficult circumstances it had yet faced after 26 March 1999, and in an unclear and unstable partnership with NATO where different NATO member states had very different views of the relationship.[52]

10

ALLIANCE WITH NATO AND DEMOBILISATION OF THE KLA

It is American involvement in Europe, through NATO and the Marshall Plan, that has, paradoxically, provided Western Europe with such capacity as it currently possesses to act as a unified political entity.

Philip Bobbitt[1]

Throughout twentieth century history, superpowers like the United States and Russia suffered continual difficulties with local client states becoming the determining agents in regional conflicts and manipulating superpower policy in particular directions. Examples are found in the Middle East with Israel filling that role for the US and Syria for Russia. The superpowers have in practice little real capacity to control what happened in many detailed political decisions by regional actors, and the tail in many cases soon begins to wag the dog. Perhaps the best example on the Russian side is Syria's invasion of Lebanon in 1976; the Soviet leaders subsequently demonstrated (after the end of the Cold War) that they had not been informed about the Syrians plans. Whether the latter was true is obviously a moot point, but it is clear that they could not control what their client state was doing at the time.

By the autumn of 1998 NATO was being drawn into the regional crisis in the southern Balkans on the Albanian side, and Russia remained the ultimate protector of Serbia. A familiar pattern was being established: a NATO commander said at the time that the Alliance had no intention of becoming the 'KLA's air force', but in reality it did so. The irony of the conflict was that airpower mattered much less in the outcome than most thought it would at the time. Helicopters as the traditional airborne adversaries of the guerrilla fighter made little difference to the VJ campaign, while the NATO bombing campaign can be said to have shown the limits of bombing as a strategic concept as much as its success. Some of the NATO equipment deployed in the campaign, such as the Apache helicopters in Macedonia, was barely up to an operational standard of airworthiness, and the crews had not been trained to fly in mountainous terrain. During the last weeks before the beginning of the air campaign on 26 March, the situation of the civilian populations in both Kosova and Serbia was rapidly deteriorating. All resources in commodities like fuel were being overtaken by the demands of the military and so food production and distribution began to be affected. The spring was often a time of flour shortages in Kosova and they were serious in 1999. This would impact most heavily upon the civilian population living in large towns like Ferizaj and Prishtina who lived mostly in apartment blocks and did not have direct access to stored supplies that the villages had in areas away from the worst of the conflict.

The air campaign would also inevitably involve the towns much more deeply in the war than hitherto. The massive main VJ army base for Kosova was within the Prishtina city boundaries on the western outskirts, and even if the NATO bombs were absolutely accurate they could well start fires that would spread into Prishtina. The MUP headquarters for Kosova was exactly in the city centre, as were the headquarters building of the Socialist Party of Serbia and the Radical Party and above all the VJ military apparatus command building. Most communications, civilian and military, depended on technical facilities in the large Post Office block about half a mile away from the VJ HQ. Most Prishtina citizens thought that these would be hit as a matter of course within a few hours of the beginning of the bombing campaign, which even the most pessimistic believed would only last a week or two before Milosevic capitulated and negotiated a VJ withdrawal. This did not take place, apart from bombing of the VJ bases. In reality, as authors and students of the air war from Ben Lambeth to Ivo Daalder, Michael O'Hanlon and John Labercombe have shown, the targeting limitations placed on the NATO air forces meant that major strategic targets such as those that could quickly have crippled the Milosevic war machine were not touched until late in the air campaign, so that, for instance, the Prishtina Post office communications complex was eventually hit by a cruise missile only as late as 24 May,[2] almost two months after the air war started. Tony Blair observed in his memoirs, 'Basically Kosovo demonstrates the fundamental, unavoidable and irredeemable limitation of a pure air campaign against a determined opponent who cares little about losing life.'[3] In the light of studies of the air war by professionals, it would be more accurate to conclude that a determined regime can hold out against bombing for long periods if the targeting is not focused properly on major strategic targets.

The official US Army study of the Kosovo conflict is entitled *Disjointed War—Military Operations in Kosovo, 1999*, a highly appropriate title in view of the course of events.[4] The campaign was in the view of the authors a 'war of constraints', where the enormous technical capabilities of NATO were never properly used until much later than they could have been, by which time tens of thousands of civilians had been killed, 'disappeared', injured or displaced and the VJ and MUP had run amok in fulfilling the objectives of 'Operation Horseshoe' and much older Serbian nationalist ambitions to drive the Albanians out of Kosova.[5] As Bacevich and Cohen observe in their study, with perhaps unintentional irony:

Many in the NATO leadership and member governments remained hopeful that a show of force would compel the Serbian government to yield. There was that abiding belief ... that the campaign will last two nights and after that two nights, Mr Milosevic would be compelled to come to the table, said one senior US General.[6]

This was clearly wishful thinking, and many senior commanders in the US realised how fragile the consensus was within the alliance for any military action in support of the Kosova Albanians. The split across the Atlantic was the basic division in NATO, with most Americans believing that Kosova was the final act in the disintegration of Yugoslavia and that the war should as far as possible lead to the rapid fall of the Milosevic regime, even if that meant a temporary Allied occupation of Serbia, while others wished to see a Yugoslavia survive in which the displacement of Milosevic was not an immediate priority. The US Army had no wish to use ground troops in the conflict at all, and there were profound differences between Wesley Clark as SACEUR and US Army General Mike Short who was in charge of the US army contingent. Indeed, as the RAND study authors point out, the Clinton administration was reluctant to use US troops in any post-conflict peace keeping operation at all, and many of the army generals and swathes of the Pentagon bureaucracy took their lead from the administration on this issue.[7] Many senior British officers strongly disliked Clark and what he represented, some because of simple and essentially minor personality issues, as with Jackson. There were in addition a small minority of dogmatic pro-Serb 'traditionalists' and more common non-interventionists. The numerous basically pro-Serb officials in the UK Ministry of Defence used the 'special relationship' to quietly try to brief against Clark in Washington and undermine him. The always strong pro-Israel lobby in the US Administration and on Capitol Hill were mostly still wedded to the old Yugoslavia and did not wish to see the overthrow of Milosevic, particularly the sections linked to the Likud party in Tel Aviv.[8] In Europe and some sections of the State Department, there was pressure to keep Ibrahim Rugova going as a possible future leader, and dealings with him were deputed to NATO Secretary General Javier Solana. They met regularly once the bombing campaign started, with a key meeting on 18 May where the future political structure of a United Nations administration was discussed, and Rugova gave an undertaking to postpone the independence issue.[9]

In retrospect it is possible to see these and similar forces as likely to encourage Milosevic to hold out for as long as possible if Serbia could endure the air campaign, gambling on NATO allies' lack of will to countenance the ground option. Although Serbian intelligence was not what it had been, it was nevertheless quite efficient in the United States and major European capitals, particularly Brussels, and Milosevic knew there were important opinion-constituencies with little enthusiasm for the war and less for Kosova independence. As the RAND authors observe, 'whatever the political merits of resisting any ground operation planning, it did have serious military consequences.'[10] They were particularly serious for the KLA who for the previous five months had enjoyed a relatively protected position under the terms of the KVM. The KLA leaders, even the most educated and best informed like Xhavit Haliti and Hashim Thaci, had little sense of how they were to be subjected within a short time to standard British and other counterinsurgency techniques that were also based on the political perspective that Kosova was not going to become independent (otherwise KLA demobilisation would not have been enforced: if Kosova was to become independent, the KLA would have quickly become the nucleus of a future national army).

Within hours of the first bombs falling on Yugoslavia, the VJ moved heavy armour that had been stored in bases in Novi Sad, in the Sandjak and at Vranje in the Preshevo Valley into Kosova. The early Tomahawk cruise missile attacks against Yugoslav air defences had little or no effect in Kosova. Of the fifty-one targets in the original strike plan, few were in or even near Kosovo, and some, such as those on Sombor air base on the Hungarian border, were almost as far away from Kosova in Serbia as it is possible to be.[11] During the first night most of the Yugoslav MiG-29s took off but soon took losses and never again mounted significant opposition to the NATO forces. Land attack missiles were fired from the UK submarine *Splendid* in the Adriatic. This and other activity certainly indicated Allied seriousness but had little or no effect against the widely dispersed VJ units on the ground, where battalions had been split down into company-sized units with only a few armoured vehicles each. Deception, in the form of mock-up vehicles made of cardboard and wood, was extensively used throughout the air campaign, drawing on old Yugoslav doctrinal traditions.[12]

In these conditions a perfect opportunity was provided for the MUP and VJ to move against remaining civilian communities and intensify the ethnic cleansing processes. In general the VJ took the lead in the countryside, while MUP activity was focused on the towns. The former took the expected form of artillery assaults on areas where the KLA was believed to be, but already the KLA insurgents had also sensibly split their resources down into small units and were also increasingly using towns like Vushtrri, Ferizaj and Mitrovica to fade away into invisibility, sometimes shedding uniforms and lying low and awaiting developments in the bombing campaign. But the Sword of Damocles hung over Prishtina. The Communist showpiece capital with its docile petit-bourgeoisie and many former collaborators with the Titoist dictatorship (and even the Milosevic regime) had seen many vicissitudes over the years since 1990 but had always managed to avoid the most unpleasant consequences of collaboration with the Yugoslavist Communist project. Now every building was shaken by huge explosions as the VJ base on the urban fringe was bombed, and hundreds of cardboard decoy vehicles caught fire sending a pillar of smoke into the sky to rival those from the Kosovo Polje power station chimneys. Vil-

lages near the city in hitherto peaceful areas to the east of Prishtina like
Mramuer e Busi were shelled and the inhabitants driven out.[13] MUP
police filled the streets, searching for known militants, and many families took refuge in their cellars. The radical student leader and close
collaborator of Demaci Albin Kurti was an early target for arrest, and
was eventually detained on 27 April.[14]

Balkan history has many ironies but few rival those experienced in
the NATO bombing campaign. Prishtina had not only avoided the
atrocities of the villages but almost any serious consequences of the
war at all. That situation was about to change, yet it did so slowly. The
decisions taken by NATO in the bombing campaign were also in part
decided expressly on the basis of protecting Kosova towns, so that they
could be used as centres of governance in a post-conflict 'peacekeeping' period, reflecting the Communist problematic of the 'radical' Kosova countryside against the 'responsible' town. A similar archaism
pervaded the British forces operations in 'taking' Prishtina from the
Provisional Government Hashim Thaci had declared in April 1999,
because in reality the KLA had never really controlled the city in any
meaningful sense at any stage of the conflict. KFOR's excessive focus
on Prishtina meant there were few or no troops to establish order in
the countryside and protect remaining Serbs from Albanian reprisals
and attacks on their monuments.[15] In many ways the UNMIK mission
after 1999 was not only ineffective and suffocated by practical contradictions, as Whit Mason and Ian Oliver have shown so clearly, it was
also the last Titoist project in the Balkans, and many of its roots lie in
the obsolete and Yugo-nostalgic political assumptions in the international community in the late wartime period.[16]

The fate of the KLA during the air campaign was inextricably linked
to that of the remaining civilian population. As soon as the air campaign started, the VJ prioritised ethnic cleansing of major urban centres outside Prishtina. In the main these were towns that commanded
important road junctions. At a centre like Suva Reka in the south-west,
with three main roads junctions nearby, the VJ had moved in as soon
as the KVM mission had evacuated on 22 March. As Julia Kristeva has
pointed out, 'crossroads' dominate the Balkans from the centre, places
of 'monstrous intimacy'. Such places are dangerous to totalitarian rulers as enabling popular intercourse and mobility and need to be
destroyed as a priority.[17] Shootings began by the roadside crossroads
and people started fleeing the town. This was the precursor of the mass

expulsion of nearly all the Albanian 90 per cent of the town's population on 24 March. As the OSCE report put it, 'the main offensive involved the killing of a large number of civilians, which lasted for just a few days.'[18] The perpetrators were a mixture of VJ, MUP police, Serbian reservists from Nis, and local Serbian civilians, some wearing balaclava helmets and with Arkan's 'Tiger' patches on their arms, and armed with Kalashnikovs, hand grenades, knives and pistols. The local population fled in panic, with different Serbian militias, soldiers and police firing on them from different directions and many were killed in the ensuing mayhem. The local KLA unit attempted to hold on to one quarter of the town but withdrew on 25 March when faced with overwhelming odds. In nearby villages most people had already fled to the forests after being advised of the imminent ethnic cleansing by the KLA. Some left and went to Albania, a wise decision in view of the cold weather and poor food supply that would take the lives of many children and old people in the next weeks of fugitive life. Many of the objectives of 'Operation Horseshoe' were already beginning to be attained, and the bombing campaign with its ineffectual operations suited the Serbs very well. As Vladimir Stambuk, Milosevic's Vice President of Yugoslavia, had observed: 'a small scale bombing would be a great pretext and alibi for us to continue with the persecution of the Albanians and the Serb opposition as well because in times of war nobody can ask anything …' [19]

The ethnic cleansing process was accompanied by widespread extortion, beatings and individual killings. Multiple rapes, sexual violence and the use of women for forced labour were also noted by investigators in the post-war period.[20] In the main, the Serbian forces attempted to move people in blocks of ten to twenty thousand people at a time from their habitations onto the main roads in the direction of Albania and Macedonia, and some to Montenegro also.[21] Small KLA units were often powerless to act in this process, and their only hope was to retreat into the forests themselves, in a repeat of the summer 1998 experience, and wait for better times to regroup. The NATO bombs were a great encouragement to the young soldiers, in many ways the only source of optimism they had. The Free Kosova radio station was still functioning and the vast fire that had engulfed the Prishtina VJ base on 27 March was widely known.

In general the scale of the Serbian assault on the Albanian population left the KLA helpless. A town like Ferizaj was typical of those that the war had hardly touched until then. In the early war period a kind of apartheid had prevailed where during the day the 85 per cent Albanian majority was able to work and open shops and businesses while at night they never left their homes and only Serb bars and clubs were open. The situation deteriorated rapidly after 20 March, with the VJ and MUP making a show of force after the exit of the KVM. Between 21 and 24 March the local Serb and Roma[22] civilians were armed and joined VJ and MUP units in demolishing Albanian shops and businesses in an orgy of violence that left the town terrorised, and on the last day of the month the uniformed Serbs ordered the mass evacuation of the Albanian population to Macedonia. Whole areas of the town were emptied systematically, street by street. Ferizaj was an early example of a prompt NATO air response, as the scale and ferocity of the assault on the population alerted NATO target planners. On 8 April, the nearby 'Milan Zecar' military barracks was bombed, but it had little effect on Serb ground operations and by the end of the month most of Ferizaj was empty.

A generally systematic pattern of activity was adopted by the Serbs which strongly points to the existence of an overall plan, whether it was called 'Operation Horseshoe' or by some other name. This applied particularly to operations against Albanian villages. Heavy armoured vehicles surrounded the houses and would give a warning to leave, often by throwing grenades into a house and killing a number of people at random. In other cases there was shooting into the air, often by armed local Serb civilians working with the soldiers and MUP. After the warning time had expired, the Serbs would attack the village. The movement of the Serb forces usually created panic among the inhabitants, who would flee into nearby fields or woods. Sometimes Serb paramilitaries such as the Radical Party militia of Vojislav Seselj, the 'White Eagles', would stay in a village after the VJ had left and systematically strip the houses of all valuables before burning them down and killing the cattle and sheep. Often a corridor would have been left open, and so the villagers would have to flee in a particular direction, always towards Albania or Macedonia. Elderly people who stayed behind as they were unable to flee or face forest life were killed. The initial force of the Serbian assault reached its height about ten days after the start of the bombing campaign, with large massacres such as those of almost the entire male population of Krushe (Mala Krusa) at Celina near Prizren, along with many children under 14, and a 106-year-old man on 25 March.[23] The population fled towards Albania after being driven out before they had the opportunity to bury their dead. [24]

As news of these and similar events spread in early April, many urban communities of Albanians who had remained in Kosova split up as family units, with the familiar pattern of women leaving with the children and trying to reach safety outside the country and the men heading for the mountains. As many as 100,000 people were on the move in the middle of the month. By the end of April this had led to a large increase in KLA recruiting, as the men had seen appalling events and wished to take revenge on the Serbian assault and fight back. Although refugees were flooding into Albania, this was not accompanied by any significant number of Albanian citizens coming forward to fight for Kosova. Perhaps only ten or fifteen Albanians actually joined the KLA in the entire course of the conflict, as the illuminating memorial volume for the dead Albanian volunteer Indrit Cara indicates. Thus the first month of the air war was something of a Pyrrhic victory for the VJ. The infantry assaults certainly destroyed Albanian residential communities but they did not have the same effect on the KLA. Local KLA commanders faced again many of the same problems of new and untrained recruits as they had faced in the spring of 1998 with the arrival of these new recruits, mostly ex-town dwellers, who wanted guns and uniforms. They were holed up in small units in the forest and waiting for the bombing campaign to force a VJ retreat. They had lived easier lives than the villagers in their shops and offices and were not as attuned to physical hardship. In one respect only was the practical situation better than in 1998, in that now there was a reasonable small arms and Kalashnikov supply, which there had not been the preceding year. By the nature of circumstances, new recruits were often in uniform and in action within days of having joined a unit, often against overwhelming Serbian forces. Few actually overcame the practical difficulties and got productively involved.

It is instructive to look at the KLA casualty statistics for this and earlier periods in areas such as Ferizaj, which until March 1999 had not been deeply involved in the war. The town came under the Operative Zone 9 'Nerodimes' organisational structure of the KLA, which in the course of the war took about 193 fatalities. Of these, no less than 161 were in 1999, most in the March to May period, compared with only 32 in the entire 1997–99 period.[25] Only three of the 193 were from Ferizaj families, despite the town having more than 85 per cent of the population of the Operative Zone. No doubt there were many patriotic people in the town who would have liked to resist the invasion, but by the time they attempted to get involved it was often too late to do so. As elsewhere in the war, the vast majority of KLA soldiers came from the villages and the mass population displacement of the bombing campaign period did not alter this fact. It is certain that the days between 24 and 30 March produced the highest casualty figures for the KLA in the entire conflict. Human feeling often compelled units to make a stand and fight against overwhelming odds and bear the heavy consequences rather than retreat to the relative safety of the forests.

Within the VJ the NATO bombing campaign appeared to solve many longstanding and pressing problems. On 24 March, under wartime legislation, the MUP police had been subordinated to the VJ under General Pavkovic in a unified command, so fulfilling one of Pavkovic's most dearly held ambitions. This produced a force of over 50,000 uniformed men. On the first two days after 24 March, the 15th Armoured Brigade from Prishtina and the 211th Armoured Brigade from Serbia secured the Prishtina-Podujeve road, so 'solving' a long standing problem that had existed for months. The 11th Armoured, and 37th and 125th Motorised Brigades swept into Drenica, and the 125th then went into southern Kosova. [26] The VJ had been operating throughout the conflict, as indeed it had throughout the Croatian and Bosnian conflicts, without any clearly defined or agreed national defence doctrine. For much of that time it was in theory unclear what the nation actually was; Yugoslavia, which was disintegrating, or Serbia. The bombing campaign offered an opportunity for restoring the VJ traditional position in society, as defenders of Serbia, and it had to physically defend itself in Kosova to be successful. There were a number of critical issues to overcome, of which manpower was the most important. It has been estimated that during the 1998–99 period no less than 22,000 conscripts failed to answer the conscription draft for service in Kosova. [27] International sanctions against the country were still inhibiting the import of necessary spare parts and imported military equipment. Money was often short, and most soldiers, non-commissioned officers and officers were paid late. Barracks were in poor physical condition. In these circumstances, which have been compared since the war in Serbia to those of the declining Tsarist Russian army in the First World War, patriotism was a valuable form of ammunition.

The VJ leadership was able to mobilise it quite successfully, in the third phase of the war. NATO intervention between 24 March and 12 June was seen differently at street level in Serbia from the preceding phases of the Kosova conflict, which most Serbs outside Kosova tried to forget or neglect. NATO brought the Kosova war into Serbia itself. The high proportion of bombing targets outside Kosova shocked public opinion, particularly when bombs destroyed basic civic infrastructure such as the Pancevo oil refinery on the Danube, bridges, train stations and civilian factories producing important export goods such as textiles. It was, above all, a sign of the failure of the anti-terrorist campaign. Many intelligent Serbs knew the KLA was small, and hitherto had believed that the expansion of the 400-strong Special Counter-Terrorist Unit (SAJ) to 1,000 men for the Kosova conflict, plus the VJ and MUP, would easily suffice for the counter-insurgency task.[28] To judge from the information reaching the British Embassy from its UDBA intelligence contacts, this was the belief also in key state institutions.[29] There seems to have been little practical cooperation or intelligence sharing between the UDBA and the VJ army intelligence at this stage in the conflict.

In the west, many KLA fighters temporarily retreated into Albania. This was not simply a matter of expediency, as the foreign military trainers in Kruma and elsewhere were encouraging them to do so before proceeding with the reorganisation of the army in cooperation with members of the General Staff. The KLA faced another period of reorientation and renewal, as it had in the KDOM/KVM mission period, and the existence of the neighbouring kindred state was required to achieve this. The arrival of Agim Ceku as commander had improved the KLA's image with the foreign military missions and he had an extended network of contacts dating from his role in the war in Croatia.[30] He took up his post in favourable circumstances. As Ramush Haradinaj has written, the great achievement of the Rambouillet talks process from the Albanian point of view was not the written agreement itself but the sense of unity for the prosecution of the war. The last decisive influence of Rugova had been firmly marginalised by Rambouillet. For Ramush Haradinaj and the other senior zone commanders who had been persuaded to sign the agreement by Thaci and Krasniqi without having read it or being fully aware of its contents, this was very important. The Rambouillet deal involved major concessions on the Albanian side, in fact it was the beginning of Albanian retreat on key political demands that was to continue over the next few years.[31] But it was more important then to have political unity for the NATO war option. As Haradinaj has observed, 'The political unity forged there helped us better prepare for the ensuing Serb offensive': or, more simply, the politics of the Bukoshi-Rugova world in Kosova did not matter any more except as part of a wider national coalition.

In reality his optimism was to be ill-founded and very short lived. The LDK did not join the Provisional Government of Kosova that Thaci founded in the first week in April and the unity of the Rambouillet delegation was broken. The 'Provisional Government' is largely forgotten now, and did not amount to very much after June 1999, but it was a clear and concrete call to all Kosova Albanians to side with the KLA and its allies to determine the future of Kosovo. Hashim Thaci was raising a hammer to drive the first nails into the coffin of Rugova's party. Yet the KLA was an army, not a new administrative force, and its claims to be the only legitimate force rang hollow. Thaci, Haliti and the Drenica inner circle had been badly prepared—they did not have a 'shell' political party waiting after liberation, and as a result, the field in Prishtina was left clear for political rivals after June 1999. In terms of insurgency and revolutionary theory, the paradigm of an urban insurrection in Kosova had finally been totally abandoned, in favour of the construction of an orthodox army, symbolised by the arrival of General Ceku as leader.[32]

Ibrahim Rugova did not venture back to Kosova until several weeks later. As Samantha Power has observed in her biographical study of the work of the United Nations leader Sergio Vieira de Mello, 'One major issue had been left unresolved: After Serb forces departed, who would run Kosovo? Kosovo's ethnic Albanian majority, which had operated its own informal, underground government structures since the province was stripped of its autonomy in 1989, was eager to take over, but the Russians would not allow it.' In the meantime the internationals on the ground tried to grasp the reality. In a symbolic assertion of authority, the 'Bank of Dardania' was closed down by NATO/KFOR. The decision by Rugova set the scene for many of the setbacks the Albanians encountered in the months and years after June 1999 and the entry of NATO ground forces into Kosova. Critics of the British paratroopers in Prishtina have claimed that General Mike Jackson took it upon himself to break up the Thaci/KLA government. In fact, although Jackson initially had a difficult personal relationship with Thaci, it was really Rugova and the LDK, under largely Italian and Vatican tutelage, that achieved this by refusing to take part in a united Albanian front when dealing with the international community.[33] As Power also points out, 'the UN staff had done no advance planning to lead what, by the look of it, would be both the most ambitious political mission in the organisation's history since the Bosnian and Rwandan debacles.'[34]

Ramush Haradinaj himself enhanced his already high reputation as a commander in this period, and laid the foundations for his future political career. Dukagjini KLA forces regrouped and focused on the defence of the Koshare corridor. His local commander Agim Ramadini was a very brave and effective soldier who made an extraordinary contribution to the war here before he was killed, gun in hand. The entire struggle for Koshare has reached a position in the Kosova Albanian popular mind not far short of the Prekaz massacre of the Jashari family in March 1998.[35] Fighting conditions above Koshare were very difficult for the KLA soldiers, on high open windswept moorland without the forest cover of the lower valley. Casualties were very high, logistics were difficult and food supplies were often irregular.

In a strange fashion, the Koshare corridor and the conflict over it that continued for weeks between April and June 1999 confirmed the original Belgrade perception of the war as an Albanian-originated insurgency, which in essence it was not. The threat of a surge of KLA fighters re-entering Kosova from Albania via Koshare confirmed their deepest fears. The little village lies at the head of the steep Batusche valley leading up from the Decani-Gjakova road to the border with Albania, 7 km up a narrow dirt road through beech and fir forest. It was, in Serbian terms, in the heart of bandit country, an open sore that allowed fighters easy access to safety in Albania and the supportive local Tropoja population there with their own warrior traditions. The main road below had been fought over continuously since March 1998, and the border protection zone defences had been destroyed by the KLA in June 1998 and never rebuilt. A small VJ building about a kilometre below the border was manned but it was a lonely and vulnerable post.

It did not take long for the NATO command to conclude that a wider useful role could be developed there for the guerrilla force. There was clearly no prospect of reconciliation between Thaci and the KLA, and Rugova and the LDK, and NATO concluded that as the KLA and what it represented would be the dominant force on the ground after the war, it was necessary to work more closely with it.[36] The bombing campaign in the west and Dukagjini in particular was not going well, with the VJ well dispersed and dug in and largely invisible from the air as the heavy spring leaf cover came to the forests. The VJ and MUP also used urban refuges like empty factories in the middle of Albanian-majority towns like Gjakova that could not be targeted because of the risk of major collateral damage to civilians. There were a few large-scale fixed targets, like the Prishtina VJ base, but they were quickly exhausted as significant targets. The USAF could not yet get agreement within NATO for targeting strategic targets in central Prishtina. The priority was to find a way to draw the VJ out into the open so that it could be bombed. The battle for Koshare fulfilled this need, as on the Albanian side of the border the KLA was consolidated and built up with foreign advice and this meant that the Belgrade VJ command had to face the threat of a possible invasion. Minds were further concentrated by the disastrous bombing error on 29 April when NATO jets bombed a column of Albanian refugees near Decani on horses and carts and killed over fifty people.

Politics were also playing a part elsewhere with KLA development. The 'Atlantic Battalion' of KLA volunteers from the United States was leaving New York in the third week in April with much publicity and many media comparisons with the International Brigade in the Spanish Civil War.[37] The hundred-plus volunteers did not make a significant difference militarily, although many fought very bravely in and around Mount Pashtrik, but the unit had a massive symbolic importance in several dimensions. It was above all a symbol of the unity of the large and wealthy but politically fissiparous Albanian-American community of over three hundred and fifty thousand people behind the war. For the public in Albania, it showed that open support and commitment from citizens of the world's only superpower was coming, when the ineptitude of the Nano government before November 1998 had destroyed what little confidence in the war they may have had.[38] The volunteers were loud, cheerful, colourful, very American and thus an immense morale boost to the local KLA soldiers who were trying to survive in tough circumstances during the bombing campaign. Their arrival recaptured some of the heroic and romantic spirit of the early days of the KLA uprising that had tended to evaporate during the bitter survival struggles of the last year or more. The Americans also brought high-technology modern light weapons and plenty of ammunition with them, a symbol of importance for a guerrilla force that had struggled so long with munitions deficit. Many were very amateur soldiers but in the circumstances of the time that did not matter very much. The Byronic ideal of self-sacrifice in a Balkan cause does not require military competence, only drama and moral and political commitment. That was absent on the Serbian side. There were, by this stage of the war, few Serbian volunteers going south from Serbia to 'defend' Kosova. The 'Tigers' controlled by Arkan and the 'White Eagles' of the Radical Party were less paramilitary militias than small armed gangs, some of only a few men seeking plunder on the coat-tails of the MUP and VJ, a pale shadow of the forces of hundreds of Serbian volunteers involved at various stages in the Croatian and Bosnian wars. As an example, the 'White Eagles'' entire strength in Prizren is thought to have amounted to only about thirty men, although it was sufficient for them to cause bloody havoc in the town after the arson attack on the League of Prizren building in the first days after 26 March. Many Prizren Serbs threw in their lot with them, a terrible decision that led to their ejection from their homes in June 1999 and a life of exile.

By the end of April, the number of KLA soldiers probably amounted to about 18,000 men and women, of all ages, from raw teenagers to men of seventy or more. They were scattered all over Kosova, and perhaps only 3,000 were directly involved in the Dukagjini and Koshare fighting, but there were enough for the situation and they played a sufficiently productive role for the KLA to finally establish itself as part of the victorious coalition with NATO when the Serbs left after the Chernomyrdin agreement in mid-June.[39] Some had played a role in helping NATO in bombing targeting, as Lambeth noted in his RAND study, but always their main role was to force VJ units into the open. The battle for Mount Pashtrik was in a sense lost, but as he writes, 'Ultimately the VJ forces managed to repulse the KLA assault on Mount Pashtrik. To do so, however, they had to come out of hiding and move in organised groups, making themselves potential targets, especially for A-10's, on those infrequent occasions when they were detected and approved for attack by the ABCCC or the CAOC.'[40]

Ultimately, assessment of the strengths and weaknesses of what the KLA did and did not achieve in the west in this period depends on much wider issues of whether it was wise for NATO to have started the air campaign at all without a credible ground intervention threat. US General Mike Short pointed out after the war that 'although NATO was not formally allied with the KLA, the fact that the latter had begun to operate with some success in the end made the Yugoslav army come out and fight and try to blunt the KLA offensive ... and once they moved, or fired their artillery, our strikers learned where they were and could go in for the kill.'[41]

The KLA, in this sense, was all that NATO had, and it provided a final opportunity for the force to validate itself and contribute to the liberation of Kosova. As the climax of the bombing campaign approached there was more and more active cooperation between British Special Forces soldiers operating in the 'Operation Horn' framework and groups of KLA units. Some quite substantial engagements were fought, like that reported in the London *Sunday Telegraph* by Andrew Gilligan, which took place on 12 June just as NATO forces were entering Kosova.[42] Gilligan pointed out that as the bombing campaign had gone on,

SAS-KLA patrols inside Kosovo had become increasingly common towards the end of the war, despite British denials. The British soldiers ... drew on the local knowledge and experience of their KLA companions ... in the final days of the air campaign, according to US sources, another joint KLA-SAS patrol had already achieved a notable success by pinpointing a concentration of more than 400 Serb troops in wooded ground near the Albanian border. Using secure radios the patrol called in American bombers, which attached the Serb positions, causing what one official described as 'mass devastation'—the worst military casualties of the war.

In terms of the lonely conspiratorial meetings of the LPK and Kosova Liberation Army pioneers of the 1980s like the Gervalla brothers and the martyrs of Drenica in 1998 like the Jashari family, it seemed that a dream had been fulfilled. As Daalder and O'Hanlon have written, 'A reasonable degree of KLA/NATO coordination was only sensible ... using intermediaries such as the Albanian military, and possibly working through the CIA rather than direct military channels, the alliance knew what the KLA's general patterns of operation were by the war's end.[43]

The Kosova Albanians' force was fighting shoulder to shoulder with some of the finest and most legendary infantry soldiers in the world, the British SAS, for the liberation of their nation from Yugoslavia. Two legends had met, the supreme military skills of the SAS and the national legends of the Kosova Albanians. Above them in the sky, the might of American air power was fully integrated with their ground war. The USAF had indeed become, in the derogatory phrase, 'the KLA air force', and was happy to do so. Yet as in a preceding generation of Albanian Partisan warfare, the victory gained was soon to have a bitter taste.[44] The issue goes back to the dilemma Alia and others faced in 1990 about the kind of liberation army that would be needed in Kosova. The KLA in its NATO alliance became complicit in a view of the international order of an essentially conservative nature. The KLA drew in its origins on the Enverist tradition but the course of the war drew it away from any social revolutionary objectives (along the Official IRA model) towards what its Marxist critics have seen as a populist-nationalist force (the Provisional IRA model) and then became the agent of a capitalist Kosova firmly integrated within Western-controlled globalised neo-liberal structures.[45]

The war ended with the well known process of negotiations in which Russia's Special Representative for Yugoslavia and founder of GAZPROM Viktor Chernomyrdin (1938–2010) was central, persuading Milosevic that there was no future in his military campaign. Without Russian support, Milosevic's cause was lost. The acceleration of the NATO bombing campaign to include strategic targets meant that increasingly important industrial and infrastructure assets in Serbia were now being destroyed, and NATO was clearly prepared to take the kind of risks in hitting sensitive targets that led to the mistaken bombing of the Chinese Embassy in Belgrade on May and would in due course be prepared to target Milosevic himself. These processes did not involve the KLA at all, although they were no doubt very welcome to the leadership and the rank and file alike. There was no option for the Serbian dictator but to withdraw from Kosova and hope to secure the increasingly shaky future of his government within Serbia itself. The army withdrew as the Military-Technical agreement provided, and left delirious crowds of Albanians celebrating in the streets of every town and village in Kosova. The KLA marched into the main towns, to cheering crowds and dancing and music went on far into the night. It seemed to be the fulfilment of a centuries old dream for the majority community. Yet the more astute amongst them knew that the future held many complex decisions, in an endlessly complex political and economic reality. The Albanian government ordered the closure of the remaining few FARK camps in Albania and in a paramilitary sense, the KLA were the masters of all they surveyed.[46]

But as so often in wars, the relationship between the guerrilla force and the formal army was difficult and could be contradictory, and in many situations there were political complications. An interesting parallel can be found from the Second World War in the joint struggle of the Allied 8th Army in Italy with the Italian Communist-led Partisans against the German occupiers. After Mussolini was dead and Axis rule had collapsed, the once allied Partisans were soon regarded as a political threat by Churchill, Eisenhower and the 8th Army command and were expelled from positions of local authority in towns and cities they had jointly liberated. A similar process was soon to be targeted against the Kosova Liberation Army. There was no legal place for the April 1999 'Provisional Government' in United Nations Security Council Resolution 1244 which provided the basis for the international community activity in the post-intervention period, and no authority for what the KFOR head Mike Jackson and the UN Representative Bernard Kouchner regarded as a 'parallel' government to the international administration. Yet it is unlikely that the embryo international administration in the early summer of 1999, and KFOR, could have resisted a well-led and united mass movement of the Albanians demanding immediate independence, perhaps through a quick and locally organised referendum. But the outbreak of petty political rivalries among some of the victorious KLA leaders, the comprehensive leadership failure of Ibrahim Rugova and the focus of some LPK leaders like Ahmeti and Veliu on considering future military action in Macedonia fatally weakened the impulse towards an independent Kosova. Hashim Thaci had no means of preserving the Provisional Government from the forces that wished to destroy it.

In the villages the processes of ethnic revenge proceeded virtually unchecked, as in many KFOR areas virtually all available forces were concentrated in urban barracks and it would have been impossible in any case to cover all of Kosova's often remote and difficult countryside. In some cases local KLA commanders put pressure on Serbs to go, in other areas it was simply a matter of inter-communal revenge after the active participation of ethnic Serbs in serious acts of violence against their Albanian neighbours in the wartime period. The officials and collaborators of the Milosevic system in Kosova certainly did not need encouragement by the KLA or anyone else to leave, as they knew they had no future in a democratic Kosova; the same was true of the section of the Roma who had scavenged actively in the houses and properties of displaced Albanians whilst they were refugees. As the Friedrich Naumann Stiftung think-tank pointed out in its analysis of the KLA and its demobilisation, 'It is disputed whether there was a coordinated strategy of "purging" Kosova by the KLA leadership'.[47] Wars have winners and losers and the Albanians were now the winners and the Serbian and Roma minorities the losers. The Serbs had controlled Kosova throughout the twentieth century against the wishes of the majority community there and lost control at the end of it. In their view, a secret conspiracy against their country had succeeded in depriving them of their most treasured historic territory.

11

PRESHEVO AND THE MACEDONIAN SEQUEL
2000–2001

Here among you have I risen	*Ne mes tuaj kam qendruar*
And aflame am I now blazing	*E jam duke perveluar*
Just a bit of light to give you	*Qe t'u ap pakeze drite*
That I change your night to daytime	*Natene t'ua benj dite*

Naim Frasheri, *The Words of the Candle*

After the time of celebration and the mass return of refugees to their homes, the rest of the summer of 1999 was a time for urgent reconstruction tasks. Ex-KLA soldiers sat for long hours with colleagues trying to discern the intentions of the international community. A priority was the formation of political parties, with the Swiss-based KLA spokesman Bardhyl Mahmuti leading the field by holding a party formation conference in Prishtina as early as July 1999. The formal demobilisation of the KLA proceeded without delays, culminating in a victory parade in September. General Mike Jackson's tight timetable for demobilisation was achieved without difficulty. The atmosphere in the cities was relaxed but the increasing inter-communal violence and the flight of Serbs were beginning to lead some internationals to turn their sympathies away from the Albanians and towards the now displaced Serbs. The northern *opstina*s of Kosova, north of the Ibar river, had become a refuge for war criminals and undesirables from the

Milosevic administration and were never brought under proper control by the United Nations or KFOR. Tensions grew rapidly on all sides, over many issues, and the autumn and winter of 2000–2001 was a time of acute social upheaval in the Kosova Albanian world.

The more intelligent among the Albanian political community in Prishtina had anticipated difficulties in the situation of the Provisional Government with the arrival of NATO/KFOR and the United Nations UNMIK administration, but few at the time of the Rambouillet conference before the bombing campaign had foreseen the reversal of fortune for the Kosova Liberation Army after the summer of 2000 and formal demobilisation.[1] The Thaci-led Provisional Government was destroyed by a combination of incompetence and indecision and a sophisticated counter-insurgency policy under KFOR's British commander General Mike Jackson, agreed also in the NATO capitals.[2] Jackson and Kouchner were throughout acting under their legal rights within UN Security Council Resolution 1244 but that did not make their decisions any more welcome to many in the Albanian majority community. General Jackson's central concern was establishment of control over the population of Prishtina.[3] He was well aware of the reprisal attacks on Serb families and monuments in the hinterland but KFOR did not have sufficient forces on the ground to prevent them, although no-one wished to admit this fact. The Prishtina internationals were determined to prevent the Albanians from establishing an untrammelled nationalist government under the control of ex-KLA figures. The United Nations UNMIK mission leaders shared these objectives. The conflict with NATO SACEUR Wesley Clark over the Russian provocation at Prishtina airport was public and unpleasant and Jackson was subjected to some very critical comment in the US press. Although the resilient Jackson saw it all as part of the rough and tumble of military leadership life in a conflict zone, the ever-present if often subliminal anti-Americanism in some parts of the British Whitehall establishment seized on it all as a way to try to extricate themselves from a US-led Kosova intervention policy which many of them had never privately supported.

There were also many practical problems within Prishtina itself. Thaci was well intentioned but young and inexperienced and did not have a proper political staff. Many Provisional Government 'ministries' were empty offices with the detritus of Milosevic-period papers scattered all over the floor. Above all, the decision of Rugova and the

LDK leadership not to join the Thaci government fatally undermined Thaci's position, as Jackson and many foreign observers soon realised. The familiar Kosova problem of state absence reasserted itself. Even if Thaci had had the political authority to form a government, there would not have been a functional local state to base it upon. Jackson sometimes had a poor personal relationship with Thaci, who considered privately that in many ways Jackson was out of the political control of Tony Blair and London.[4] Thaci was still thinking in terms of the more positive aspects of the Rambouillet deal for the Albanians and was slow to recognise how the internationals were changing the agenda with the main objective of removing the KLA heritage from the political scene in Prishtina. Jackson's British army Paratroopers, who were the main infantry regiment in Prishtina, were expert professional peacekeepers but opened fire on a pro-KLA demonstration in Prishtina in July and killed two young men.[5] A chasm of misunderstanding was opening between Albanian nationalists (not just the KLA) and the international staff in the United Nations administration in Prishtina.

Confronting and facing down the Thaci 'government' was a high risk strategy for KFOR and UNMIK, but it was successful. The mainstream of thought in NATO was that Ceku could be relied upon to 'deliver' the rest of the KLA, as he duly did, and in return establishment of a small national guard type force, the Kosovo Protection Corps (KPC), would be allowed. On 19 September the KLA was formally demobilised and ceased to exist, and a Victory Parade was held. It was an emotional occasion for the soldiers, few of whom could have sensed what difficult days lay ahead. The mixture of amateur and professional soldiers, tractor drivers and doctors in brown camouflage fatigues, all marched proudly through the middle of Prishtina in bright sunshine through cheering crowds ten deep on the pavement and seemed to a casual observer to be masters of all they surveyed.

The Provisional Government leader Hashim Thaci had also been unprepared for the pincer movement that KFOR and the UNMIK chief Kouchner used to undermine his position. He was, after all, a very young man with no previous experience in the jungle of Balkan politics or of the duplicity of major powers over small country politicians. He was probably unaware that even a statesman as committed to the Kosova Albanians as Tony Blair had given little thought to the independence issue.[6] He had not understood the farsighted background British strategy to tame and neutralise the Kosova Albanian military movement that had evolved since the summer of 1998, and the full significance of the arrival of Ceku on the scene. If the Kosova war was a war of conspiracies, it is quite appropriate to describe the machinations of the Serb-sympathisers within NATO, the EU and the international community as a conspiracy against Kosova independence. On 14 June, in an interview with a Prishtina newspaper, Thaci said quite clearly in response to a question about the future of the KLA that 'The KLA will be transformed into an army that will defend the territory of Kosova',[7] and a few days later the *International Herald Tribune* ran a front page story with a picture of Thaci under the headline 'NATO to consider new Kosovo Army', but the text actually said that the KLA had agreed to disband.[8] The contradictions of victory were becoming apparent. Jackson and the British military felt that the situation would be decided by creating *de facto* realities on the ground, as the Russians had shown at Prishtina airport, and proceeded accordingly. Seeing the drift of events, many Albanians in the countryside where KFOR held little effective power did the same, and drove out many of their Serb neighbours and attacked their churches and other buildings. In a certain sense, the war had not ended.[9]

The irony of the situation was that neither Jackson nor Thaci was anything like as much in control of the KLA as they both wished to believe, and much of the 'demobilisation' was purely nominal. The KLA as a formal army was metamorphosing into an armed people. Some KLA soldiers had already handed in their uniforms, if not their guns, and were on their way home to attend to very urgent domestic rebuilding and farm restocking tasks, but most kept their weapons and hid them. An unimpeded flow of small arms was coming over the border from Albania, and many returning refugees bought guns from traders in Kukes or Bajram Curri before returning home. It was in the three or four months after June 1999 that the fabled Albanian arsenal was rebuilt, much of it from ex-1997 uprising magazine depletion. Above all, there was plenty of ammunition on sale. Some weapons supply was also available from abandoned VJ army magazines and military depots which were quickly looted by local people. Although KFOR and UNMIK were able to demobilise the KLA and bring down the Thaci government, they were unable to stop the Albanian population restoring their traditional heritage of small arms possession in households.

The summer of 1999 wore on, with regular visits by international dignitaries following that of Tony Blair, but the little tree Blair planted near the Prishtina sports centre was already torn out of the ground. In the countryside life for the ex-soldiers seemed simpler, without the acute political tensions of the towns. Virtually all Serbs had gone from western Kosova and few remained elsewhere except north of the Ibar river in Mitrovica and Zvecan *opstina*s. There was much work to do in the rural areas, and in all Balkan wars there is a time for fighting and a time for work to maintain life. It was too late to plant a harvest but many farm animals could be saved from among those that had survived the conflict. Foul wells could be cleaned out and disinfected. Major international NGOs like CARE International brought in resources to reconstruct damaged but usable housing. Oxfam drilled new water holes. Rural life pieced itself together while politics became focused on the capital. The underground organisations like the LKCK and LPK were very much still in existence, and they had become legal political parties with offices in the new Prishtina. Revolutionary ardour was being replaced by the pleasures of legal operations and respect from many internationals after so many years in the dangerous political twilight. The LKCK's role in the early Provisional Government had been a target for British ire, with its system of 'block' political representatives seeming reminiscent of Communist-type practices, and the sophisticated LPK Swiss-Albanian Diaspora businessmen who had arrived in Kosova in the summer in large cars were stereotyped as gangsters and probably drug dealers by the KFOR army establishment. On the other hand, there was little KFOR could do to control events and before long large houses were being built among the ruins of old Serbian party officials' houses on Dragodan hill to house the victorious KLA commanders. This was not at all unpopular with the Albanian majority who felt that it was all a just reward for what the KLA had achieved in the war.

The intelligence material provided from London and Washington to the NATO/KFOR commanders and the nascent UNMIK administration did nothing to prepare them for the social revolution that the exit of the Serbian administration had released. The 'new men' of the wartime generation were displacing the old administrative elite from major jobs. Thousands of people from impoverished rural environments in Drenica and elsewhere who had been at the heart of the war moved to Prishtina and other towns to occupy empty flats left by Serbian officials who had fled. Many had fought in the KLA, and a new society was developing where those excluded from power and social and economic status for three generations were taking over the city. Membership of the KLA had given these people high social status in their villages and soon a new informal power network in a very Kosova sense had begun to appear, based on war and kinship loyalty and economic self-interest, a new parallel structure that all the efforts of the UNMIK administration over several years between 1999 and 2008 could do little to disturb. In many respects, KFOR faced the traditional problem of all Yugoslav armies in Kosova, of insufficient infantry manpower to try to control an increasingly sceptical and critical Albanian majority population.

The international administration saw the KLA formally demobilised in the late summer months, and after a difficult start Thaci and Jackson and Kouchner established much clearer relationships and a *de facto* understanding. Thaci, had, after all, been a signatory of the original KLA demobilisation agreement. The internationals were thus very unprepared for the opening of the conflict in the Preshevo valley that followed in the autumn. Preshevo, known to Albanians as Kosova Lindore, Eastern Kosova, is on the eastern border of Kosova and Serbia, and is a flat, wide valley that carries through it all the main rail and road links between Belgrade, Nis and the Mediterranean. Preshevo town had a large majority of ethnic Albanians in the old Yugoslavia, along with Bujanoc and other small centres to the north. It lies immediately to the south of the hardline nationalist Serbian town of Vranje. Preshevo had always been part of Kosova geographically and culturally since Ottoman times, but the Kosova border had been changed by Tito in 1947 to give a wider non-Albanian majority corridor for the strategic transport routes. The importance of the valley was enhanced after 1991 with the arrival of the Former Yugoslav Macedonia/Republic of Macedonia as an independent state, and Preshevo valley formed a narrow conduit for the roads and railway running down from Nis to Thessaloniki between the two closely affiliated states of Greece and Serbia.

Between the summer of 1998 and June 1999 Preshevo Albanians had endured the same serious human rights violations, random violence and in particular mosque burnings as those living elsewhere in Kosova. The Islamic heritage has always been a more substantial cultural factor in Preshevo than in other parts of Kosova, ever since the defeat of Mullah Idris Gjilan's Ballist revolt against Communism ended in 1951.[10] The social structure encouraged radicalism, with many historical resemblances to the world of displaced and declassed Ottoman *beys* and *agas* in the hills around Struga and Ohrid.[11] After the overwhelming Serbian victory in the Balkan Wars at Kumanovo in 1912, to the south in Macedonia, Albanians involved with the Ottoman system fled and took refuge in Preshevo hill village life. An intense cultural nationalism pervaded the villages around Kumanovo. The new Yugoslav identity as citizenship and nationality was forced upon the Albanians, and preserving their Islamic religious traditions became synonymous with being an Albanian. The onslaught against the mosques and undefended villages was particularly severe in April 1999.[12] In the Gjilan region, the KLA had no capacity to defend the houses and mosques against the VJ heavy armour operating on familiar home territory, and there was ideal tank country in much of the land.

During the summer of 1999 little happened in Preshevo to encourage the Albanians, apart from a mostly Saudi-financed repair and reconstruction programme for the mosques.[13] Although there was no formal local KLA structure, small arms began seeping into the valley from Kosova. Many Serbian paramilitaries had retreated to Preshevo after June and NATO's arrival, including Arkan's soldiers retreating into Vranje, the little tobacco town north of the Preshevo valley and a long-time centre of Serbian nationalist extremism. Milosevic reinforced the army at the large Preshevo bases. It did not take long for the dynamic development that the KLA had experienced in the Gjilan region in the bombing campaign period to spill over the border. The Serbs after losing control of Kosova were angry and revengeful and the Preshevo Albanians had few means of defending themselves or securing their communities. The valley became a contested border, part of the longstanding wider problem of the instability of Serbia's southern borders for much of the twentieth century.[14]

The Preshevo guerrilla movement, the Ushtria Clirimitare e Presheves Medvegjes dhe Bujanocit (UCPMB), was originally formed in the autumn of 1999 by a very small group in Gjilan, akin to the way the original KLA was formed; it was centred around Jonuz and Shafket Musliu, both longstanding LPK members with Preshevo family roots. Both had fought in the KLA in Kosova. Random attacks on Serbian security personnel and army reservists in Preshevo had already taken place, and attempts to sabotage VJ vehicles.[15] The US Army-controlled sector of Kosova had a more or less open border with limited patrolling and dense forests in many places made guerrilla movement easy. The UCPMB was formed when the KLA was still on the crest of a wave, but almost as it was breaking. The UCPMB immediately ran into a number of operational difficulties, although many recruits quickly came forward. It did not have ideal links with the new political leadership in Prishtina, as most activists came from a generally LDK background and among the key movers and shakers in the war support machine in the Diaspora, virtually none came from Preshevo. Apart from one or two prominent individuals like the writer and journalist Vehbi Bajrami, very few in the US Albanian Diaspora came from Preshevo. There was a certain war-weariness developing in some parts of the Kosova Albanian community, and the ground for a new war had not been well prepared with the Western media.

Few Western journalists had ever visited Preshevo before the conflict or knew anything about the region, apart from seeing little villages with white minarets out of the train window on the way down from Nis to Skopje. There had been no media coverage whatsoever of the ethnic cleansing and violence there in the bombing campaign period. Hundreds of people had fled the villages in the hills around Bujanoc and Preshevo town itself. Most important, those in Prishtina who did know something about the details felt privately that it was a doomed struggle, where a small UCPMB force would face overwhelming VJ armed forces acting out of their own bases on their own territory, as they saw it. There was little or no possibility of the UCPMB obtaining the key asset of positional advantage that has determined the outcome of so many guerrilla wars.[16] The VJ had it to start with and never lost it throughout the brief conflict. Subjective factors also played part in some Albanian perceptions that limited the immediate activist support the UCPMB needed. Preshevo people in Kosova have a reputation akin to the Irish of the Albanian world, charming but irresponsible, quick to pick a fight if offended and maybe liable to do crazy things. In many minds in more conservative Kosova families in the old-fashioned LDK dominated orbit around Gjilan, these were powerful negative images of the UCPMB. Some support did come, often from unexpected quarters, with volunteers coming to fight in the UCPMB from Prizren, recalling the period when imams linked to Mullah Idris had fled to Prizren after the end of the fighting in Preshevo in 1950–51. Some young men of the south-west died in UCPMB uniform a generation later, as the northern KLA cemetery in Prizren indicates in its grave memorials. The French, British and other European armies were being fed propaganda from Serbian contacts that the insurgency in Preshevo was openly 'Islamic' and they felt the Americans were being naïve in indulging its growth in their sector.

The appetite for revenge was nevertheless strong in Preshevo itself and by January 2000 a regular pattern of shooting incidents and attacks on police posts had developed, and small firefights in the forested areas between VJ and UCPMB soldiers. The 70,000 ethnic Albanians living there had many longstanding and justified grievances against Belgrade and they felt their time had come to put themselves on the international community Balkan map by the time-honoured method of armed revolt. At a local and tactical level the UCPMB was a more effective KLA-descended guerrilla force than some of its critics have allowed. The UCPMB was adept with mines, unlike the early KLA, and soon began to take out VJ vehicles and block border access routes. It also had some 120mm mortars, and recoilless anti-tank weapons which they were capable of using effectively.[17] The UCPMB no doubt hoped that the developing conflict would see NATO come in on the Albanian side, as in Kosova. This did not take place. A major change in atmosphere and policy towards the region was under way in the international community throughout 2000, as American focus turned towards Serbia and the 'Miles plan' to bring down the Milosevic regime and return Serbia to democracy within a new Yugoslavia.[18] New Kosova insurgencies were a nuisance and unwelcome in this context, as they only reinforced the power of the hard right and Milosevic in Belgrade. The arrival of the Bush administration in January 2001 strongly reinforced these tendencies, with a desire in Washington by the new government to see the Kosova intervention as a Clinton project with which many did not want further association.

Fighting intensified in Preshevo in the summer of 2000, but was inconclusive. The UCPMB was perhaps suffering from the fact that in the main Kosova war period, it had been part of the Karadakut (Gjilan region) KLA Operative Zone and never had a prior military identity of its own to build upon. There were many mutual misunderstandings between Preshevo and Gjilan. Local Preshevo people were often expecting much more help from Gjilan than actually came and some people in Gjilan could not understand why the old Preshevo political leadership with its links to Belgrade was allowed to be involved in the peace talks with NATO.[19] The UCPMB was effective at hit and run tactics but the geography of the valley and the poor political leadership in the towns did not lead to a mass movement in the Albanian community in support of the guerrillas. It was not possible to establish any significant liberated base area in Preshevo, there was no equivalent area to Drenica in the early stages of the Kosova war or Shipkovica in Macedonia in 2001, and the UCPMB was dependent for most of its supplies on materials moved in from Kosova. It was thus very vulnerable to a tightening of border security and a clampdown by NATO forces within Kosova. In essence this is what happened, and in the autumn of 2000 a military stalemate was reached, although a new offensive developed after Christmas and ran into January and February 2001.

The small leading group of often American-trained UCPMB soldiers commanded some very young, raw and inexperienced recruits and there were severe limits to what could really be achieved. The British military and most European militaries within KFOR were strongly critical of the Americans for having allowed the insurgency to develop in the first place. After the overthrow of Milosevic many UCPMB fighters felt that the future was uncertain and the Musliu leadership was under pressure from within Kosova to wind down the war for the winter and await developments with Belgrade.[20] Many of the UCPMB men came from ex-KLA backgrounds and were members of the newly formed Kosova Protection Corps (KPC). They had joined the UCPMB expecting to precipitate rapid NATO intervention, and when it did not materialise were uncertain of their role. The little guerrilla force had made a strategic misjudgement in putting so much hope on NATO, and although they fought well and effectively at the tactical level, had few options to prolonging the war against their big northern neighbour. They did not have the capacity, or the vision, to undertake the sabotage of the big bridges on the north-south road and rail lines to cut the strategic through routes that would almost certainly have prompted direct NATO intervention. These were the only real targets in the Preshevo valley. Yet the military situation to the south, in the FYROM/ Republic of Macedonia, was quite different and soon the Preshevo conflict began to evolve seamlessly into what became the war in Macedonia in 2001.The formal ceasefire and surrender of the UCPMB took place on 24 March 2001 and NATO allowed the VJ to move infantry to reoccupy all the ground safety zone, but although this was seen as a major victory over Albanian insurgency by many in NATO and a long-overdue 'turn to the Serbs' by a few parties, it was irrelevant to the wider regional conflict.

After the overthrow of Milosevic in September 2000 the new Kostunica government appointed Nebojsa Covic to develop a plan to defuse the conflict and put post-Milosevic Serbia's relations with the Albanians on a new footing, and the 'Programme for the Solution of the Crisis in the Pcinja District' resulted in early 2001.[21] It was a thoughtful, well written document that showed the new Belgrade government's grasp of public relations, and it appealed to the internationals in Kosova who wanted to do something to 'reward' the new Serbian government and show the Serbian people that they were now friends. The inscribed Serbian view of the history of Preshevo was cleverly written and adopted without hesitation by NATO and the new Dutch negotiator, Peter Feith. The Serbs also had the advantage of a pliable older generation Albanian leader, the Mayor of Preshevo Riza Halimi, who was a social conservative with a record of collaboration with Belgrade and operated outside the new Albanian paramilitary tradition. Covic had been heavily involved in trying to defuse the Preshevo crisis for some time, and had almost been killed in fighting in Licane.

The crucial event to end the fighting and the rise of the UCPMB was the NATO/US decision to close the demilitarised zone along the Kosova-Preshevo border which had been a safe haven for the UCPMB. It was duly imposed at a diplomatic level, in what the Serbian leader Zoran Djindjic called 'our first victory for ten years'. The UCPMB appeared to have been defeated and demobilised without significant achievement, as the provisions for local democracy set out in the Agreement were largely nominal and most have never been observed, let alone enforced.[22] Although it was a little time before the events of 11 September 2001 in New York, the atmosphere in the international community about insurgency with possible Islamic identities or links was changing. The arrival of hard-line right-wingers in senior posts in the Bush administration was a background factor in the US that assisted the Serbs in Preshevo.

The end of the fighting in Preshevo overlapped with the beginning of the 2001 war in Macedonia. Important leaders of the KLA were unemployed after 2000 and there was increasing concern at the direction of Bush administration policy when the US expert Sean Sullivan was finally replaced as chief international community negotiator by Peter Feith. The LPK leadership was very concerned at the pattern of events in Macedonia and there is some evidence to suggest that there was already consideration being given to opening a new front in Macedonia with a new military force.[23]

Another major factor that played into the hands of more militant Albanians was the reversal of policy over Kosova independence that was beginning to transform the political atmosphere in Prishtina. The political leadership around Thaci, Haliti and Haradinaj had begun to see the full extent of the internationals push for a 'Yugoslavist' solution to the crisis over Kosova's status and the abandonment of any prospect at all of a promised referendum on independence. They felt cheated and betrayed, after having agreed at Rambouillet to postpone an independence referendum for a period. Now it seemed the Holy Grail of independence was being withdrawn from view altogether. The attractions of a war in Macedonia were obvious to many of them, to cut this Gordian knot and show NATO that it could not neglect the Albanian national cause. Albanians still suffered gross human rights violations and poor democratic rights under the Macedonian government system and many young people had seen what had been achieved in Kosova by military methods against much tougher government opposition than existed in Skopje. There were capable soldiers ready to fight in some numbers, unlike the too-small core of the UCPMB in Preshevo. There was a substantial weapons arsenal that had been moved over the border before the summer 1999 demobilisation of the KLA into Tetovo and elsewhere in western Macedonia, and the Macedonian army was an incompetent and badly trained force with low morale and poor organisation. Macedonia had a long tradition of underground Albanian organisations and in the mountains the Ballist tradition had never been as thoroughly or systematically repressed as in Kosova. After the 1968 protest demonstrations the Levizje e Shqiptareve ne Maqedoni, the League of Albanians in Macedonia, had been founded; it was ostensibly a human rights lobby organisation but in practice had a radical nationalist agenda.[24]

Above all, Macedonia was the home territory of Fazli Veliu and Ali Ahmeti, two of the founders of LPK in its modern form, and Ahmeti was still in Albania for much of the time with access to the old KLA munitions and recruitment network he had controlled in 1998–99.[25] Veliu was moving from his Swiss home base back to Macedonia when he was arrested in Germany on 13 February. It was an ominous event but attracted little publicity at the time. He had made the error of attempting to enter Germany from Switzerland via Bavaria, a part of the country with a tough police force with a long history of anti-Albanian surveillance and a wider political culture that outside liberal

Munich was unsympathetic to any Albanian exile political organisation other than the Kosova Democratic League.[26] Bavaria had been the only part of Germany to try seriously to ban fundraising for the KLA in 1998–99.[27] Within neighbouring Macedonia political tension was rising and the Interior Minister Lupo Boskovski was an adventurist figure who was determined to make his political career to the top and the prime minister's post on the basis of crushing the nascent Albanian insurgency. It suited him to have an insurgency to crush.

The Macedonian army had been hampered in its development in some respects after independence in 1991 by the United Nations arms embargo that continued until 1996, and was short of everything except light weapons. On paper it was made up of about 18,000 regular soldiers and 85,000 reservists but in many ways this was only a notional strength and far fewer were actually present in barracks, trained or properly organised. The Interior Ministry police was a much more formidable, if smaller force of 7,600 men, along with the 'Lions' and 'Wolves' special police units, modelled on the Serbian JSO anti-terrorist units.

It was a potent mixture, and by February 2001 Macedonian military intelligence was beginning to realise the full extent of the possible threat. Skopje was awash with rumours of sightings of uniformed Albanian fighters in the woods on the slopes of the Black Mountains north of Skopje and the eastern end of the Shar range above Tetovo. The international community and NATO were not attentive. They were full of pride at the success in controlling and demobilising the Preshevo insurgency and, with the cooperation of the new government in Belgrade, proud of the success of the Covic plan. This led to a degree of complacency. By all counts, the basic conditions for a successful uprising were in place by March 2001, as events showed. In the little village of Tanusche which was bisected by the Kosova-Macedonian border a minor land dispute about grazing rights across the border erupted into violence. A few weeks before, at the end of January, a grenade attack had destroyed a police post by the roadside at the little village of Tearce on the Tetovo to Kosova main road. Tearce was near Poroi, a very militant village which had contributed several soldiers to the KLA in Kosova.

The fighting in Tanusche spread rapidly through the hill villages nearby and towards Haracinje above Skopje. The new force, the National Liberation Army, was led in the formal military sense by

General Gezim Ostreni, a burly ex-JNA officer from the western mountain town of Dibra on the border with Albania who had deserted and fought in the Kosova war.[28] Ali Ahmeti was the political soldier on the ground, akin to Hashim Thaci's position in the Kosova war, but with a higher personal visibility during the conflict in Sipkovica where he held regular press conferences. Fighting rapidly spread in March to Tetovo where the full incompetence of the Macedonian army was exposed and Ali Ahmeti moved from Albania to formally establish the headquarters of the NLA in the mountain village of Ship-kovica, on the heights above Tetovo town.[29] Ahmeti and Ostreni had made a careful study of the weaknesses of the original KLA as a military force in the winter of 1999–2000. The National Liberation Army in Macedonia had a distinctly different structure and ethos. It was, in a general sense, a pure guerrilla army with none of the associations of the armed Kosova people that the KLA had in some of its multiple guises. It was conceived as a small mobile force that was well armed and could quickly expose the weaknesses of the Macedonian army with its lumbering heavy vehicles, lack of air presence and helicopters (as the war developed they had to be obtained from Ukraine), and badly trained and ill-motivated men. It was selective in its recruitment in order to avoid the competence and command structure problems in Kosova. The political leadership of the guerrillas was clear and united around the Swiss LPK veterans Veliu and Ahmeti, and there was no collaborationist leader in Albanian Macedonia like Rugova in Kosova who could divert the war effort. The PDSH party of Menduh Thaci and Arben Xhaferi had been heavily involved in the Kosova war and refugee crises and although Xhaferi had something of a pacifist and internationalist thread in his political outlook as well as nationalism, the PDSH never became something separate from the NLA support mechanisms. The NLA started off as about 250 men, most of whom had fought in Kosova and some in Preshevo valley, and it grew to over 3,000 by the end of the conflict in August 2001. It was divided into six brigades, of varying sizes, with most fighters concentrated around Tetovo and Gostivar.

The NLA drew on the fighting experience of senior ex-KLA soldiers most of whom had been through the Koshare battle experience in the spring of 1999 and had learned a great deal from UK and US soldiers and military contractors. It was quite elitist and some volunteers were turned away if they were felt to be too young and inexperienced, unlike some of the callow youths in the UCPMB who had to fight bravely against often impossible odds. The geography suited the insurgents, unlike that in Preshevo. Shipkovica was a classic guerrilla mountain refuge, high above Tetovo and its Ottoman castle at Selce with a full view of all of the city and easy to defend with only one main asphalt road leading up to it. Paths behind the village led over the mountains across to the border with Albania only about twenty miles away where the Macedonian army had no ground presence at all. The NLA could be kept supplied by horse and mule from Albania, although as the conflict developed this was not generally necessary. The positional advantage factor always aided the NLA compared with the lumbering and inefficient heavy armour of the Macedonians in the Tetovo streets below. They attempted to shell NLA positions in and around Tetovo Kale, the rambling Byzantine and Ottoman ruined fortress above the town, but made little impression on it.

The beginning of the insurrection in Macedonia was in fact precipitated by the Slav-Macedonians, however prepared the LPK leadership and the nascent army may have been for conflict.[30] The police and army attack on Tanusche resulted in the death of an Albanian villager. Gun battles had developed lasting two hours or more after 26 February and the Macedonian 'Wolves' anti-terrorist unit was sent into the village. The Skopje government was clearly looking for a military solution but seems to have been unaware of the systematic prior preparations for war that the National Liberation Army (NLA) leadership group had been making. The National Democratic Party (NDA), a small Albanian party with Ballist roots in Macedonia, appears to have decided on the war option as early as 1999, but memoirs of ex-NLA soldiers show that at this stage Ali Ahmeti was against opening a front in Macedonia and seems to have envisaged that happening only as late as 2004 or 2005.[31] Nevertheless the NDA retained some minor military ambitions and capacity and it was the NDA supporter and ex-KLA Kacanik valley soldier Xhezair Shaqiri (Commander Hoxha) who led armed men into the village in February 2001 to try to defend it.[32] He was soon followed by others, such as the ex-KLA soldier Nuri Bexheti from the prominent Bexheti family in Tetovo who also brought new soldiers, who had been preparing to fight for some time, with them. The first official NLA communiqué appeared on 23 January 2001, claiming responsibility for the Tearce police station attack. It was a gauntlet thrown down to the international community.[33]

The new force urgently desired and needed publicity. Earlier armed actions in Macedonia such as the bombing of Kicevo police station in 1999 had attracted little attention, as did the subsequent attacks on police stations in Skopje and Oslomej in January 2000. Although Fazli Veliu was blamed in the Skopje press for personally orchestrating these attacks, this seems very unlikely as he was then held in solitary confinement in prison in Germany. Whatever the leadership issues, there was no doubt that another serious conflict based on an Albanian insurgency was looming, and it was not hard for both Kosovars and Tirana Albanians to see that it might not be difficult to make it a military success and so reverse the backsliding of the international community on the Albanian national question in Kosova. In Prishtina, the winter of 2000–2001 was perhaps the high point of the process of policy reversal towards Belgrade that was taking place in UNMIK and KFOR, with eyes on the Bush administration's new priorities.

The NLA army emerged in a formal sense in NLA Communiqué number 4 dated 24 April 2001, by which time it was clear that Ahmeti had been appointed military leader by the small leadership group. This was a job Shaqiri (Hoxha) would have liked but he did not possess the necessary political connections or military stature to get it. It is interesting to speculate whether this would have happened if Veliu had not been so long in prison in Germany. Veliu was Ahmeti's uncle, a founder of LPK in the early 1980s, and a superb underground organiser. He was in Irish terms 'a sea green incorruptible nationalist' and in the normal course of things would have been regarded as the senior figure and likely NLA leader. On the other hand, Ahmeti had the practical experience of running the KLA logistics in Albania for two years which had given him very clear and definite practical ideas on how the Macedonian war should be conducted, and he had a genuine if somewhat quixotic talent for soldiering. He was also photogenic and adept with the media, whereas Veliu looks like the average middle-aged Tetovo shopkeeper in a sombre suit and can be uncommunicative with those he does not know. Veliu excelled as the intellectual and organiser and was used to life in the underground and in the shadows.

They were nevertheless a formidable combination, with extensive family links to the newly emerging radical Albanian villagers in southwest Macedonia who were very poor and suffered serious human rights problems with the Skopje government. The prevailing culture was rural and quite conservative and dominated by the small rituals of

Sunni Islamic daily life in the villages. Life was hard and emigration for the intelligent almost inevitable. There was an extensive Diaspora in the United States and this was quickly mobilised, with one Texas-based restaurant owner alone giving more than half a million dollars to the new army.[34] The Macedonian army maintained a large base at Kicevo and it was soon to be drawn into the emerging conflict. The focus of the war in the early weeks was north of Skopje and then, after violence erupted in Tetovo, it spread south along the main road towards Ohrid. The Macedonians tried to safeguard the road against the NLA by cutting down the trees on either side, a tactic developed on the advice of NATO military advisers, but this had little effect. The Skopje army had nothing like enough men to make an impression on the NLA which simply faded into the vast and mostly uninhabited western Macedonian deciduous forests between Gostivar and Ohrid and reappeared to threaten the road when the Macedonians had left for barracks. The dense leaf cover that was growing as the spring advanced was sufficient to prevent the occasional Macedonian helicopter from locating them.

The efficient advance of the rebels caused consternation in most parts of the international community and as a sop to Belgrade, and to try to close down the NLA supply line from the Preshevo valley into Macedonia, the Yugoslav army was allowed back into hitherto prohibited areas of the Kosova border zone on 8 March. This had no effect on the Macedonian NLA at all, as by the time it had happened all likely soldiers from the UCPMB were already in NLA uniforms and ranks. Within about three weeks, the Macedonians had lost control of all of the country west of this road to the border with Albania apart from garrison-held areas in Struga and Ohrid towns themselves. International community concern focused on the security of the big Mavrovo hydroelectric dams which supplied a substantial part of the FYROM/Republic of Macedonia's electricity. Sabotage could have caused catastrophic flooding, but in the event the NLA left them alone. As NLA control spread down the Black Mountains slopes to within a few miles of the capital, Skopje, the government of Boris Trajkovski and Lujpjo Georgievski was torn between the urge for negotiations and a settlement along Preshevo lines, and the desire for a clear military victory. Trajkovski was closely controlled by the international community and was inclined to conciliate but he was opposed by the confrontational instincts of Boskovski and IMRO leader Lujpjo Georgievski. Their views prevailed and on 22 March Trajkovski was forced to

THE KOSOVA LIBERATION ARMY

announce a new security initiative against the rebels. Macedonian soldiers launched an offensive in and around Tetovo but with little result. The NLA had survived the key first two months of the war without serious mishap and by the beginning of April a sense spread throughout the region that the Albanians were on a winning roll and had surmounted the problems of failure in Presheva.

On that same day, 22 March, NLA guerrillas had started fighting in daylight in the town for the first time and it was clear the battle for Tetovo was never going to be won by the Macedonians.[35] A few days before, on 17 March, a Macedonian army helicopter had crashed near the ski resort at Popova Shapka (Kodra Diell) above Tetovo, killing and injuring policemen. In the town old Bulgarian T-72 tanks attempted to impose themselves but had no organised infantry backup and achieved virtually nothing. In order to keep the initiative, all the NLA had to do was draw the Macedonians into open combat where international military observers could soon see their incompetence. The Skopje government did not keep any anti-insurgent credibility for very long, as the changing character of the International Crisis Group reports on the conflict indicates, and by mid-April it was clear that the NLA had passed within a few weeks all the basic tests of survival, positional advantage and tactical sophistication that it had taken the original KLA well over a year to learn.

Large refugee movements started out of Tetovo town and by the beginning of April perhaps 25,000 people from in and near it were on the move. Some even went to Kosova, a mirror image of the popular movement out of Kosova into Tetovo in 1998 and 1999. The generally very satisfactory situation on the ground from the point of the NLA (apart from the loss of a few defence posts in villages south of Tetovo) was unaffected by the arrival of a large international community delegation in Skopje headed by NATO General Secretary George Robertson and American Ambassador Christopher Hill, long a veteran of Macedonian crises and seen by the NLA as highly critical of Albanian nationalist ambitions. The delegation duly declared its support for the Macedonian government security crackdown[36] Robertson said the Skopje government had acted with 'commendable restraint but also with determined fairness'.[37]

Military experts did not agree; *Jane's Defence Weekly* analyst Zoran Kusovac observed the 'procrastination and slow troop build-up' of the Macedonians and was sceptical about what they had achieved.[38] In many ways the NATO chief's and diplomat's visit had played straight into the NLA's hands. The diplomacy was isolated from the realities on the ground and had little effect. The Albanians had been able to set the agenda from the start of the conflict and continued to do so, seizing both political and military advantage. With NATO there was disarray with conflicting views on whether any intervention to stop the war might be attempted and if so, how it might be done. The German military had the most local knowledge as they had been in a small UN peacekeeping force there before the war started, and most German officers thought the Macedonian cause was already lost. The borders were open. Ahmeti had correctly guessed that the international community forces on Macedonia's borders would not attempt to engage the NLA because of the need to avoid possible casualties, and new NLA supply routes to and from Kosova were opened in April and worked well for the rest of the war.[39]

April 2001 was in other senses a good month for the NLA. Armed men spread across the hills around Struga and in the north-east of the country took control of villages near the major strategic town of Kumanovo. Kumanovo has a long and critical significance in twentieth-century Balkan history from 1912 when Serbian forces triumphed there against the Ottomans and established the basis for what would become the *banovina* of 'South Serbia' in the first Royalist Yugoslavia. It controls the main Athens-Belgrade motorway route and is on one of the strategic routes in the Balkans. It is also of great significance to Albanians who were a majority in the town at the beginning of the twentieth century but were driven out to surrounding villages at various stages after 1912.[40] In May and June the NLA made further steady advances, a key event being the reoccupation of Aracinovo north of Skopje in early June 2001. The brutal and savage Macedonian army assaults on civilians that took place there when the army tried to drive them out finally turned remaining world opinion against Skopje and the strategy of a military solution. Ali Ahmeti was able to deliver the NLA in the various negotiations that followed as the more militant Commander Hoxha was outmanoeuvred. The basis for the transition of the NLA from a small and fairly successful insurgent army to Ali Ahmeti's personal political party took place in these weeks.[41]

In these circumstances the priority for the international community was to begin negotiations and force an end to the conflict. NATO troops had in a certain sense stopped the war spreading into Skopje by

243

mid-May by taking control of NLA positions to the north of the city, although they had not disarmed the NLA soldiers. This stabilisation plan was a priority for the NATO high command in Brussels as the social structure of Skopje with its predominantly Albanian and Muslim north and Slav and Orthodox south sectors of the city had all the ingredients for another Sarajevo. The Macedonian army could easily have moved heavy armour onto the hills below the Monastery of Pantelimon south of the city and begun shelling the Albanian districts north of the river if they had been better organised and led. Equally the NLA could have swept into the city from the north if they had not been impeded by NATO protecting the Slav population south of the Vardar river. There were divisions emerging among the Albanian leaders, between those who wanted to fight on with a maximalist platform and effectively split and federalise or cantonise the country, and more moderate voices. The latter, mostly in and around Xhaferi and Thaci's party, feared that a split of the Republic of Macedonia/FYROM would only aid the long-term ambitions of Greece in Macedonia.[42] No cantonisation or federalisation plan existed, a weakness in LPK prior planning for the NLA offensive.

There were also practical military questions to consider. The NLA had no clear view on what to do with fighting in majority-Macedonian districts. It was probably easily capable of occupying some such areas, around Kicevo for example, at the high tide of its success in midsummer. The terrain there (for example around Makedonski Brod) was very open with a low population, vast forests and no easily defensible potential bases. NLA soldiers would have been vulnerable to attack from the air, and by this stage of the war the Skopje government had obtained mercenary pilots and helicopters from Ukraine for this purpose. Most NLA soldiers had no wish to occupy land that seemed to belong to the majority ethnic group. They were happy to fight bravely and well to clear the Macedonian army from 'their' parts of the country but that was generally the height of their ambitions. The political leaderships around either Ahmeti or Thaci/Xhaferi had no clear plan to put forward to the international community on how to formally cantonise or split the country, and from the world's point of view the whole issue recalled the failed attempts to produce cantonal solutions to end the Bosnian conflict.[43]

Arben Xhaferi's long international experience and elder statesman role was used by the international community in the talks that were held at the lakeside resort of Ohrid to try to negotiate a deal to end the fighting.[44] This was less difficult than it might first appear. For Xhaferi the talks were an opportunity to restore his political primacy in the Albanian leadership in Macedonia, now threatened by Ahmeti. The Macedonians knew that they did not have the firepower to crush the NLA and Ahmeti realised that while some of his soldiers, including General Ostremi, were unhappy about the prospect of a ceasefire, about as much as could reasonably be obtained by military force had been obtained by early August and a stalemate had developed.[45] The NLA easily controlled all the land west of the Skopje-Tetovo-Gostivar main road. Control of the road in the Mavrovo mountains was contested but was basically in the hands of the NLA, while south in the lowlands towards Struga and Ohrid an unstable 'no man's land' existed. The Albanian population had taken some severe pressure in southern towns like Bitola (Monastir) where the mosque had been burned down and many famous buildings wrecked. Most Albanians had left Ohrid and moved to Struga where they felt safer. Ethnic Macedonian villages were heavily armed, albeit with light weapons, and were ready to move on their ethnic Albanian neighbours in what they saw as a fight for the survival of their country. The NLA was capable of a very full control of territory and protection of the Albanian population north of Mavrovo, but this was not the case to the south. As this was Ahmeti's home territory he was open to pressure to wind down the conflict. In his personal ideology he retained a strong attachment to the socialist ideal of a new egalitarian Macedonian and 'people's' state and in his heart did not wish to see it split with unpredictable and unforeseeable results, and he was persuaded that the Ohrid Accords offered a fair role to the Albanians in society.[46] His critics saw his long exile in Switzerland as a cause of an unduly sentimental and favourable image of what a reformed Macedonia might become.

General Ostremi came from the hill town of Dibra very close to the border with Albania, and this was perhaps a factor in his more intransigent thinking; Albanians there had long been under severe pressure from Skopje and the proximity to Albania itself with the latter border only a few miles away inevitably gave rise to thoughts of national unification. As all concerned well understood, the Macedonians would have to concede most practical control of the west to the Albanians but would fight for Skopje as their capital, and there could be no certainty about what the outcome of such a battle might be.

Despite a number of violent incidents such as the death of ten Macedonian soldiers in an ambush just outside Skopje on 8 August after the Macedonians killed five Albanian rebels the previous day, the war wound down as talks reached a conclusion.[47] On 17 August the first British and French NATO troops arrived, on 22 August NATO authorised the full deployment of a 3,500-strong force, and soon afterwards the Ohrid Accords were signed giving major human rights advances to the Albanians. The peacekeeping force began collecting weapons from the insurgents. Some declined to hand in their weapons and formed a new underground organisation, the AKSH, the National Army of the Albanians, with a specifically Ballist political agenda. Another rite of passage in the long odyssey of the KLA and its descendant organisations was being enacted. It was a very long way and a very long time indeed from the lonely hopes of the early German- and Swiss-based pioneers of the 1970s and 1980s. By July 2002 Ali Ahmeti and Fazli Veliu had formed their own political party and within a year they were partners in the government of the Republic of Macedonia/FYROM. Their insurgency had been a resounding success; well led militarily with very low casualties and well judged politically throughout.[48] Unlike the JNA and the VJ, the KLA had shown itself to be capable of transforming itself to meet the needs of the times and the different theatres of war where it operated. Yet the ex-LPK organisers turned open politicians would find themselves facing the same dilemma as their old comrades in Kosovo, finding that the skills to run secret organisations in the underground are different from those of government.

12

EPILOGUE

At Rome, meanwhile, Lentullus was carrying out Catiline's orders. He worked, personally, or through agents, on all whose character or fortunes seemed to mark them as fit instruments for revolution, not confining himself to citizens, but approaching all sorts and conditions of men, providing they could be of service in the rising.

Sallust, The Conspiracy of Catiline[1]

There are many problems established state authorities face in resisting a determined and well organised insurgency, whether in ancient Rome or twentieth century Yugoslavia. Intelligent rulers know this and this knowledge can often soon lead to paranoia. The effect of belief in conspiracy theories is usually paranoia, but in turn that does not mean that conspiracies do not exist.[2] In December 1992 Slobodan Milosevic's wife, the Sociology professor and hardline Communist Mira Markovic, observed in her Belgrade newspaper column that:

A civil war has been raging in Yugoslavia for a whole year now. Admittedly, it has not spread to all the former territories, but we have no longer any reason to believe that it will not. This classic civil war was preceded by several years of a special civil war. The bankrollers and masterminds of this special war against Yugoslavia and in Yugoslavia were located outside our country, but were able to recruit an army inside it. Long has it been apparent that the leaders and ideologists of separatist and nationalist movements and their followers have either consciously or unconsciously served as a fifth column, as a lever by means of which Yugoslavia was brought down and its peoples catapulted into war'.[3]

In her rambling analysis of the Yugoslav crisis at that time, Markovic illustrates some of the Serbs' deepest fears. She is suffused with a pessimistic sense that the country is at the mercy of superpower machinations, and there is little or nothing the Belgrade leadership can do to stop the conflicts spreading. She sees the main threat as military, a force or forces created from 'outside' Yugoslavia to destroy it by conspiring with disaffected minorities. Several years later this was still how the Belgrade government saw the KLA. The Serbs saw they were a stronger nation than Albania, where they believed the threat emanated from, and could defeat it by military means. The fact that the most powerful military alliance in the world, NATO, might be prepared to tolerate or even assist a nationalist resistance movement was quite beyond their imagination in those days.

The declaration of Kosovo independence in February 2008 appeared at one level to mark the end of a long and tortuous conflict which had been one of the most intractable problems in the southern Balkans in the twentieth century. Yet many Serbs have yet to come to terms with this reality and over a wider terrain, geographical and intellectual, come to terms with the failure of the Greater Serbia project. Most history of the conflict that has been published in Serbia is in more or less total denial about most major events in the ground conflict. As James Gow put it, 'The Serbian project ultimately came to nothing'.[4] Five years later Kosova's independence has been recognised by over 80 countries in the United Nations and the predictions in some quarters of a violent Kosova Serb reaction to the decision have been misplaced. Kosova has taken its place in the so-called Grand Strategy of the United States. This was after a war which, in the view of some commentators, was the first to be 'fought not for traditional security and economic objectives but for new institutional and ideological ones.'[5] It is doubtful if this is or was the case. Dominance of the Adriatic coast of the Mediterranean is vital to United States and NATO power projection into the Middle East and the Caucasus, given the importance of sea power in the projection of US power generally.

At the same time the Western Balkans as a whole is in something of an indeterminate state and there is an absence of security structures in the region. In the light of the major crisis in Greek finances that developed in late 2009 and came to the fore in 2010 it is far from clear what the prospects for further enlargement of the European Union in the Balkans will be, (after the membership of Croatia), or whether European Union membership if achieved will have as much influence over events as its proponents claim. The form of limited and controlled independence put forward in the Ahtisaari plan for Kosova independence did not envisage the creation of a Kosova army, and the demobilisation of the Kosova Protection Corps and the creation of the Kosova Security Force has not eased these dilemmas, as they are only small and limited national guard type forces, pale shadows of the KLA in its heyday.[6]

It is generally believed that the United States and the United Kingdom were in favour of a Kosova army in the new state that would not seek to disavow the KLA inheritance and the US Department of Defence had prepared a plan for an army as early as 2004/2005, but the policy option was later ruled out under the Ahtisaari negotiations by some of the European Union nations. It was believed the proposal would be unacceptable to Serbia and prevent the signing of the Ahtisaari plan.[7] The general model envisaged in Washington was based in some respects on the post-1945 German Bundeswehr: for a period the officer corps would include non-national officers from NATO nations and in practice the level of Kosova-led operational autonomy would be constrained. Thus, although formal independence has been achieved, many of the same splits in the international community that have always existed regarding Kosova independence still exist, and they have prevented the creation of a Kosova army and the completion of the sovereignty process. The problem of the KLA inheritance remains unresolved. Much of the logic of the position of some European Union nations would imply a highly Belgrade-centric view of the region, and also in some quarters a sense that the independence decision was a mistake and is in some sense reversible. In response to these and similar views, and the continuing Serbian campaign for the partition of Kosova, there is always the possibility of reactivation of the KLA inheritance.[8]

Although it is not generally stated in public by politicians or diplomats, there is both passive and active complicity in the government project in Belgrade to keep Kosova as weak and unsuccessful as possible and to hope for the time, however distant, when the Kosovars themselves will see that they are better off as part of Serbia. Other actors in Belgrade politics, such as ex-President Vojislav Kostunica, change little over the years. He puts forward an unchanging and classic Serbian nationalist line, as does most of the Serbian Orthodox

Church. Thus the concessions made to Serbian sensibilities between 2006 and 2008 in the Ahtisaari process have not produced any greater realism towards the Kosova issue, or any movement on the Serbian side. In contrast, the Kosova Albanian majority has made continual and major concessions to the international community and Serbia ever since the summer of 1999, with the failure of the original Thaci 'Provisional Government' to declare or hold a referendum on independence, the demobilisation of the Kosova Liberation Army with no real guarantees of what might replace it, and the numerous concessions to international community viewpoints on security in the TMK under Agim Ceku's command. The deal over the Preshevo Valley conflict in late 2000 was on terms highly advantageous to Belgrade.[9] There is also the issue of the shabby treatment given to ex-soldiers of the KLA in the first demobilisation and the subsequent political manipulations of successor organisations. It was only in Macedonia under the quality political and military leadership of Veliu, Ahmeti, Thaci, Xhaferi and Ostremi that it was possible to start to reverse these setbacks.

The creation of a Kosova army to complete the independence process and enable the state to achieve the full respect of its neighbours remains an urgent priority in Albanian eyes. The strength of the NATO KFOR force has dropped dramatically in the period since independence, from about 34,000 men and women to less than 10,000 in 2013. This is well below the infantry strength numbers most independent judges consider necessary to control civil disorder in Kosova, whatever its origin. Although the size and efficiency of the Kosova Border Police and the internal police have improved a great deal in these years, there is no effective security presence at all on most of the Kosova border with Serbia, and little heavy armour or other serious military capacity in the event of serious internal public order problems or external threat from the north. The monopoly on heavy armour that the VJ held throughout the wartime period remains today. Kosova is in many ways a new phenomenon in the Balkans, a new state which has achieved existence through a successful insurgent war and with the help of the world's most powerful military alliance. Yet an ancestral problem remains, the central strategic position of Kosova and its implications. Kosova has not achieved its full development post-independence because of strategic constraints. This is clearly because of the different views of the modern equivalents of the Great Powers of the past in the region, the United States and the United Kingdom on one hand and the

European Union on the other. In the European view there is a balance of interests to be maintained and in some senses little has changed since the Serbian historian Stojanovic wrote in his study of the Congress of Berlin and its aftermath, 'The proportion of power of the Great Powers had to be preserved in the East despite the transformations that were taking place there. To this all other interests were subordinated: the destiny of the Christians as well as that of Turkey.'[10]

The period of bitter nationalist rivalry that was to follow the 1878 Congress, and resurfaced after the end of communism, will, it is to be hoped, not be repeated in the twenty-first century, but the recurrent patterns in Balkan history do not entirely disappear over time. As it is a creation of the military arm of the West, the North Atlantic Treaty Organisation ensured that Kosova is intrinsically rooted in the Western world, but that world is in many ways as divided as ever. New nation states have never been welcomed since the end of the Cold War by many of the old European elites whose outlook was based on centralism and elements of the planned economy in their own countries, like France, Italy and Spain. Turkey is now reappearing as a new independent foreign policy factor in the Balkans with generally positive attitudes towards the completion of the Kosova sovereignty process.

At the heart of the story is the need to make a realistic evaluation of what the Kosova Liberation Army achieved and what its legacy will be. In his recent work *The Insurgent Archipelago: from Mao to Bin Laden*,[11] John Mackinlay sees all modern insurgencies as children of the work of Mao Tse-tung, who established their classical form with his dictum that insurgency is '80 per cent political and 20 per cent military'. There is the obvious question of how far the KLA was ever fully a 'Maoist' insurgency in military practice, except that it had its roots in the Kosova countryside in Drenica and Dukagjini. The prototype was adapted by the LPK/KLA from its definitely ideological Marxist roots in the early 1980s through a fairly successful transition to an advanced populist insurgency where local self-initiative by the majority population in defence of their houses and farms made it politically impossible for the Serbs to succeed with their ethnic cleansing ambitions. The military side of the insurgency was a brilliantly successful example of the power of 'propaganda by deed' for the insurgent in the sacrifice of the Jashari family at a key stage in the KLA campaign.[12]

It remains doubtful, though, whether the Kosova Liberation Army ever achieved the classic Titoist Partisan paradigm (itself derived from the Bolshevik experience) of a movement that grows so rapidly and universally among the workers and peasants as to fulfil the Titoist criteria of 'turning the insurrection into a total national war.'[13] The Kosova Albanians did seize the political high ground, and the numerous and concerted attempts by the opponents of Kosova independence in NATO and UNMIK in the post-2000 period, and other international factors, have never been able to displace the KLA's secondary political apparatus from the central and determinate place in Kosova Albanian politics, as Hashim Thaci's assumption of office as the first Prime Minister after independence in 2008 demonstrates. The LPK and its allies and supporters were there before the war, they helped start and sustain the war. They miscalculated and stumbled in Preshevo in 2000–2001 but triumphed in Macedonia in 2001; they remain influential today.

The KLA in its history has also demonstrated the correctness of the observation made many years ago by C.E. Callwell that the insurgent always has the strategic advantage in a conflict, while the counter-insurgent merely has tactical advantage.[14] This was a particular factor in the KLA's war against the VJ under Slobodan Milosevic's control because it so happened that Milosevic as a politician was a superb tactician in maintaining himself in power but had little strategic concept of where his policies might lead Serbia and Yugoslavia.[15] This political blindness exacerbated the weaknesses of his overall military strategy and in turn the VJ military response to the KLA.

The political side of the insurgency has had a less happy development in Kosova itself, although, as indicated above, many of these problems were being overcome in the last weeks of the Preshevo stage of the Serbian-Albanian conflict and were finally surmounted and superseded in the FYROM/Republic of Macedonia in 2001. The distinct nature of Kosova Albanian politics and the fact that there were major opinion constituencies, principally in the Kosova Democratic League, that had not taken part in the war and were to varying extents complicit in Rugova's denial of the validity of the war option itself, meant that the international community always had a platform for attempts to deny those politicians who had emerged from the KLA political legitimacy. The key targets in this respect were and to some extent still are Hashim Thaci and Ramush Haradinaj, but there also many others. The entire saga of the removal of Ramush Hardinaj as a legitimately elected Prime Minister and the subsequent Haradinaj trial at the ICTY at The Hague, and the humiliating nature of his rearrest on charges on which he had already been acquitted, is impossible to understand except in the context of political manipulation of the Prishtina political scene by international community figures anxious to promote particular political developments in Serbia.[16] The ICTY has been used to try to maintain Belgrade hegemony in the region.

In the main the theorising of the ICTY as a conflict resolution tool took place in Blair's United Kingdom where a particularly narrow and schematic understanding of the rule of law in international relations was promoted, in many ways a throwback to the early days of 'End of History' frenzy after 1990.[17] The 'rule of law' as an advocacy concept has replaced the obviously discredited concept of the 'New World Order' but performs the same structural function in discourse. As nobody can be against the 'rule of law' it is a timeless construct, although in practice at the ICTY it conceals cynical political manipulation of Kosova elites by governments. The rule of law is itself debased through its use in this way. The question is bound to arise of whether the impulses that lay behind the Kosova insurgency are exhausted. Optimists argue that they are, and that the conditions that gave rise to the KLA are long superseded by the departure of many of the Kosova Serbs, the fall of Milosevic, and Kosova independence in 2008. Pessimists will note the stagnation in much of Kosova, denial of Kosova independence in Belgrade and some sections of the international community, the limits to sovereignty under the Ahtisaari Plan, the absence of a Kosova army, continuing issues in Preshevo, tensions in the FYROM/Republic of Macedonia, rapidly growing unemployment and vast differences in wealth.

Underlying many of these concerns is the question of the alleged wider clash between the Christian and Islamic worlds in the wars in Iraq and Afghanistan and the possibility that any future Kosova conflict would involve questions of religion. There are many models of Islamic insurgency in the world. One of the great achievements of the Kosova Liberation Army was that it avoided involvement with any element of Islam, and Serbian claims that it was involved were highly counterproductive for Belgrade.[18] It is an open question whether that would be the case in the future, given the failure of the international community to establish full sovereignty in Kosova. Islam was the 'ghost in the machine' for the Kosova Liberation Army that was never actually there. The weakness, cynicism and incompetence of the UNMIK international administration after 1999 with its shabby treatment of many ex-KLA soldiers may have given rise to a degree of cynicism about Western secular democratic politics as a whole. This contains many dangers for the future if the Kosova Liberation Army inheritance is not adequately integrated into the new state institutions through an effective NATO-allied armed force.

Always in the background is the fact that it will take time to overcome the bitter inheritance of the Milosevic regime in Belgrade and the Balkan region generally, probably a longer time than the international community has so far understood. As Sallust observed in ancient Rome:

But what manner of men are they who have made themselves rulers of the state? They are evildoers whose hands are red with blood. Covetous beyond measure and stained with guilt, they are none the less swollen with pride, and there is nothing that they will not sell: honour, reputation, natural affection, every virtue indeed—as well as every vice—is to them a source of profit.[19]

Until the Serbian people face the question of what happened to their country in the years after 1987 and the moral and political degeneracy of the Milosevic period, it is likely that the Kosova Liberation Army inheritance will thrive. Memorials to the sacrifices of the KLA men and women are now dotted all over the Kosova landscape, polished granite slabs with photographs in enamel of departed young people from mostly modest families. They are a reminder of a tangible and close history. Kosova Albanians do not feel secure in their current relationship with post-Milosevic Serbia. They know that throughout its history Serbia has been an expansionist nation with regional hegemonic ambitions and shifting and changing borders. The danger with the denial by the international community of full sovereignty under the Ahtisaari plan is that elements in Serbia may in the future seek to reopen the Kosova border issue. In a sense they are already doing so through their promotion of the partition concept in Kosova north of the Ibar river, a policy with direct linear ancestry to the Milosevic period. In the majority of cases throughout Balkan history, when the borders of Serbia have changed they have done so as the result of war.

The Kosova Albanians are also so far in a position very similar to the Balkan peoples' situation after the First World War when the achievement of the nation state, as Michael Barratt Brown puts it, 'even one large enough to be economically viable for capitalist development, left most of the Yugoslav peoples after 1919 no better off than before and in many cases with the same foreign companies exploiting them on their land and in the mines and factories.'[20] The process of full emancipation of Serbia and Kosova from the burden of the shared past within globalisation has yet to be achieved. It is questionable whether current NATO policies are in keeping with the new situation on the ground, or whether NATO has yet, as Glenny observes, to 'address the effects, not merely of a three month air war in 1999, but of 120 years of miscalculation and indifference since the Congress of Berlin.'[21] There is perhaps nothing that symbolises this more clearly than the fact that there are still well over a thousand Kosovar Albanians missing and presumed dead in Serbia, ten years after the war. It seems Belgrade has remembered Niccolo Machiavelli's well known dictum, that a dead man cannot contemplate vengeance, and the generous but naïve cooperation the Kosova Albanian leaders gave to the international community in the Rambouillet period over demobilisation of their unique army in 1999 was essentially misplaced.[22]

In the Balkans, the attractions of the political underground and political conspiracy are always present. The liberal theory of the binary opposition between true history (bourgeois electoral praxis) and untrue conspiracy history (illegal anti-state activity) does not hold in the Balkans or elsewhere in Eastern Europe. The heritage of the LPK shows that in the right circumstances, small underground groups can develop wider political movements that lead to successful insurgencies. For the young men and women who are often the instigators, it can seem at first an easy process. The novelist Donna Tartt gives an imaginary example:

'Though after all your Xenophon and Thucydides, I dare say there are not many young people better versed in military tactics, I'm sure, if you wanted to, you'd be quite capable of marching on Hampden town and taking it over by yourselves.'

Henry laughed. 'We could do it this afternoon, with six men,' he said.

'How' said everyone at once.

'One person to cut the phone and power lines, one at the bridge over the Battenkill, one at the main road out, to the north. The rest of us could advance from the south and west. There aren't very many of us, but if we scattered, we'd be able to close off all the other points of entry,'—here he held out his hand, his fingers spread wide—'and advance to the centre from all points.' The fingers closed into a fist. 'Of course, we'd have the advantage of surprise,' he said, and I felt an unexpected thrill at the coldness of his voice.'[23]

In the real life case of Kosova, Freddie Mehmeti, a Chicago-based Homeland Calling activist, later wrote:

I was convinced that handful of people can do miracles. I had faith in the KLA. My teenage experiences in Montenegro taught me that a small group of people can do miracles if they have the will. It may take a long time, but eventually their movement can grow. I was actually surprised that the KLA grew much faster than I expected.[24]

Thus the conspiracy becomes the history and escapes the fictional.

ILLUSTRATIONS

Fig. 1: The Tradition of Kosova Resistance.
Fig. 2: The Jashari Brothers: Founding Fathers of the KLA.
Fig. 3: Adem Demaci in prison, about 1980.
Fig. 4: The Underground Press: 'The Voice of Kosova'.
Fig. 5: Armed uprising in Albania: Gjirokaster, 1997.
Fig. 6: A Kosova army forms: KLA female recruits, 1998.
Fig. 7: New soldiers under canvas: Dukagjini, 1998.
Fig. 8: The refugee crisis, Kukes, Albania, 1999.
Fig. 9: Gaoled student leader Albin Kurti, Prishtina.
Fig. 10: Hashim Thaci in Prishtina, 1999.
Fig. 11: From soldier to politician, Ramush Haradinaj, 1999.
Fig. 12: International peacekeepers, Turkish soldiers in Prizren, 1999.
Fig. 13: The price of war, excavating a mass burial, rural Kosova.
Fig. 14: Prishtina memorial ceremony, 1999.
Fig. 15: Macedonian sequel: Ali Ahmeti in the mountains, 2001.
Fig. 16: LPK leader Fazli Veliu and NLA recruits, Shipkovica.

Fig. 1: The Tradition of Kosova Resistance

Fig. 2: The Jashari Brothers: Founding Fathers of the KLA

Fig. 3: Adem Demaci in prison, about 1980

ZËRI i KOSOVËS

ORGANI I LEVIZJES POPULLORE PER REPUBLIKEN E KOSOVES

Viti IX i botimit
Nr. 3, mars 1990

KOMUNIKATE

Popull shqiptar,

Populli ynë, pasardhës i ilirëve përballoi gjatë shekujve pushtimin e asimilimin dhe të gjitha metodat e tjera të shumta. Gjatë tërë historisë sonë ne luftuam me guxim kundër të gjithë atyre që synuan të na pushtojnë atdheun. Pos kundërvënies pushtuesve romakë e bizantinë, populli ynë iu kundërvu edhe pushtimeve të perandorive serbe të shekujve XIII-XV, duke përballuar asimilimin dhe serbizimin e Kosovës.

Me luftën heroike populli ynë nuk u mposht as nga Perandoria Otomane. Deri sa forcat shqiptare luftonin kundër pushtuesve osmanë, ushtria ekspansioniste serbe e malazeze pushtoi viset që ua kishte dhuruar Kongresi famëkeq i Berlinit, më 1878, nën pretekstin se po çlironin viset ballkanike nga sundimi osman.

Që kur mbretëritë shoviniste serbo-malazeze pushtuan Kosvën, populli ynë nuk e pushoi rezistencën.

Gjatë luftërave ballkanike e gjerë më 1921 u zhdukën 36 mijë shqiptarë. Gjatë Reformës Agrare 27.II.1919, 10.904 kolonistëve u janë ndarë 8987 hektarë tokë, ndërsa serbëve vendas u janë dhënë 27.713 hektarë. Vetëm gjatë 3 vjetëve të para të Mbretësirue SKS, përveç mijëra të shpërngulurve, të burgosurve, e të plaçkiturve u mbytën mizorisht 12.777 shqiptarë. Nga viti 1912 e gjer më 1941 u shpuerngulën për në Turqi 500.000 shqiptarë, ndërsa në tokat e tyre u vendosën 24.000 familje kolonësh serbo-malazeze, sipas Elaboratit të të Vasa Çubriloviçit, mars 1937. Teza aq shumë e përhapur sot për gjoja Kosovën serbe është pa bazë edhe për arsye të faketeve të sipërpërmendur, edhepër arsye se sipas regjistrimit 1921 struktura kombëtare në Kosovë ishte: serbë-ortodoks 94.300, ose 22 për qind, serbë-muslimanë 13.500 ose 3 për qind, arnautë 280.000 ose 66 për qind, turq 3.3000, dhe 5.000 të tjerë.

Shpërthimi i LDB përkohësisht pengoi zbatimin e Elaboratit të Çubriloviçit. Por, shpëngulja e popullit tonë u vazhdua nga Rankoviçi.

Pushtuesit serbo-maqedono-malazezomedhenj, për më pak se dy dekada zhdukën fizikisht mijëra shqiptarë dhe shpuerngulën për Turqi 400.000 të tjerë, ndërsa në vend të tyre u vendosën 54.000 kolonë serbomalazez.

Shpërngulja e shqiptarëve është e vazhduar me anë të metodave perfide edhe gjatë dy dekadave të fundit, gjatë së cilës periudhë janë shpërngulur 250.000 shqiptarë në të katër anët e botës.

Popull shqiptar,

Kur delegati nga Kosova më 15 dhjetor 1937, në Kuvendin e Serbisë bëri pyetje në emër të bazës rreth qëndrimeve fashiste të V. Çubriloviçit, nuk iu dha përgjigje dhe pyetja e tij u hodh poshtë, nga neoçubrilloviçët, si e pabazë! Ndërsa sot të tërbuar, pas manifestimeve gjithëpopullore të popullit tonë, gjatë janar-shkurtit të këtij vitit, srbomëdhejtë sërish po e shohin ëndrrën e paraardhësve për kolonizimin e sërishëm të Kosvës, duke vendosur 100.000 serbomalazez dhe duke i shpërngulur 300.000-400.000 «emigrantë» shqiptarë. A është i realizueshem ky ideal cionist?

Jo! Gjarpijtë e gjakut, siç i quajti serbomëdhenjtë, simboli i rezistencës sonë kombëtare, Adem Demaçi, tash një shekull nuk kanë lënë metodë pa përdorur për realizimin e qëllimeve të errëta.

Por gjaku i dëshmorëve shqiptarë nuk ka lejuar pustimin e tokës së të parëve.

Duke pasur parasysh këtë përvojë historike, me këta usht.shqiptarë të përbetuar, **Lëvizja Popullore për Republikën e Kosovës**

THERRET

Që ta ngritim zërin kundr planeve djallëzore të politikës aktuale dhe të mos e lejojmë kolonizimin e sërishëm të Kosovës.

Lufta jonë e drejtë demokratike e paqësore, ka bërë që të kemi përkrahjen e opinionit demokratik ndërkombëtar dhe vazhdimi i saj patjetër do të kurorëzohet me fitore.

Rrofte populli ynë liridashës i pamposhtur!

Rrofte opinioni demokratik ndërkombëtar!

Lavdi dëshmorëve puer liri!

Kosova Republikë!

Prishtinë, 7.III.1990

VETEM NE REPUBLIKEN E TYRE SHQIPTARET MUND TE NDIHEN TE BARABARTE

Intervistë me shokun Adem Demaçi botuar në gazetën «Veçernji List» të Zagrebit të datës 24.2.1990, me titull «Milloshevici punon për ne». Intervistën po e botojmë në tërësi. Nëntitujt janë të gazetës «V. List».

KAM QENE KUNDER DHUNES DHE ATENTATEVE
—Gëzoni famën e ideologut të se-

peratizmit në Kosovë. Njëkohësisht keni munguar në. të gjitha konfliktet më të mëdha—në ato të 1968, 1981, 1988, e deri më sot, edhe atë me alibinë e përkrye: keni qenë në burg.

—Po, kjo është situatë tepër paradoksale. Përse? Duhet hyrë në thelbin e çështjeve. Çfarë është konflikti në

Jugosllavinë e sotme? Klasa burokratiko-parazite ka përshkuar gjithë shoqërinë... Xhidoja thotë se kjo është «klasë e re», por nuk thotë se çfarë është. Kjo klasë burokratiko-parazite për ta zgjatur pushtetin e vet, në munges-së të armiqve duhet t'i trillojë, e nëse veç ata ekzistojnë, duhet t'i ngritë dhe t'i paraqesë në prizmë të shtrembër, vetëm e vetëm që të mund të arsyetojë vetveten. Kjo klasë patjetër duhet të krijojë prej armikut gogol, na e trilloje atë, duke arsyetuar mizoritë e veta —mbajtjen e njeriut 30 vjet në burg. Logjika e kësaj klase është logjikë e ngurtë, devijuese, antidialektike. Kundërshtarët e saj mundohet t'i prezen-

(Vijon në faqen 3, 4 dhe 5)

Fig. 5: Armed uprising in Albania: Gjirokaster, 1997

Fig. 6: A Kosova army forms: KLA female recruits, 1998

Fig. 7: New soldiers under canvas: Dukagjini, 1998

Fig. 8: The refugee crisis, Kukes, Albania, 1999

Fig. 9: Gaoled student leader Albin Kurti, Prishtina

Fig. 10: Hashim Thaci in Prishtina, 1999

Fig. 11: From soldier to politician, Ramush Haradinaj, 1999

Fig. 12: International peacekeepers, Turkish soldiers in Prizren, 1999

Fig. 13: The price of war, excavating a mass burial, rural Kosova

Fig. 14: Prishtina memorial ceremony, 1999

Fig. 15: Macedonian sequel: Ali Ahmeti in the mountains, 2001

Fig. 16: LPK leader Fazli Veliu and NLA recruits, Shipkovica

APPENDIX A

MILITARY ORGANISATION IN WARTIME KOSOVA, MARCH-MAY 1999

KOSOVA LIBERATION ARMY

General Headquarters   Kukes, Albania
General Staff Headquarters   Prekaz, Kosova

OPERATIONAL ZONES   Commander

Zone 1—Drenica   Sami Lustaku

Brigades: 111 'Fatmir Ibishi', 112 'Sherif Jonuzi', 113 'Muje Krasniqi',114, 'Fehmi Lladrovci

Zone 2—Llap   'Remi' (Rrustem Mustafa)

Brigades: 121 'Shaban Shala',122 'Zahir Pajaziti'

Zone 3—Dukagjini   Ramush Haradinaj

Brigades 131 'Jusuf Gervalla', 132 'Myrte Zenelli', 124 'Adrian Krasniqi, 134 'Bedri Shala', and 136 Brigade

Zone 4—Shala   Rahman Ramaj

Brigades 141 'Mehe Uka', 142 'Azen Galica'

Zone 5—Pashtrik

Brigades 151 'Zahir Pajaziti' and 152 'Shala'

Zone 6—Nerodime   Shukri Buja

Brigades 161 'Ahmet Kaqiku', 162 'Agron Bajrami'

Zone 7—Kara Dagh

Brigades 171 'Kadri Zeka', and 172 and 173 Brigades

KOSOVA LIBERATION ARMY: ADMINISTRATIVE DIRECTORATES: NOVEMBER 1997

G1	Personnel	Adem Grabovci
G2	Security and Information	Kadri Veseli
G3	Operations	Beslim Zyrapi
G4	Logistics	Xhavit Haliti
G5	Civil-Military Relations	Rame Buja
G6	Communications	Muse Jashari
G7	Finance	Lahi Ibrahimi
G8	Public Security	Fatmir Limaj
G9	Politics	Hashim Thaci
Inspector General		Rexhep Selimi
Spokesman		Jakup Krasniqi

YUGOSLAV ARMY (NIS COMMAND CENTRE)

Commander   General Nebojsa Pavkovic

FORCES

Mixed Artillery Brigades 150 and 202
7 and 311 AF SAM Regiments

Nis Corps:

211 Armoured Brigade and 4 Motorised Brigade, Reserves 2 and 805 Motorised Brigades, 50 Light Infantry Brigade, 203 Mixed Army Brigade.

Leskovac Corps:

Reserves 89 and 135 Motorised Brigades, 21 and 42 Artillery Brigades

APPENDIX A

Prishtina Corps:

52 Engineers regiment, 52 Military Police Battalion, 52 Signal Regiment, 15 Armoured Brigade, 78,125 and 549 Motorised Brigades, 243 Mechanised Brigade, 58, 175 and 354 Light Infantry Brigades, 52 Mixed Artillery Brigade, 62 Mixed Artillery Brigade, 102 Mixed Artillery Brigade, 53,55 and 57 Border Brigades.

In addition, various Special Forces and Anti-Terrorist Units, mainly from Leskovac and Uzice, reconnaissance and Military Police Units. Timok Task Force:
9 and 148 Motorised Brigades.

BORDER INCIDENTS IN THE 'FIRST OFFENSIVE' PERIOD[1]

1 January 1998–1 August 1998

Number of alleged illegal crossings and border incidents

Illegal crossings—from the FRY	166
Illegal crossings—in the FRY	355
TOTAL	521

Border incidents classified by types

Air space violation	5
Territory violation	8
Territorial waters violation	2
Removal of border markings	1
Infiltration of subversive groups	68
Other	3
TOTAL	87

Weapons seized at border of FRY/Republic of Albania

Different types of rifles	947
Machine guns	161
Mortars	7
Large mortars	26
Anti-aircraft guns	3
Portable rocket launchers	65
Hand grenades	3,295
Ammunition and small arms ammunition	348,954
Mortar shells	484

Grenades for portable launchers	289
Mines	132 kg
Anti-tank mines	55

APPENDIX B

KOSOVA PEOPLE'S MOVEMENT (LPK) AND POPULAR FRONT FOR A KOSOVA REPUBLIC (LPRK): CHRONOLOGY AND DEVELOPMENT

Chronology and Development

Spring 1981	Mass demonstrations for a Kosova Republic in Prishtina and other Kosova towns and cities.
July 1981	Formation of Popular Front for a Kosova Republic (LPRK) by Hydajet Hyseni, Mehmet Hajrizi and Nezir Myrtaj.
17 January 1982	Murder of the Gervalla brothers and Kadri Zeka, near Heilbronn, Germany.
17 February 1982	Formation in Turkey by exiles of the League for a Socialist Republic of Albanians in Yugoslavia (LSRAY).
May 1982	Formation of LSRAY in Switzerland by Xhafer Shatri.
Summer 1982	Formation of LSRAY in Kosova by Gafurr Elshani, Shaban Shala and others. LSRAY begins to set up clubs for exiles in Switzerland and Germany.
1983	The newspaper *Zeri I Kosoves* is printed in Switzerland. Arrest of Zijah Shemsiu and

	Sami Kurteshi for arms dealing between Switzerland and Yugoslavia.
1984	Editorial collective for *Zeri I Kosoves* formed, including Hasan Mala and Emrush Xhemajli.
1985	LSRAY adopts new name, the Popular Front for a Kosova Republic (LPRK).Formation of LPRK in Prekaz, Drenica by Adem Jashari, Sami Lushtaku, Jakup Nura and others.
November 1986	Establishment of LPRK Exterior in Zurich, Switzerland.
July 1987	Meeting of LPRK in Zurich agrees party statues, elects Fazli Veliu, Xhavit Haliti, Emrush Xhemajli as leaders.
1987–1989	LPRK develops organisation in Kosova Diaspora.
1988–1989	LPRK begins sabotage of telephone and electricity lines linking Kosova with Serbia and Macedonia.
1989	Formation of the military council of LPRK. LPRK organises demonstrations against loss of Kosova autonomy. Activists of the LPRK organise the armed '*Llap Ceta*' in Podujeve.
1990	LPRK activity against loss of Kosova autonomy.
October 1991	Third Congress of LPRK in Drenica. Name changed to Kosova Peoples League (LPK). Gani Thaci and Azem Syla join leadership group.
November 1991	Meeting between LPK leaders Xharvit Haliti, Xharvit Haziri, Ahmet Haxhiu and Albanian President Ramiz Alia in Tirana.
December 1991	Formation in Zurich of coordinating body to support armed resistance in Kosova.

1991–1992	LPK member Fehmi Lladrovci moves to Zagreb to work with deserting Albanian soldiers in Croatia.
May 1992	LPK branch founded in Peje. Delegation of LPK leaders meet ASP leader Fatos Nano in Zurich.
1993	Foundation of the Homeland Calling Fund in Switzerland.
April 1993	LPK *ceta* including Hashim Thaci, Bilal Sherifi and Adnan Asllani begins armed actions in Drenica. 29 July: 4th Congress of LPK adopts programme for the armed struggle in Kosova.
August 1993	Mass arrests of alleged LPK members in Prishtina.
1994	Reorganisation of LPK in Switzerland. Fazli Veliu and Muhamet Kelmendi become the heads of political organisation Xhavit Haliti, Azem Syla and Ali Ahmeti heads of Special Operations.
1993–1995	Establishment of LPK in all main Kosova cities and regions.
November 1994	First FX communiqué of LPK military committee issued in Aarau, Switzerland.
1994–1996	Development of LPK framework for a Kosova Liberation Army.
March 1997	In Germany military committee of LPK appoints Fehmi Lladrovci to form a support group of soldiers for Adem Jashari in Drenica. Ali Ahmeti deployed to assist Ramush Haradinaj after death of Luan Haradinaj.
April 1997	LPK in Prishtina join with underground group led by Dr Muhamet Mehmeti and student leader Muhamet Mavraj.

August 1997	LPK HQ in Albania established at Golem, near Durres as supply base for Drenica.
January 1998	LPK leadership approves design of KLA emblems and uniform in Switzerland.
March 1998	Most of the LPK leadership moves to Albania. Prioritises supply of satellite telephones and technical equipment to the KLA. Veliu remains in Switzerland.
May 1998	First major shipment of arms to KLA from LPK via Struga, in FYROM/Republic of Macedonia.
December 1999	*Zeri I Kosoves* starts to appear daily in Prishtina.
January 2000	LPK initiates aid for the UCPMB fighting in the Preshevo valley.
March 2000	In Gjilan Jonuz Musliu, a LPK activist forms the Political Council for Preshevo, Medvegje, and Bujanoc.
April–December 2000	LPK joins coalition with AAK in Kosova.
July 2000	250 delegates meeting in Prishtina approve new statues for LPK.
February 2001	LPK publishes a programme for a liberation of the Albanians in Macedonia. Ex-KLA soldiers of Macedonian origin form National Liberation Army.

APPENDIX C

THE PROGRAMME OF THE PEOPLE'S MOVEMENT
FOR THE REPUBLIC OF KOSOVA (LPRK)[1]

Introduction

The Albanian people, descendants of the Illyrians, have faced throughout the centuries, invasion, attempts at assimilation and all kinds of other actions by numerous would-be conquerors, while living themselves in their present autochthonous territories. During their entire history they fought bravely against all those who invaded their Motherland, and those who attempted to exterminate or assimilate it.

As in the case of the earlier Roman, Byzantine and other invaders, our people opposed the invasions of the Serbian Empire in the 13th and 14th centuries, resisting the assimilation and Serbianisation of Kosova. The Albanian people also took part in the Battle of Kosova in 1389, in an alliance of the Balkan peoples, in a resistance front to the Ottoman invaders. The almost five hundred years of Ottoman enslavement struck our people hard but they did not hesitate to confront the superpower of the time. Indeed, the heroic resistance of our people obstructed the invasion of Central Europe by the Ottoman forces, and so contributed to the defence of European civilisation.

Our people was formed and developed simultaneously within the weakening of the Ottoman Empire, with the spread of Enlightenment ideas of the European renaissance and of the capitalist element in social life. National consciousness grew in the struggle against the Ottoman invaders.

In the second half of the nineteenth century, our people threw up a galaxy of patriots in our National Renaissance which further developed its will to struggle against the Ottoman invaders and gain national independence. At the time when its destiny was being determined, our people mobilised around the Albanian League of Prizren, founded on 10th June 1878. This League fought for the defence of Albanian interests at the Congress of Berlin, led to the uprising for autonomy and independence, and defended our territories from partition and conquest by neighbouring chauvinist states, behind which stood the great imperialist powers of the time. Tsarist Russia, by means of the Treaty of San Stefano and with the support of the Great Powers, denied to our people the right to form its own national state with the aim of using its territory for imperialist expansion.

While the rebel forces led by the Albanian League of Prizren were fighting against the Ottoman invaders, the Serbian and Montenegrin armies attacked the Albanian rebel forces from the rear in order to occupy those territories granted to them by the infamous Congress of Berlin. Thus, the Serbian armies attacked, massacred and expelled the ethnic Albanian population of Fuschegropa (in Jablanica in Kosova), and of the districts of Nis, Prokuple, Leskovac, Toplica, Vranje and elsewhere, while the Montenegrin armies attacked the Albanian territories of Plava, Gucia, Hoti, Gruda and Tivar.

Successive uprisings attained national dimensions during the years 1908–1912. The fruit of these uprisings and the patriotic activity of the Albanian diplomacy was the Declaration of National Independence on 28th November 1912. At the time when our people were making decisive attempts to gain liberation, the chauvinist armies of the Balkan coalition, under the pretext of liberating the Balkan lands from Ottoman occupation, occupied and dismembered our territory.

The Ambassador's Conference sponsored by the imperialist Great Powers, which took place in London in 1913, recognised this occupation and left more than half of the territory of Albania under the rule of the chauvinist kingdoms of Montenegro and Serbia. This historical injustice, against the resistance and numerous protests of our people, was confirmed by the Versailles conference of 1919, which created the Kingdom of the Serbs, Croats and Slovenes. This Kingdom, like the Serbian and Montenegrin armies during the Balkan wars and the First World War, continued the same policy of denationalisation, displacement and physical extermination of our people.

Since the chauvinist kingdoms of Serbia and Montenegro occupied Kosova, our heroic people have not ceased its resistance. Uprisings for freedom and independence were carried out in the form of well known insurgent struggles such as the Kacak movement. This national liberation movement was led by the Kosova Committee.

* * *

The outbreak of the Second World War found the people of Kosova wearied by the heavy oppression under the yoke of the bourgeois-monarchist Yugoslavia. The policy which the Greater Serbia activists had pursued towards our people had been condemned by the Communist Party of Yugoslavia, which recognised the right to national self-determination of the component states and peoples. The CPY upheld this correct position at its third Congress, at its 5th national conference, and during the Second World War up to the Second Assembly of the Yugoslav Anti-Fascist Council of National Liberation (ASNOM), when the leadership of the CPY and the Yugoslav Partisan Army betrayed the Albanian people.

At this meeting, where the foundations of the state power of the present Socialist Federation of Yugoslavia were laid, nothing was said about the Albanian people of Kosova. No Albanian delegate took part, and in opposition to the will of our people, it was decided that Kosova and its regions should be forcibly retained as a colony.

At the time when the foundations of the future Federal Republic were being laid, the Kosova district committee of the CPY summoned the first and founding Conference of the National Liberation Council for Kosova, which took place from 31st December 1943 to 2nd January 1944 in Bujan, in the highlands near Gjakova in Kosova. It was attended by 43 Albanian and 8 Serbian and Montenegrin delegates. The conference unanimously approved a resolution which clearly expressed the desire and determination of our people to unite with the Mother Country of Albania. They considered the Communist Party of Albania, the Communist Party of Yugoslavia (the CPY), the Albanian National Liberation Army (ANLA), the Yugoslav National Liberation Army (JNA) and their allies—the Soviet Union, Britain and the United States—guarantors of this. The decisions taken at Bujan further mobilised the will of our people to throw themselves into the general national liberation uprising against the Nazi fascist occupiers, in which more than 50,000 Albanian fighters took part and thousands of martyrs sacrificed their lives.

At this time, when in pursuit of the Nazis, the Kosovar brigades went to the aid of the peoples of Yugoslavia and shed their blood for their freedom, Serbian and Montenegrin and Macedonian Partisan divisions, instead of acting in the same way, invaded free Kosova and cruelly massacred the defenceless population. With the ensuing proclamation of martial law on Kosova, the Yugoslav leadership trampled on the historic decisions of Bujan. In this way Kosova was again occupied.

* * *

In order to subjugate our people more easily, the Belgrade government partitioned Kosova between the Republics of Serbia, Macedonia and Montenegro, just as bourgeois-monarchist Yugoslavia had divided it into 'banovina' (provinces) before the Second World War. Kosova was, therefore, not only occupied but was prevented from enjoying equal rights with the other federal units within the framework of the Socialist Federation of Yugoslavia. Following the example of the Yugoslavia of the Karageorgevich monarchs, the Yugoslav leadership revived the 1938 agreement between the Turkish and Yugoslav governments for the expulsion of the Albanians. This chauvinist-colonialist policy was exercised according to the formulae of the notorious Serbian Cultural Union, whose President, Vaso Cubrilovic was appointed Minister without Portfolio in the then Belgrade government. In accordance with these formulae, actions such as 'Otkup' (the compulsory purchase of Albanian peasants produce by the Yugoslav state), forced agrarian reform and coercive actions were carried out leading to the death or expulsions of thousands of Albanians who were beaten to death or otherwise humiliated.

During this time our national flag, language, education and identity was prohibited. In parallel with this, intensive exploitation of Kosova mineral resources was intensified. In the struggle for power, the Croatian-Slovenian leadership defeated the Greater Serbian clique led by Alexander Rankovic, and after 1956 brought an easing of the policy of terror and genocide, and of the deportation of and discrimination against our people.

* * *

At this difficult time, the sons of our people undertook broad and organised measures of resistance. As a result of and a reaction to this oppressive policy, the demonstrations of 1968 were organised in which people from all parts of the Albanian districts determined the right to use the national flag, and for a Kosova republic, a University and for the release of political prisoners. The Belgrade regime bloodily suppressed these demonstrations. But later, out of fear of a repetition of these mass protests, the Belgrade government was obliged to accede to some of the above demands. So Kosova obtained the right to use the flag and the language, (although only in its own districts), together with the right of an autonomous entity, and also Prishtina University was founded then.

Our people won these rights with blood and sacrifices, in struggle against backward views resulting from severe oppression, and for the sake of its ardent desire for knowledge. The broad education of the new generation began, even though only the minimal conditions for this existed.

The intensification of economic backwardness, the continuous fall in the standard of living, the growth of unemployment on one hand, and the growth of the national and class consciousness of the people unwilling to live in such conditions resulted in a sharp rise in revolutionary determination, particularly among the young, to struggle in an organised way for rights due to our people.

As a result of these struggles, in 1974 the Belgrade regime was forced to grant in Kosova (but not in the other regions of Serbia, Montenegro and Macedonia inhabited by an Albanian majority) the status of an 'Autonomous District', although this autonomy was always limited to education and culture. Meanwhile the aggressive supporters of a Greater Serbia were gaining in influence and in 1989 unleashed a military police terror and suppressed the judicial status of the Autonomous District of Kosova which remained a component part of Serbia. In this way constitutional rights acceded to Kosova by the 1974 Constitution were annulled. During all this time staged political trials and the persecution of patriotic and revolutionary elements in the population continued. However, the organised resistance of our people to the many gaolings and special courts grew ever stronger. Through publications, pamphlets, slogans they opposed the savage robbery of their wealth and the violation of their national and democratic rights, together with all the diabolical measures of the state aimed at disorientating and corrupting the youth.

As a direct result of this organised revolutionary activity and of the deepening of the gulf between impoverished Kosova and the rest of the country, in spring 1981 demonstrations had broken out. Protests grew in the succeeding years, culminating in the mass strikes of 1988 and 1989 which embraced the whole people, in which all strata of the Albanian population took part

The revolutionary forces, being in tune with the flow of events, led the people and in their name, demanded that Kosova be accorded the status of a Republic within the framework of the Yugoslav Federation, and they put forward other demands based on the Constitution of the Socialist Federal Republic of Yugoslavia.

Character, aims and motives of the people's movement for the Republic of Kosova

1. The political, judicial and economic system established in 1946 and 1963, together with the Constitution of 1974 and the constitutional amendments of 1989, originated from the cliques in power and their aim that the state should be authoritarian and centralist. By the constitutional changes of 1989, the position of Kosova and the Albanian people was established in accordance with the national-chauvinist views of Serbia, Macedonia and Montenegro.

2. The enslavement of the Albanian people by Serbian, Macedonian and Montenegrin chauvinists, that is of Kosova under Serbia and the other Albanian areas under Macedonia and Montenegro—is based on political, judicial and economic formations. It is in every way equivalent to enslavement by a colonial power.

3. In these conditions the government of the SFRY has not only intensified political discrimination, violence and terror but in collaboration with the army and police an in opposition the will of the Albanian people, has suppressed the Constitution of the Autonomous District of Kosova and placed it under the rule of Serbia. With great speed laws have been imposed which deprive Kosova of all its rights, intensify violence and sanction a system of military and police dictatorship.

4. The position of Kosova under Serbia, and of the other Albanian areas under Macedonia and Montenegro, is that history, education, language and culture of our people have been virtually proscribed, and they have been deprived of freedom of speech, assembly, and of

organisation, and of every national and democratic right in an attack on our identity. Our people are no longer designated as a Nation, but as a 'national minority'

5. This anti-Albanian policy reveals not only the chauvinist aims of those Serbianising Kosova and establishing a unitary system of Greater Serbian hegemony, but also the wider plan hatched up between Moscow and Belgrade to dominate the peoples of the Balkans and prepare an attack on the Peoples Socialist Republic of Albania.

6. Alongside the oppression, the denial of national and democratic rights and the capitalist relations of production, the Albanian people in Yugoslavia are also suffering colonialist exploitation. The more the military machinery is modernised, the more technical progress enters production, the deeper the economic crisis in Yugoslavia grows—the more intense grows the exploitation of our resources and the more the state tries to place the burden of the crisis on the backs of the working masses.

7. Through its colonialist policy, the Belgrade government is carrying out a systematic plunder of the wealth of Kosova, of its raw and semi-processed materials; it is making enslaving investments, building factories only to benefit Serbia and Montenegro, and it is intensifying the rate of extraction of surplus value from labour, as well as the economic and political migration of the Albanians.

8. The more the national consciousness of the Albanian population grows, the more severe the terror caused by the rulers grows, but is countered by the growing determination of the people to solve the national question.

9. The demonstrations, strikes and violent clashes of the spring of 1981, of November 1988, and of February, March and May 1989 were the direct continuation of our people's uninterrupted struggle for freedom, equality and republican status, and evidence of its rising intensity. These popular struggles did not have any chauvinist, reactionary, separatist or counter-revolutionary character, as the Belgrade government alleges. They were a consequence of the unbearable state in which the Albanian population found itself, and the savage colonialist exploitation imposed on our working masses.

10. The demand for Republican status for Kosova, for democratic and national freedom and rights, and for better living conditions is for

rights which are realisable under the Constitution. The national question remains unresolved for the Albanian population of Yugoslavia. The demand for Republican status is correct and supported by the entire Albanian population. The establishment of this Republic would place our people on an equal level with the other peoples of the Socialist Federal Republic of Yugoslavia.

11. The Albanian people of Kosova possess all the characteristics which constitute a nation. They have a common history, language, territory, economic life, psychological make-up and culture which establish that they are a nation and not, as the advocates of a Greater Serbia allege, merely a 'national minority' or a 'nationality'. In fact, by numbers, the Albanian population is the third largest constituent of Yugoslavia.

12. Republican status would make possible rapid economic and cultural development and confirm the Albanian people as a nation within Yugoslavia.

13. Republican status for Kosova would in no way harm the peoples of Yugoslavia or the administration of the Federal state (the SFRY).On the contrary, it is in the interests of the peoples and Republics of the SFRY. Republican status is also in the interests of the Serbs, the Montenegrins and Macedonians who live in Kosova, since it will free them from the manipulations and pressures imposed upon them by the Belgrade regime to adopt a hostile and aggressive stand towards our people.

14. The demand for the formation of the Republic of Kosova is correct and in the spirit of the Yugoslav Constitution. The punishments meted out to those who demand a Kosova Republic are unlawful.

15. The demand for republican status for Kosova does not impair the territorial integrity of the SFRY.

16. The formation of the Republic of Kosova is in conformity with the Charter of the United Nations and the Helsinki Final Act and presents no danger to peace in the Balkans. On the contrary, peace in the Balkans would be further stabilised.

17. Even though this demand is correct and our demonstrations have been peaceful and disciplined, the lackeys of Greater Serbia and Macedonian and Montenegrin chauvinists have ordered their suppression by the army, the militia and the Special Police. Consequently, the Belgrade government must bear responsibility for the

bloodshed, for the murder of demonstrators, for the imprisonments, and for the generally fascist measures applied in Kosova.

18. The political aim of the Greater Serbian activists is not only the Serbianisation of Kosova on the basis of the shameful new Constitution of Serbia, but a return to the system of Rankovic with an expansion of the military to secure its hegemony over all Yugoslavia. This is to be realised by cooperation with Russian social-imperialism against the peoples of Yugoslavia and the Balkans. In these conditions, the mobilisation of the Albanians, with their militant patriotic spirit, their unity, their faith in their own capacity, has increased and they are going forward on the road of determined struggle to realise their national and democratic rights.

19. The aim of the People's Movement for the Republic of Kosova (LPRK) is that Kosova, inhabited by a majority of Albanians, should be accorded the status of a Republic of the Socialist Federal Republic of Yugoslavia (RSFRY).

The political demands

With these facts in mind, the LPRK demands the realisation of the following national and democratic rights:

1) The granting of the status of a nation to the Albanian people in Yugoslavia.

2) The formation of the Republic of Kosova within the framework of the Socialist Federal Republic of Yugoslavia to include the areas inhabited by an Albanian majority now under Serbia, Macedonia and Montenegro.

3) An amnesty for the Albanian political prisoners and for political supporters of the demand for the Republic of Kosova.

4) The facilitation of the return to their homes of the Albanians driven out by violence and terror.

5) The withdrawal of occupying troops and Belgrade secret service agents.

6) The recognition of the right of freedom of speech, of the Press, and of assembly and political organisation.

7) The institution of a proportionate number of Albanian officers and non-commissioned officers in the army to the number of Albanians in the general population, so our people can make an equal contribution to the other Federal nationalities.

8) The adequate representation of Albanians in leading roles in civilian state occupations in the Federal state.

The economic demands

With the aim of removing the colonial oppression of Kosova, the LPRK demands:

1) Autonomous economic and trade enterprises, like those of the other SFRY republics.
2) All natural resources (above and below ground) to be placed under the control of the state authorities of the Republic of Kosova.
3) Industrial enterprises should be constructed in Kosova for manufacturing products from Kosova raw materials.
4) All contracts involving colonial exploitation to be annulled.
5) Kosova should receive its own income from within the SFRY budget.
6) Conditions should be created to increase employment and to assist the return of emigrants.

Immediate issues

Working to create the Republic of Kosova, the LPRK organises resistance in every factory, village, school, and neighbourhood for the defence of the national, political, economic and social rights of the working class, the peasants, the young people, the women and the intellectuals and opposes the pillaging of Kosova resources and defends the material and spiritual culture of our people.

1) For the realisation of these demands and aims, LPRK gives priority to the organisation of illegal activity, but the LPRK will also utilise legal forms of struggle where possible.
2) The LPRK organises emigrants abroad against the occupation. It sees the workers at home and abroad at the core of the progressive forces.
3) The LPRK opposes the Yugoslav League of Communists and its treacherous mass organisations, such as the Socialist League of the Working People, the Socialist Youth League and the Trade Union League. They are tools of the occupiers. LPRK will work to unmask their treacherous leaderships and recruit the masses manipulated by them.

4) The LPRK is opposed to reformism and bourgeois legalism, but at the same time, it opposes anarchist and terrorist methods of struggle which seriously harm and compromise our just cause.

5) The LPRK opposes the efforts of the enemy to use religion, revenge feuds and family conflicts to divide our people.

6) The LPRK opposes efforts to promote enmity on the part of the Albanian people towards Socialist Albania. It will publicise the successes achieved in all fields by the People's Socialist Republic of Albania.

7) The LPRK highly values the correct stand of the PSR of Albania towards the demands of our people for the formation of a Kosova republic within the SFRY. This stand in no way constitutes 'interference in the internal affairs of Yugoslavia' but is a natural interest in the defence of the part of the Albanian people who live within Yugoslavia, and it is within international law.

8) The hysterical campaign which Belgrade has undertaken against Socialist Albania is unilateral, despicable and dangerous, and rests on the expansionist philosophy of Greater Serbian nationalism.

9) The LPRK opposes all efforts of the Serbian, Macedonian and Montenegrin occupiers to alienate our people from the other Yugoslav peoples. The LPRK does not confuse the people of SFRY with their chauvinist leaders, but considers them, particularly the working class and the revolutionaries as allies in the struggle for equal rights and freedom.

APPENDIX D

THE PROGRAMME OF THE KLA

On 27 April 1998 when the KLA war in Kosovo had begun to take shape, the KLA General Staff issued a political statement in which it stated:

The Albanian people in Kosovo are living in great peril and under great pressure from Serb forces that are working towards the complete isolation and destruction of the KLA and then of the Albanian people as a whole. Our freedom-loving people gave birth to the KLA to oppose the Serb foe and to prove to the democratic world that it is able to fight for its freedom and to gain victory. In view of the existing situation and with regard to its operational activities against Serb forces, the General Staff, aware of its historic obligations, has come out with the following positions.

1. The KLA represents the totality of the armed forces of Kosovo and other occupied lands; its objective is to liberate and unite Albania's occupied territories.
2. The KLA struggle has a defensive and liberation character. Its goal from start to finish has not been war itself, but freedom and peace for the people. It is with this in mind that it will fight and make sacrifice.
3. The KLA rigorously denounces terrorism and other forms of violence against the civilian population and those in captivity. The KLA will respect the international conventions of the United Nations and the War Convention.

4. The KLA belongs and will forever belong to the people. Our country must, and has a historical obligation to assist those parts of the country that have been occupied. The KLA will accept the assistance of and will co-operate closely with the international community.

5. The KLA has funds of its own that are supported voluntarily by the people through mechanisms such as *Atdheu në Rrezik* (Fatherland in Peril) and *Vendlindja Thërret* (Homeland Calling), etc.

6. We are in a war situation and call upon political parties and liberation forces to unite on the battlefront against Serb forces.

7. The KLA is willing to negotiate with the foe only under international mediation and only once occupation forces have withdrawn from Albanian territory. Any agreement reached without the approval of the KLA is invalid.

8. We invite the Albanian media to provide an objective view of our struggle. The KLA is not interested in publicity for profit and will not allow itself to be misused or misinterpreted.

9. For the sake of peace in the region, we appeal to international decision-makers and, in particular, to the United States and the European Union, to exert pressure upon the occupants and to give their support to the just war of the Albanian people in Yugoslavia.[1]

APPENDIX E

UNDERTAKING OF DEMILITARISATION
AND TRANSFORMATION OF THE KLA: 20 JUNE 1999

Signed on 20 June 1999

1. This Undertaking provides for a ceasefire by the UCK, their disengagement from the zones of conflict, subsequent demilitarisation and reintegration into civil society. In accordance with the terms of UNSCR 1244 and taking account of the obligations agreed to at Rambouillet and the public commitments made by the Kosovar Albanian Rambouillet delegation.
2. The UCK undertake to renounce the use of force to comply with the directions of the Commander of the international security force in Kosovo (COMKFOR), and where applicable the bead of the interim civil administration for Kosovo, and to resolve peacefully any questions relating to the implementation of this undertaking.
3. The UCK agree that the International Security Presence (KFOR) and the international civil presence will continue to deploy and operate without hindrance within Kosovo and that KFOR has the authority to take all necessary action to establish and maintain a secure environment for all citizens of Kosovo and otherwise carry out its mission.
4. The UCK agrees to comply with all of the obligations of this Undertaking and to ensure that with immediate effect all UCK forces in Kosovo and in neighbouring countries will observe the provisions of this Undertaking, will refrain from all hostile or provocative acts,

hostile intent and freeze military movement in either direction across International borders or the boundary between Kosovo and other parts of the FRY, or any other actions inconsistent with the spirit of UNSCR 1244. The UCK in Kosovo agree to commit themselves publicly to demilitarise in accordance with paragraphs 22 and 23, refrain from activities which jeopardise the safety of international governmental and nongovernmental personnel including KFOR, and to facilitate the deployment and operation of KFOR.

5. For purposes of this Undertaking, the following expressions shall have the meanings as described below:

   a. The UCK includes all personnel and organisations within Kosovo, currently under UCK control, with a military or paramilitary capability and any other groups or individuals so designated by Commander KFOR (COMKFOR).

   b. «FRY Forces» includes all of the FRY and Republic of Serbia personnel and organisations with a military capability. This includes regular army and naval forces, armed civilian groups, associated paramilitary groups, air forces, national guards, border police, army reserves, military police, intelligence services, Ministry of Internal Affairs, local, special, riot and anti-terrorist police, and any other groups or individuals so designated by Commander KFOR (COMKFOR).

   c. The Ground Safety Zone (GSZ) is defined as a 5-kilometre zone that extends beyond the Kosovo province border into the rest of FRY territory. It includes the terrain within that 5-kilometre zone.

   d. Prohibited weapons are any weapon 12.7mm or larger, any anti-tank or antiaircraft weapons, grenades, mines or explosives, automatic and long barrelled weapons.

6. The purposes of this Undertaking are as follows:

   a. To establish a durable cessation of hostilities.

   b. To provide for the support and authorisation of the KFOR and in particular to authorise the KFOR to take such actions as are required, including the use of necessary force in accordance with KFOR's rules of engagement, to ensure compliance with this Undertaking and protection of the KFOR, and to contribute to a secure environment for the international civil implementation presence, and

   c. After 29 days, the retention of any non automatic long barrelled weapons shall be subject to authorisation by COMKFOR.

d. Within 30 days, subject to arrangements by COMKFOR, if necessary, all UCK personnel, who are not of local origin, whether or not they are legally within Kosovo, including individual advisors, freedom fighters, trainers, volunteers, and personnel from neighbouring and other States, shall be withdrawn from Kosovo.

e. Arrangements for control of weapons are as follows:

 i. Within 30 days the UCK shall store in the registered weapons storage sites all prohibited weapons with the exception of automatic small arms.
 30 per cent of their total holdings of automatic small arms weapons will also be stored in these sites at this stage. Ammunition for the remaining weapons should be withdrawn and stored at an approved site authorised by COMKFOR separate from the assembly areas at the same time.

 ii. At 30 days it shall be illegal for UCK personnel to possess prohibited weapons, with the exception of automatic small arms within assembly areas, and unauthorised long barrelled weapons. Such weapons shall be subject to confiscation by the KFOR.

 iii. Within 60 days a further 30 per cent of automatic small arms, giving a total of 60 per cent of the UCK holdings, will be stored in the registered weapons storage sites.

 iv. Within 90 days all automatic small arms weapons will be stored in the registered weapons storage sites. Thereafter their possession by UCK personnel will be prohibited and such weapons will be subject to confiscation by KFOR.

f. From 30days until 90 days the weapons storage sites will be under joint control of the UCK and KFOR under procedures approved by COMKFOR at the JIC. After 90 days KFOR will assume full control of the sesites.

g. Within 90 days all UCK forces will have completed the processes for their demilitarisation and are to cease wearing either military uniforms or insignia of the UCK.

h. Within 90 days the Chief of General Staff UCK shall confirm compliance with the above restrictions in writing to COMKFOR.

j. The provisions of this Undertaking enter into force with immediate effect of its signature by the Kosovar Albanian representative(s).

k. The UCK intends to comply with the terms of the United Nations Security Council Resolution 1244, and in this context that the international community should take due and full account of the contribution of the UCK during the Kosovo crisis and accordingly give due consideration to:

i. Recognition that, while the UCK and its structures are in the process of transformation, it is committed to propose individual current members to participate in the administration and police forces of Kosovo, enjoying special consideration in view of the expertise they have developed.

ii. The formation of an Army in Kosovo on the lines of the US National Guard in due course as part of a political process designed to determine Kosovo's future status, taking into account the Rambouillet Accord.

This Undertaking is provided in English and Albanian and if there is any doubt as to the meaning of the text the English version has precedence.

Cross-Border activity

7. With immediate effect the UCK will cease the movement of armed bodies into neighbouring countries. All movement of armed bodies into Kosovo will be subject to the prior approval of COMKFOR.

Monitoring the Cessation of Hostilities

8. The authority for dealing with breaches of this Undertaking rests with COMKFOR. He will monitor and maintain and if necessary enforce the cessation of hostilities.

9. The UCK agrees to co-operate fully with KFOR and the interim civil administration for Kosovo. The chief of the General Staff of the UCK will ensure that prompt and appropriate action is taken to deal with any breaches of this Undertaking by his forces as directed by COMKFOR.

10. Elements of KFOR will be assigned to maintain contact with the UCK and will be deployed to its command structure and bases.

11. KFOR will establish appropriate control at designated crossing points into Albania and the FYROM.

Joint Implementation Commission (JIC)

12. A JIC will be established in Pristina within 4 days of the signature of this Undertaking. The JIC will be chaired by COMKFOR and

will comprise the senior commanders of KFOR and the UCK, and a representative from the interim civil administration for Kosovo.

13. The JIC will meet as often as required by COMKFOR throughout the implementation of this Undertaking. It may be called without prior notice and representation by the UCK is expected at a level appropriate with the rank of the KFOR chairman. Its functions will include:

   a. Ensuring compliance with agreed arrangements for the security and activities of all forces;

   b. The investigation of actual or threatened breaches of this Undertaking;

   c. Such other tasks as may be assigned to it by COMKFOR in the interests of maintaining the cessation of hostilities.

Demilitarisation and transformation

14. The UCK will follow the procedures established by COMKFOR for the phased demilitarisation, transformation and monitoring of UCK forces in Kosovo and for further regulation of their activities. They will not train or organise parades without the authority of COMKFOR.

15. The UCK agrees to the following timetable which will commence from the signature of this Undertaking:

   a. Within 7 days, the UCK shall establish secure weapons storage sites, which shall be registered with and verified by the KFOR;

   b. Within 7 days the UCK will clear their minefields and booby traps, vacate their fighting positions and transfer to assembly areas as agreed with COMKFOR at the JIC. Thereafter only personnel authorised by COMKFOR and senior Officers of the UCK with their close protection personnel not exceeding 3, carrying side arms only, will be allowed outside the assembly areas.

   c. After 7 days automatic small arms weapons not stored in the registered weapons storage sites can only be held inside the authorised assembly areas.

Other international organisations, agencies, and non-governmental organisations and the civil populace.

16. The actions of the UCK shall be in accordance with this Undertaking. «The KFOR» commander in consultation, where appropriate,

with the interim civil administrator will be the final authority regarding the interpretation of this Undertaking and the security aspects of the peace settlement it supports. His determinations will be binding on all parties and persons.

Cessation of hostilities

17. With immediate effect on signature the UCK agrees to comply with this Undertaking and with the directions of COMKFOR. Any forces which fall to comply with this Undertaking or with the directions of COMKFOR will be liable to military action as deemed appropriate by COMKFOR.

18. With immediate effect on signature of this Undertaking all hostile acts by the UCK will cease. The UCK Chief of General Staff undertakes to issue clear and precise instructions to all units and personnel under his command, to ensure contact with the FRY force is avoided and to comply fully with the arrangements for bringing this Undertaking into effect. He will make announcements immediately following final signature of this Undertaking, which will be broadcast regularly through all appropriate channels to assist in ensuring that instructions to maintain this Undertaking reach all the forces under his command and are understood by the public in general.

19. The UCK undertakes and agrees in particular:
   a. To cease the firing of all weapons and use of explosive devices.
   b. Not to place any mines, barriers or checkpoints, nor maintain any observation posts or protective obstacles.
   c. The destruction of buildings, facilities or structures is not permitted. It shall not engage in any military, security, or training related activities, including ground or air defence operations, in or over Kosovo or GSZ, without the prior express approval of COMKFOR.
   d. Not to attack, detain or intimidate any civilians in Kosovo, nor shall they attack, confiscate or violate the property of civilians in Kosovo.

20. The UCK agrees not to conduct any reprisals, counter-attacks, or any unilateral actions in response to violations of the UNSCR 1244 and other extant agreements relating to Kosovo. This in no way denies the right of self-defence.

21. The UCK agrees not to interfere with those FRY personnel that return to Kosovo to conduct specific tasks as authorised and directed by COMKFOR.

22. Except as approved by COMKFOR, the UCK agrees that its personnel in Kosovo will not carry weapons of any type:
    a. Within 2 kilometres of VJ and MUP assembly areas;
    b. Within 2 kilometres of the main roads and the towns upon them listed at Appendix A;
    c. Within 2 kilometres of external borders of Kosovo;
    d. In any other areas designated by COMKFOR;

23. Within 4 days of signature of this Undertaking:
    a. The UCK will close all fighting positions, entrenchments, and checkpoints on roads, and mark their minefields and booby traps.
    b. The UCK Chief of General Staff shall report in writing completion of the above requirement to COMKFOR and continue to provide weekly detailed written status reports until demilitarisation, as detailed in the following paragraphs, is complete.

NOTES

FOREWORD TO THE PAPERBACK EDITION

1. See A. Ulunyan, 'Slavjanovedenije', *Slavonic Studies* 1, January 2013, Institute of History of the Russian Academy of Sciences, Moscow. Also, 'Balkanweb', www.balkanweb.com/kultur, 5 March 2013.

ACKNOWLEDGEMENTS

1. Carla del Ponte (with Chuck Sudetic), *Madame Prosecutor*, New York, 2009.
2. See E. Ceku, *Shekulli I Ilegales Proceset Gjyqesore kunder Ilegales ne Kosove: Dokumente*, Prishtina,2004, S. Kecmezi-Basha, *Levizja Ilegale Partiotike Shqiptare ne Kosova (1945–1947)*, Prishtina, 1998; also the writings of Bajram Kosumi and other ex-political prisoners on this subject.
3. S. Sullivan, *Be Not Afraid, You Have Friends in America*, New York City, 2004, and R. Sadiku, *Lidhja Kosovare 1949–1999*, Prishtina, 2006.
4. A leader of the KLA support structures in New Jersey and in the Second League of Prizren in the USA.
5. For Qira's career, see Chapter 1.
6. See Z. Qira, *Cell 31*, New York, 1979 and other Qira books.

INTRODUCTION

1. N. Machiavelli, *On Conspiracies*, London, 2010. For a cogent view of the relevance of Machiavelli to revolutionary theory and organisation, see L. Althusser, *Machiavelli and Us*, London, 1999. The discussion of Hegel and his thinking on the unification problems of the national state is particularly relevant to Yugoslavia in the twentieth century.
2. J. Pettifer, *Kosova Express*, London and Madison, 2005, *Ekspresi I Kosoves*, Prishtina and New York, 2006; J. Pettifer and M. Vickers, *The Albanian Question—Reshaping the Balkans*, London and New York, 2007.

287

3. Procopius, *The Wars*, Cambridge, 1981.
4. N. West, *The Secret War for the Falklands*, London, 1997.
5. D. Tartt, *The Secret History*, New York, 1992.
6. See G. Arndt and others, *Orientalism and Conspiracy—Politics and Conspiracy Theory in the Islamic World*, London, 2010. Also J. Swire, *Bulgarian Conspiracy*, London, 1939, for the classic pre-World War II account of the Macedonian revolutionary/insurgent/terrorist movement (depending on ideological standpoint) as a Sofia-financed criminal conspiracy. Swire is an acute commentator, but his study is permeated throughout with Serbian and Greek views of Balkan history that were universal in the British elite at that time.
7. T. Hill, *The Hidden*, London, 2009, pp. 40 ff.
8. D. Aaronovitch, *Voodoo Histories: How Conspiracy Theory has Shaped Modern History*, London, 2009. This book has many valuable insights, particularly on issues such as the ideological role of the Protocols of the Elders of Zion, but does not clearly define what is meant by a political conspiracy in modern society and elides the fact that many real conspiracies have existed and do exist. It is, for instance, perfectly arguable that the Iraq war was in essence a political conspiracy by a particular ruling group against the Iraq government where historical truth on major issues, e.g. the alleged existence of WMD, was grossly distorted. See also D. Pipes, *Conspiracy*, New York, 1997.
9. There is a conceptual link between Philby as a spy, a 'secret agent', and Philby as the alleged or real defender of Enver Hoxha's Albania from MI6/CIA overthrow attempts. See paper by T. Winnifrith in *Albania and the Balkans—Essays in Honour of Sir Reginald Hibbert*, publication forthcoming.
10. On the issue of myth and the KLA, see J. Pettifer, The Kosova Liberation Army: The Myth of Origin', in M. Waller, K. Drezov and B. Gokay (eds), *Kosovo: The Politics of Delusion*, London and Portland, 2001.
11. See Sallust, *The Conspiracy of Catiline*, and Procopius, *The Secret History*.
12. Aaronovitch, op. cit., p. 7.
13. See M. Todorova, *Imagining the Balkans*, London, 1994 and other works. Although there is much to be learned from Todorova's writings, in my opinion she does not really face up to issues such as the importance of assassination and conspiracy in the recent Balkan political tradition. Some of her critics have claimed that as she is a Bulgarian, there are issues in her work conditioned by her view of the Internal Macedonian Revolutionary Association (IMRO) in the history of modern Bulgaria. IMRO is usually seen as the first 'modern' terrorist organisation, as in the writings of Duncan Perry and others.
14. Sabrina P. Ramet, *Thinking about Yugoslavia—Scholarly Debates about the Yugoslav Breakup and the Wars in Bosnia and Kosovo*, Cambridge, 2005.
15. See I. Roberts *Razgovori s Milosevicem*, 'PUBLIKUS', Begrade, 2012.
16. The nearest to a conventional history book is Jakup Krasniqi's *Kthesa e Madhe UCK*, Prishtina, 2006, although it is a limited and conventionally-minded book that does not generally touch on anything not already well known to students of the subject.

17. See J. Eyal, ed., *The Warsaw Pact and the Balkans*, London, RUSI, 1989, section by Klaus Lange on Albania. The book was noteworthy for the first publication in English of JNA Colonel Hlaic's notorious list of the thirteen different oppositional tendencies which were the most dangerous enemies of Yugoslavia.

18. See paper by Charles J. Dick, 'Maskirovka in Yugoslav Military Thinking', 1999 (www.csrc.mod.uk).

19. See J. Pettifer, *The New Macedonian Question*, London and New York, 1998.

20. See F.W. Walbank, *The Decline of the Roman Empire in the West*, London, 1946, pp. 20 ff., and much succeeding work.

21. As with the ithyphallic statues placed on the boundaries of the early classical *polis*.

22. As I. Paperela points out in Eyal (op. cit.), for Belgrade rulers the great advantage of using the army against the enemies of Yugoslavia was that its enemies always appeared to be tangible and 'knowable' if seen in military terms.

23. See C.M. Woodhouse, *The Struggle for Greece 1941–1949*, London, 1976, p. 286.

24. The nationalist Balli Kombetar was founded in the early stages of the Second World War and remained independent of the other, mostly Communist-led resistance groups. It fought against Yugoslav and Albanian Communism from its inception. See Chapter 2.

25. See Fredric P. Miller, Agnes F. Vandome and John McBrewster, eds, 'Socialist Federal Republic of Yugoslavia', *VDM*, Mauritius, 2009, for basic military information and documentation.

26. For a general account, see Benjamin J. Lambeth, *NATO's Air War for Kosovo*, RAND, Santa Monica, 2001. Also John Labercombe's unpublished study for MoD/DSTL of the RAF air war.

27. For detail, see G.S. Simjanic. *Agresija NATO*, Belgrade, 2009. This illuminating book on the air war marks the beginning of serious study of the Kosova war by the Yugoslav military establishment.

28. There is of course the wider issue focused on the debate among military historians of the twentieth century about what the real impact of bombing has been in wars in general. In Britain this has often focused on the role of Bomber Command in the Second World War and the fate of German cities such as Dresden. Bombing then was often linked to the notion of 'punishment' of enemy civilian populations, and in Serbia in the 1999 air campaign 'punishment' of the Serbian population for supporting the Milosevic regime.

1. THE ORIGINS OF A GUERRILLA ARMY

1. J.B. Tito, *Selected Military Works*, Belgrade, 1966.

2. See C. Daase, 'Clausewitz and Small Wars', in H. Strachan and A. Herberg-Rothe, eds, *Clausewitz in the Twenty First Century* Oxford, 2007, p. 183. Also Clausewitz, *Schriften*, Berlin, 1812.

3. For a contemporary picture of Yugoslav pastoralism, see E.H. Carrier, Water and Grass: *A Study of the Pastoral Economy of Southern Europe*, London,

1932. Also M. Verli, *Reforma Agrare Kolonizuese ne Kosova 1918–1941*, Bonn, 1991, and *League of Nations Conference on Rural Life National Monographs Yugoslavia*, 1939, Geneva.

4. See I. Inalcik and D. Quataert, eds, *An Economic and Social History of the Ottoman Empire 1300–1914*, Cambridge, 1994.

5. L. Lyde and A. Mockler-Ferryman, *The Balkan Peninsular: A Military Geography*, London, 1905.

6. L. Bashkurti, *National and European Identity of the Albanians*, Tirana, 2006, pp. 113 ff.

7. See A. Dragnich, ed., *Serbia's Historical Legacy*, Boulder, 1994.

8. For Byzantium, see L. Clucas, *The Byzantine Heritage in Eastern Europe*, New York, 1988.

9. There is no satisfactory history of the Mitrovica/Trepca/Zvecan mines or the Kosova mining industry in any language. For a good contemporary survey see International Crisis Group Balkans report No. 82: *Trepca: Making Sense of the Labyrinth*, Washington-Prishtina, 28 November 1999. Little has changed in the basic situation in the mines in the intervening years. The best guide to the colonial mentality in pre-1939 London regarding Yugoslav extractive industry assets is the Annan papers from the old Royal School of Mines library which are now housed in Imperial College, London library. Noel Annan (1916–2000) was a trusted British establishment figure with an agreeable Bloomsbury dilettante style but with only an amateur knowledge of the mining industry, and his observations are more useful on the social and political issues than on the mines. Also, D.A. Wray, *The Geology and Mineral Resources of the Serb-Croat-Slovene State*, London, 1921. In the early days the Trepca owners were interested in their own history, see L. Saleman, *Yugoslavia The Ancient Mining Laws and Customs*, Trepca, 1926.

10. For a coherent if nationalist statement of the mainstream Serbian view of this history as it affected policy in the Milosevic period, see P. Simic, *The Kosovo and Metohija Problem and Regional Security in the Balkans*, Institute of International Politics and Economics, Belgrade, 1994.

11. The Kosova Albanians like all Albanians claim descent from the ancient Illyrians, who were some of the earliest inhabitants of the Balkans before the Roman and Slav invasions. For an account of the Illyrians by a British authority, see J. Wilkes, *The Illyrians*, Oxford, 1992. For the Albanians' own views, see A. Buda, ed., *The Albanians and their Territories*, Tirana, 1985, and the work of more recent authors such as Neritan Ceka.

12. For ancient Delphi as a war memorial see P. Cartledge, *Agesilaos and the Crisis in Sparta*, London, 1987.

13. Late antiquity and Byzantium was an important period for the genesis of modern Balkan transport routes and military border topography. See P. Stephenson, *Byzantium's Northern Frontier*, Cambridge, 2000.

14. E. Isambert, *Orient Grèce et Turquie D'Europe*, Paris, 1884.

15. See E. Zachariadou, ed., *The Via Egnetia under Ottoman Rule*, Rethymnon, 1996 for the later period. For general data on Albanian and Kosova roads in

antiquity and the medieval period, see W. Shtylla, *Rruget dhe Urat e Vjetra ne Shqiperi*, Tirana, 1997.

16. See J.B. Tito, *Selected Military Works*, Belgrade, 1966. One of Tito's less noticed qualities was his extensive knowledge of Balkan military history and military geography, something that may have assisted him in the Partisan campaign and then in preserving his government. For a sympathetic early picture of Tito in action that captures the atmosphere of the beginnings of socialist Yugoslavia, see G. Bilainkin, *Tito*, London, 1949. For an Albanian view highly critical of Hoxha's early links with Tito in the Partisan period, see N. Plasari and L. Malltezi, *Politike Antikombetare e Enver Hoxha*, Tirana, 1996.Also Hoxha's own work, *The Titoites*, Tirana, 1981.

17. A. Zhelyazkova, *Albania and the Albanian Identity*, Sofia, 2000.

18. See N. Todorov, *The Balkan City 1400–1900*, Seattle, 1983.

19. B. Tomasovic, *Life and Death in the Balkans*, London, 2009.

20. E. Hobsbawm, *Bandits*, London, 1969.

21. See H. Incalik, op. cit.

22. L. Althussser, in *For Marx* paper 'Contradiction and Overdetermination', pp. 114 ff. As Sue Clegg observed in an appreciation of Louis Althusser's (1918–90) life and work, the French Marxist philosopher's influence on political movements was often indirect, and 'some individual insights could be used without accepting the whole package'. In the intellectual background of the 1980s, his view of Stalinism as based on the theoretical error of economism seemed relevant to the left wing of Kosova Albanian nationalists, as the Albanian leaders of the Yugoslav League of Communists in Kosova had continually sacrificed 'idealism' (the Albanian nationalist agenda) for 'economism', (the real/alleged economic benefits for Kosova of staying within the Yugoslav framework). See 'The Remains of Louis Althusser', in *International Socialism*, London, 1991.

23. There is no satisfactory in-depth history in a west European language of Kosova under Royalist Yugoslavia. There is surprisingly little quality work published in Albanian or Serbian either, even local studies. Vickers and Malcolm (op. cit.) both provide excellent general background. For an account of Belgrade's more or less identical *modus operandi* in neighbouring Macedonia, see N. Boskovska, *Das Jugoslawische Makedonien 1918–1941: Eine Randregion zwischen Repression und Integration*, Weimar and Vienna, 2009.

24. Ref. H. Seton Watson, *The East European Revolutions*, New York, 1956, pp. 144 ff.

25. For a reliable general picture of the relationships between the Partisans and the British Special Operations Executive, see H. Williams, *Parachutes, Patriots and Partisans: The Special Operations Executive and Yugoslavia 1941–1945*, London, 2003.

26. See *History of the Party of Labour of Albania*, 8 Nentori, Tirana, 1982.

27. See R. Hibbert, *Albania's National Liberation: The Bitter Victory*, London, 1991.

28. Perhaps the classic example in the Second World War was the joint British-Greek resistance operation to destroy the Gorgopotamos Bridge in Thessaly in 1943.

29. For an interesting personal memoir by an Albanian member of the International Brigades, see S. Luarasi, *Ne Brigadat Internacionale ne Spanje*, Tirana, 1996. It is perhaps revealing that it hardly touches on guerrilla war military leadership issues, and it was unpublished until eleven years after Enver Hoxha's death, probably because Luarasi was a close associate of the disgraced Partisan commander and Albanian Communist leader Mehmet Shehu.

30. An exception was Mullah Idris Gjilan in the fighting in Preshevo between 1944 and 1949.

31. In many ways the Partisans had transformed themselves from an army to a party after 1945. The great majority of prominent Macedonian Communists under Tito were from a Partisan army background, like General Mitre Apostolski. The army was a popular career for Macedonians under Titoism. Perhaps Lazar Kolichevski was the only top Macedonian CPY leader who espoused a non-Partisan political identity.

32. For detail, from a pro-Communist viewpoint, on the Albanian Partisan movement, see V. Hoxha, *Aradha Partizane 'Zejnel Hajdini'*, Prishtina 1973, and F. Hoxha, *Beteja perfundimtare per Clirimin e Kosoves*, undated publication, Prishtina. Fadil Hoxha's memoirs and later writings are much less reliable sources and he undoubtedly exaggerates the size of Partisan detachments and influence.

33. N. Malcolm, *Kosova*, London, 1998, pp. 310 ff.

34. M. Vickers, *Between Serb and Albanian: A History of Kosovo*, London, 1998, pp. 141 ff.

35. There are numerous works in English on the Partisan war in Yugoslavia. The best introductory account for the political/military issues is F.W. Deakin, *The Embattled Mountain*, Oxford, 1971.

36. An account of the development of Soviet guerrilla warfare models derived from the Spanish experience is in A.K. Starova, *Behind Fascist Lines*, New York, 2001.

37. See Hibbert, op. cit.

38. See M. Radulovic, *Tito's Republic*,Wrotham, 1948. Radulovic's book is a little known and neglected work. Radulovic was a British ex-8th army officer of Serbian descent who became a journalist after demobilisation and was Reuters correspondent in Belgrade between 1945 and 1947. He was a perceptive witness of many important events and described the totalitarian apparatus Tito set up to stay in power, both before and after the break with Stalin. As he was anti-monarchist, he lacked a support constituency in Balkan circles in London post-1948 and his book largely disappeared without trace.

39. See the autobiographical diaries from 1943 of the senior Kosovar Communist Fadil Hoxha, *Kur Pranvera Vonohet*, Prishtina, 1980.

40. See Radulovic, op. cit., pp. 221 ff. He goes on to observe, correctly, that 'The Yugoslav-Albanian pact which provided for the abolition of customs barri-

ers between the two countries and the coordination of economic and military plans was considered in Belgrade as the first step towards union in the Balkans.'

41. As late as 1958, in a book written by the prominent and intelligent Swiss journalist Ernst Halpern, *The Triumphant Heretic Tito's struggle against Stalin*, it was possible to omit any mention of the Kosova question at all in Yugoslavia and even to deny that the Albanians were a majority of those living there.

42. There is a very large journalistic and scholarly literature on the Tito-Stalin split in 1948 and its complex implications for the region. A few of the documents discovered in the Russian archives in Moscow were published in Albania in 2002 as Y. Minxhozi, ed., *Leter e panjohur e Enver Hoxha mbi Kosoven— Dokumenta te Arkivave Ruse'*, which illustrate the Albanian leader's stance on some issues.

43. The policy culminated in the 1954 'Treaty of Alliance between Greece, Turkey and Yugoslavia'. See Tito, *Selected Speeches and Articles 1941–1961*, Belgrade, 1963, p. 147. Tito saw the Treaty as part of his wider deals with the West, and an attempt to work towards the 'elimination of this hotbed that is the Balkans'. It shows the Yugoslav dictator's characteristic political skill in his dealings with the West, in which the gross human rights violations against the Albanians and other nationalities in Yugoslavia were obscured by a largely meaningless international treaty involving NATO members and interests.

44. General D. Ojdanic, 'The Army of Yugoslavia has passed a historic examination', in *The Army of Yugoslavia*, Belgrade 1999, pp. 5 ff.

2. THE UNDERGROUND WAR 1950–1990

1. S. Gjecov, ed., *The Code of Lek Dukagjini*, New York, 1989.

2. See declassified CIA document, US State Department, 11 May 1950, 'Evaluation of Soviet-Yugoslav relations' (1950), in *From 'National Communism' to National Collapse: US Intelligence Community Estimative Products on Yugoslavia, 1948–1990*, NIC publications, Washington, 2006. The degree to which US perceptions of and policies towards Albania were and are related to issues of sea power should never be underestimated.

3. See M.Verli, *Kosova ne Fokusin e Historise*, Tirana, 2003.

4. This continued as a factor right through the Titoist period and entered into the support structure for the Milosevic regime, particularly in rural southern Serbia.

5. For a good general statement of Soviet diplomatic views, see D. Chuvakin, 'Star Hours in Soviet-Albanian Relations', *International Affairs*, Moscow, Vol. 37 No. 8, 1991. For a dated but serious study that is very sympathetic to Tito, see also S. Clissold, *Yugoslavia and the Soviet Union 1939–1973*, Oxford, 1975, also N. Beloff, *Tito's Flawed Legacy*, London 1985, a prescient account by a senior British journalist of some of the issues.

6. Ref: Unpublished documents in MFA archives, Moscow. Dimitri Chuvakin (1903–1997) was the main Ministry of Foreign Affairs influence on Comintern

Albanian policy for many years after he joined the MFA in 1938. He was Stalin's Ambassador in Tirana from 1945 to 1952, and from 1952 to 1958 Deputy Head of the Balkan department in the MFA. The Chuvakin documents cast
doubt on the views put forward by Noel Malcolm in his book *Kosovo*, London, 1998 that Hoxha was always completely subservient to Stalin over Kosova (pp. 319 ff.).

7. D. Chuvakin, 'Star Hours in Soviet-Albanian Relations', *International Affairs*
Vol. 37 No. 8, 1991.

8. D. Chuvakin, 'Star Hours in Soviet-Albanian Relations', *International Affairs*
Vol. 37 No. 8, 1991.

9. From Diary of Dimitri Chuvakin, section July 1949, op. cit.

10. A senior KGB official, Nina Smirnovna (1928–2001), was the KGB official in
charge of them. She later became a prominent historian and MFA expert on
Albania in post-communist Moscow in the 1990s, and author of a history of
Albania.

11. See the numerous works of the Tirana-based historian Meringlen Verli for
studies of Kosova's general economic history after 1945.

12. See unpublished PhD thesis by Elidor Mehili, Princeton University History
Department. For defence issues, see Y. Molla, *Plani Sekret per Kosoven*,Tirana,
2006. The Soviets, like NATO two generations later, were primarily interested
in the Albanian coastline.

13. For a fine picture of similar settlement processes in post-First World War Kosova, see B. Tomasovic, Life *and Death in the Balkans*, London, 2009.

14. For Qira's own account of these events, see *Cell 31*, New York, 1979. His
objective and informative book is the main source for this period and until the
Albanian intelligence archives are fully opened in 2040 is likely to remain so.

15. See N. Malcolm, op. cit., pp. 321 ff.

16. Qira, Z, Cell 31, op. cit.

17. For Fadil Hoxha's own view of the critical year of 1943, see his publication
Kur Pranvera Vonohet Fragmente nga Ditare-1943, Prishtina, 1980. It is an
interesting human story and a good picture of wartime conditions but illustrates clearly the political ignorance and naivety of most Kosova Partisans
about Tito's real post-war intentions.

18. These *bey* and general Ottoman survivals under Titoism were not confined to
Kosova. For a good picture of the surviving Albanian 'power families' in western Macedonia late in the Second World War, and how their political networks
operated, see 'Albania, Macedonia and the British Military Missions, 1943 and
1944', paper by Reginald Hibbert in J. Pettifer, ed., *The New Macedonian
Question*, London and New York, 1998.

19. Other pro-Russian Kosova Albanians were detained for some years after 1949
in the Goli Otok forced labour camp on an island in the Adriatic, along with
much of the Montenegrin party and military leadership. There is an extensive
Serbian, Bosnian and Montenegrin literature on Goli Otok but often the books
neglect to mention that pro-Soviet Albanians who were against the Resolution
were also detained there, as well as alleged IMRO and pro-Bulgarian sympa-

thisers from Macedonia and other real and alleged anti-Tito dissidents. Although the existence of Goli Otok was well known in the West, there is no record of any protest against it made on human rights grounds by Tito's Western backers in Europe, although there were some in the United States. For a Montenegrin picture of life in Goli Otok see T. Nikcevic, *Goli Otoci Jova Kapicica*. Kapicica was a JNA officer who fell foul of Tito in 1948 but was subsequently rehabilitated.

20. Qira himself was well aware of the many ironies in the life of the political activist in the Albanian cause. As his later reflection shows, in his book on the main incidents that interest him in Albanian twentieth century history, *Ujqit ne Frak* (Wolves in Tail Coats), Tetovo, 1999, it was rare for the Albanians to be able to trust their friends. In the USA in the 1990s he worked as manager for the Rentokil company in New York and found cleaning jobs for KLA recruits on the run from Kosova while they did their military training.

21. It is worth noting that the official history of the Albanian Communists, *The History of the Party of Labour of Albania*, Tirana, 1980 makes no mention of the Kosova issue at all in its account of the 1948 crisis and the break with Tito. As its critics have claimed, it is a history of Albania, not of the Albanians.

22. James Klugman wrote two booklets on Yugoslav developments after 1945 when he was a senior British Communist Party official. In *Yugoslavia Faces the Future*, London, 1947, he puts forward a call for British support for Tito over difficult issues such as the future of Trieste. In *From Trotsky to Tito*, London, 1951, his polemic on the 1948 events, he echoes the most Stalinist line. His account of the Titoists in their struggle for leadership of the Albanian party and their attempts to displace Enver Hoxha as leader contains no mention of Kosova at all, and he shows little knowledge or interest in Albania or Kosova.

23. See Halil Katana, *Kudusi Lama Gjenerali I Luftes*, Tirana, 2002, and Lama's own account of the war, *Kosova dhe Ushtria Clirimtare*, Tirana, 2005. It is worth remembering that Lama and fellow officers of his generation were trained in the Tirana Military Academy as young men in the 'pro-China' period of the APL and would have known Maoist texts on people's war at cadet age. In the main, though, the Chinese, even in the 'Red Guard' period, did not have much direct input into the Academy, preferring to offer 'star' officers visits to Beijing to learn Chinese, and to deal with equipment supply.

24. See Averil Cameron and James Pettifer, *The Enigma of Montenegrin History: The Example of Svac*, Tirana, 2008. Also K. Prasniker and A. Shober, *Kerkime Arkeologjike ne Shqiperi ne Shqiperi dhe Mal te Zi*, Vienna, 1919, republished in Tirana in 2003.

25. See H.K. Haug, *Creating a Socialist Yugoslavia*, London, 2010 for background on the Titoist view of the party in resolving the national question in Yugoslavia. See also P. Shoup, *Communism and the Yugoslav National Question*, New York and London, 1968 for an informed introductory analysis, but one imbued with the general assumptions of the Titoist leadership of the time.

26. In many ways the Kosovar Albanians with the LPRK in the 1980s had to go

through the same processes as the original founders of the Albanian Party of Labour (PLA) in Albania early in the Second World War. There are many parallels between the way the Albanian Partisan movement developed guided by the PLA after 1942–43 and the way the KLA developed from the LPK after 1996. See paper by Klaus Lange in J. Eyal, op. cit., and R. Bailey and B. Fischer, op. cit.

27. See *Flamuri*, Rome, 28 November 1966, Le Monde, 23 September 1966, *The Times*, 22 September 1966.

28. There is a massive new literature on Balli Kombetar in Albanian post-Communism. The political heritage is very contentious. See S. Kecmezi-Basha, op. cit. for a sound general guide to the period. Also V. Xhemali, *Forcat Kombetare ne Mbrothe te Shqiperise Ethnike 1941–1945*, Tetovo, 2006, and I. Dobra, *Lufta e Drenices 1941–1945 dhe ND SH Deri 1947*, Prishtina, 1997. Many biographical studies of activists are hagiographical and should be used as sources only very critically.

29. See S. Gashi, *Adem Demaci: A Biography*, Prishtina, 2010.

20. For an excellent account of Haxhiu and his radical nationalist political ambiance in the 1960s and 1970s, see I. Neziri, *Ahmet Haxhiu nje jete te tere ne levizjen ilegale*, Prishtina, 2001. Unlike some of the more hagiographic volumes to appear in Kosova post-1999 about KLA precursors, the book catches very well the political complexities and dilemmas of Haxhiu and his associates, and the centrality of Switzerland as a place of refuge for his generation of militants.

31. Gashi, op. cit., pp. 10 ff.

32. See S. Gashi, op. cit. This well-illustrated book is a sophisticated and reliable short study that will open up many avenues for future investigators.

33. Turkey closed its borders to new immigrants from Yugoslavia in 1930, largely in response to the world economic crisis and spiralling unemployment.

34. See R. and R. Batoku, *Organizata BTSH 1959*, Peja, 2004.

35. For details of settlement numbers and locations, see Ozgur Baklacioglu, N., *Dis Politika ve Goc*, Istanbul, 2010.

36. See Hakif Bajrami, *Dosja Demaci*, Prishtina, 2003.

37. The theories of insurgency the Cuban revolution produced, e.g. Guevara's *La Guerra de las Guerrillas*, Havana, 1960, were not known until much later in Yugoslavia and never published in Albania. It is very unlikely they had any influence on Demaci and his associates at an ideological level. Later on, the Cuban model of a very small number of insurgents being able to act as the catalyst for an uprising was very attractive to the LPRK/LPK radicals pre-1990, and probably remained in the political subconscious afterwards.

38. See the valuable collection of articles illustrating this process in the revolutionary press in Kosova, in S. Kecmezi-Basha, *Shtypi Ilegal Shqiptar ne Kosove (1945–1999)*, Prishtina, 2009.

39. In my opinion, the 1968 demonstrations in Prishtina and elsewhere in Kosova are an often underestimated element in the mixture of forces and events for change that led to the 1974 Yugoslav constitution. This may be because, unlike

what happened in most street demonstrations in twentieth-century Kosova, there was no widespread violence or major loss of life and members of all ethnic groups were participants. For records of the trials afterwards, and statements of the Kosova Communists, see E. Ceku, *Demonstratat e Vitit 1968 ne Arkivin e Kosoves*, Prishtina, 2009.

40. *Rilindja*, Prishtina, 1 December 1968.
41. See B. Berisha, *Fundi I hje Aventure Politike*, Tetovo, 1998.
42. For information on the 1967–68 protests in a key area of Kosova, see F. Pushkolli, *Llapi gjate Historise*, Prishtina, 1998. Pushkolli demonstrates clear links between the old Ballist organisations such as the Second League of Prizren who still had a few underground activists in the Llap region and Demaci's Marxist allies in the LBRSH, an indication that Demaci's imprisonment had failed to dent his political influence.
43. Milo Djukanovic (1962–) became the first Prime Minister of an independent Montenegro in 2004 and remains a powerful figure in Montenegro at the time of writing. His role as a Milosevic protégé in the League of Yugoslav Communists youth organisation in the 'anti-bureaucratic revolution' phase in 1986–89 made his initial political fame.
44. For details, see Sadik V Krasniqi, *Lufta per Clirimin e Kosoves (1997–1999)*, Prishtina, 2009.
45. S. See Kecmezi-Basha, *Organizatat dhe grupet ilegale ne Kosove 1981–1989*, Prishtina, 2003.
46. See M. Hajrizi, *Historia e nje Organizate Politike Dhe Demonstratat e Vitit 1981*,Tirana, 2008.
47. At the same time, later in the year in Tirana a publication was issued, *The Status of a Republic for Kosova is a Just Demand*, 8 Nentori, Tirana, 1981. This has a significantly different 'spin' on events from that of earlier Tirana material, with a fair degree of recognition of the politics of the demonstrators.
48. See M. Vickers, *Between Serb and Albanian: A History of Kosovo*, pp. 208 ff. for a clear account of the social and political repression in the early 1980s. Mahmut Bakalli (1936–2006) had close British links and for many years after his ejection from power was promoted by the UK as a future Kosova leader under democracy. He was popular with some KLA leaders as a principled nationalist figure who had not subscribed to the illusions of Rugova, and in his later years enjoyed the status of an elder statesman in Prishtina. Even by Kosova standards, he was an exceptionally heavy smoker and his gravelly voice was famous on radio and television.
49. See M. Hajrizi, *Histori e nje organizate Politike dhe Demonstratat e Vitit 1981*, Tirana, 2008.
50. For Kosumi's own account of these years, see Kosumi, B., *Letersia nga Burgu*, Tirana, 2006, and other writings and publications.
51. Later KLA political spokesman in Geneva in the wartime period. See Chapter 6 ff.
52. See M. Vickers, op. cit., p. 225.
53. For a good picture of the background in Germany during these and succeeding

years, from an LDK perspective, see J. Buxhovi, *Kthesa Historike Vitet e Germanise dhe Epoka e LDK*-s, Prishtina, 2008. It is particularly good on the dilemma the LDK founders had in choosing between Rugova and Rexhep Qosja as leader after the LDK was formed (p. 217 ff.).

54. See M. Dreshaj-Baliu, *Jusuf Gervalle—Jeta dhe Vepra*, Institut Albanologik I Prishtina, 2002. Also E. Ceku, *Struktura politike e Ilegales se Kosoves*, Tirana, 2006. The LNCKVSJ was primarily important for discussing openly for the first time in its underground press material, the exact model of insurgent army that would be needed to liberate Kosova. It also had international contacts, in French, Austrian and German Marxist-Leninist organisations. The militants involved were top priority targets on Serbian blacklists for many years. It is likely the Serbian security service was involved in the assassination of the ex-LNCKVSJ member and KLA leader Smalj Hajdaraj (1951–2002) in the Rugova Pass. He was a 1980s Gervalla associate and veteran of Goli Otok political prison. Hajdaraj had been a KLA battalion leader in the Pass in the wartime period, and a popular and widely respected figure. See N. Kelmendi, *Vrasja e Deputetit*, Prishtina, 2003. This source has useful biographical information but is highly selective and unreliable on Hajdari's early political activities and his later relationship with the LDK. It was an early sign of the political degeneration within UNMIK in 2002 that Hajdaraj's death was blamed on 'organised crime' and never properly investigated.

55. For details on the LPRK/LPK relationship, see Chapter 6.

56. Ukshin Hoti (1943–?) disappeared while in Serbian custody serving a five-year sentence for political offences in May 1999. He is assumed to be dead, but the circumstances and time of his death are unknown. He resigned from the LDK in 1992, and then worked with the more specifically Balli Kombetar opposition tradition and was in the UNIKOMB group with close Skopje and Tetovo links. His most important writings are on the philosophical basis of Albanian nationalism, *The Political Philosophy of the Albanian Question*, Tirana, 1995. See F. Dalipi, *Ukshin Hoti per Kauzen Kombetare*, Gjilan, 2000.

57. Ramush Haradinaj (1968–), born in Gllogjan, Dukagjini. Active in LPK while in Swiss and French exile. Zone Commander in Dukagjini in the war, founder/leader of the Alliance for Kosova party (AAK) in 2000. Member of the Kosova Assembly and Prime Minister 2003–04. Tried at ICTY for war crimes and acquitted, 2005. Leader of Opposition in Kosova Assembly post-independence from 2008. He was subsequently tried again for alleged war crimes at the ICTY and eventually acquitted in 2012. He has resumed the leadership of the AAK party in Kosova.

58. Hashim Thaci (1968–). Born in Broje, Drenica. Attended Prishtina University and joined LPRK as a secret member, see Ch. 3, note 39.

59. Adem Jashari (1955–98) was born in Prekaz I Ulet, the son of a schoolteacher, and became a fighter against Serbian rule in Kosova from an early age. His family defended their house from Serbian attack in 1991 and he subsequently worked in various capacities in the LPRK, LPK and the KLA before his death in March 1998.

60. Xhavit Haliti (1956–) was born in Novo Selo, near Peje. As a student radical he worked with Ahmet Haxhiu's group in the LPRK. He clashed with the Serbian police and fled to Switzerland after a shooting incident. Member of the founding group of LPK Exterior in Zurich and member of KLA General Staff. KLA chief in Tirana in the wartime period. Member of the Kosova Assembly 2000–.

61. Ali Ahmeti (1959–). Born in Zagos, Kicevo district, FYROM/Republic of Macedonia. Imprisoned for language rights agitation, escaped to Kosova, helped form Marxist-Leninists of Kosova organisation, and then to fled to Switzerland in 1984. Member LPK Exterior, head of logistics for the KLA in Albania in the wartime period, founder of the National Liberation Army in Macedonia in the 2001 conflict, Deputy Prime Minister and leader of BDI party in Skopje government, 2003–.

62. Fazli Veliu (1945–) was born near Kicevo in FYROM/Republic of Macedonia. He was a founder of LPK and effective head of LPK Exterior in Switzerland throughout the pre-war and wartime period. Active in the 2001 Macedonian conflict, he became a senior member of Ali Ahmeti's BDI party. He was also founder of the 'Macedonian Albanians of the Diaspora' organisation which played an important role in funding the 2001 National Liberation Army. To understand his thinking, the most important work is F. Veliu, *LPK dhe UCK: Nje Embleme nje Qellim*, Tirana, 2001.

63. See Jusuf Gervalla, *Kenget e Moshes*, Prishtina, 2004.

64. Swiss constitutional and democratic rights for political refugees are often little understood. See J.-E. Lane, *The Swiss Labyrinth: Institutions, Outcomes and Redesign*, London, 2001 for general background.

65. J. Kristeva, *Crisis of the European Subject*, New York, 1980. Also, for past background, Larry Wolff, *Inventing Eastern Europe: The Map of Civilisation on the Mind of the Enlightenment*, Stanford, 1994.

66. Fazli Veliu (1945–), see footnote 62 above.

67. See Appendix C to *Programme of the People's Movement for the Republic of Kosova*, English publication by The Albania Society, Ilford, 1989. This document is in fact the Second Programme. The First Programme was approved by the First General Assembly of the PMRK/LPRK in July 1987 and published in the organ of the PMRK/LPRK *Zeri I Kosoves*, Aarau, Switzerland, No. 7, 1987.

68. G. Fiori, *Antonio Gramsci: Life of a Revolutionary*, London, 1970.

69. Mazower, M., *The Balkans*, London, 2000.

70. See M. Stankova, *Georgi Dimitrov: A Biography*, London, 2009. Dimitrov had the great advantage over all other Balkan Communist leaders that he was of the 'Old Bolshevik' generation, who received their initial political education before the Stalinist deformations of Marxism.

71. It is hard to generalise, as some Marxists texts were published and available easily to the general populations while others were in practice only available to those who attended higher party schools or the Institute of Marxist-Leninism. Only *Das Kapital* was really widely available in Albania along with

numerous renditions of Enver Hoxha's own 'interpretative' works. Lenin's *What is to be Done'* was also in wide circulation. The Party of Labour eventually published a 71-volume *Vepra* of Hoxha's Collected Works just after his death in 1985. Texts from the revival of Marxism in Western countries in the 1970s and 1980s were unobtainable, as were the writings of authors from within the Communist tradition, like Gramsci's, that were regarded as revisionist. Even during the 'pro-Chinese' period in Albania in the late 1960s and early 1970s few of Mao's works were ever translated into Albanian or published there.

72. Op. cit., p. 23.
73. They are buried in Germany, in Bad Canstadt cemetery, outside Stuttgart near the Mercedes Benz factory.
74. See N. Ragaru and K. von Hippel, *Understanding the Albanian Diaspora*, Paris and London, 2002, pp. 55 ff.
75. There is as yet no satisfactory book, even of a basic narrative character, on the Gervalla brothers and their contribution to the national movement.
76. In an interview in Zurich in April 2003, Avdyl Gervalla, one of the two surviving brothers, then a journalist on *Bota* Sot newspaper, made clear to me that he saw the future of Kosova as still between Communists and nationalists, and that the faith of the Swiss Diaspora in the LDK as a political force capable of opening up the war option had been destroyed by the errors of Bujar Bukoshi after 1992. See Chapter 3.
77. It has been estimated that by 1997 about 500 million DM was raised for political purposes in Germany by the Albanian Diaspora. Until 1997 most of this money went to the Bukoshi-controlled '3 per cent' Fund and details on what happened to it are not available.
78. The Yugoslav secret police at the end of the 1980s believed it was fighting a splinter organisation also, the 'Organizaten e Frontit te Resistences', which allegedly had a headquarters in Kosova in Decani. It is not possible to find independent verification for these claims. See T. Gecaj, *Kolona s'ndalet...!*, Prishtina, 2002. Gecaj's book is a good account of the Odyssey many Swiss-based militants took before they eventually ended up fighting for the KLA, mostly after the spring of 1998.
79. Discussion: Hashim Thaci with James Pettifer, Prishtina, 14 March 2003. There was no Trotskyist tradition in Kosova Albanian politics which in his youth might have involved Thaci. This was in contrast to some Balkan cities, e.g. Zagreb, in particular. Those inclined to this orientation (few in number) tended to involve themselves in the trade union movement in the Mitrovica and other mines.
80. This continued on occasion up until 1999. See *Bota Sot*, Zurich, 11 July 2000. In essence, in the view of the Right it was a fight about whether the Albanian secret service should control the development of the Kosova Liberation Army. The evidence for this view is yet to be fully convincing.
81. For the general crisis atmosphere, see Amnesty International report, *Recent Events in the Autonomous Province of Kosovo*, London May, 1989

82. By far the best source for this period is N. Gjeloshi, *Kosova ne Udhekryq' 89*, a gripping and well researched account of the turmoil in Prishtina and Mitrovica in 1988 and 1989.

83. See M. Vickers, op. cit., pp. 224 ff.

84. For a representative view of how this was seen in Britain at the time, see Ed Steen, 'Yugoslav protesters hail Milosevic as the new hero', *The Independent*, London, 16 September 1988.

85. Interview Ramiz Alia/James Pettifer, Tirana, 2007.

86. For a reliable general picture of Alia's views in this period, see B. Shala *et al.*, *Une, Ramiz Alia*, Prishtina, 1992. See also obituary of Alia by Miranda Vickers in *The Guardian*, Friday 7 October 2011.

87. It is noticeable that most recently published popular history of the 1998–99 war in Serbian stresses the 'anti-terrorist' element, e.g. the works of an author like Milovan Drecun.

88. See J. Gow, *Legitimacy and the Military: The Yugoslav Crisis*, London, 1992, pp. 118 ff.

89. See N. Gjeloshi, op. cit. for the complexities of the early Vatican role. Some leading clerics in Rome, for instance Mgr Claudio Celi, had Albanian connections and were happy to talk about support for independence as early as 1992 but few of the Kosova Albania leaders seemed to realise that Celi's views were far from representative and that entrenched pro-Belgrade sentiment ruled in many areas of the Vatican bureaucracy and almost universally in the Vatican diplomatic service.

90. For a general account of the role of Diasporas in the early years, see P. Hockenos, *Homeland Calling—Exile Patriotism and the Balkan Wars*, Cornell, 2003. Hockenos is more reliable as a source and as an analyst on the northern Yugoslav republics, less so on Kosova and Macedonia.

3. A NEW FORCE IN A NEW BALKANS 1990–1995

1. 'Precis des Guerres de Cesar', J. N. Marchand, ecrit sous la dictee de L'Empereur, Paris 1836.

2. T. Wintringham, *How to Reform the Army*, London, 1939.

3. Conrad, J., *Under Western Eyes*, London 1947, p.107.

4. *The Guardian*, London, 29 January 1990.

5. The best detailed documentation of the period of Serbian repression after the introduction of the emergency laws in 1990 is in *Yugoslavia: Human Rights Abuses in Kosovo 1990–1992*, Helsinki Human Rights Watch, New York, 1992 and in *Dismissals and Ethnic Cleansing in Kosovo*, International Confederation of Free Trade Unions, Brussels, 1992.

6. *Observer*, London, 4 February 1990.

7. This use of the military by Milosevic in this period is rarely described satisfactorily or accurately in any of the current textbooks covering recent Kosova history. Thus the burden of responsibility for the descent of Kosova into violence and war in the late 1990s is not properly apportioned, giving the uninitiated

reader the impression that it was mainly the KLA that brought violence and conflict to Kosova. This myth has remained widely current in the minds of international administrators in post-war Kosova. It is significant that there is no mention whatsoever of the use of Yugoslav military forces in Kosova between 1989 and 1996 against the majority Albanian community in the historical section of the UNMIK *Guide to Kosovo* that was given to all new UNMIK international administration staff after 1999.

8. All LDK publications from the 1990s reflect this political perspective, although Rugova's universalist views on the role of the organisation came to be doubted by many members over time.

9. See N. Gjeloshi, op. cit., pp. 54 ff. (Ref fn 15).

10. W. Zimmerman, *The Origins of a Catastrophe*, New York, 1996, p. 80. Zimmerman of course begs many questions; most of all, he expresses the deeply mistaken idea that Albanian nationalism was a 'new' phenomena and a reaction to Milosevic, with the implication that a more moderate ruler could have held on to Kosova.

11. Interview with James Pettifer, Tirana, see above.

12. This was a main preoccupation of British foreign intelligence officials in 1991–92.

13. Interview, Tirana, July 2005.

14. See B. Hanley and S. Millar, *The Lost Revolution: The Story of the Official IRA and the Workers Party*, London, 2010.

15. www.lpk-kosova.com/historiku.html and Appendix.

16. The LDK Information office in Prishtina reported that 'The village (Prekaz I Ulet) is completely blocked off and shots are being heard. The foretold measures of the Serbian police over the unprotected Albanians in this cold winter are being realised.' LDK Information Bulletin, Prishtina, 30 December 1991.

17. For a sound general account of the development of the LPK in this and earlier periods, see B. Islami, *E Fshehta e Hapur e Kosoves*, Prishtina, 2001. It is a very strong source on personalities, the LPK/LKCK and LPK/KLA relationships and some individual political trajectories, such as that of Xhafer Shatri in Switzerland, but less clear on ideological issues.

18. See F. Mehmetaj, *Adrian Krasniqi-Rexha—Nje jete e nje vdekje per atedhe*, Prishtina, 2001. From this and other sources which although limited do appear reliable, there was much more activity in the formation of the early KLA in and around Peje than the more Drenica-centric accounts of the war history would acknowledge. Krasniqi-Rexha was eventually shot dead by the Serbian police in an ambush near Peje on 16 October 1997, just before the KLA became a public force. It was alleged he was carrying bombs to blow up a nearby police post.

19. Gjirokastra was (and remains with some citizens) a centre of support for Hoxhaist sentiment.

20. See ICTY papers, Limaj trial, Day 40.

21. Author's translation from text in Kecmezi-Basha, S., *Levizja Ilegale Patriotike Shqiptare ne Kosove (1945–1997)*, Prishtine, 1998.

22. See N. Gjeloshi, op. cit., pp. 128 ff.
23. See Gjeloshi, op. cit., pp. 215 ff. It is not clear whether Tudjman and his associates had discovered that Lladrovci was not a Catholic but was from a Muslim family. He became one of the most influential KLA commanders in the early stages of the war and was killed in fighting in 1998. He is generally regarded as an attractive and disinterested idealist and a fine soldier and was a major loss to the KLA. See also Agim Zogaj's material on the difficulties a future KLA senior commander had with many Croats, in *Deshmi per Rrugen e Lirise Dailog me Naim Maloku*, Prishtina, 2000, pp. 66 ff. It is clear that the considerable amount of money that had been collected in Switzerland and Germany by late 1991 for weapons purchase—at a time when, according to Maloku, an AK-47 only cost 125 dollars—was completely wasted.
24. For an absorbing background book about Lladrovci's life and death, and that of his wife and fellow KLA fighter Xheva (Krasniqi), see B. Islami, *Perjetetesia e Dyfishte*, Tirana, 2008. Lladrovci made a strong impression on all he met, with the BBC correspondent David Loyn comparing him to a contemporary version of the Albanian culture hero Skanderbeg, pp. 53 ff.
25. The most important source for this and much later history involving the Roman Catholic Church and pro-KLA Catholic Albanians is Nike Gjeloshi, *Kosova 1999 As Republike e Proklamuar, As Autonomi e Imponaur*, Tirana, 2004. Gjeloshi is from a prominent northern family and was closely involved in senior positions in and around the LDK as soon as it was founded, and for a time was deputy to Bukoshi in the 'Ministry of Defence'. He came to strongly disagree with many decisions taken by Bukoshi, although he did not become critical of Rugova until a much later stage. This will be an important source for early Vatican attitudes towards Kosova after 1990. Gjeloshi became a highly committed supporter of the KLA during its development period and his book is an objective and well written account with perceptive eyewitness accounts of many important meetings and events, although it would be improved if the lengthy digressions giving his views about Mother Teresa, Pope John Paul II and other prominent Catholics had been shortened or omitted. For the official Vatican position on later stages of the conflict, see *The Holy See and the Crisis in Kosova*, Vatican City, 2002, a work that raises as many questions as it answers.
26. See A. Zogaj, *Dialog me Naim Maloku*, Prishtina, 2000. Maloku had become a strong critic of Bujar Bukoshi in the 1996–97 period within the LDK and had opposed the formation of FARK. This valuable and candid source also gives good insights into the operations of the Yugoslav KOS security service in Croatia, the personalities around assassinated Ahmet Krasniqi and the military leadership of FARK in 1998 and the turmoil surrounding the shooting of Azem Haydari in Tirana in the summer of 1998. See Pettifer/Vickers, *The Albanian Question-Reshaping the Balkans*, op. cit., pp. 168 ff. For an illuminating illustration of Bukoshi's views in this period, on the key issue of his attitude to the 1997 uprising in Albania, see *Zeri*, Prishtina, 5 April 1997.
27. The role of FARK is very controversial throughout its existence. See Chapters

5 and 8 to 10. For well sourced information on the Panalbanian Assembly, see *Arena*, Skopje, Nos 7 and 8, January 2010. There is a large and usually propagandist literature in Kosova, most of it hostile to the FARK and its military leader Tahir Zemaj. See, for instance, E. Luma and D. Krasniqi, *Keshtu beri Tahir Zemaj*, Prishtina, 2001. The main pro-Zemaj, pro-FARK apologia book is A. Ahmetaj and S. Krasniqi, *Keshtu Foli Tahir Zemaj*, Prishtina, 2001. At The Hague Kosova Prime Minister Hashim Thaci described Zemaj as only a 'common criminal' (ICTY papers, Limaj trial, Thaci witness statement). The detailed role played by FARK soldiers in the conflict has yet to be investigated on any objective basis. Anecdotal evidence would suggest the FARK may have contributed something to the liberation of Peje but played a very negative role in border logistics, in Albania, in the fighting at Rahavec and around Prizren at later stages of the conflict. In his interviews Ramush Haradinaj is highly critical of the FARK. See *A Narrative about War and Freedom*, pp. 129 ff. He points out the difficulty KLA commanders had in establishing the *modus operandi* of the FARK: 'I never knew where the power struggle, or the political struggle, started, and where it was going.' It is also unclear how far Zemaj actually 'commanded' the FARK in any normal military sense.

28. Some deserters also went straight to Albania, although few later played any significant later role in the KLA. See J. Pettifer, *Kosova Express*, London and New York, 2004, pp. 51 ff.

29. See Kosova Information Centre, *Albanian Democratic Movement in Former Yugoslavia: Documents 1990–1993*, Prishtina, 1993.

30. For the post-1990 period, see M. Vickers and J. Pettifer, *Albania: From Anarchy to a Balkan Identity*, London and New York, 1996.

31. B. Bukoshi (1947–). Born Suva Reka, qualified as a medical doctor. A founder of the LDK and first 'Prime Minister' of the Rugova 'government' after 1991. For basic information on the career of Bujar Bukoshi in Germany in the Milosevic period, see P. Hockenos, *Homeland Calling: Exile Patriotism and the Balkan Wars*, Cornell, 2003. This book is not a trustworthy source on many topics and contains factual errors, but gives a good impression of how Bukoshi was seen in Germany at that time.

32. The Belgrade government was much more realistic about what the onset of the LDK 'government' represented than most Kosova Albanians. See, for instance, article in the SPS party newspaper *Politika*, 2 March 1991, 'Kosovo and the end of Enverism'. The article envisaged a possible separatist uprising which Rugova and the LDK would be unable to prevent in the spring of 1992.

33. For detail, see James Pettifer and Miranda Vickers, *The Albanian Question—Reshaping the Balkans*, London and New York, 1997.

34. Interview with Shaip Latifi, president of the LDK in Zurich 1992–95, 25 April 2003, and with Xhervat Mazrekaj, editor of *Bota Sot* newspaper, Zurich, 9 June 2005.

35. See J. Pettifer and M. Vickers, *The Albanian Question: Reshaping the Balkans*, pp. 129 ff.

36. Report of Amnesty International, London, 2 February 1993. Also, Amnesty International report *Ethnic Albanians Trial by Truncheon*, February 1994.
37. Ramush Tahiri is Ali Aliu's son-in-law.
38. See article by James Pettifer, *The Scotsman*, Edinburgh, 22 December 1992, 'An army which is ill-equipped to fight'.
39. See S. Zejnullahu, *Lufta per Kosoven (Flet Komandant Remi)*, Prishtina, 2001.
40. See Gjeloshi, op. cit., pp. 59 ff.
41. Interview with Shaip Latifi, Zurich, 25 April 2003. Latifi was forced into Swiss exile after losing his job as a mining engineer at Trepca, and became President of the LDK in Zurich for a period in the early 1990s.
42. Hashim Thaci (1968–). Born in Buroje in Drenica. Member of LPRK as student leader at Prishtina University, moved to Zurich in 1991, studied history and political science at Zurich University. Returned to Kosova 1993, took part in attacks on Serbian police posts with early KLA groups, sentenced to 22 years imprisonment *in absentia*. Political Spokesman for the KLA 1998–99, set up the first Provisional Government of Kosova April 1999, leader of the PDK party in Kosova Assembly 1999–. Prime Minister 2008–.
43. See J. Pettifer, *A Concept for a New Reality Dialogue with Hashim Thaci*, Prishtina, 2001, and conversations Hashim Thaci-James Pettifer, 2000–2004. The emphasis on 'sleeper' recruitment seemed to be a particular priority for the LPRK. The LPK later had a more open membership, although this may be because a high proportion of membership was in the Diaspora, particularly Switzerland where membership did not involve the serious physical and security dangers that it did in Kosova.
44. A. Bekaj, *The KLA and the Kosova War*, Berlin, 2010. This is a useful general introduction to the history, although weak on some ideological issues.
45. Thaci had been president of the newly formed independent students' union in Prishtina University after 1989. His history teacher has observed that he was a less than assiduous student 'with his mind on other things', but he did show interest in Kosova history in the Second World War (Interview with Professor Nada Boskovska, Zurich, 2 February 2010).
46. Gjeloshi, op. cit., pp. 217 ff.
47. See Fazli Veliu, *UCK nga Betaja ne Beteje*, Tetovo, 2005.
48. Fatmir Humolli (1965–), born in Donje Ljupche village near Podujeve, joined LPK in 1985, joined LKCK in 1991, active in building KLA in Kosova 1992–97, sentenced to eight years in gaol *in absentia* in 1997, attended military training and recruiting in Albania in 1998, member of Llap KLA command. From 2001 member of the Kosova Assembly for LKCK.
49. See G. Geci, *Lufta pa Maska Drenica 1991–1999*, Prishtina, 2001. This is an interesting memoir, but needs to be read very critically. Geci did not like or get on with the LPK leadership, particularly Xharvit Haliti, whom he accuses of 'Stalinist paranoia' (p. 7). Geci says he is putting forward the view of an average KLA soldier but in fact is as political as many he criticises. His observations are most useful as a source in conveying the confusion of the wartime period and the difficulty a committed and brave man like Geci had in fitting

into structures developed by others who knew each other well over a long period beforehand, as the LPK members usually did. He does not understand that LPK internal security had been essential for its survival in conditions of illegality, although he may well be right in seeing it as an obstruction to independent initiatives in the war.

50. A.K. Starinov, *Behind Fascist Lines*, New York, 2001.

51. B. Hamzaj, *A Narrative about War and Freedom (Dialogue with Commander Ramush Haradinaj)*, Prishtina, 2000.

52. It is worth recalling that Seselj in the United States then was not regarded as the war criminal and violent extremist that merited his ICTY indictment. He was seen in some quarters, mainly in the Republican Party in the mid-West, as an anti-Communist who deserved serious consideration. The 118th session of the Ohio Senate gave him an award for 'outstanding human rights achievement' in 1989. See *Velika Serbija*, Belgrade, November 1995.

53. See *Security and Defense Policy of Republic of Albania*, Republic of Albania Council of Defense, Tirana, 1995. A. Copani, 'New Dimensions of Albania's Security Posture', *Nato Review* 44 (2), March 1996.

54. The best picture of the development of the radical wing of the movement in this period is in F. Pushkolli, *Hasan Ramadani (1948–1994)*, Prishtina, 2004.

55. D. Sejdiu, *Kush ishte Zahir Pajaziti?* Prishtina, 2001.

56. See J. Pettifer and M. Vickers, *The Albanian Question*, London and New York, 1997 for a detailed analysis of the uprising.

57. See the publications of General Kudusi Lama, a key figure in the Tirana army leadership. In *Kosova dhe Ushtria Clirimtare*, Tirana, 2005, he sets out an interesting and fairly comprehensive picture of the relationship between the Albanian armed forces and the KLA. He focuses mainly on the later 1998–99 period.

58. Discussion with L. Bashkurti, Tirana, 2009.

59. R. Haradinaj, *A Narrative on War and Freedom*, Prishtina, 2002.

60. See Gjeloshi, op. cit.

61. For more detail, see Christopher Deliso, *The Coming Balkan Caliphate: The Threat of Radical Islam to Europe and the West*, Westport, 2007, pp. 29 ff. This is a highly angled book with often arbitrary interpretations of events but contains some useful source material if critically evaluated. The account of the origins of the LPK in Turkey is inaccurate, for instance, and would appear to depend on recycled Serbian propaganda.

62. An interesting picture of this world is provided in Nathan Pali's postgraduate thesis 'The Church of Jesus Christ Latter Day Saints Enters Albania 1992–1999', see Brigham Young University website, www.home.bgu.edu, 2008.

63. For background, see J.-E Lane, *The Swiss Labyrinth Institutions, Outcomes and Redesign*, London, 2001.

64. Some had prominent political roles, like Bardhyl Tirana, President Jimmy Carter's personal lawyer.

65. For an excellent account of these years, see F. Pushkolli, *Hasan Ramadani (1948–94)*, Prishtina, 2004.

66. As the official history of the Albanian Party of Labour observes, pertaining to events in 1943 in the Second World War, 'in the Partisan *ceta*s the masses of the people saw for the first time the champions of their own interests.' The situation was much the same in central and western Kosova after 1995.

67. See R. Mustafa, *Deshmoret e UCK-se Zona Operative e Lapit*, ed. S. Zhitia, Prishtina, 2001. The arrest of Remi on alleged extortion charges was a clear fabrication by UNMIK and NATO/KFOR intelligence officials as a means of trying to break the remaining influence of the KLA in the Podujeve region. At this time the odd idea of an east-west partition of Kosova was current in these circles, and Llap militancy was an obstacle to these plans. Remi was subsequently acquitted and is now a Kosova Member of Parliament in Hashim Thaci's governing PDK party.

68. This ideology has a very long history, going right back in various guises to the beginnings of twentieth century colonisation of Kosova. See B. Tomasovic, *Life and Death in the Balkans*, London, 2006, pp. 10 ff for a fine picture of Serbian security force activity in the 1920s and 1930s.

69. See, for instance, material on the Rama family who were subjected to a Serbian massacre in Llap in March 1999, X. Rama, *10 Deshmoret e Familjes Rama*, Prishtina, 2004.

70. See Zejnullahu, *Lufta per Kosoven—Commander Remi Speaks*, Prishtina, 2001. Remi is one of the ex-KLA commanders who is a thoroughly reliable factual source on most aspects of the war. His book was soon withdrawn from sale after publication, which in the odd, intensely pro-Yugoslavist atmosphere of the UNMIK administration at the time is perhaps not surprising. Others have speculated that this was because he notes the role of the imams in KLA recruitment centres in Podujeve.

71. See Hank Perritt's collection of wartime songs.

72. The only mention I have found of a specific Islamic influence on the development of the war in my research for this book is in Rrustem Mustafa's (Commander Remi) account of recruitment to the Llap KLA forces, where young men were put forward from the Podujeve *madrese*. See above.

4. PREPARATION FOR BATTLE: A HANDGUN ARMY?

1. S. Vukmanovic-Tempo, *Revolucija koja tece*, Belgrade, 1971.

2. D. Djordjevic and S. Fischer-Galati, *The Balkan Revolutionary Tradition*, New York, 1981, p. xv.

3. *About the Events in Kosova*, 8 Nentori, Tirana,1981.

4. See R. Holbrooke, *To End a War*, New York, 1998, and interviews by James Pettifer with State Department and ex-State Department officials.

5. See S. Dede, *The Counter Revolution within the Counter Revolution*, Tirana, 1983.

6. See F. Ajvazi, '*Portreti I Luftetarit te Lirise*, Prishtina, 2000. This little book is one of the best guides to the psychology of the ordinary KLA soldier, who felt impelled to volunteer and fight. It also conveys a sense of the magnitude of the

events unfolding that made an individual seem irrelevant and unimportant, and it is a reliable source on the circle of military command around Haradinaj in Dukagjini region.

7. See B. Kondis, 'A British Attempt to Organise a Revolt in Northern Albania during the Greek-Italian War', in *Greece and the Wars in the Balkans (1940–1941)*, Thessaloniki, 1992.

8. T. Garton Ash, 'Is Kosovo the Albanian apocalypse?' *The Times*, London, 19 March 1997.

9. *Misioni I Climirit*, Tirana, 1998, Vol. II, pp. 128 ff.

10. Syleman Selimi (1970–). Born Arceve village in Drenica, joined LPK 1996, conscript in Yugoslav army 1997–98, later head of KLA HQ General Staff from summer 1998 until April 1999 when he was replaced by Agim Ceku, in 2001 Deputy Commander Kosova Protection Corps (TMK). His uncle is Rexhep Selimi.

11. M. Jackson, *Soldier: The Autobiography*, London, 2007. Many British army officers were puzzled when they arrived in Kosova in the summer of 1999 to discover the lack of explosive usage by the KLA in the war. In doctrinal terms, it was central to all their understanding of successful insurgency practice since the Boer War. See *British Army Review*, No. 148, Warminster, Winter 2009/2010.

12. See article by Miranda Vickers, 'Balkan powder keg ready to explode', *The Independent*, London, 8 July 1996. The realistic observation in the story that Rugova was now 'a tired and withdrawn man' brought very adverse comment in London official quarters. Also, by the same author, 'Kosovo on the brink of abyss', *The European*, London, 20 June 1996.

13. See F. Pushkolli, *Mbrojtja Kombetar e Kosoves*, Prishtina, 1991. This was a very influential work in some Western intelligence circles who saw it as providing a textbook for the Kosova uprising many expected in the winter of 1991–92. Also D. Sejdiu, *Kush ishte Zahir Pajaziti*, Prishtina, 2001, and F. Pushkolli, *Zahir Pajaziti Hero I Kombit*, Prishtina, 2001. In Belgrade the whole issue was seen as one of the survival of Enver Hoxha's ideas of PanAlbanian revolution which some suspected had persisted during the time of Ramiz Alia. See, for instance, media comment on events such as the article 'Kosovo and the end of 'Enverism'. *Politika*, 2 March 1991.

14. 'Yank' Levy, *Guerilla Warfare*, London, 1941.

15. For the complete texts, see G. Elshani, *Ushtria Climitare e Kosoves Dokumente dhe Artikuj*, Prishtina, 2003. An earlier edition was published in Aarau, Switzerland in 2001.

16. See, for instance, James Pettifer, 'Tensions are mounting in Kosova', *Wall Street Journal Europe*, 24 May 1996.

17. Milosevic had always envisaged the option of a return to old colonisation processes in Kosova. This long predated the war, see S. Milosevic, *Godina Raspleta*, Belgrade, 1989, pp. 152 ff. As with Hitler's *Mein Kampf*, the dictator stated many of his future political objectives in published works that ought to have been more widely read in the international community.

18. For background see an important interview with the Swiss-based LPK activist Bardhyl Mahmuti in P. Denaud and V. Pras, *Kosovo—Naissance d'une lutte armée UCK*, Paris, 1998.

19. F. Trgo, in *Tito's Historical Decisions*, Belgrade, 1980, pp. 14 ff.

20. See T.E. Lawrence, *Seven Pillars of Wisdom* and other writings. For Soviet guerrilla warfare theories developed in the Spanish Civil War, see A.K. Starinov, *Behind Fascist Lines*, New York, 2001.

21. There is a voluminous, mostly anthropological literature on the *Kanun*, its re-emergence after Communism and its role in modern Albanian and Kosova life. For general background, see the writings of Antonia Young and Robert Elsie.

22. See G. Geci, *Lufta Pa Maska*, Prishtina, 2001.

23. From N. Imeraj, *UCK Troje T'Bashkuria KLA A United Nation*, Tirana, 2000.

24. See Human Rights Watch, *A Week of Terror in Drenica*, New York, 1999, and OSCE Publication *Kosovo/Kosova As Seen As Told*, Vienna, 1999 and other publications.

25. It is perhaps interesting to note that there was virtually no accurate information on the nature of these informal leadership structures or their history available to the NATO KFOR forces which entered Kosova in 1999 or the incoming UNMIK international administration. See, for instance, the International Crisis Group publication, *Who's Who in Kosovo* (2000), which is helpful and illuminating about the political leadership but has almost no information at all about the military or security leadership of the KLA.

26. See Anon., *Humbjet e policies Serbe gjate luftes ne Kosove*, a pirated Albanian language edition of a Serbian police-origin memorial volume to those killed between 1992 and 2000 in the conflict.

27. Quoted in *VIP News* Belgrade, 24 May 1998.

28. VIP News Belgrade, 7 August 1996.

29. Mother Teresa (1910–97) was born Gonxhe Bojaxhiu to an Albanian family living in Skopje, Macedonia. Her Missionaries of Charity Order was founded in 1946.

30. *VIP News*, Belgrade, 4 November 1996.

31. R. Haradinaj, quoted in *A Narrative about War and Freedom*, Prishtina, 2000.

32. Ali Ahmeti later became a leading politician in Skopje after the 2001 conflict in the FYROM/Republic of Macedonia and Emrush Xhemajli is currently a member of the Kosova Assembly for the Socialist Party of Kosova.

33. The Haradinaj 'myth' has always been that Ramush Haradinaj never left Kosova during the war. This is certainly true if the 'war' period is defined as starting in November 1997.

34. In his war interviews Haradinaj observes that Konushevski was a key figure in KLA logistics and supply and moved continually through the entire conflict between Albania and Kosova. Haradinaj surmises he was killed by 'a Serbian hand' but with Albanian local traitors possibly involved as executioners. This is a convincing argument. The circumstances of the killing would very strongly suggest the involvement of foreign intelligence capacity in locating of the victim through cellphone trace use. The Prishtina journalist Baton Haxhiu goes

somewhat further in his book *Lufta Ndryshe*, Prishtina, 2008 and points the finger at local Albanians operating within the OSCE framework on the border in 1998 and seeking to steal the arms from their truck. Konushevski himself had some background of involvement with the SHIK security agency in Albania and this organisation was heavily factionalised in the wartime period, often with different groups working for different external national intelligence agencies, particularly the Greek. See J. Pettifer and M. Vickers, *The Albanian Question*, op. cit.

35. *A Narrative about War and Freedom*, op. cit., pp. 27 ff.
36. R. Radinovic, *The Military and Strategic Importance of Kosovo and Metohija for the Federal Republic of Yugoslavia*, op. cit., pp. 177 ff.
37. The incursion in 1915–16 has the strongest purchase on the Albanian popular memory. See S. Tchernoff., *Serbs in December 1915*, London, 1916 and T. Judah, *The Serbs: History, Myth and the Destruction of Yugoslavia*, Yale, 1997.
38. One senior British paratroop officer interviewed described the VJ as a 'crap army', adding that in some senses the KLA was also a 'crap insurgency' (September 2010). It is an interesting issue how far the first may have given rise to the second.
39. See many recent local studies, such as H. Saraci, *Ortakolli ne Driten e Luftes Climitare*, Prishtina, 1999.
40. V.I. Lenin, *Works Vol. VIII*, p. 305 (Russian edition).
41. See S. Vukmanovic, *How and Why the People's Liberation Struggle of Greece met with Defeat*, London, 1985.
42. It is often forgotten that in many areas of Kosova there was an exact correspondence between the old Communist party membership and the 'new' LDK membership, as ceremonies of exchanging the old CPY cards for the LDK party cards were popular.
43. See M. Pirraku, *Mulla Idris Gjilani dhe Mbrojtja Kombetar e Kosoves Lindore 1941–1951*, Prishtina, 1995. It is surprising that this major historical work has never been translated into English or a major West European language in view of the value it would have had in improving understanding of the background to the Preshevo conflict in 2000–2001.
44. See J. Pettifer, *Kosova Express*, op. cit., pp. 60 ff. and *The Holy See and the Conflict in Kosova*, Rome, 2000. Roberts was subject to criticism in the US and parts of the UK press in particular for his relationship with the Serbian leader.
45. See J. Pettifer and M. Vickers, *The Albanian Question*, London, 2007 for a detailed analysis of the 1997 events in Tirana and their relationship to the Kosova war.
46. See Z. Rexhepi, *Partia Demokratike Shqiptare Lindja Zhvillimi dhe Veprimtaria*, Tetovo, 2004.
47. For background on the failure of democratic reform in the FYROM/Republic of Macedonia in the early 1990s see G.-H. Ahrends, *Diplomacy on the Edge*, Washington, DC, 2007.

48. The best account of these relationships is in a Tetovo journalist's book, Beqir Berisha, *Fundi i nje Aventure Politike*, Tetovo, 1998.
49. See for instance *Washington Times*, 8 May 1996.
50. *Rilindja*, 6 July 1996.
51. Kosova refugee settlement in Albania in the Zogist period had been localised around Durres and the neighbouring little town of Shijak.
52. See Kadri Rexha's fine biographical study of Edmond Hoxha, *Pushke Lajmetare*, Prishtina, 2002.
53. BBC Monitoring, 13 January 1997, ICTY document No: U0038669.

5. AUTUMN 1997: THE WAR IS DEFINED

1. For information on the Kosova Liberation Army war dead, see the series *Fenikset e Lirise Deshmoret e Ushtrise Climitare te Kosoves*, eleven volumes published to date, Prishtina, 2001–12.This is a valuable reference work on the war victims. There is as yet no general study of the sociology of KLA recruitment. The book reinforces the view that the overwhelming majority of KLA volunteers were from poor or middle rural backgrounds or from provincial towns. On a numerical basis, Prishtina is very under-represented. For the Dukagjini region, see a similar volume, H. Hasani (ed.) *Te Pavdekshmit e Dukagjinit Desjmoret e UCK-se te ZOD*, Peje, 2002. For a very scholarly and well researched book on the Llap region, see S. Zhitia, *Deshmoret e UCK-se Zona Operative e Llapit*, Prishtina, 2000.
2. *Bulletin of the Ministry of Information of the Republic of Kosova*, No. 321, 7 December 1997.
3. *Jane's Intelligence Review*, March 1998, London.
4. For the decline in the Albanian army after 1990, see C. Dennison Lane, *Once upon an Army—the Crisis in the Albanian Army 1995–1996*, G-114, CSRC, RMA Sandhurst, 2002. www.defenceacademy.mod.uk and E. Leci, *Eliminimi I Lidership Ushtarak*, Tirana, 2002. Also C. Dennison Lane, 'The Disintegration of the Albanian Army', *Mediterranean Quarterly*, Volume 9, No. 2, Summer 1998.
5. See Daniel T. Canfield, 'The Russian-Chechen Wars', *Joint Force Quarterly* 51, 2008, Joint Chiefs of Staff, National Defence University, Washington, DC.
6. S. Woodward, *Balkan Tragedy*, Washington, DC, 1995.
7. See J. Gow, *Legitimacy and the Military*, op. cit.
8. See, for example, publications from Belgrade such as *Terrorism in Kosovo and Metohija and Albania—White Book*, Belgrade, 2008. This booklet which was published in September 1998 makes no geographical distinctions at all in the KLA's areas of operations between Albania and Kosova.
9. See H. Husaj, *Dubrava Rruga Drejt Vdekjes*, Peje, 2006, an interesting little book on the Dubrava prison atrocity in which numerous inmates were murdered by Serbian paramilitaries on 22 May 1999. Apart from the human rights issues, it is also (perhaps unintentionally) revealing about Rugova's efforts to renew

links with the old Balli Kombetar in Albania in the wartime period, and gives a good picture of the political prison regime in the late 1990s in Kosova.

10. There is already a very large literature, mostly in Serbian or English, about the psychology and mentality of Milosevic. For a reliable and balanced general book, see L. Sell, *Slobodan Milosevic and the Destruction of Yugoslavia*, Durham, 2002, also A. Le Bor, *Milosevic: A Biography*, London, 2002 and D. Doder and L. Branson, *Milosevic: Portrait of a Tyrant*, New York, 1999.

11. This mentality was certainly not confined to 'Balkan' political and military actors in the conflicts. The role of the revival of interest within the British army, diplomatic corps and media in Rebecca West's *Black Lamb and Grey Falcon* as a 'canonical' guide to the region, though it was written over seventy years before the 1990s conflicts, is significant; interest was also revived in works structuring the 'living past' in the contemporary present, like Robert Kaplan's *Balkan Ghosts*.

12. See J. Gow, *The Serbian Project and its Adversaries*, London, 2002 for a well informed if occasionally somewhat abstract analysis of this period from the wider strategic point of view. As Gow points out, since Milosevic and Stoyacic are both dead and Stanisic turns out to have been a US contact (although possibly not in this period of the conflict), it is unlikely that the details of the decision will ever be known. At this stage in his dictatorship Milosevic, like many similar rulers before him, preferred to work by telephone instructions and meetings and avoid written documentation of his decisions. The existence of the ICTY war crimes tribunal may have played a part in this. Defenders of the Serbian government have always denied that such a comprehensive strategy for the ethnic cleansing of Kosova ever existed.

13. See additional material on this issue in my book *Kosova Express*, op. cit., pp. 140 ff.

14. See Appendix reproducing the Programme of the Kosova Liberation Army.

15. See D. Eudes, *The Kapetanios Partisans and Civil War in Greece, 1943–1949*, London, 1972.

16. Interview with Xhavit Haliti, Kosova, 2004.

17. Of course KLA leaders considered Zemaj as only a criminal using the war for personal aggrandisement. See remarks by the KLA political spokesman and now Kosova Prime Minister Hashim Thaci in his statement to the ICTY in the trial of ex-KLA leader Fatmir Limaj, ICTY records, www.icty.com. Also negative statements by Ramush Haradinaj and others.

18. The Rugova Pass mountain border area with Montenegro is a possible exception but it was not very important in Kosova-wide terms for most of the war, as Albania itself was so easily accessible nearby.

19. Reporters arriving in Kosova who had covered the Bosnian war often expected the KLA to be quickly destroyed from the air. See, for instance, report by Kurt Schork for Reuters, 8 April 1998. The most likely reasons for the relative absence of helicopters from much of the conflict were simply shortages of fuel and spare parts.

20. Interview with Ivor Roberts, Belgrade, 1995. Ivor Roberts was a prominent figure in Foreign Office Balkan deliberations in this period under John Major's Conservative government in the UK.
21. For more detail, see Pettifer and Vickers, *The Albanian Question: Reshaping the Balkans*, London and New York, 2010.
22. Pettifer and Vickers, op. cit., p. 98.
23. BBC Monitoring Brief EE/3126A/6, 16 January 1998.
24. There were no foreign or local media to witness the Likoshan events. The best eye witness account in English is in *We Witness.../Edhe ne Deshmojme...*, Tetovo, 2000: 'The Massacre of Likoshan' by Mevledin Neziri, a local construction worker.
25. See A. Loyd, *Another Bloody Love Letter*, London, 2007, pp. 18 ff.
26. There is a veritable mountain of material in Albanian on the Jashari family and their deaths, most of it (understandably) hagiographical and often vague and inaccurate. This does not apply only to the Albanian-language literature. The characterisation in Tim Judah's book *Kosovo War and Revenge* of Adem Jashari as an uneducated man who happened to hate Serbs and enjoyed killing them is far from the mark. The most reliable biographical source book is by B. Hamzaj and F. Hoti, *Jasharet*, Prishtina, 2003. The interview in it with Rifah Jashari, one of the few surviving members of the family, is important in that it illustrates the Turkish geographical dimension to the family's political activities. This would have brought them particular opprobrium with the Serbian secret police and intelligence apparatus and may account in part for the enthusiasm and vigour the Serbian authorities showed in destroying the family.
27. Interview with Lt Colonel Philip Cox, ex-British Army, 2010. For a lively if very pro-Serbian and often speculative book with chapters on the SAS and the Balkans, see C. Jennings, *Midnight in some Burning Town*, London, 2004. He demonstrates, perhaps unintentionally, the prevailing ideology in some of the British army officer corps who saw themselves fighting Albanian 'extremism' without any very clear idea of the Albanian political culture.
28. 'About the Events in Kosova', *8Nentori*, Tirana, 1981.
29. See Pettifer, *Kosova Express*, op. cit.
30. A stray bullet almost killed the British journalist Vaughan Smith during the Prekaz fighting. It lodged in his cellphone in a shirt breast pocket.
31. See the ICTY trial records and the very useful and comprehensive volume published by the OSCE in Vienna in 2000, *Kosova As Seen As Told*.
32. See D. Anjelkovic (ed.), *Kosova Crucified*, Belgrade, 2000 for an account of this period from the Serbian side; for the spring 2003 events see D. Kovadinovic, *The March Pogrom*, Belgrade, 2004. The major Russian scholarly work on the damage to monuments is A. Lidov (ed.), *Kosovo: Orthodox Heritage and Contemporary Catastrophe*, Moscow, 2007.
33. Fazli Veliu has written extensively on the war in Macedonia in 2001 and the role and genesis of the NLA there as an insurgent force. He has been a little more circumspect about his earlier political life at the centre of LPK/KLA support operations in Switzerland in the Kosova war. For the latter, see F. Veliu,

UCK nga beteja ne beteje—Mesazhe te Paperfunduara, Tetovo, 2003. He describes his persecution by the Skopje authorities before the 2001 conflict started in F. Veliu, *I Perndjekur ne Shkup ne Perendim*, Tirana, 2001 For the public positions of the LPK in the most important wartime period, see F. Veliu, *LPK dhe UCK: Nje embleme nje qellim*, Tirana, 2001.

34. In a sign of LPK concern that the Swiss government decision might at some future point be reversed, the Homeland Fund chief Jashar Salihu opened up a parallel operation in Denmark in the next months. Salihu had been a political exile in Copenhagen for some time after he was released from gaol in Yugoslavia in the late 1980s.

35. Interview with British government official, May 2001, and discussions with Swiss diplomat, July 2002.

36. See B. Hamzaj, *A Narrative about War and Freedom (Dialogue with Commander Ramush Haradinaj)*, Prishtina, 2000. Haradinaj also claims to have been in touch with sympathetic Swiss military officers between 1991 and 1993 and to have received some military training in Switzerland.

37. Swiss army development had evolved in the nineteenth and the early twentieth century with two main elements: first, the right of male citizens to bear arms and keep them at home, originally linked to the admiration the leaders of the nineteenth century Confederation had for the US Constitution, and second, a way of life where in the mountains, rural inhabitants needed small arms to protect flocks in a pastoral economy. A third factor was the general utility in defence doctrine of an armed people for a small country surrounded by powerful neighbours. For the Kosovars, all these seemed powerful parallels to their own situation and thinking, where interfering Hapsburgs in Swiss history were replaced by hegemonist Serbia and Yugoslavia. See G. Grimm, op. cit.

38. Fehmi Agani (died 1999) was a senior sociology professor and author who was one of an influential group of Albanian leaders of the Communist party in Kosova in the 1980s from the western town of Gjakova. Then he was a close associate of the Kosova party chairman Mahmut Bakalli; see Pettifer, *Kosova Express*, pp. 204 ff. Agani was murdered by Serbian forces when attempting to leave Kosova in April 1999. For information on the crisis in the Kosova Communist party leadership involving Bakalli in the late 1980s, see Vickers, op. cit.

39. In my experience, these were nearly all people who had been connected with Bujar Bukoshi's 'Defence Ministry' in the 1990s.

40. Zemaj was eventually assassinated in Kosova in January 2003. For an anti-Zemaj account of events, see E. Luma and S. Krasniqi, *Keshtu Beri Tahir Zemaj*, Prishtina, 2001. It is impossible to verify many of the allegations about Zemaj, particularly after his violent death. For a hagiographic portrait, see A. Ahmetaj and S. Krasniqi, *Keshtu foli Tahir Zemaj?* Prishtina, 2001. It is more interesting as a source on the FARK attempts to take over leadership of the war effort in the summer of 1998 in Tirana, and the background to the murder of 'Minister of Defence' Ahmet Krasniqi there, than anything else.

6. A LIBERATED DRENICA AND MILOSEVIC'S FIRST OFFENSIVE

1. Mao Tse-tung, *On Guerilla Warfare*, Champaign, IL, 2000.
2. Interview with British diplomat who served in the Belgrade Embassy in 1998, August 2010. Some members of the Embassy staff decided to make direct contacts with the media to highlight the dangers in events, as they felt much prior reporting to London had not reflected the seriousness of the situation. The main sources hitherto had been UDBA staff in Belgrade.
3. See J. Pettifer, Kosova Express, op. cit., pp. 39 ff.
4. ICTY documentation, Limaj trial, 13 January 2005.
5. These mule tracks and non-metalled roads are not shown on any modern maps. The only good map/guide to the 'secret roads' of pre-industrial age Kosova that often continue to exist is to be found in the Austro-Hungarian army military guidebook, *Detailbeschreibung des Sandjaks, Plevlje und des Vilayet Kosovo*, Vienna, 1899. I am grateful to the staff of the Austrian National Library in Vienna for locating a copy of this rare work.
6. For general background on the history of this issue, see Robert C. Austin, *Greater Albania: The Albanian State and the Question of Kosovo 1912–2001*, Budapest, 2004. For a popular account of the Serbian view, see J.M. Canak (ed.), *'Greater Albania': Concepts and Possible Consequences*, Institute of Geopolitical Studies, Belgrade, 1998. This depends for most of its information on a more scholarly but equally tendentious work, D. Borozan, *Greater Albania—Origins, Ideas, Practice*, Institute of Military History of the Yugoslav Army, Belgrade, 1985. Both depend on the *idée fixe* that all Albanian nationalism depends on outside Power support for its existence.
7. See *Srpsko Jednistvo*, Belgrade, November 1995 issue. Arkan's supporters claimed that a large pre-1912 Serbian population had been driven out of Junik at the time of the formation of the first Royalist Yugoslavia. There is no independent evidence for this view. The only substantial urban concentration of Serbs in this part of Kosova was in Peje (Pec).
8. *Albanian Daily News*, 10 March 1998.
9. There are many books and war memoirs in Albanian describing the long struggle for Koshare. For a reliable general account, see M. Cetta, *Me UCK ne Koshare*, Prishtina, 2002; V. Rustemi, *Nuhi Tairi Legende e Gjalle e Betejes se Koshares*, Skopje, 2006. The latter is an important source on the significant group of Macedonian-origin participants who took part in the Koshare fighting on a Pan-Albanian basis.
10. See James Pettifer, 'Kosovo gunmen force Serb police to beat retreat', *The Times*, 8 January 1998. In retrospect it is a moot point whether the Serbs had lost 'control' of much of western Kosova as I and others on the scene then felt they had. It is arguable that they had never really had it in many places after about perhaps 1990 in the later Yugoslav period.
11. AFP, Paris, 3 April 1998.
12. BBC Monitoring, EE/3115/A9 3 January 1998.
13. ICTY court records, Limaj trial judgement, pp. 20 ff.

14. See R. Luxemburg, *Die Mass Strike*, Berlin, 1922.

15. *Koha Ditore*, Prishtina, 24 July 1998.

16. It is clear that in some militant areas such as Kacanik, immediately north of the Macedonian border and Skopje, moves were afoot to develop the KLA well before the General Staff's arrival, and clearly the KLA leadership suffered from some of the same local intelligence 'black holes' about what was happening as the Serbs. In these matters like many others, the ICTY 'narrative' in the Limaj trial judgement is deeply misleading in its picture of the war. For a cogent account of the development in the Kacanik Gorge and vicinity, see H. Kurtaj, *Shungullon Gryka e Kacanikut*, Kacanik, 2000. Although this belongs to the often hagiographical 'local war memorial' genre of books, it has much useful information on the wider issues, as seen from an interesting perspective of a well known militant centre that was far from the border with Albania. Nationalism in the area is explicable in terms of historic traditions—the hill villages above the Gorge were always very poor, in Ottoman times the Gorge was known as a haunt of robbers and bandits, and after the Drenica catastrophe in 1945, some Drenica people who had served forced labour sentences found refuge in Kacanik and subsequently jobs in the quarrying industry and the Hani I Elezit (General Rankovic) cement factory. Much of the first Kacanik KLA was wiped out by the VJ in mid-July 1998 and it was reformed after the Racak massacre in January 1999 as part of the KLA Brigade 161 'Ahmet Kacaku', working closely with larger Brigade 162, 'Agim Bajrami'. It took heavy casualties for the second time in April and May 1999 during the NATO bombardment when the VJ was struggling to retain control of the Gorge as the main route between Prishtina, Ferizaj and Macedonia. The Kacanik battles could have been transformed if the KLA had used explosive munitions to destroy the main bridge at Palaj, although this would have been unhelpful for NATO in the summer of 1999 when ground forces entered Kosova.

17. For a sound general account of KLA development in this region in the early stages of the conflict, see H. Matoshi (ed.), *Gallapi gjate Rrjedhave te Historise*, Prishtina 2010. The author's writings would suggest there was little intelligence available to the Serbs about what was happening in this remote area of the eastern Kosova hill country and Belgrade seemed slow to realise that here, as elsewhere, the development of the KLA by May 1998 had become Kosova-wide.

18. Interview with Vaughan Smith, ex-Frontline Television, September 2010.

19. S. Avramov, 'The Post-war restructuring of Europe-Manipulation of Kosovo and Metohija', in *Kosovo and Metohija: Challenges and Responses*, Belgrade, 1997.

20. Subsequently Greek Foreign Minister in the New Democracy government until 2009.

21. For further background on Greek collaboration with the Milosevic regime involving allegations of assassinations of ethnic Albanian activists in Europe, see T. Michas, *Unholy Alliance: Greece and Milosevic's Serbia*, College Station, 2002.

22. International Crisis Group, *Kosova Spring*, 20 March 1998, Prishtina-Sarajevo.
23. See 'Massive pro-Kosovo rally unites Albanian political parties', *Gazeta Shqiptare*, Tirana, 7 March 1998. Exceptions to the general poor media coverage of events in Europe at this stage were the London weekly *The Economist*, and the *Neue Zürcher Zeitung* in Switzerland, which maintained comprehensive and objective reporting throughout the conflict.
24. See the collection of secret police documents from Yugoslav Interior Ministry archives, *Dosja Sekrete e UDB-se Emigracioni Shqiptar 1944–1953*, Prishtina, 2004.
25. Montenegrin soldiers seem to have been particularly important in this trade, perhaps a symbol of the looming crisis between Belgrade and Podgoritsa in the post-Milosevic years.
26. 18 Serbian families are said to have left Decani on 14 April (ICTY documents, Limaj trial, Day 18).
27. ICTY evidence, Limaj trial, Day 19.
28. See H. Katana, *Kudusi Lama Gjenerali I Luftes*, Tirana, 2002. Katani's book is a well researched and reliable source. It indicates that after the chaos in early 1997, the Nano government had made a sensible decision in keeping General Kudusi Lama in command of the Kukes Infantry, although his functional forces seem to have been extremely limited and he relied mostly on his dominant personality and good local contacts to get things done. He had good relationships with President Rexhep Meidani and Minister of Defence Sabet Brokaj, who was one of the few senior ministers in that government not under Greek tutelage. He seems to have had little contact with Prime Minister Fatos Nano throughout the emergency period. Interior Minister Neritan Ceka also had little influence on events in Kukes region. In theory an Albanian army brigade with seven battalions was supposed to be there but in practice there was nothing near this strength.
29. According to some sources, no less than 4,000 tons of munitions were stored in the little town of Kukes at this time.
30. At this point there was some discussion in the more traditionalist elements of the diplomatic community, e.g. around the Swedish envoy Karl Bildt and the ex-British Ambassador to Belgrade Ivor Roberts, that an international military force ought to be sent to help the Serbs seal the border. The idea, apart from the politics, foundered on ignorance of the practicalities of the geography and terrain.
31. See the well known television film, *The Valley*, BBC UK 1998 for a graphic picture of these intense local confrontations.
32. *Bujku*, Prishtina, 29 April 1998.
33. The whole issue of Western indifference to, and even implicit collaboration, with the use of illegal anti-personnel mines by the VJ has yet to be explored properly in the public domain, ten years after the war. Most journalists and ECMM monitors active in Kosova in this period knew that they were being used, but there is no record of any statement about this issue from any NATO

member government. It is particularly strange regarding the UK government, as the anti-mines campaign was very strong in the UK following the Princess of Wales's death in 1997 and was openly espoused by Prime Minister Tony Blair. See Pettifer, *Kosova Express*, op. cit.

34. See J. Pettifer, 'We Have been here Before', *The World Today*, London, April 1998.

35. The general timing of this 'opening to the KLA' from London seems to have run largely in parallel with the change of US policy instituted by Secretary of State Madeleine Albright. A military assistance and advisory programme for the future army was agreed, under the codename 'Operation Horn'. Richard Holbrooke's thinking about the US leadership role in Kosova can be seen in an article he wrote in the *New Yorker* magazine ('Why are we in Bosnia?', 18 May 1998). Holbrooke wrote: 'If the United States does not lead, its European allies could falter as they did in the early part of the decade. Indeed, since the end of this year, the old pattern has threatened to repeat itself, in Kosovo, an Albanian Muslim region in Serbia, Serbian police have cracked down on ethnic Albanians. This time, though, the United States immediately condemned the aggressors, and Secretary of State Albright called for fresh sanctions against Belgrade. "We will keep all options open to do what is necessary to prevent another wave of violence from overtaking the Balkans", she said in March. As Kosovo reminded us, there will be other Bosnias in our lives.' At this stage of the conflict, there was perhaps greater internal unity in State department leaders' thinking than later in the year.

36. A. Bekaj, op. cit., pp. 18 ff.

37. See R. Haradinaj, *A Narrative about War and Freedom*, op. cit., pp. 56 ff.

38. Once again Belgrade was very poorly informed. Yugoslav intelligence staff did not seem to read what was in the Western newspapers. Journalists were consistently reporting that LDK village bosses were supporting the new army. See, for instance, Philip Sherwell, 'Kosovo's peasants prepare for battle', *Sunday Telegraph*, London, 23 March 1998.,

39. See R. Thomas, 'Choosing the Warpath', *The World Today*, London, May 1998.

40. KIC 334, London, Kosova Information Office, 30 March 1998.

41. Haliti has subsequently been criticised for this but it should be borne in mind that FARK was beginning to emerge as a force in Tirana and northern Albania in the late spring of 1998 and as an expert on the politics involved and the past role of the FARK in Albania, Haliti was aware of the need to restrict FARK development as far as possible. Haliti had the key quality in this Tirana context of being able to cope with and up to a point get along with Albanian Socialist Party Prime Minister and government leader Fatos Nano. Haliti had an unenviable task for the KLA in dealing with Nano, who gave often contradictory instructions to his ministers about policy towards the KLA (Interview with ex-Interior Minister Neritan Ceku, Tirana, March 2002).

42. See article about Haliti in *Klan* magazine, Tirana, 22 March 2000.

43. See I. Neziri, *Ahmet Haxhiu nje Jeta te tere Levizjen Ilegale*, Prishtina, 2001, p. 133.

44. Other ex-KLA sources suggest that it was not until about the time of the autumn 1998 KDOM international observer mission that the Dukagjini region had a properly integrated member of the General Staff.

45. *The Times*, London, 28 April 1998.

46. For a general appraisal of the situation in Albania in this period, see International Crisis Group document *The View from Tirana: The Albanian Dimension of the Kosovo Crisis*, ICG, www.intl-crisis-group.org, 9 July 1998. The main author was Miranda Vickers.

47. Research interviews with ex-US and UK Defence Intelligence Agency/Defence Intelligence Service officials, 2006.

48. For the atmosphere in Prishtina at the time, see Pettifer, *Kosova Express*, op. cit., p. 163. Most observers saw it as a limp farce, with NATO planes often not even entering Kosova airspace.

49. Politics may also have been involved. Suva Reka was the home base of the LDK leader Bujar Bukoshi. For a picture of the war around the town and the development of the KLA there and around Prizren, see M. Elshani, *Betejat e Lavdishme te Brigades 123 Ditar Lufte*, Prizren, 2001 although it is stronger on the 1999 NATO intervention period than on earlier times.

50. See relevant material in the ICTY records of the Limaj trial.

51. *Daily Telegraph*, London, 27 July 1998.

52. According to some accounts, this was the first successful use of anti-tank mines by the KLA in the war. This may be the case but evidence is lacking. In his generally reliable account, Katana suggests that regular mining of roads and tracks against Serbian armour did not really start until February–March 1999. See H. Katana, *Tri Dimensioned e Luftes Clirimtare te Kosoves*, Tirana, 2002. It may be that the arms embargo on the KLA was much more effective in preventing the supply of these and similar munitions than it was in restricting AK-47 Kalashnikov and handgun supply. It is likely that most of what did eventually reach the KLA came from Albanian army sources.

53. It emerged in Prishtina after the war that it would have been possible for the KLA to close off the water supply to the main VJ base outside Prishtina if they had been organised to do so. This would probably have applied to other Yugoslav security installations also.

54. For detail on the development of the conflict in Vushtrri there is a large and generally reliable literature. See H. Saraci, *Masakrat Serbe ne Komunen e Vushtrrise 1998–1999*, Prishtina, 2005 for an emotional but professionally researched picture of the human costs of the war in the town. The journals and reports (publication forthcoming) of the 1999–2004 Vushtrri United Nations administrator C. Dennison Lane give a cogent account of the immediate postwar period that illuminates many aspects of the war. D. Simnica, *Heriozmi I Kreshtave te Shales*, Prishtina, 2000 is an interesting diary account by a female KLA leader active in the rural region between Vushtrri and Mitrovica. It is clear from what she writes that the town was largely a no-go area for the VJ

then. Lane, post-November 1999 was often the only US administrator at a senior level in UNMIK and his reports are likely to cast much light on the internal tensions in UNMIK in this period.

7. SUMMER 1998: GOLGOTHA AVOIDED

1. I. Jonuzi-Krosi, *Golgotha Shqiptare (1946–1952)*, Tetovo, 2007.
2. '62 Days of Hell in Decani', Kosovapress.com
3. See *VIP News*, No. 1293, 20 July 1998, Belgrade. *VIP News* was taken as a canonical source of news during the war, in fact during the entire 1992–2005 period by the diplomatic community in Belgrade. Its editor Bratislav Grubacic attempted to remain as independent as possible in often very difficult circumstances.
4. See S. Shala, *Lufta e Logjes 1998 Monographi*, Peje, 2006.
5. The incident bears out the remarks of a defence witness, Robert Churcher, at The Hague in a later stage of the Limaj trial, that the KLA had no clear conception of the nature of a military command structure at this stage at all. Churcher evidence 25 May 2005, ICTY.
6. ICTY papers, Limaj trial, Day 69.
7. ICTY papers, Limaj trial, witness statement by Hashim Thaci, 24 September 2005. Presumably Thaci is referring to the leadership that day, rather than the rank and file.
8. Tom Walker (1963–2004) was a prominent journalist for the News International newspapers in the Balkans in the 1990s. He was sympathetic to the Serbs in the war.
9. The perceptions of the KLA in mainstream Serbia were heavily influenced by symbolic identifications from the past. See I. Colovic, *The Politics of Symbol in Serbia*, London, 2002 for a very interesting study of the wider processes in Serbian society after 1989.
10. 'Operation Horn' remains a top secret operation and many details of its activity are unclear.
11. For a lively if often speculative and very inaccurate account of British SAS military involvement, see C. Jennings, *Midnight in Some Burning Town British Special Forces Operations from Belgrade to Baghdad*, London, 2004.
12. O. Heilbrunn, *Partisan Warfare*, London, 1962.
13. See R. Qosja, in *La Question Albanaise*, Paris, 1995 for the best formulation of this concept as it was later seen in the US liberal orbit.
14. The British liked to see themselves as 'moderates' in Yugoslav matters, compared to 'extreme' Americans. I remember a conversation in 1998 on the appointment of Sir David Hannay as Tony Blair's foreign policy adviser. It was welcomed by the senior diplomat concerned as Hannay was 'good at calming down the Yanks over Bosnia'.
15. The response of NATO Secretary General Javier Solana to the Rahavec events was that 'the restraint shown by parties in the Kosova crisis was the result of

NATO's willingness to act in Serbia's southern province in the event of an escalation of the conflict': *VIP News*, 20 July 1998.

16. See Crosland evidence to ICTY, Limaj trial, Rule 70 Witness statement, 5 December 2000. Colonel John Crosland was British Defence Attaché at the Belgrade Embassy and a very objective and professional observer of events, although his access to the conflict zones was sometimes restricted by the Belgrade authorities. The very early timing of his statement is interesting, and indicates that the British government, at least, were anticipating that Limaj would be indicted at The Hague fully three years before the actual event. It is a further illustration of how in fact the ICTY agenda and activity were mostly controlled from London, as part of a lawyer-led manipulative 'conflict resolution mechanism'. Crosland, reporting to the Defence Intelligence Service (DIS) as a DA in Belgrade, was able to have major personal influence over the data agenda that reached the British government. The KLA leadership seems to have known little or nothing about the role of British intelligence outside the Foreign Office until the sometimes difficult encounters between Hashim Thaci and General Mike Jackson in the power struggle for control of Prishtina in the summer of 1999 (Pettifer/Thaci conversations 2001–2004).

17. Krasniqi evidence to ICTY, witness statement to Limaj trial, 4 May 2004.

18. See R. Hibbert, *Albania's National Liberation: The Bitter Victory*, London, 1991, and B. Fischer, op. cit.

19. Bardhyl Mahmuti (1960–). Born in Tetovo, in FYROM/Republic of Macedonia. Moved to Prishtina 1972, graduated Prishtina University, imprisoned after 1981 student demonstrations, moved to Switzerland where he studied for a PhD in political science at Lausanne University. Joined LPK Exterior in Switzerland. His perceptive observations about the history of the conflict can be found in P. Denaud and V. Pras, *Kosovo: naissance d'une lutte armée UCK: Entretiens avec Bardhyl Mahmuti*, Paris and Montreal, 1999. He attempted to found his own political party in summer 1999 in Kosova but then worked with Hashim Thaci and the PDK.

20. For more detail, see D. Heinriksen, *NATO's Gamble: Combining Diplomacy and Airpower in the Kosova Crisis 1998–1999*, Annapolis, 2007. Also B. Lambeth, *NATO's Air War for Kosovo*, RAND, Santa Monica, 2001.

21. There is, of course, a long literary tradition in these matters. As long ago as 1909, when John Buchan's famous spy novel *The 39 Steps* was published, Buchan wrote in it about a story about Balkan revolution in *The Scotsman* acting as the catalyst for a revolution to take place.

22. For the world of the Grand Hotel, see *Kosova Express*, op. cit.

23. The refugee situation has inspired a large literature by foreign authors, e.g. Booth, but less from Albanian writers (particularly women who bore the brunt of the hardships), and I am unaware of any work by Serbian or Montenegrin writers at all on the refugee experience. See S. Gashi (ed.), *Historite Tmerrit 1998–1999* for a good picture of the time by a group of Kosovar women who were displaced. A prevailing bogus myth in UNMIK after the war (one of many) was that Kosova women were sometimes forced into internal exile and

woodland life by their men. Gashi's authors show conclusively that this was not the case and women, as carriers of much historical family memory in oral historical tradition were able to inspire even quite young adolescents to take part in the war and execute Serbs. In turn this patriotic activity led to an improvement in the traditionally subservient position of these women in many rural families in the post-war period.

24. ICTY papers, Limaj trial.

25. See also Amnesty International documents, *A Human Rights Crisis in Kosovo Province June 1998*, London, 1998.

26. *Jane's Intelligence Review*, April 1999, London.

27. 'Muslimmedia.com', London, 1 September 1998. This site with its roots in the Bosnian war became increasingly influential in the summer of 1998, with its view that the West wished to see the defeat of the KLA by Milosevic and Serbian rule over Kosova reasserted within the 'autonomy' framework of the old .1974 Yugoslav constitution. The astute military commentary on events has led to some speculation that the material on the site was sourced from a Middle East government.

28. The name of the British operation to support the KLA development was 'Operation Horn'. See Chapters 8 to 10.

29. Agim Ceku (1959–). Born in Cyshk near Peje. Fought with Croatian forces in 1991 against the JNA, wounded in 1993, achieved rank of Brigadier in Croatian army. Resigned in Zagreb in February 1999 to fight in Kosova.

30. The LKCK also seems to have been a particular target of London and European opprobrium after June 1999. The LKCK policy of appointing 'block' representatives for security watches in local residential districts and blocks of flats was seen as 'Communist' by the British leadership of KFOR in Prishtina in the summer of 1999, and some LKCK members were arrested in Prishtina that summer. The question of the political control over Jackson from London, or lack of it, is likely to be a subject of a debate by future historians.

31. F. Maclean, *Disputed Barricade: The Life and Times of Josif Broz Tito*, London, 1957, pp. 175 ff. There is much published material of an often very controversial nature about Maclean's role in putting Tito into power and the general politics of the situation. See the writings of Michael Lees, Jasper Rootham, Nora Beloff and others. These bitter controversies among ex-British Special Operations staff resurfaced in the post-1990 period in London.

32. J. Kampfner, *Blair's Wars*, pp. 41 ff.

33. In interviews after the war both Ramush Haradinaj and Hashim Thaci observed to me that the KLA was 'two armies' in some aspects throughout its life. Ceku is now a PDK MP in Kosova.

34. See D. Leurdijk and D. Zandee, *Kosovo From Crisis to Crisis*, Aldershot, 2001, pp. 179 ff. for detailed chronology of NATO activity.

35. Crosland, witness material, Limaj trial. Also, Amnesty International document, EUR/70/5498, *A Human Rights Crisis in Kosovo Province*, London, August 1998.

36. *Financial Times*, London, 20 August 1998.

37. *VIP News*, 20 August 1998.

38. *VIP News*, 2 September 1998.

39. *The Times*, 8 September 1998.

40. See M. Cetta, *Me UCK ne Koshare*, op. cit., pp. 72 ff. It seems likely that Krasniqi's organisational incompetence and unrealistic plans for large scale import of trucks from Switzerland, where money from the Homeland Fund was embezzled, were at least partly the cause of UCK dissatisfaction with him that led to his assassination in the summer of 1998 in Tirana.

41. *The Times*, 25 September 1998.

42. Field service regulations of the Soviet Army, 1944, Chapter XVII, 'Partisan Operations', Moscow, 1944.

43. See R. Maksutaj, *Isniq through the Centuries*, Prishtina, 2002. This is a very well researched local study with excellent Ottoman and Communist-period sections, though the ancient history section is full of ill-informed speculation about the Illyrians.

44. Isniq claims a strong patriotic history and to have sheltered the Albanian nationalist hero Isa Boletini when he was fleeing from the Serbs in 1908. In the late 1920s and early 1930s much of the area around the village was dominated by outlaw gangs under the control of Beke Ademi and his family. The outlaws in the main were from families whose land had been taken by Serbian colonists. The village was burnt in the first week of September 1998.

45. This was not the case in the cultural sphere where some of the most prominent pro-KLA singers and artists were women, like Leonora Jakupi.

46. D. Siminca, *Heroizmi I Kreshtave te Shales Ditari Lufte*, Prishtina, 2000.

47. A well known statue of the 'Woman of Epirus' stands as a memorial to this activity in central Thessaloniki.

48. See James Pettifer, 'Winter bites early in Kosovo', *Sunday Times*, London, 27 February 1998; James Walsh, 'Agony in the Wilderness', *Time* magazine, New York, 5 October 1998.

49. See *Kosova Express*, op. cit.

50. *Daily Telegraph*, London, 2 October 1999.

51. For detail, see Pettifer and Vickers, *The Albanian Question*, op. cit., pp. 168 ff. It has recently emerged that a main reason for Krasniqi's killing was linked to allegations that he had appropriated money for a large truck convoy of aid raised in Switzerland. Many other conspiracy theories abound about this event, e.g. that Krasniqi had a strong connection with Bosnian Muslim activists in Sarajevo and had encountered difficulties with the Albanian government of Fatos Nano as a result. For a sympathetic account of Krasniqi's life and activity, see article by Skender Zogaj in *Reviste Ushtarake Organ I Ministrise se Mbrojtjes te Republikes se Kosoves*, Issue No. 2, Tirana, October 1998. It is certainly true that the Ambassador of Bosnia-Herzegovina to Albania was the only foreign diplomat to attend his funeral.

52. See S. Zejnullah, *War for Kosova: Commander Remi Speaks*, Prishtina, 2001.

The Llap KLA 115th. Brigade in many ways made its name with this encounter and its aftermath, but it was very lucky as many of its soldiers were new recruits and there was a shortage of weapons and ammunition. The terrain was also far from ideal for an ambush.

53. Interviews with British FCO and MoD officials, 2007–2009. It seems to have taken Robin Cook some time after his arrival as Foreign Secretary to realise the way the pro-Serb opinion lobby in the FCO operated.

54. For Demaci's own retrospective view of his role at that time, see *Kosova ne Udhekrya Intervista me Adem Demaci*, ed. B. Selimi, Tirana, 2005. It is also interesting on other topics, such as the 1997 events in Albania.

55. Albin Kurti (1975–) was in jail in Serbia in the later wartime period. After 2006 he became leader of the Vetevendosje movement in opposition to the Ahtisaari Plan for controlled independence.

56. See S. Sullivan, *Be not Afraid for You Have Sons in America*, op. cit.

57. Florin Krasniqi (1964–). Born in village of Vranoc, south of Peje. He emigrated to the United States in 1988. His brother Adrian was a member of the LPK and joined a Peje KLA group in 1996. He was killed in fighting near Klicina in October 1997, the first KLA soldier to die in uniform. Florin Krasniqi then set up the main arms smuggling channel from the US to the KLA. For small arms transit data in general, see www.gunpolicy.org/firearms/region/kosovo. Academic debate has been unduly influenced by ill-founded assumptions about assault rifle supplies. There are numerous works on the AK-47 family of weapons, and the life and work of the great Soviet designer Mikhail Kalashnikov. The Albanian product was in effect an exact copy of the Russian original. See C. J. Chivers, *The Gun*, New York, 2010, p. 214ff.

58. See S. Sullivan, op. cit., pp. 156 ff. This was probably the most important success for the AACL in its history. See www.aacl.com

59. *Der Spiegel*, 18 September 1998.

60. He was suffering from a crisis with his diabetes (JP/AD interview, 20 July 2005).

61. See *Kosova Express*, op. cit., pp. 175 ff.

62. The role of the camps in Kukes as a catalyst for British and other foreign thinking about involvement has not been sufficiently explored so far in the literature of the war. In his evidence to the British House of Commons committee hearings on Kosova in 2000, 'Operation Allied Harbour' commander Major General John Reith compared the dangers with the KLA in the camps to the Palestinian *intifada* (Evidence, 12 May 2000). He points out correctly that the camps were within Serbian artillery range. His psychology is illustrative at a deeper level of the fear of Islamic radicalism that was often in the background of British military elite thinking about the Kosova conflict. His evidence also confirms that the main way the 'Operation Harbour' authorities communicated with the KLA was through the Albanian Intelligence Service SHIK. It seems fairly clear from reading between the lines of his evidence that he was prohibited by Whitehall from holding direct meetings with KLA leaders.

63. *VIP News*, 16 September 1998.

64. *Evening Standard*, London, 20 October 1998. Also *Kosova Express*, op. cit., pp. 194 ff. and Philip Smucker, 'Serbian show of force threatens Kosovo cease-fire', *Daily Telegraph*, London, 20 October 1998; see also *Kosova Express*, op. cit., pp. 201 ff.

65. *The Economist*, London, 24 October 1998.

66. The Mission did not reach strength until at least the end of January 1999, if then. See OSCE *Newsletter*, Vol. 5 No. 11, OSCE, Vienna. The first UK monitors did not arrive until 6 November 1998, only 11 out of a designated strength of 200. See *The Guardian*, London, 7 November 1998.

67. Interview with British ex-KVM observer Mike Moreland, based near Prizren, 1999. The OSCE-led KVM has had a bad press, understandably, for the hapless and ineffectual verification mission in the 1998–99 winter, but it did contribute substantially to Kosova by mine clearance in the post-war period. See KVM Mine Action Centre, maic@osce-kvm.org.

68. International Crisis Group, *Kosovo's Hot Summer*, ICG Balkans Reports, No. 41, 2 September 1998.

69. See Nuset Pllana, *Rruga e Lirise—The Path to Freedom*, Prishtina, 2000 for a good account of the development of the KLA radio station, Radio Free Kosova. The funds for the radio came from wealthy Macedonian-Albanian KLA supporters, via the Preshevo valley, an omen for the future. See Pllana, op. cit., pp. 141 ff. Transmissions began on 4 January 1999.

70. *A Week of Terror in Drenica: Humanitarian Law Violations in Kosovo*, New York, 1999.

71. The VJ itself in early August was clearly preparing the ground for a possible incursion, with wild propagandist media claims that as many as 300 Albanian army officers had been infiltrated into Kosovo to fight with the KLA (see VJ army newspaper, *Vojska*, 7 August 1998).

72. See Pettifer and Vickers, *The Albanian Question*, op. cit. Also International Crisis Group briefing, ICG Tirana, 1 October 1998.

73. See Pettifer and Vickers, *The Albanian Question*, op. cit.

74. See internal ICG assessment by Laura Rosen, 9 October 1998.

8. THE GATHERING STORM—AUTUMN 1998

1. S. Sullivan, quoting Brooklyn KLA leader and organiser Florin Krasniqi, in *Be Not Afraid, You Have Sons in America*, New York, 2004. See also film *The Brooklyn Connection: How to Build your own Guerilla Army*, www.filmstransit.com. Sullivan's superbly researched book gives a fine account of the KLA and the role of Florin Krasniqi in New York but does not reflect fully the wider US Albanian Diaspora activity in support of the war.

2. The importance of the little town of Vushtrri and the surrounding locality as a focus for the war in its final months cannot be overestimated. Vushtrri held the key for the security of the Mitrovica-Prishtina main road. See H. Saraci, *Masakrat Serbe ne Komunen e Vushtrrise 1998–1999*, Prishtina, 2005, for an

emotional but well researched account of Serbian war crimes and human rights violations there. The worst massacre was in the village of Martiraj on 2 May 1999. Also the diaries of the UNMIK Vushtrri administrator 1999–2004 C. Dennison Lane, publication forthcoming.

3. *VIP News*, 7 October 1998.
4. This definition has achieved near-canonical status in most post-2000 publications about the war in Belgrade, where the KLA is defined as an Al Qaeda ally and surrogate and a Muslim terrorist force. See, for instance, Milovan Drevic, *War for Kosova*, Belgrade, 2007, and the more scholarly Milan Milakovski and Petar Damjanov, *Terrorista Albanski Ekstremista*, Belgrade, 2002. These authors are Macedonian and much of the text is about the Macedonian Albanian National Liberation Army in 2001. From the point of view of military history, these assumptions are useful to nationalist Serbs insofar as they obviate the need for clear-headed analysis of what actually happened to the VJ in the Kosova War. Both books are flawed conceptually insofar as they suggest a pattern of formal military organisation in the KLA that often did not exist.
5. KIC *Kosova Daily Report* no. 1586, Prishtina, 18 October 1998.
6. *VIP News*, 19 October 1998.
7. *Sydney Morning Herald*, 15 October 1998.
8. *Daily Telegraph*, London, 21 October 1998.
9. The information on this subject appears to be one of the sections of Perritt's book which can be regarded as a reliable source. H. Perritt, op. cit., pp. 91 ff.
10. Veliu has written extensively about the war, but less about LPK itself. See F. Veliu, *LPK dhe UCK: Nje embleme nje Qellim*, Tirana, 2001.
11. This community is large and complex. Albanians have lived in Turkey for hundreds of years. For general settlement issues in the twentieth century, see N. Ozgur Baklacioglu, *Dis Politika ve Goc: Balkanlardan Turkiyeye Arnaut Gocleri 1919–1980*, Istanbul, 2010. In the twentieth century the main inward migration has been from the Cameria district of north-western Greece and from Kosova. For the Cham issue, see M. Vickers, publications with www.csrc.mod.ac.uk, also J. Pettifer, *Woodhouse, Zervas and the Chams*, Tirana, 2009 for British policy in the Second World War period. The centre of Kosova-origin settlement in Istanbul is in the districts near Bajram Pasha international bus station. There are also very large numbers of Turkish citizens with some Albanian element in their descent, particularly in the army. For the Preshevo smuggling route, see H. Perritt, op. cit.
12. For an excellent general picture of the Albanian emigration in Turkey, see N. Baklacioglu, *Dis Politika ve Goc Yugoslavya'dan Turkiye'ye Goclerde Arnavutlar (1920–1990)*, Istanbul, 2010.
13. Turkish-based Albanians and people of Albanian descent were probably more important in the Macedonian conflict than in the Kosova war. There were important links with the *tekkes* in Turkey which had been set up in the 1920s emigration.
14. For a competent short history of the PDSH and its evolution, see Z. Rexhepi, *Partia Demokratike Shqiptare Lindja Zhvillimi dhe Veprimtara*, Tetovo, 2004.

Also *Kosova* Express, op. cit., pp. 205 ff. The ease with which the munitions route was set up depended on the fact that the FYROM/Republic of Macedonia had been an important centre of small arms transfer throughout the ex-Yugoslav wars and professional arms dealers operated under the cover of other business organisations there.

15. See *The Albanian Question*, op. cit., pp. 171 ff.
16. Swisscom mobile phones played a vital role in the conflict, and in the view of some actors, were as symbolically as important as the high-technology sniper rifles from the USA. The Serbs did not have—nor, in all probability, did most Western nations—the telephone intercept technology to break into the Swiss voice codes.
17. Arben Xhaferi (1948–2012) was born in Tetovo and studied philosophy at Belgrade University, and was a leader of the 1968–69 student protest movement there. Until 1990 he was in the Prishtina media, and then moved to the FYROM/Republic of Macedonia where in 1992–93 he worked with Menduh Thaci to transform the radical wing of the old Party for Democratic Prosperity into a new political force. He was joint leader with Thaci of the PDSH for many years.
18. Menduh Thaci (1960–) was born in the village of Gllatocice, north-west of Tetovo, which straddles the current Kosova-FYROM/Republic of Macedonia border. He studied law at Skopje University and became politically active in the PDP. With Arben Xhaferi he overthrew the old leadership of this party in 1993, and he has dominated the successor PDSH party with Xhaferi in Tetovo ever since. Thaci became full party leader in 2008.
19. There were also some Gorani with a tradition of service in the Yugoslav police and military. Milosevic encouraged this, as a foil to the Albanians.
20. There is no reliable writing on the foreign police missions deployed in Albania, FYROM/Republic of Macedonia and Kosova since 1991. The field is dominated by grandiose claims of success, absence of reliable statistics and propaganda of various kinds. This is usually designed to obscure the high costs and modest achievements of these police missions.
21. For a pro-FARK account of this period, which is interesting in revealing the links between the FARK and the Democratic Party in Tirana, see M. Bucpapaj, *Partia Demokratike dhe Ceshtja Kombetare*, Tirana, 2000.
22. See S. Smilanic, op. cit.
23. ARTA Prishtina, 20 October 1998, and Reuters, 22 October 1998.
24. See *Kosova Express*, op. cit, pp. 202 ff.
25. Media Centre Prishtina, Bulletin, 26 October,1998
26. S. Zejnullahu, op. cit.
27. T. Judah, *War and Revenge*, Yale, 2002.
28. B. Hamzaj, *A Narrative about War and Freedom*, op. cit, pp. 116 ff.
29. Matthew McAllester's speculations about the residual strength of the blood feud among the Albanians in Peje as a factor in the war in the north-west of Kosova may equally well apply to Decani and Gjakova families. See M. McAllester, *Beyond the Mountains of the Damned—The War inside Kosovo*, New

York, 2001. This objective and very balanced account of the war in and around Peje is another good book that was unfortunate in the timing of its publication, at the height of the bizarre UNMIK campaign to force Kosova back towards Yugoslavia.

30. See McAllester, op. cit.

31. Ref. N. Gjeloshi, op. cit. Even at this late stage, Gjeloshi and other ex-LDK people in Zurich in the leadership were preoccupied by the problem of what to do about the role of Bujar Bukoshi. Gjeloshi speculates that Bukoshi was still playing a negative role by preventing the full strength of German-based Albanians' money from being mobilised behind the KLA fundraising effort.

32. See B. Simms, *Unfinest Hour—Britain and the Destruction of Bosnia*, London, 2001.

33. See, for instance, the ICTY witness statement of the British verifier C.J. Clark, who was based at Brezovica (Shterpce). He is an objective observer in his work but his statement contains statements such as 'the KLA were responsible in most cases for breaking the Holbrooke agreement', and 'the SAJ forces that I described above were well trained in counter-insurgency tactics and were highly disciplined.' He does, however, also comment that 'there was a lot of pressure by the OSCE to get the mission up and running and as a consequence a lot of unsuitable people were employed who did not have the necessary skills for the mission' (ICTY document, Limaj trial, dated 21–23 March and 5 July 2001).

34. A US Air Force assistance plan, Operation Determined Guarantor, had been set up to protect the verifiers but it is not clear what its role would have been in any real crisis. See B. Nardulli *et al.*, *Disjointed War: Military Operations in Kosovo 1999*, Arlington, 2002. This study was produced for the US Army and is a very thoughtful, balanced and informative work.

35. For a good impressionistic picture of this world, see Rose, *'Fighting for Peace'*, London, 1996.

36. On a personal note, I recall visiting a KVM base near Ferizaj in December 1998 and being questioned for over an hour on alleged Arab Muslim 'Mujahidin' who the verifiers thought were living in the town. The vocabulary used obviously came straight from Serbian secret intelligence placed propaganda.

37. *VIP News*, 11 November 1998.

38. *VIP News*, 17 November 1998. There was always substantial over-representation, in relation to proportions in the Yugoslav population, of Montenegrins in the upper ranks of the JNA and VJ.

39. Sami Lustaku (1961–) was born in Prekaz near the farm of the Jashari family. He fought in all the early stages of the war after military training in Albania in the mid-1990s. In the later stages he was commander of the KLA in the Prizren region. His family is one of the most influential in the Drenica and in Hashim Thaci's PDK party. Since 1999 he has occupied various senior posts in the Kosova Protection Corps and other institutions.

40. B. Magas, *The Destruction of Yugoslavia*, London, 1993, p. 292.

41. See C.J. Clark, ICTY witness statement, op. cit.

42. For earlier period background see J. Gow, op. cit.
43. *VIP News*, 17 December 1998. The statement was accurate but only reflected a reality that had existed for perhaps two months. See S. Sullivan, op. cit. for an illuminating account of how US Albanian Diaspora money was now being routed directly to Xhavit Haliti in Tirana by Florin Krasniqi and others.
44. Discussions James Pettifer/Shaun Byrnes, June 2011.
45. See *Kosova Express*, op. cit., pp. 204 ff.
46. See *From 'National Communism to National Collapse*, op. cit.
47. See W. Clark, *Waging Modern War*, op. cit.
48. One of the main advantages US intelligence had over the EU nations in understanding the Kosova war was the strength in depth and excellent organisation of the CIA and DIA in Switzerland, where the agencies were often more tolerated than those of EU nations such as France and Italy.
49. On 14 September the Kosova Council for Rights and Freedoms had announced that 1,221 Albanians had been killed since 15 January 1998, and about 900 people were missing. The UNHCR estimated the number of displaced people at 270,000.
50. In Jennings, op. cit. there is various speculation that the SAS was unwilling to get involved in Kosova. There is no independent evidence for this view that I am aware of.
51. See C. Jennings, op. cit.
52. See M. Jackson, *Soldier*, op. cit. Jackson's view of the British intelligence content in the KVM was that 'we sent in a recce party, disguised as monitors, who provided us with intelligence reports, both political and military'.
53. Interview with Miranda Vickers, ICG analyst Tirana, London, 2008.
54. *Kosova Daily News*, 28 December 1998.
55. Rustem Mustafa (Captain Remi), born 27 February 1971 at Perpallac near Podujeve. Joined the Llap *ceta* in 1993, after resigning from the LPK. Active in the war after 1996, commander of 5th. Operative Zone of the KLA in 1998–99.In 2000 Major General in the KPC. Arrested by UNMIK 2001, gaoled and then acquitted. Mustafa then joined Hashim Thaci's PDK party, and is currently a member of the Kosova Assembly.
56. *Kosovo News*, 24 December 1998.
57. See S. Zejnullahu, op. cit., pp. 80 ff. The contribution of the Humolli family as a backup mechanism to Remi's command was very important in these events. In politics most family members had been broadly associated with the LKCK in the pre-war period.
58. OSCE spokesman Mons Nyberg, quoted in VIP News, 30 December 1998.
59. KDOM *Daily Report*, 28 December 1998.
60. See K. Zilliacus, *Tito of Yugoslavia*, London, 1952. Zilliacus was a left-wing Labour MP who strongly backed Tito in the split in 1948, unlike some of his Parliamentary colleagues.

9. RACAK TO RAMBOUILLET: JANUARY-MARCH 1999

1. ICTY Limaj trial papers, 19 November 2004.
2. See OSCE publication *Kosovo/Kosova: As Seen, As Told*, Vienna, 2000, and *Kosova Express*, op. cit. p. 226.
3. William G. Walker (1935–). Born in Kearney, New Jersey. Held a succession of US diplomatic posts in South and Central America, head of the UN Mission in Eastern Slavonia, 1997–99, head of OSCE KVM Mission 1998–99.
4. P. J. Jha, *The Twilight of the Nation State* (Introduction by E.J. Hobsbawm), London, 2006.
5. B. Nardulli, op. cit., pp. 30 ff.
6. OSCE, op. cit., pp. 371 ff.
7. *Kosova Daily Report*, 9 January 1999.
8. *VIP News*, 11 February 1999.
9. Discussions with ex-Mayor of Vushtrri, July 2003.
10. Quoted in interview 28 August 2010 with senior US KVM member.
11. In his later career this diplomat became French Ambassador to Serbia.
12. Radosavljevic was later a prominent MUP anti-terrorist commander in the war against the UCPMB in Preshevo Valley in the autumn of 2000. He was never indicted by the ICTY over the Racak events but was awarded a medal by NATO for his Preshevo 'anti-terrorist' activity.
13. *Kosova Express*, op. cit., pp. 226 ff.
14. BBC News, 16 January 1999.
15. *Daily Telegraph*, London, 27 January 1999.
16. Report of EU Forensic Team on the Racak Incident, 17 March 1999.
17. A. Campbell, *The Blair Years*, London, 2007. It is perhaps also significant that this was the first mention of the subject of Kosova at all in Campbell's record of events of the Blair period, as late in the conflict as January 1999, and confirms Kampfner's view (op. cit.) that Blair was content to go along with the Holbrooke-Hill strategy for longer than perhaps some of his modern Kosova admirers realise. His critics in Britain will see it as another example of Blair's headline-led policy orientation.
18. T. Blair, op. cit.
19. Story by James Pettifer, *The Times*, 19 January 1999.
20. *Jane's Intelligence Review*, London, February and March 1999. His observations are well informed and perceptive but reflect Belgrade assumptions about the KLA, particularly what he mistakenly considers the seismic effect of weapons imports from Albania after March 1997.
21. This plan became also the basis for the later NATO KFOR force, and was one of the reasons for some of the difficulties KFOR have encountered in the last ten years. KFOR was designed for a quite different situation to the situation it actually faced after June 1999.
22. See *Kosova Express*, op. cit and T. Judah, *Kosovo: War and Revenge*, op. cit, and the press at the time.
23. *Kosova Daily News*, 2 February 1999.

24. See B.S. Lambeth, *NATO's Air War for Kosovo A Strategic and Operational Assessment*, RAND, Santa Monica, 2001. This semi-official USAF study is an essential basic guide to the air war events.

25. In addition to Lambeth's pioneering work, there has been much further discussion of the air war. See, for instance, T. Hammond Grant, *Myths of the Air War over Serbia: Some Lessons not to Learn*, Maxwell, 2000 and C. Norton, *Operation Allied Force*, Aldershot, 2001. The media aspects of the air war are analysed from a strongly anti-war viewpoint in P. Hammond and E. Herman, *Degraded Capability; The Media and the Kosovo Crisis*, London, 2000.

26. See B. Clinton, My Life, pp. 554 ff.

27. See W. Clark, *Waging Modern War*, op. cit.

28. B. Lambeth, op. cit.

29. It must be doubted, though, if Lambeth is right in saying that this delay gave Milosevic time to prepare his air defences in their entirety. Anti-aircraft installations and missiles had already been moved to Kosova as early as October 1998, after the signature of the Holbrooke-Milosevic agreement.

30. CIA released document, 'Prospects for Post-Tito Yugoslavia', 25 September 1979.

31. International Crisis Group, Brussels, *Kosovo: Bite the Bullet*, 22 January 1999. Most of the original text had been originally drafted by the senior ICG Balkan analyst Miranda Vickers, who had been told by ICG senior representatives not to advocate open international support for the KLA in it. The final text was heavily edited in the ICG Brussels office to remove this recommendation. This report was nevertheless one of the most important and influential issued by ICG during the crisis, and highlighted how the international community was allowing Milosevic to draw them into endless 'tactical games' to use the situation for his own advantage.

32. This has continued in some historical writing about the war. See, for instance, James Gow's views expressed in *The Serbian Project and its Adversaries*, London, 2002, that 'in the absence of NATO airpower, the UCK (KLA) stood no chance against the VJ as had been demonstrated many times during the preceding year. On every occasion VJ and MUP operations had rolled back the UCK (KLA) insurgency.' Gow does not appear to see the complexity of many encounters, where the KLA were able to quickly reoccupy lost territory soon after the VJ vacated it, or that the KLA war was against the Serbian government of Kosova, of which the VJ was only an agent. In hundreds of Kosova towns and villages the KLA had destroyed any effective Serbian government presence by the autumn of 1998. War for stable territorial control within Kosova was a secondary factor.

33. In his memoirs, *War for Kosova*, Remi specifically congratulates the US army officers attached to his units and thanks them for their advice, particularly those working within KDOM. op. cit., pp. 149.

34. It is also worth noting that some of the population of the northern Prishtina had come as forced emigrants from Cameria in north-west Greece in the 1920s and 1930s and the Preshevo valley after 1947 and the defeat by the Titoists of

Mullah Idris Gjilan's Preshevo and south-east Kosova insurgency. They were not closely linked to Drenica people but had many links to eastern Kosova, and as the KLA became more established there had more commitment to its success. See M. Pirraku, op. cit.

35. Interview, S. Shala, November 1999.
36. See S. Sullivan, op. cit.
37. See R. Sadiku, op. cit.
38. *VIP News*, 8 February 1999.
39. For Thaci's general outlook and approach to politics post-1999, and some of the historical issues, see J. Pettifer, *A Concept for a New Reality Dialogue with Hashim Thaci*, Prishtina, 2001.
40. *VIP News*, 4 March 1999.
41. *VIP News*, No. 1452, March 1999.
42. *Glas Javnosti*, 4 March 1999.
43. Statement by Beatrice Lacoste, KVM spokesperson, 5 March 1999.
44. Interview with senior UK army source, August 2010, UK.
45. This promise was of course repeatedly broken by the international community, even before the eventual decision for independence in 2008.
46. Reuters, 11/12 March 1999. The relationship between Hashim Thaci and the Clinton administration spokesman James Rubin, and the situation between Rambouillet and the beginning of the NATO bombing campaign, have been explored in a publication by Rubin that was published by *Klan* magazine in Tirana: J. Rubin, *Si e Fituam Luftem*, Klan, 2000. It contains some important observations about international diplomacy during the bombing campaign and it is a pity it has not been published, as far as I am aware, in English.
47. *VIP News*, 12 March 1999.
48. *Nin* magazine, reported in *VIP News*, 18 April 1999.
49. See www.aimpress.org, Tirana, 10 May 1999.
50. Interview with senior British ex-army officer involved in 'Operation Horn', December 2009.
51. M. Albright, op. cit., pp. 398 ff.
52. Op.cit., p. 329.

10. ALLIANCE WITH NATO AND DEMOBILISATION OF THE KLA

1. P. Bobbitt, *The Shield of Achilles: War, Peace and the Course of History*, New York, 2002.
2. See I. Daalder and M. O'Hanlon, *Winning Ugly*.
3. Ibid.
4. This lengthy study by the RAND authors Bruce Nardulli, Walter L.Perry, Bruce Pirnie, John Gordon IV, and John G. McGinn is the fullest and most comprehensive study of the ground war so far published, and for a semi-official US army record is an excellent, thought provoking and very objective document. Although the focus is naturally on ground operations in Task Force Hawk, it covers in practice most aspects of the conflict in considerable detail.

5. The unpublished study made of the role of the RAF in the bombing campaign by John Labercombe for DSTL and the RAF in the UK comes to similar conclusions, particularly on the issue of the enforcement of unrealistic height limits for bombing accuracy.

6. See A.J. Bacevich and E.A. Cohen (eds), *War over Kosovo*, New York, 2001.

7. See Clinton statement made in Washington on 24 March as the air campaign began, and subsequent statements by National Security Adviser Sandy Berger (cited in Daalder and O'Hanlon, op. cit.).

8. Milosevic had a cordial relationship with the Israeli leader Ariel Sharon, and the latter's 'walk on the Mount of Olives' which inspired new conflicts in occupied Palestine was in response to the overthrow of Milosevic in 2000 in Serbia. See J. Pettifer, *Kosova Express*, pp. 177 ff.

9. These contacts were widely condemned in Kosova, and also by foreign supporters of the military campaign, particularly on the French Left. See article by Patrick Kessel, 'Some Notes on the National Question' in *Compass*, Leeds, February 1999, No. 132. Rugova was described as a speaker for the Kosova 'comprador bourgeoisie'.

10. See RAND study by B. Lambeth, Op. cit.

11. For data on the Serbian side see Simjevic, op. cit. According to the records of the Belgrade Ministry of Defence there were, between 31 March and 8 April, almost twice as many NATO bombs dropped in and near a single city, Leskovac, as in the whole of Kosova.

12. Ref. C.J. Dick, op. cit.

13. See Z. Gashi, *Ditet e Tmerrit dhe te Shpreses*, Prishtina, 2000. This is an interesting personal diary account of the sudden onset of war in a hitherto peaceful rural area. The small number of KLA fighters in the area prior to the war had mostly fought in the Llap operational zone. It shows well how the KLA became a force in the area in May-June 1999.

14. Albin Kurti (1975–) was born in Prishtina. In August 1997 he became President of the Prishtina University students union, and was one of the leaders of the 1 October 1997 mass student protest demonstration that was brutally repressed by the MUP. He was jailed in Serbia between April 1999 and 2001 after receiving a 15-year sentence for 'threatening Yugoslavia's territorial integrity'. After the war in 2005 he founded the Vetevendosje rank and file movement against the continuance of international rule over Kosova.

15. Interview with retired senior British officer who held a command position in MNB (C) in June 1999, August 2010.

16. See I. Oliver and W. Mason, *Peace at Any Price*, op. cit. In an interview with a senior US government official in Prishtina in 2008 who was in UNMIK after 1999, he expressed the view that 'It was crazy for us to try to revive a Yugoslavist solution for Kosova after 1999. But we did it.' Future historians will no doubt wish to investigate how far this was a product of the end of the Clinton administration and the arrival of the Bush administration, and how even after the fall of Milosevic there was an entrenched pro-Serb and often pro-Russian lobby of officials remaining in key positions in some Western chanceries.

17. See Dusan Bjelic's perceptive observations on Kristeva's views in *Slavic Review* 67, No. 2, Summer 2008.
18. OSCE Vienna, *Kosovo/Kosova As Seen, As Told*, Vienna, 2000.
19. Quoted by ICTY witness Radomir Tanic, in Milosevic trial, ref: P. Brooke 'Did the War on Yugoslavia *prevent* Ethnic Cleansing', in *Politics and Theology* journal, London, February 2008 issue. Tanic was active in the British and Israeli influenced 'New Democracy' party in Belgrade that was often in coalition with Milosevic between 1994 and 1997, and was part of a wider British operation to retain special influence over Milosevic. He was in a good position to observe Milosevic's evolving intentions. See also ICTY evidence in the Milosevic trial given by R. Ciaglinski (ICTY documents, p. 3224).
20. OSCE, op. cit., pp. 369 ff.
21. These mass population displacement procedures echoed the origins of 'Operation Horseshoe' in the Yugoslav military doctrinal past, when in plans drawn up to prevent a NATO invasion of Yugoslavia where the Albanian population might side with the Western invaders, they would be expelled en masse towards the Albanian Adriatic coast.
22. Known in Kosova as 'Maxhupi'.
23. OSCE material, op. cit., pp. 280 ff.
24. For a good detailed account of the conflict around Celina and Krushe, see I. Gashi and H. Fazliu, *Masakra e Celines*, Prishtina, 2000. It is clear from the eyewitness material that the VJ chose to make an example of these villages because of their proximity to the main Prizren-Gjakova main road and their activity in helping the KLA disrupt VJ convoys in the previous months, in a classic reprisal scenario of an occupying army under attack. Another useful source for the study of the war near Prizren is M. Krasniqi, *Shkelqimi i Uck-se ne Treven e Verrinit*, a careful study of events in and around the large village of Hoqe, on the road leading to the Quaf e Morina pass to Albania. Once the site of an Ottoman *han* with a long and interesting history, Hoqe was spared the worst of VJ reprisal activity after a violent attack on 11 March 1999, perhaps because of its proximity to the Shar mountains. Hoqe was active in the war from June 1998 onwards, often in association with nearby Randobrava village, north of Prizren.
25. See S. Krasniqi, op. cit., pp. 450 ff.
26. For more detail, see N. Thomas and K. Mikulan, op. cit.
27. Hamzic, op. cit., pp. 247 ff.
28. The SAJ had been founded with this original strength on 1 June 1992. For more detail see N. Thomas and K. Mikulan, *The Yugoslav Wars (2)*, London, 2006.
29. Interview with former British Embassy diplomat, August 2010.
30. An important source of Ceku's credibility was his relationship in previous days in Zagreb with the prominent Lladrovci family who were involved in the birth of the KLA in Dukagjini in 1997–98. See B. Islami, op. cit.
31. R. Haradinaj, op. cit., pp. 148 ff.

32. See A. Neuberg, *Armed Insurrection*, London, 1970, for the Comintern-derived theoretical model.

33. Jackson has made some personal comments about Kosova Albanian leaders in his autobiography, *Soldier*, op. cit.

34. See S. Power, *Chasing the Flame: Sergio de Mello and the Fight to Save the World*, New York, 2008, pp. 266 ff.

35. There is a voluminous literature in Albanian on the Koshare events. See M. Cetta, *Me UCK ne Koshare*, Prishtina, 2000, B. Gashi, *Kosharja Altari I Lirise*, Prishtina, 2006, M. Elshani, *Betejat e Lavdishme te Brigades 123*, Prizren, 2001 for generally reliable eye witness accounts. Few of the Albanian participants in the fighting seem to have known much about the role of foreign military advisers in the strategy to hold Koshare.

36. Rugova and Thaci did not actually meet at all between the Rambouillet conference in February and June that year. In May French foreign ministry officials and the Albanian Ambassador in Paris, Luan Rama, tried to engineer a meeting when both were in the city, but Rugova refused to meet. See *Albanian Daily News*, No. 1063, pp. 29–30, May 1999, Tirana. It was always difficult for fellow Albanian leaders to meet Rugova once the conflict had begun. After his death, some sections of the Kosova press have sought to obscure this, See *Bota Sot*, Zurich, 5 April 2013.

37. For a very good account of the Atlantic Battalion and its development and role, see the memoir of one of its commanders, Uk Lushi, with an Introduction by Ismail Kadare, *Shqiptaro-Amerikanet e UCK-se Kronike e Battalion 'Atlantiku'*, Prishtina, 2009.

38. See Pettifer and Vickers, op. cit.

39. See M. Cetta, op. cit. for a solid professional account, and Milazim Elshani's work on Brigade '123'. Bahri. M. Gashi's book *Kosharja Altari I Lirise* is very useful for the fighting in the April-May 1999 period. Soldiers in the KLA from Macedonia were important in the Koshare battles, see I. Memishi, *Ushtari I Lirise* for an interesting dialogue with the Tetovo-based KLA commander Taib Bejtulin.

40. Lambeth, op. cit., pp. 55 ff.

41. PBS 'Frontline', 22 February 2000.

42. *Sunday Telegraph*, 13 June 1999.

43. I. Daalder and M. O'Hanlon, *Winning Ugly: NATO's War to Save* Kosovo, Washington, DC, 2000, pp. 152 ff.

44. *Sunday Telegraph*, 1 August 1999.

45. See the views expressed by an unnamed Albanian Communist from Gjirokastra in *International Struggle Marxist-Leninist*, London, 2002, Issue 8. A member of the Party of Unified Communists of Albania (PUCA), he acknowledges that 'It is possible that some of the precursors of the UCK (KLA) might have had Marxist-Leninist elements, or even wings. It is also possible that there were and even at this moment are individual cadres in the UCK who could be considered Marxist-Leninist. But if this is so it is obvious that they have no real and visible influence on the line of the organisation whatsoever ... during the

1960's, 1970's and 1980's a great majority of national liberation movements professed to be "socialist" or "Marxist'", though in fact they were petty bourgeois or national bourgeois organisations.'

46. It is very doubtful indeed if there were really eight functioning FARK camps by this time. See S. Lipsius, 'Untergrund organisatsionen im Kosovo—Ein Uberblick', in *Sudosteuropa*, Munich, Vol. 47, 1998. Lipsius underestimates the damage done to the FARK by the arrival of international special forces trainers in Albania who sought to unify the Albanian paramilitary forces as far as they could, in practice always under KLA local commanders (discussion with ex-British SAS officer attached to training camp in Kruma, 1998–99).

47. 'Wag the Dog', on the demobilisation of the KLA, pub. Freidrich Naumann Stiftung, Bonn, 2002.

11. PRESHEVO AND THE MACEDONIAN SEQUEL 2000–2001

1. The best guide to the atmosphere of this period is Ramush Haradinaj's book, B. Hamzaj, *Paqja e Gjeneralit (Dialog me Ramush Haradinaj)*, Prishtina, 2001. This was published as a successor volume to *A Narrative on War and Freedom*, and sets out very well the mixture of incredulity, frustration and anger most Kosova Albanians felt when faced with the reality of the UNMIK administration. It is perhaps significant that unlike the first book, it was never translated or published in English. It will be an important source for the negotiations that led to the formation of Haradinaj's 'Alliance for Kosova' (AAK) party from members of different political groups (pp. 155 ff.).

2. A key figure was Jackson's Political Adviser, a senior figure from the UK Ministry of Defence, Michael Venables.

3. See Jackson's autobiography, *Soldier*, London, 2005.

4. Conversation with Thaci, June 2004, Prishtina.

5. BBC News, London, 13 June 1999.

6. Answer to question from James Pettifer, Blair visit to Prishtina, 8 July 1999. The British Prime Minister seemed surprised that my question was raised.

7. *Koha Ditore*, 14 June 1999.

8. *International Herald Tribune*, 22 June 1999.

9. See M. Angelokovic (ed.), *Kosovo Crucified*, op. cit.

10. See M. Pirraku, *Mulla Idris Gjilani dhe Mbrojta Kombetare e Kosoves Lindore 1941–1951*, Prishtina, 1995, an excellent account of the events in Preshevo at that time.

11. See Chapter 1.

12. See Bashkia Islame e Kosoves (Union of Kosova mosques), *Serbian Barbarities against Islamic Monuments in Kosova (February 1998 to June 1999)*, Prishtina, 2000, section on Preshevo valley towns and villages.

13. For an excellent account of this period, and its background in Preshevo, see M. Hajrizi, *Sprova te Clirimit*, Prishtina, 2004.

14. For a comprehensive and detailed account of the course of the conflict, see B.

Churcher, *Kosovo Lindore/Preshevo 1999–2002 and the FYROM Conflict*, CSRC RMA Sandhurst G-104, March 2002 www.defenceacademy.mod.uk

15. The best picture of the war as seen in a single village is in H. Hasani, *Dobrosini*, Bujanoc,2003. Hasani shows the lonely and isolated pattern of resistance and the characteristic pattern, as in Kosova, of the full commitment of rural communities like Dobrosin to the struggle as opposed to the inactivity in the towns.

16. See McCormick Tribune Foundation material, op. cit.

17. ref. B. Churcher, op. cit.

18. Named after Richard Miles, former US envoy in Belgrade, mainly responsible for the 'coloured' revolutions concept, e.g. the 'orange' revolution in Ukraine.

19. See S. Latifi, *Rrugetimi Neper Lugine te Presheves*, Preshevo, 2006 for an illuminating general account by a prominent local journalist of the political and military background. Also the UCPMB journal *Ushtima e Maleve* that was produced in Prishtina in spring/summer 2001 for a time. Copy No. 4 (March 2001) is interesting for a picture of the early role of NATO negotiator Peter Feith in events.

20. See R. Churcher, CSRC publications, op. cit., and J. Phillips, *Macedonia: Warlords and Rebels in the Balkans*, London, 2004 for good general narrative of events.

21. *Serbia After Milosevic: Program for the Solution of the Crisis in the Pcinja District*, Belgrade, 2001.

22. See R. Churcher, op. cit.

23. Ibid.

24. See I. Jonuzi-Krosi, op. cit., pp. 90 ff.

25. For Veliu's own account of some aspects of the war, see *UCK nga Beteja ne Beteje*, Tetovo, 2005, and for his arrest in Germany and temporary imprisonment, see *I Perndjekur ne Shkup, Qytetar ne Perendim*, Tirana, 2001.

26. For a good picture of the history of the LDK in Germany, see Latifi, op. cit.

27. See H. Perritt, op. cit.

28. In 2000 Ostreni published a book in Prishtina, *Shpresa dhe Zhgenjimi I Shqiptareve ne Maqedoni gjate dhe pas Luftes se Dyte Boterore*, an account of the fighting in western Macedonia in 1944 in the Second World War which was clearly designed to demolish what he sees as the Titoist myth of the 'liberation' of Macedonia by Tito's Partisans. It is a capable and well-researched work, although also clearly designed to prepare the way for a future conflict in Macedonia by portraying the region as subject to an illegitimate external occupation. It appeared at the time the UCPMB in Preshevo was gaining strength, also. Ostreni in many ways seeks to rehabilitate the suppressed Ballist military traditions.

29. For information on Shipkovica, see J. Pettifer, *Blue Guide to Albania and Kosova*, London and New York, 2001.

30. For a general account of NLA participation and an absorbing diary account of the conflict period, see P. Menaj, *UCK Mesazh dhe Shprese*, Tetovo, 2004. Menaj is close to Samadin Xhezairi from Prizren and the book gives interest-

ing insights into the relationship between the UCPMB supporters in Prizren and various military and political choices that later faced the NLA leaders in the June-July 2001 period. Also I. Memishi, *Ushtari I Lirise*, Prishtina, 2003, a portrait of the NLA soldier Taib Bejtulin.

31. For more detail on this period, see the excellent sources in I. Rusi, 'From Army to Party: The Politics of the NLA', in Institute of War and Peace Reporting material, *Ohrid and Beyond*, IWPR, London, 2002

32. It is worth noting that the founding group of the NDP were all ex-members of Menduh Thaci and Arben Xhaferi's PDSH party (and Commander Hoxha remained a member in some public contexts), and some in Tetovo have claimed that the NDP was set up with Menduh Thaci's knowledge in order to push his fellow-leader Xhaferi in a more radical policy direction.

33. For some rather schematic basic information on the NLA, see its website www.shqiponiapress.com

34. See *Illyria* newspaper, New York, March-August 2000 for a series of interesting articles about fundraising for the NLA in the United States and Canada.

35. See various eye witness material in the London press at the time.

36. Hill observed, 'It's very disappointing that people who were so helped by NATO actions should now become the problem'. He said it was fair to describe the guerrillas as 'outlaws'. (Phillips, op. cit., p. 97).

37. Phillips, op. cit., p. 98.

38. 3 April 2001.

39. I recall visiting high mountain Gorani villages in the Dragash (Gora) region of Kosova in late April 2001 and finding more or less free passage for guerrillas and supplies into Dragash and down to Prizren, although the whole area was supposed to have been sealed off by the Turkish army section of KFOR.

40. See Zijadin Qira's book *Ujqit ne Frak* (Wolves in Sheep's Clothing), Tetovo, 1999 for a personal account of the history in the Second World War period.

41. See Iso Rusi's article 'From Army to Party—The Politics of the NLA' in *The 2001 Conflict in FYROM—Reflections*, Institute of War and Peace reporting, June 2004, www.csrc.da.mod.uk, Defence Academy Balkans Series 04/15. Another good source is Mair Iseni, *Zhvillimet ne Maqedoni dhe Lindja e Ushtrise Clirimtare Kombetare*, Tetovo, 2003. Iseni sees the NLA as a necessary and legitimate reaction to the aggressive behaviour of the Skopje government leader Ljupco Georgievski and, perhaps rightly, points out that many of the elements in the Ohrid Accords resemble the provisions of the 'Ahrends Plan' of 1993 and could have been negotiated long before without a military conflict. See Ahrends, op. cit.

42. Conversation Pettifer/Xhaferi in Tetovo, March 2004.

43. e.g. in the Vance-Owen Plan period.

44. For detail on the course of the talks, often ironic and amusing, see K. Danaj, *Kryengritje e Pambruar*, Tirana, 2008. In a previous period, Danaj was a very senior official under Ramiz Alia in Tirana, and he sees the talks from a somewhat Olympian viewpoint.

45. For Ostreni's views see the LPK newspaper *Zeri I Kosoves*, No. 397, 4 July

2001. It is clear that the NLA war effort in the country by late May was receiving significant help from Kosova through Drenica-based TMK leaders such as Sami Lushtaku. Ostreni also focuses on defending the role of the NLA in the Kumanovo area, after local criticism that it had not been willing—perhaps not able—to take over and dominate the town like Albanian-majority towns in western Macedonia. For all his famous casual remark that the war 'had wasted two million bullets' through signing of the Ohrid Accords, he also shows himself to be a political and military realist to a LPK readership and audience. The controversy demonstrates the strategic position of Kumanovo in all Balkan wars in Macedonia from 1912 onwards.

46. See Tim Garton Ash's portrait of Ahmeti in the London *Guardian* with its controversial theme of 'the good terrorist': reproduced in *New York Review of Books*, 29 November 2001.

47. See J. Phillips, op. cit. for a reliable account of this period.

48. The best guide to this transformation is Veliu's book, *UCK nga Beteja ne Betejev—Mesazhe te Paperfunduara*, Tetovo, 2005, a diary record of events in 2001. For a semi-official British view on the issues, see 'The Kosova Liberation Army (with particular attention to its political role)', Centre for Defence Studies, King's College London, Scoping Paper 5 (for DFID), May 1999.

12. EPILOGUE

1. Op. cit., Chapter V 'The Betrayal of the Conspiracy', pp. 206 ff.

2. For discussion of this within liberal-left parameters of assumed state and political transparency, see D. Aaronwitz, *Voodoo History*, London, 2009.

3. M. Markovic, *Night and Day: A Diary*, Belgrade,1995. See also volumes such as N. Tomic *The Twilight of the West*, Belgrade, 1999.

4. See statements of the government of Borislav Tadic in Belgrade, and works such as J. Obradovic, *Ethnic Conflict and War in the Balkans: The Narratives of Denial in Post-War Serbia*, London, 2010, and J. Gow, op. cit., p. 309.

5. A. Bacevich and E. Cohen, op. cit., pp. 93 ff.

6. For a view on the situation a year after independence, see James Pettifer, *The Southern Balkans in 2009—Stability and Stasis*, www.defenceacademy.mod.uk/ research/publications/balkans

7. Interview with Pentagon officials, Washington, DC, March 2010.

8. An umbrella organisation, the National Army of the Albanians (ANA), does exist to fulfil this objective but at the time of writing most experts consider it to be a small and largely virtual organisation.

9. See N. Covic, *Serbia after Milosevic: Program for the Solution of the Crisis in the Pcinja District*, Belgrade, 2000. This hard to obtain document was heavily influenced by Americans and illustrates the 'lurch towards Belgrade' factor in the thinking of the early Bush administration very well. The view of the history of the Preshevo valley embodied in it comes straight from Serbian nationalist historiography and appears to be ignorant of the border changes in the area made to the Kosova boundaries by Tito. It nevertheless was used as the basis for the Preshevo 'settlement' by the international community. See Chapter 11.

10. M.D. Stojanovic, *The Great Powers and the Balkans 1875–1878*, Cambridge, 1939.
11. London, 2009. See also article by David Betz about Mackinlay's views in *British Army Review*, Winter 2009–2010, Warminster, 2010. Also, for an authoritative textbook on the orthodox approach to analysing and fighting Maoist model insurgency, the US Army/Marine Corps field manual FM 3–24 *Counterinsurgency*.
12. For the theorising of 'deed propaganda', see the influential works of insurgency theorist David Galula, e.g. *Counter Insurgency Warfare Theory and Practice*, Westport, 2006.
13. F. Trgo, op. cit.
14. C.E. Callwell, *Small Wars: Their Principles and Practice*, London, 1996 (3rd edition).
15. It also appears to be the theme of the forthcoming book by Fidel Castro about the Cuban revolution, *A Strategic Victory*.
16. See M. Gezhilli and R. Selmanaj, '*Haradinaj dhe Haga*', Prishtina, 2006 for a revealing account of UNMIK and NATO's shabby machinations in Prishtina at the time of Haradinaj's removal as Prime Minister and the ICTY aftermath.
17. See M. Glenny, *The Rebirth of History*, London, 1992 for a convincing rebuttal of this idea in eastern Europe. The recent publication of Campbell's diaries for the NATO war campaign period indicate Blair's important positive contributions at that stage in the war.
18. As in, for instance, *Terrorism in Kosovo and Metohija and Albania—White Book*, Belgrade, 1998, and Deliso's more recent work, e.g. his book *The New Balkan Caliphate*, op. cit. For the ongoing issues with the KLA heritage, see Isabel Strohle, 'Veterans Politics and Policies Towards the Veterans of the Kosovo Liberation Army', in Zeitschrift für Globalgeschichte und Vergleichende Gesellschaftsforschung 20 (2010), Heft. 5, Munich, 2010, pp. 87–103, and JP discussions with authors.
19. Sallust, *The Jugurthine War*, ed. S.A. Handford, London, 1963, p. 67.
20. M. Barratt Brown, *From Tito to Milosevic: Yugoslavia the Lost Country*, London, 2005.
21. Glenny, op. cit., p. 662.
22. N. Machiavelli, *On Conspiracies*, London, 2010.
23. D. Tartt, *The Secret History*, New York, 1992
24. H. Perritt, op. cit., pp. 93 ff.

APPENDIX A: MILITARY ORGANISATION IN WARTIME KOSOVA,
MARCH-MAY 1999

1. Source: *Terrorism in Kosovo and Metohija and Albania—White Book*, Belgrade, 1998.

APPENDIX C: THE PROGRAMME OF THE PEOPLE'S MOVEMENT
FOR THE REPUBLIC OF KOSOVA (LPRK)

1. The LPRK programme was approved by the first General Assembly of the LPRK
   in July 1987, and first published in Albanian in the newspaper of the LPRK,'Zeri
   i Kosoves' (Voice of Kosova), issue No 7, 1987, LPRK Exterior, Aarrau, Switzerland. It was then published as a pamphlet in June 1988.
   The text was then published in a slightly amended form by this newspaper in
   Switzerland in December 1989. This translation is based on the version published by the Albania Society of Britain in the following year, and the Albanian
   original 'Programi i Levizjes Popullore per Republiken e Kosoves', 1989. I am
   indebted to the Sud Ost Institut, Regensburg, Germany for a copy of this latter
   document, and Stuart Munro and Miranda Vickers for the Albania Society
   document.

APPENDIX D: THE PROGRAMME OF THE KLA

1. Jakup Krasniqi, *Kthesa e Madhe: Ushtria Çlirimtare e Kosovës* (Prishtina 2006),
   pp. 83–4.

BIBLIOGRAPHY AND REFERENCES

Aaronovitch, D. *Voodoo Histories*, London, 2009.
Ajgeraj, G. *Rruga e Lirise—Zafir Berisha*, Prizren, 2002.
Ahrends, G.-H. *Diplomacy on the Edge*, Washington, DC, 2007.
Alia, R. *Our Enver*, Tirana, 1987.
Albright, M. *Madame Secretary*, New York, 2003.
Allin, D.H. *et al.*, *What Status for Kosovo?* Paris, 2001.
Anjelkovic, D. (ed.) *Kosova Crucified*, Belgrade, 2000.
Anjelokovic, S. *Days of Terror*, Belgrade, 2000.
Anzulovic, B. *Heavenly Serbia: From Myth to Genocide*, New York, 1999.
Anon. *British Military Mission to Jugoslavia*, London, 1945.
Anon, *Die Armeen der Balkan-Staaten*, Leipzig, 1910.
Anon. *Humbjet e Policise Serbe gjate Luftes ne Kosove*, Prishtina, undated.
Anon. *From 'National Communism' to National Collapse: US Intelligence Community Estimative Products on Yugoslavia, 1948–1990*, Washington, DC, 2006.
Anon. (Ministry of Defence, UK) *Kosovo: Lessons from the Crisis*, London, 2000.
Anon. *Terrorism in Kosovo and Metohija and Albania—White Books*, Belgrade, 1998.
Arifi, S. *UCK ne mes te Perkrahjeve dhe Pengesave*, Gjakova, 2000.
Arsllani, I. *Distinktivi Tetovar*, Tetovo, 2008.
Ahmetaj, A. and S. Krasniqi *Keshtu Foli Tahir Zemaj?* Prishtina, 2001.
Audyli, M. and B. Kosumi *Letra nga Burgu*, Prishtina, 2004.
Auty, P. and R. Clogg *British Policy towards Wartime Resistance in Yugoslavia and Greece*, London, 1975.
Bacevich, A. and E. Cohen *War over Kosovo: Politics and Strategy in a Global Age*, New York, 2001.
Badsey, S. and P. Latawaski (eds) *Britain,NATO and the Lessons of the Balkan Conflicts 1991–1999* (with an Introduction by Geoffrey Hoon), London, 2004.

Baftiu, F. *Kosova Krize Nderkombetare*, Prishtina, 2004.

Bailey, R. *The Wildest Province: SOE in the Land of the Eagle*, London, 2008.

Bajrami, H. *Dosja Demaci*, Prishtina, 2003.

—— *Politika Serbe per Rikolonoizimin e Kosoves Me Sllave 1945–1948*. Prishtina, 2002.

—— *Programi Kombetare Politik I Shqiptareve*, Prishtina, 2002.

Baliu, B. (ed.) *Pishtaret e Lirise*, Prishtina, 2002.

Balliu, F. *The Ghoulish Lady Nexmije Hoxha*, Tirana, 2005.

Baloku, R. and R. Baloku *Organizata BTSH 1959*, Peje, 2004.

Banac, I. *The National Question in Yugoslavia*, Cornell, 1984.

—— *With Stalin against Tito: Cominformist Splits in Yugoslav Communism*, Cornell, 1988.

Barratt Brown, M. *From Tito to Milosevic: Yugoslavia the Lost Country*, London, 2005.

Bashkurti, L. *Europa Ballkani I dhe SIFA e Kosoves*, Tirana, 2006.

—— *Diplomacia Shqiptare*, Tirana, 2000.

—— *National and European Identity of the Albanians*, Tirana, 2006.

Batakovic, D. *Kosovo: La spirale de la haine*, Paris, 1993.

Batt, Judy (ed.) *Is There an Albanian Question?* Chaillot Paper No. 107, Paris, 2008.

Begovic, V. *An Answer to Comrade Cervenkov and Others*, Belgrade, 1948.

Bekaj, B. *The KLA and the Kosovo War*, Berlin, 2010.

Bekolli, Z. *Gani Helshani Veprimtar Artist Luftetar Prishtina*, 2001.

Bennett, C. *Yugoslavia's Bloody Collapse*, London, 1995.

Berisha, B. *Fundi I nje Aventure Politike*, Tetovo 1998.

Baze, M. *Shqiperia dhe Lufta ne Kosove*, Tirana, 1998.

Bilainkin, G. *Tito*, London, 1949.

Binaj, A. and B. Polo, *Buzheti dhe Shpenzimet per Mbrojtjen*, Tirana, 2002.

Bishop, R. and E. Crayfield, *Russia Astride the Balkans*, London, 1949.

Bislimi, M. *Tahir Meta—Monograpfi*, Prishtina, 2004.

Blair, T. *A Journey*, London, 2010.

Blitz, B. (ed.) *War and Change in the Balkans*, Cambridge, 2006.

Bobbitt, P. *The Shield of Achilles: War, Peace and the Course of History*, New York, 2002.

Boja, R. (ed.) *Serbian Barbarities against Islamic Monuments in Kosova*, Prishtina, 2000.

Booth, K. *The Kosovo Tragedy: The Human Rights Dimension*, London, 2001.

Borici, G.L., *Ex Yougoslavie entre la violence et la paix*, Tirana, 2007.

Boskovska, N. *Das Jugoslawische Makedonien 1918–1941*, Weimar and Vienna, 2009.

Brankovic, C. *Alexsinac—City of Peace*, Belgrade, 2000.

Brovina, F. *Cry for Kosova*, Prishtina, 1999.

Buckley, M. and Cummings, S. (eds) *Kosovo Perspectives of War and its Aftermath*, London, 2001

Buckley, W.J. (ed.), *Kosovo: Contending Voices on Balkan Interventions*, Grand Rapids, 2000.

Bucpapaj, M. *Partia Demokratike dhe Ceshtja Kombetare*, Tirana, 2000.

Bunker, R.J. (ed.) *Criminal-States and Criminal-Soldiers*, Abingdon and New York, 2008.

Buxhovi, J. *Kthesa Historike Vitet e Germanise dhe Epoka e LDK-s*, Prishtina, 2008.

Bylykbashi, I. *Kronike (1981–1995)*, *Chronicle (1981–1995)*, Prishtina, 1996.

Callwell, C.E. *Small Wars: Their Principles and Practice*, Lincoln, Nebraska, 1996.

Cameron, A. and J. Pettifer *The Enigma of Montenegrin History: The Example of Svac*, Tirana, 2009.

Campbell, A. *The Blair Years*, London, 2007.

Canak, J. *Greater Albania: Concepts and Possible Consequences*, Belgrade, 1998.

Cani, B. and C. Milivojevic *Kosmet ili Kosova*, Belgrade, 1996.

Carpenter, T.G. *Nato's Empty Victory: A Postmortem on the Balkan War*, Washington, DC, 2000.

Carrier, E.H. *Water and Grass: A Study in the Pastoral Economy of Southern Europe*, London, 1932.

Ceku, E. *Mendimi Politik I Levizjes Ilegale ne Kosove 1945–1981*, Prishtina, 2003.

——— *Shekulli I Ilegales Proceset Gjyqesore kunder Ilegales ne Kosove Dokumente*, Prishtina, 2004.

——— *Struktura Politike e Ilegales se Kosoves*, Tirana, 2006.

——— *Demonstratat e Vitit 1968 ne Arkivin e Kosoves*, Prishtina, 2009.

Cetta, M. *Me UCK ne Koshare*, Prishtina, 2002.

Chiclet, C. *Les communistes Grecs dans le guerre. Histoire du Partie Communiste de Grèce, 1941–1949*, Paris, 1987.

Chivers, C.J., *The Gun*, New York, 2010.

Churcher, B. *Kosovo Lindore/Preshevo 1999–2002 and the FYROM Conflict*, RMA Sandhurst CSRC G-104, 2002.

Clark, H. *Civil Resistance in Kosovo*, London, 2000.

Clark, W. *Waging Modern War*, New York, 2002.

——— *A Time to Lead*, New York, 2007.

Clayer, N. *Aux Origines du nationalisme albanais*, Paris, 2007.

Clinton, B. *My Life*, New York, 2004.

Clucas, L. *The Byzantine Heritage in Eastern Europe*, New York, 1988.

Clunies-Ross, A. and P. Sudar *Albania's Economy in Transition and Turmoil, 1990–97*, Aldershot, 1998.

Cocaj, N. *Bartesit e Lirise Haxhi Hoti*, Has, 2000.

Cohen, G. *Karl Marx's Theory of History—A Defence*, Oxford, 1978.

Colovic, I. *The Politics of Symbol in Serbia*, London, 2002.

Constitution of the Republic of Kosovo, Prishtina, 2008.

Cordesman, A.H. *The Lessons and Non Lessons of the Air and Missile Campaign in Kosovo*, Westport, CT, 2001.

Cosic, D. *Kosovo*, Belgrade, 2004.

Covic, N. *Serbia after Milosevic: Program for the Solution of the Crisis in the Pcinja District*, Belgrade, 2001.

Cuni, M. *Reportazhe Lufte*, Prishtina, 2002.

Daalder, I.H. and M.E. O'Hanlon *Winning Ugly: NATO's War to save Kosovo*, Washington, DC, 2000.

D'Alema, M. *Kosova-Italianet dhe Lufta*, Tirana, 2004.

Dalipi, F. *Ukshin Hoti per Kauzen Kombetare*, Gjilan, 2001.

Danaj, K. *Populli I Tradhtuar*, Tirana, 1998.

——— *The Clinton Doctrine and the Twenty First Century*, Tirana, 2001.

——— *Kryengritje e Pambaruar*, Tirana, 2008.

Dauti, D. *Lufta per Trepcen*, Prishtina, 2002.

——— *Reflektime Shqiptaro-Britanike*, Prishtina, 2001.

Davis, D. and A. Pereira (eds) *Irregular Armed Forces and their Role in State Formation*, Cambridge, 2002.

Dede, S. *The Counter Revolution within the Counter Revolution*, Tirana, 1983.

Dedijer, V. *Jugoslovensko-Albanski Odnosi (1939–1948)*, Belgrade,1949.

Deliso, C. *The Coming Balkan Caliphate*, Westport, CT, 2007.

Denaud, P. and V. Pras *Kosovo: naissance d'une lutte armée UCK*, Paris, 2000.

Detrez, R. *Kosovo: de Uitgesteide Oorlog*, Antwerp, 1998.

——— *Kosova (Lufta e Shtyre)*, Tirana, 2004.

Dimitrevic, B. *Jugoslavia I NATO*, Belgrade, 2003.

Dixon, C. and O. Heilbrunn, *Communist Guerilla Warfare*, London, 1954.

Djokic, D. (ed.) *Yugoslavism: Histories of a Failed Idea 1918–1992*, London, 2003.

Dobra, I. *Lufta e Drenices 1941–1945 dhe NDSH deri 1947*, Prishtina, 1997.

Doder, D. and L. Branson, *Milosevic: Portrait of a Tyrant*, New York, 1999.

Drevic, M. *Arigi Kosovski*, Belgrade, 2005.

——— *Rat na Kosovo*, Belgrade, 2007.

Dreyer, J.T. *The PLA and the Kosovo Conflict*, Carlisle, PA, 2000.

Djordjevic, D. and S. Fischer-Galati, *The Balkan Revolutionary Tradition*, New York, 1981.

Dragnich, A. (ed.) *Serbia's Historical Heritage*, Boulder, 1994.

Duka, V. *Qytetet e Shqiperise ne Vitet 1912–1924*, Tirana, 1997.

Dyrmishi, D. *Veprimtaria e Bandave dhe e Organizateve Opozitare Ilegale ne Shqiperi (1944–1948)*, Tirana, 2003.

Elshani, G. *Ushtria Clirimitare e Kosoves, Dokumente dhe Artikuj*, Prishtina, 2003.

Elshani, H. *Ceta e Bruksellit (Mendime dhe Opinione)*, Peje, 2007.

Elshani, M. *Betejes e Lavdishme te Brigades 123 Ditar Lufte*, Prizren, 2001.

Elsie, R. *Kosovo: In the Heart of the Powder Keg*, New York, 1997.

Emerllahu, S. *et al. Edhe ne Deshmojme: And We Witness*, Tetovo, 2000.

BIBLIOGRAPHY AND REFERENCES

Eudes, D. *The Kapetanios: Partisans and Civil War in Greece, 1943–1949*, London, 1972.

Eyal, J. (ed.), *The Warsaw Pact and the Balkans, Moscow's Southern Flank*, London, 1989.

Fahti, S., A. Graf and L. Paul *Orientalism and Conspiracy*, London, 2010.

Fejza, E. (ed.) *Vushtrri me Rethine*, Vushtrri, 2003.

Ferizi,J. *Kosova nuk eshte Serbi*, Prishtina, 2001.

Fiori, G. *Antonio Gramsci: Life of a Revolutionary*, London, 1970.

Fischer, B. *Albania at War 1939–1945*, West Lafayette, IN, 1999.

——— *Balkan Strongmen: Dictators and Authoritarian Rulers of South East Europe*, Lafayette 2007.

Freundlich. L. *Albania's Golgotha*, Prishtina, 2010.

Fowler, W. *The Secret War in Italy: Special Forces, Partisans and Covert Operations 1943–1945*, Hersham, 2010.

Friend, M. *No Place Like Home: Echoes from Kosovo*, San Francisco, 2001.

Fyson, G., A. Malapanis and J. Silberman, *The Truth about Yugoslavia*, New York, 1993.

Galala, D. *Counter Insurgency Warfare Theory and Practice*, Westport, 2006.

Gashi, B. *Muje Krasniqi nje Jete per Liri*, Prishtina, 2002.

——— *Kosharjia Altari I Lirise*, Prishtina, 2006.

Gashi, I. (ed.) *The Denial of Human and National Rights of Albanians in Kosova*, New York, 1992.

Gashi, I. and H. Fazliu *Masakra e Celines*, Prishtina,2000.

Gashi, S. *Adem Demaci: A Biography*, Prishtina, 2010.

Gashi, Sanije *Historite Tmerrit 1998–1999*, Prishtina, 2009.

Gashi, Z. *Ditet e Tmerrit dhe te Shpreses (Ditari I luftes dhe pasojat e Offensives Serbe ne Mramuer e Busi)*, Prishtina, 2000.

Gecaj, T. *Kolona s'ndaled....!*, Prishtina, 2002.

Gentile, G. *How Effective is Strategic Bombing? Lessons learned from World War II to Kosovo*, New York, 2001.

Gerguri, M. *Aget Gerguri dhe Levizja NDSH (1945–1947)*, Prishtina, 2007.

Gervalla, J. *Kenget e Moshes*, Prishtina, 2004.

Gezhilli, M. and R. Selmanaj *Haradinaj dhe Haga*, Prishtina, 2006.

Gjeloshi, N. *Kosova ne Udhekryq'89*, Gorle, 1997.

——— *Kosovo, 1999*, Tirana, 2004.

——— *Kosova ne Udhekryq '89*, Gorle, 1997.

Glaurdic, J. *The Hour of Europe: Western Powers and the Breakup of Yugoslavia*, London, 2011.

Glenny, M. *The Rebirth of History*, London, 1990.

——— *The Balkans: Nationalism War and the Great Powers*, London, 2000.

Gligorijevic, M. *Serbia after Milosevic: Program for the Solution of the Crisis in the Pcinja District*, Belgrade, 2001.

Golemi, S. *UCK-ja dhe Kadareja*, Prishtina, 2004.

Golemi, S. and D. Goxhai *Rruga qe me coi ne radhet e UCK-se*, Tirana, 2000.

BIBLIOGRAPHY AND REFERENCES

Gordy, E. *The Culture of Power in Serbia*, University Park, Pennsylvania, 1999.

Gow, J. *Legitimacy and the Military: The Yugoslav Crisis*, London, 1992.

────── *The Serbian Project and its Adversaries*, London, 2003.

Goxhai, D. (Shpetim Golemi) *Rruga qe me coi ne radhet e UCK-se*, Tirana, 2000.

Greicevci, R. *Pushka*, Prishtina, 2002.

────── *Limaj, Celiku I Paqes*, Prishtina, 2004.

Grimm, R. *Geschichte der Schweiz in ihren Klassenkampfen*, Zurich, 1977.

Guevara, E. *La Guerra de las Guerrillas*, Havana, 1960.

Hadzic, M. *The Yugoslav People's Agony: The Role of the Yugoslav People's Army*, London, 2002.

Hajrizi, M. *Sprova te Clirimit*, Prishtina, 2004.

Hajro, A. et al., *Historia e Artit Ushtarak te Luftes Antifashiste Nacional Clirimitare te Popullit Shqiptar*, Tirana, 1989.

Halperin, E. *The Triumphant Heretic: Tito's Struggle against Stalin*, London, 1958.

Hamzaj, B. *A Narrative about War and Freedom (Dialogue with Ramush Haradinaj)*, Prishtina, 2000.

────── *Paqja e Gjeneralit (Dialog me Ramush Haradinaj)*, Prishtina, 2001.

Hamzaj, B. and F. Hoti *Jasharet*, Prishtina, 2003.

Harbinson, R. (ed.) *My Name Came Up*, London, 2000.

Hasani, H. *Te Pavdekshmit e Dukagjinit Deshmoret e UCK-se te ZOD*, Peje, 2002.

Hasani, H.H. *Dobrosini*, Bujanoc, 2003.

Hashim, A. *Small Wars: An Interpretive Analysis of Theory and Practice*, London, 2010.

Headley, J. *Russia and the Balkans*, London, 2008.

Heilbrunn, O. (Foreword by C.M. Woodhouse) *Partisan Warfare*, London, 1962.

Heinemann, A. and W. Paes, *Wag the Dog: The Mobilisation and Demobilisation of the Kosova Liberation Army*, Bonn and Skopje, 2000.

Hehir, A. (ed.) *Kosova, Intervention and Statebuilding*, Abingdon and New York, 2010.

Henriksen, D. *NATO's Gamble: Combining Diplomacy and Airpower in the Kosovo Crisis 1998–1999*, Annapolis, 2007.

Hibbert, R. *Albania's National Liberation Struggle: The Bitter Victory*, London, 1991.

────── *Albania's Emergence onto the Balkan Scene*, Thessaloniki, 1997.

Hobsbawm, E.J. *Bandits*, London, 1969.

Hodge, C. *Britain and the Balkans*, London, 2006.

Holohan, A. *Networks of Democracy: Lessons from Kosovo, for Iraq, Afghanistan and Beyond*, Stanford, 2005.

Holbrooke, R. *To End a War*, New York, 1998.

Hoti, U. *The Political Philosophy of the Albanian Question*, Tirana, 1998.

Hoxha, E. *L'"Autogestion" yougoslave: théorie et pratique capitalistes*, Paris, 1979.

—— *With Stalin: Memoirs*, Tirana, 1979.

—— *The Titoites*, Tirana, 1982.

—— *Laying the Foundations of the New Albania*, Tirana, 1984.

Hoxha, F. *Kur Pranvera Vonohet*, Prishtina, 1980.

Hoxha, S.F. *Qamil Hoxha "Drini"*, Gjakova, 2009.

Hurd, D. *Memoirs*, London, 2003.

Hyde, D. *The Roots of Guerrilla Warfare*, London, 1968.

Ignatieff, M. *Virtual War: Kosovo and Beyond*, London, 2000.

—— *Empire Lite*, London, 2004.

Ingrao, C. and T. Emmert *Confronting the Yugoslav Controversies*, West Lafayette, 2009.

Institute of History, Prishtina *The Kosovo Issue—A Historic and Current Problem*, Tirana, 1996.

International Crisis Group *Reality Demands: Documenting Violations of International Humanitarian Law in Kosovo 1999*, Brussels, 2000.

—— *After Milosevic*, Brussels, 2001.

Isambert, E. *Orient Grèce et Turquie d'Europe*, Paris, 1881.

Iselini, M. *Zvillmet ne Maqedoni dhe Lindja e UCK*, Tetovo, 2003.

Islami, B. *Perjetesia e Dyfishte*, Tirana, 2006.

—— *Fshehta e Hapur e Kosoves*, Prishtina, 2001.

Islami, M. *Vasil Shanto*, Tirana, 1981.

Istrefi, N. *Naser Shatri—Ulqit Ilire*, Prishtina, 2001.

Jacgagi, N.V. *Qemal Stafa, sa vie et sa lutte*, Tirana, 1973.

Jackson, M. *Soldier: The Autobiography*, London, 2007.

Jakupi, A. *Two Albanian States and National Unification*, Prishtina, 2004.

Jashari, R. 'Zeri i Lirise', Prishtina, 2009.

Jha, P. S. and Hobsbawm, E. J. *The Twilight of the Nation State*, London 2006.

Jokic, A. (ed.) *Lessons of the War in Kosova: The Dangers of Humanitarian Intervention*, Ormskirk, 2003.

Joksimovich, V. *Kosovo Crisis: A Study in Foreign Policy Mismanagement*, Belgrade, 1999.

—— *Kosovo is Serbia*, Belgrade, 2009.

Jonuzi-Krosi, I. *Golgotha Shqiptare I (1946–1952)* and *II and III (1952–1963 and 1963–1970)*, Tetovo, 2007 and 2008.

Jennings, C. *Midnight in some Burning Town*, London, 2004.

Judah, T. *The Serbs: History, Myth and the Destruction of Yugoslavia*, Yale, 1997.

—— *Kosovo: War and Revenge*, Yale and London, 2002.

—— *Kosovo: What Everyone Needs to Know*, Oxford, 2008.

Jurisevic, C. *Blood on my Hands*, Melbourne, 2010.

Kabo, P. *Autoritarizem ne Tranzicion*, Tirana, 2006.

Kacza, T. *Zwischen Feudalismus und Stalinismus*, Berlin, 2007.

BIBLIOGRAPHY AND REFERENCES

Kadare, I. *Il a fallu ce deuil pour se retrouver*, Paris, 2000.
———— *Koha Barbare*, Tirana, 2000.
———— *Mbi Krimin ne Ballkan*, Tirana, 2011.
Kadare, I. and U. Hoti *Bisede Permes Hekurash*, Tirana, 2000.
Kadishani, J. *Bajram Cukovci-Curri*, Prishtina, 2007.
———— *Lufta e Celise se Siceves dhe Komandant Shaban Sadiku*, Prishtina.
Kadishani, J. and T. Mrijaj *Ngjarje dhe Portrete Historike*, Prishtina, 2004.
Kadolli, A. *Ore Kombetare*, Prishtina, 2001.
Kaloshi, A. *Bytyci*, Tirana, 2004.
Kampfner, J. *Blair's Wars*, London, 2006.
Kapo, H. *Vepra (I)*, Tirana, 1980.
Karaqi, G. *Miremengjes Atdhe*, Prizren, 2000.
Katana, H. *Kudusi Lama Gjenerali I Luftes*, Tirana, 2002.
———— *Tri Dimensioned e Luftes Clirimtare te Kosoves*, Tirana, 2002.
Kecmezi-Basha,S. *Levizja Ilegale Patriotike Shqiptare ne Kosove (1945–1947)* Prishtina, 1998.
———— *Shtypi Ilegal Shqiptare ne Kosove (1945–1999)*, Prishtina, 2009.
King, I. and W. Mason, *Peace at Any Price*, London, 2006.
Kitson, F. *Low Intensity Operations*, London, 1971.
Klugman, J. *et al. Yugoslavia Faces the Future*, London, 1947.
Klugman, J. *From Trotsky to Tito*, London, 1951.
Kojadinovic, D. (ed.) *The March Pogrom 2004*, Belgrade 2004.
Kola, H. *Genocidi serb ndaj Shqiptarët ne viset e tyre ethnike ne Jugosllavi 1941–1967*, Tirana, 2000.
Koliopoulos, J. *Brigands with a Cause*, Oxford, 1987.
Konechni, G. and S. Georgiev, *Historical Dictionary of the Republic of Macedonia*, London, 1998.
Kosovo—International Aspects of the Crisis (in Russian), Moscow, 1999.
Kosovo and Metohija Documents and Facts, Belgrade, 1995.
Kosova Historical Institute *Kosova*, Prishtina, 1992–1996.
Kosova Information Centre *Albanian Democratic Movement in Former Yugoslavia: Documents: 1990–1993*, Prishtina, 1993.
Kostovicova, D. *Kosovo: The Politics of Identity and Space*, London, 2005.
Kosumi, B. *Letersia nga Burgu*, Tirana, 2006.
Kraja, M. *Mirupafshim ne nje Lufte Tjeter*, Prishtina, 2003.
———— *Vite te Humbura*, Prishtina, 2003.
Krasniqi, A. *Kline me Rrethine ne Valet e Historise*, Klina, 2002.
Krasniqi, J. *Kthesa e Madhe UCK*, Prishtina, 2006.
Krasniqi, M. *Kosova pas 22 Januarit 1998*, Prishtina, 2000.
Krasniqi, M.D. *Shkelqimi I UCK-se ne Treven e Verrinit*, Prizren, 2002.
Krasniqi, S.V. *Lufta per Clirimin e Kosoves (1997–1999)*, Prishtina, 2007.
Kurtaj, H. *Shungullon Gryka e Kacanikut*, Kacanik, 2000.
Lama, K. *Kosova dhe Ushtria Clirimtare*, Tirana, 2005.
Lambeth, B. *NATO's Air War for Kosovo: A Strategic and Operational Assessment*, Santa Monica, 2001.

———— 'Lufta e UCK-se ne Zon', Prishtina, 2012.

———— 'Ne Rrugen e Lirise—Dokumente', Prishtina, 2012.

Lane, C.D. *Once Upon an Army: The Crisis in the Albanian Army, 1995–1996*, www.csrc.org, RMA Camberley, 2002.

Lane, J.-E. *The Swiss Labyrinth: Institutions, Outcomes and Redesign*, London, 2001.

Laqueur, W. *Guerrilla Warfare: A Historical and Critical Study*, New Brunswick, 1976.

Latifi, H. and L. Sermoxhaj *Hogoshti (Monografi)*, Prishtina, 2002.

Latifi, S. *Dialog ne Theatrin Levizes*, Prishtina, 2002.

———— *Rrugetimi neper Lugine te Presheves*, Preshevo, 2006.

Lauka, I. and Imeri, E. (eds) *Shqiperia ne Dokumentet e Arkive Ruse*, Tirana, 2006.

Lazri, S. and J. Malo *Dans les prisons et les camps de concentration de la Yougoslavie*, Tirana, 1960.

Lebor, A. *Milosevic: A Biography*, London, 2002.

Leci, E. *Eliminimi I Lidershipit Ushtarak*, Tirana, 2002.

Lees, L.M. *Yugoslav-Americans and National Security during World War II*, Urbana and Chicago, 2007.

Leuenberger, U. and A. Maillard, *Les Damnés du troisième cercle—les Kosovares en Suisse 1965–1999*, Geneva, 1999.

Leurdijk, D. and D. Zandee, *Kosovo: from Crisis to Crisis*, Aldershot, 2001.

Levy, 'Yank' *Guerilla Warfare*, London, 1941.

Lidov, A. *et al. Orthodox Heritage and Contemporary Catastrophe*, Moscow, 2007.

Liotta, P.H and C.R. Jebb, *Imagining Macedonia: Idea and Identity*, Westport, 2004.

Lleshi, H. *Vite Njerez Ngjarte*, Tirana, 1996.

Loyd, A. *Another Bloody Love Letter*, London, 2004.

Luarasi, S. *Ne Brigadat Internationale ne Spanje*, Tirana, 1996.

Lupe, N. *Te Drejtat Ne Kosove*, Belgrade, 1998.

Lyde, L. and A. Mockler-Ferryman *The Balkan Peninsular*, London, 1905.

Maclean, F. *Disputed Barricade*, London, 1957.

Maksutaj, R. *Isniq through the Centuries*, Prishtina, 2002.

Malcolm, N. *Kosovo*, London, 1998.

Maloku, E. *Gjuha e Stuhise Qershor 1998—Kallnor 1999*, Prishtina, 2002.

Maloku, E. (ed.) *The Expulsions of Albanians and Colonisation of Kosova*, Prishtina, 1997.

Mao Tse-tung, *On Guerilla Warfare*, Champaign, IL, 2000.

Marantzidis, N. *Dimokratikos Stratos Elladas 1946–1949*, Athens, 2010.

Markovic, M. *Night and Day: A Diary*, Belgrade, 1995.

Markovic, N. and M. Jovanovic *War Daily Reviews*, Belgrade, 2000.

Markovski,V. *Goli Otok, The Island of Death: A Diary in Letters*, Boulder, 1984.

Matoshi, H. *Gallapi*, Prishtina, 2010.

Mazower, M. *The Balkans*, London, 2000.

MacKenzie, S.P. *Revolutionary Armies in the Modern Era—A Revisionist Approach*, London, 1997.

McAllester, M. *Beyond the Mountains of the Damned: The War inside Kosovo*, New York, 2002.

McConville, M. *A Small War in the Balkans: British Military Involvement in Wartime Yugoslavia 1941–1945*, London, 1986.

McCormack Tribune Foundation, *Irregular Warfare Leadership in the 21st Century*, Wheaton, IL, 2007.

Mehmetaj, F. *Adrian Krasniqi-Rexha (Nje jete e nje vdekje per atedhe)*, Peje, 2001.

——— *Rapsodia e Heronjeve te UCK*, Prishtina, 2006.

Menaj, P. *UCK Mesazh dhe Shprese*, Tetovo, 2001.

Memishi, I. *Ushtari I Lirise Taih Bejtulin*, Prishtina, 2003.

Mertus, J. *Kosovo: How Myths and Truths Started a War*, Berkeley, 1999.

Michas, T. *Unholy Alliance: Greece and Milosevic's Serbia*, College Station, 2005.

Mijalokovic, M. and P. Daminov *Terorizam Albanski Ekstremista*, Belgrade, 2002.

Milo, P. *Greater Albania—Between Fiction and Reality*, Tirana, 2000.

——— *Kosova nga Rambuje ne Pavaresi*, Tirana, 2009.

——— *Ditari I nje Ministrite Jashtem Konflikti I Kosoves 1997–2001*, Tirana, 2009.

Milosevic, S. *Godina Raspleta*, Belgrade, 1989.

Minxhozo, Y. (ed.) *Leter e Panjohur e Enver Hoxha mbi Kosoven Dokumenta te Arkivave Ruse*, Tirana, 2002.

Mjeku, M. *Kosova ne Dimrin e Vitit 1945*, New York, 2002.

Moisiu, A. *Midis Nanos dhe Berishas (Vol I-III)*, Tirana, 2007–2009.

Molla, Y. *Plani Sekret per Kosoven*, Tirana, 2006.

Motes, Mary *Kosova-Kosovo: Prelude to War 1966–1999*, Redland, Florida, 1998.

Mrijaj, T. and K. Kapinova *Lidhja e Prizrenit 1962–2002*, New York, 2002.

Mucolli, Z *Hertica*, Prishtina, 2000.

Muja, S. *Tragjedi e Papare ne Historine e Njerezimit ne Luften e Kosoves*, New York, 2001.

Mulaj, K. *The Politics of Ethnic Cleansing in the Balkans*, Lanham and Plymouth, 2010.

Murati, S. *Serbia kunder Serbise*, Tirana, 2005.

Murtezai, E. *Fehmi Agani*, Prishtina, 2000.

Muzarku, I. (ed.) *Quo Vadis Eastern Europe? Religion, State and Society after Communism*, Ravenna, 2009.

Myrtaj, N. *Jehone Lufte*, Prishtina, 2002.

——— *17 e 18 Marsi 2004*, Prishtina, 2004.

Nardulli, B. *et al. Disjointed War: Military Operations in Kosovo 1999*, Arlington, 2002.

BIBLIOGRAPHY AND REFERENCES

Nasi, L. *Aspekte te Shtypjes Kombetare e Politike te Shqiptare e Politike te Shqiptare ne Kosove, 1981–1986*, Tirana, 2011.

Naumann, F. *The Mobilisation and Demobilisation of the Kosovo Liberation Army*, Bonn/Skopje, 2001.

Nazarko, M. (ed.) *Presidenti Meidani dhe Kosova*, Prishtina, 2000.

Nazi, L. *Ripushtimi I Kosoves Shtator 1944–Korrik 1945*, Tirana, 1994.

Neuberg, A. *et al.*, *Armed Insurrection*, London, 1970.

Neziri, I. *Ahmet Haxhiu hje Jete te Tere ne Levizjen Ilegale*, Prishtina, 2001.

Nicevic,T. *Goli Otoci—Jova Kapecica*, Sarajevo and Belgrade, 2010.

O'Neill, B. *Insurgency and Terrorism Inside Modern Revolutionary Warfare*, Dulles, VA, 1990.

O'Neill, William G., *Kosovo: An Unfinished Peace*, International Peace Academy, New York City, 2002.

Obradovic, J. *Ethnic Conflict and War Crimes in the Balkans: The Narratives of Denial in Post-Conflict Serbia*, London, 2010.

OSCE *Kosovo/Kosova: As Seen As Told*, Prishtina, 1999.

Osmani, J. *Kolonizimi Serb I Kosoves*, Prishtina, 2000.

Osmani, S. *Gjenocidi Serb ne Kosove*, Tirana, 1999.

Osservatore Romano, *The Holy See and the Crisis in Kosovo*, Vatican City, 2002.

Ostremi, G. *Shpresa dhe Zhgenjimi Shqiptareve ne Maqedoni Gjate dhe Pas Luftes se Dyte Boterore*, Prishtina, 2000.

Ozgur Baklacioglu, N. *Dis Politika ve Goc: Balkanlardan Turkiyeye Arnaut Gocleri 1919–1980*, Istanbul, 2010.

Pacolli, B. *Nga sfida ne Sfide*, Prishtina, 2010.

Palmer, S. and R. King *Yugoslav Communism and the Macedonian Question*, Hamden, 1971.

Palushi, P. *Kukesi ne 79 Dite*, Tirana, 1999.

——— *Muharrem Bajtaktari ne Vitet 1945–1946*, Tirana, 1998.

Papatheorodou, A. *Oi Mousoulmanoi Tsamides—UCK*, Thessaloniki, 2002.

Pavlovic, M. *et al.* *Gerila na Balkani*, Tokyo-Belgrade, 2007.

Pellegrin, P. *Kukes* Stockholm, 1999.

Perolli, G. *Konference e Bujanit*, New York, 2002.

Perritt, H.H. *Kosovo Liberation Army: The Inside Story of an Insurgency*, Urbana, 2008.

Perry, D.M. *The Politics of Terror: The Macedonian Revolutionary Movements 1893–1903*, Durham, NC, 1988.

Pesmanoglu, S. *Kosovo Dvostruka Hibris*, Belgrade, 2005.

Petritsch, W. *Zielpunkt Europe:Von den Schluchten des Balkans und den Muhen der Edene*, Vienna, 2009.

Pettifer, James, *Dialogue with Hashim Thaci*, Prishtina, 2004.

——— *Kosova Express*, London and Madison, 2004.

——— *Blue Guide Albania and Kosovo*, Budapest, 2008.

Pettifer, James (ed.), *The New Macedonian Question*, London and New York, 1998.

Pettifer, James and Miranda Vickers, *The Albanian Question—Reshaping the Balkans*, London and New York, 2007.

Phillips. D.L. *Liberating Kosovo*, Cambridge, Massachusetts, 2012.

Phillips, J. *Macedonia: Warlords and Rebels in the Balkans*, London, 2004.

Pirraku, M. *Mulla Idris Gjilane dhe Mbrojtja Kombetar e Kosoves Lindore 1941–1944*, Prishtina, 1995.

———— *Per Kauzen Shqiptare 1997–1999*, Prishtina, 2000.

———— *Tivat 1945*, Prishtina, 1993.

Plasari, N. and L. Malltezi, *Politike Antikombetare e Enver Hoxha*, Tirana, 1996.

Pllana-Prishtina, N. *Luftoi per te jetuar te tjeret Agim Bardh Zenelli*, Prishtina, 2001.

Podrimi, A. (ed.) *Bashkekohesit per Agim Ramadanin*, Prishtina, 2001.

Polovina, Y. *Nje Kolonel Midis Tiranes Dme Prishtines*, Tirana, 2007.

Ponte, Carla del with C. Sudetic, *Madame Prosecutor*, New York, 2009.

Popov, N. (ed.) *The Road to War in Serbia*, Budapest, 1996.

Popovic, S. *et al. Kosovski cvor dresiti ili Seci?* Belgrade, 1990.

Power, S. *Chasing the Flame: Sergio de Mello and the Fight to Save the World*, New York, 2008.

Pozzi, H. *Black Hand over Europe*, London, 1935.

Prasniker, M. and A. Shober *Kerkime Arkeologjike ne Shqiperi dhe Mal te Zi*, Vienna, 1919.

Prifti, P. *Remote Albania: The Politics of Isolation*, Tirana, 1999.

Pridham, G. and T. Gallagher *Experimenting with Democracy: Regime Change in the Balkans*, London, 2000.

Procopius, *The Secret History*, London, 1962.

———— *The Wars*, Cambridge, 1981.

Prorok, C. *Ibrahim Rugova's Leadership*, Vienna and Frankfurt, 2004.

Pushkolli, F. *Zahir Pajaziti Hero I Kombit*, Prishtina, 2001.

———— *Arrestimi I General Remit*, Prishtina, 2002.

———— *Hasan Ramadan (1948–1994)*, Prishtina, 2004.

Qira, Z. *Cell 31*, New York, 1979.

———— *Ujqit ne Frak*, Tetovo, 1999.

Qosja, R. *La Question albanaise*, Paris, 1995.

Radinovic, R. *et al. Kosovo and Metahija Challenges and Responses*, Belgrade, 1997.

Radulovic, M. *Tito's Republic*, Wrotham, 1948.

Ragaru, N. and K. von Hippel *Understanding the Albanian Diaspora*, Paris and London, 2002.

Rajak, S. *Yugoslavia and the Soviet Union in the Early Cold War: Reconciliation, Comradeship, Confrontation, 1953–1957*, Abingdon, 2010.

Rama, L. *Nen jijen e eklipsit*, Tirana, 1999.

Rama, X. *Fshati Kolaj gjate Historise*, Prishtina, 2001.

Ramet, S. *Nationalism and Federalism in Yugoslavia, 1962–1991*, Bloomington, 1992.

—— *Balkan Babel: The Disintegration of Yugoslavia*, Boulder, 1995.

—— *Thinking about Yugoslavia*, Cambridge, 2005.

—— *The Three Yugoslavias: State Building and Legitimation 1918–2005*, Washington, DC, 2006.

Ramet, S., Listhaug, O. and Simkus, A. (eds) *Civic and Uncivic Values in Macedonia: Value Transformation, Education and Media*, Basingstoke: Palgrave Macmillan, 2013.

Randjelokovic, S (ed.) *The Army of Yugoslavia*, Prishtina, 1999.

Randjelovic, S. (ed.) *Trace of Inhumanity: NATO Aggression on Civilian Population and Facilities in Yugoslavia*, Belgrade, 1999.

Ranke, L. von *A History of Servia and the Servian Revolution*, London, 1852.

Rankin, R. *The Inner History of the Balkan War*, London, 1931.

Rappaport, H. *Conspirator: Lenin in Exile*, London, 2009.

Record, J. *Beating Goliath: Why Insurgencies Win*, Dulles, 2007.

Reinhardt, K. *KFOR Streitkrafte für den Frieden*, Frankfurt, 2002.

Reljin, M.V. and M. Knezevic *Kosovo and Metohija: Challenges and Responses*, Belgrade, 1997, Tirana, 1995.

Republic of Albania Council of Defense *Security and Defense Policy of Republic of Albania*, Tirana, 1996.

Reuter, J. *Shqiptare ne Jugosllavi*, Tirana, 2003.

Reuter, J. and K. Clewing *Der Kosovo Konflict*, Munich, 2000.

Rexha, K. *Pushke Lajmetare*, Prishtina, 2002.

Rexhepi, F. *Gjilani me Rrethine gjate Luftes se Dyte Boterore (1941–1945)*, Prishtina, 1998.

Rexhepi, Z. *Kabashi*, Prishtina, 2003

—— *Partia Demokratike Shqiptare Lindja Zhvillimi dhe Veprimtaria*, Tetovo, 2004.

Risospastis (collective authorship), *H. Tixponh Epopiia toy Dhmokratikoy Stratoy Ellades 1946–1949*, Athens, 1988.

Roberts, I. *Razgovori s Milosevicem*, Belgrade, 2012.

Rose, M. *Fighting for Peace*, London, 1998.

Ross, S. *The War in Kosovo*, Hove, 2000.

Rukiqi, M. *Krijues dhe Bartes te Tregimeve Popullore ne Drenice*, Prishtina, 1998.

Rumsfeld, D. *Known and Unknown: A Memoir*, New York, 2011.

Rustemi, V. *Nuhi Tairi Legende e Gjalle e Betejes se Koshares*, Skopje, 2006.

Sadiku, R. *Lidhja Kosovare 1949–1999*, Prishtina, 2006.

—— *Ajet Rushiti*, Chicago, 2010.

Saleman, L. *Yugoslavia: The Ancient Mining Laws and Customs*, Trepca, 1926.

Sallust, *Bellum Catilinae* (Transactions of the American Philological Association Texts and Commentaries) Oxford, 2007. Translation by S.A. Hanford, in Penguin Classics, London, 1964.

Sarafis, S. *Greek Resistance Army*, London, 1980.

BIBLIOGRAPHY AND REFERENCES

Shrader, C. *The Withering Vine: Logistics and the Communist Insurgency in Greece, 1945–1949*, New York, 1999.
Schmidt-Neke, M. *Entstehung und Ausbau der Konigsdiktatur in Albanien (1912–1939)*, Munich, 1987.
Scotto, G. and E. Arielli *La Guerra del Kosovo*, Rome, 1999.
Sejdiju, N. *Te Renet nuk Vdesin Kurre*, Tetovo, 2003.
Sejdiu, D. *Kush ishte Zahir Pajaziti?* Prishtina, 2001.
Sell, L. *Slobodan Milosevic and the Destruction of Yugoslavia*, Durham, NC, 2002.
Selm van, J. (ed.) *Kosovo's Refugees in the European Union*, London, 2000.
Seton-Watson, H. *The East European Revolution*, New York, 1956.
Shala, B. *Vitet e Kosoves 1998–1999*, Prishtina, 2000.
Shala, B. *et al. Une, Ramiz Alia*, Prishtina, 1992.
Shala, S. *Lufta e Logjes 1998*, Peje, 2006.
Shatri, M. *Kosova ne Luften e Dyte Boterore 1941–1945*, Tirana, 1997.
Shatri, M. and X. *Nje Gur per Varrin e Ushtarit Qe e Vrane*, Prishtina, 2011.
Shehi, Z. *Indrit Cara 'Ushtar Kavaja'*, Tirana, 2007.
Shoup, P. *Communism and the Yugoslav National Question*, New York and London, 1968.
Simic, P. *Route to Rambouillet: Kosova Crisis 1995–2000*, Belgrade, 2000.
Simms, B. *Unfinest Hour—Britain and the Destruction of Bosnia*, London, 2001.
Simnica, D. *Heroizmi I Kreshtave te Shales*, Prishtina, 2000.
Sinani, S. *Kosova ne Syrin e Ciklonit*, Tirana, 1999.
Smilanic, G.S. *Agresija NATO*, Belgrade, 2009.
Sokoli, A. *Kosova Dialog*, Tirana, 1999.
Sorensen, J. *State Collapse and Reconstruction in the Periphery*, New York, 2009.
Solzhenitsyn, A. *Lenin in Zurich*, London, 1975.
Spahiu, N. *Shqiptare dhe Serbet ne Luften Finale per Kosoven*, Prishtina, 2000.
Standish, A. *Kosovo One Year On*, London, 2000.
Starinov, A.K. *Behind Fascist Lines*, New York, 2001.
Styskalikova, V. *Terrorismus Nebo Guerilla*, Prague, 2006.
Sullivan, S. *Be not Afraid, for you Have Sons in America: How a Brooklyn Roofer Helped Lure the US into the Kosovo War*, New York, 2004.
Swire, J. *Bulgarian Conspiracy*, London, 1939.
Tahiri, B. *Drenica nje Shekull Trimerie*, Prishtina, 2001.
——— *Adem Jashari Legjende e Legjendave*, Prishtina, 2001.
Tahiri, E. *The Rambouillet Conference*, Peje, 2001.
Tchernoff, S. *Serbs in December 1915*, London, 1916.
Thomas, N. and K. Mikulan *The Yugoslav Wars (2)*, London, 2006.
Tierney, J.J. *Chasing Ghosts: Unconventional Warfare in American History*, Dulles, VA, 2007.

BIBLIOGRAPHY AND REFERENCES

Tito (Josif Broz) *Selected Speeches and Articles*, Belgrade, 1963.

───── *Selected Military Works*, Belgrade, 1966.

Tomic, N. (ed.) *The Twilight of the West*, Belgrade, 1999.

Trgo, F. *et al.*, *Tito's Historical Decisions*, Belgrade, 1980.

Troebst, S. *Conflict in Kosovo: Failure of Prevention?* Flensburg, 1998.

Ukimeri, B. *Legenda e Bjeshkeve te Nemura te Dukagjinit 1998–1999*, Prizren, 2003.

Ukshini, S. *Kosova dhe Perendimi*, Prishtina, 2000.

───── *Nga Lufta ne Paqe*, Prishtina, 2004.

───── *Kosova ne politiken jashtme te BE—se 1991–2007*, Prishtina, 2008.

Vankovska, B. and H. Wiberg *Between Past and Future: Civil-Military Relations in the Post-Communist Balkans*, London and New York, 2003.

Vaso, A. and S. Anagnosti *Albania The Great Shelter: The Kosovo Emergency and How it was Faced by Albanian Non-Governmental Organisations*, Tirana, 1999.

Veliu, F. *LPK dhe UCK: Nje embleme nje quellim*, Tirana, 2001.

───── *UCK nga beteja ne beteje*, Tetovo, 2005.

───── *I Perndjekur ne Shkup ne Perendim*, Tirana, 2001.

Verli, M. *Kosova ne Fokusin e Historise*, Tirana, 2003.

───── *Reforma agrare kolonizuese ne Kosove*, Tirana, 1992.

───── *Shfrytezimi Ekonomik I Kosoves 1970–1990*, Tirana, 1994.

Vickers, Miranda, *The Albanians: A Modern History*, London, 1996.

───── *Between Serb and Albanian: A History of Kosovo*, London, 1998.

Vladsavijevic, N. *Serbia's Antibureaucratic Revolution: Milosevic, the Fall of Communism and Nationalist Mobilisation*, Belgrade, 2008.

Vucinic, W. and R. Emmert *Kosovo: Legacy of a Medieval Battle*, Minnesota, 1991.

Vukaj, S. *Rusia dhe Kosova*, Tirana, 2007.

Vukmanovic, S. *How and Why the People's Liberation Struggle in Greece Met with Defeat*, London, 1985.

Waller, M., K. Drezov and B. Gokay, *Kosovo: The Politics of Delusion*, London, 1999.

Walsh, L. *Uprising in Albania*, London, 1997.

Weller, M. *The Crisis in Kosovo 1989–1999*, Cambridge, 1999.

Williams, H. *Parachutes, Patriots and Partisans: The SOE and Yugoslavia, 1941–1945*, London, 2003.

Winchester, S. *The Fracture Zone: A Return to the Balkans*, London, 1999.

Wintringham, T. *How to Reform the Army*, London, 1939.

Woodward, S. *Balkan Tragedy: Chaos and Dissolution after the Cold War*, Washington, DC, 1995.

Wray, D.A. *The Geology and Mining Resources of the Serb-Croat-Slovene State*, London, 1921.

Xhemali, V. *Forcat Kombetare ne Mbrotje te Shqiperise Etnike 1941–1945*, Tetovo, 2006.

───── *Xheme Hasa me Vullnetare ne Mbrojtje te Shqiperise*, Tetovo, 2007.

Zametica, J. *The Yugoslav Conflict*, London, 1992.

Zekaj, R. *The Development of Islamic Culture among the Albanians in the Twentieth Century*, Tirana, 2002.

Zejnullahu, S. *Lufta per Kosoven (Flet Kommandant Remi)*, Prishtina, 2001.

—— *War for Kosova (Commander Remi Speaks)*, Prishtina, 2001.

Zhelyazkova, A. *Albania and the Albanian Identity*, Sofia, 2000.

Zeri I Popullit (Edition) *The Status of a Republic for Kosova is a Just Demand*, Tirana, 1981.

Zilliacus, K. *Tito of Yugoslavia*, London, 1952.

Zimmerman, W. *Origins of a Catastrophe*, New York, 1996.

Zogaj, A. *Dialog me Naim Maloku*, Prishtina, 2000.

Zogaj, G. and Taci, S. *Deshmovet dhe te Renet e-uck nga shqiperia*, Prishtina, 2013.

Zogaj, P. *Uncivil War*, Tirana, 1998.

Zutic, N. *Vatikan I Albanci*, Belgrade, 2000.

Other publications and newspapers

Albislam, Tirana 2002–.

Arena, Skopje 2009–.

Balkan Review, Thessaloniki 1994–95.

Balkan Studies, Thessaloniki 1985–.

Bota Sot, Zurich 1992–.

British Army Review, Warminster 1992–.

Compass, Leeds, 1997–.

Epocha e Re, Prishtina, 1999–.

Eurobalkans, Aegina, 1994–95.

Flamuri, Rome, 1962–.

Foreign Affairs, Washington, 1990–.

Gazeta Shqiptare, Tirana, 1992–.

Intervju, Belgrade, 1991–.

International Affairs, London, 1992–.

International Struggle Marxist-Leninist, Leeds, 2000–2002.

Joint Forces Quarterly 1998–.

Journal of Slavic Military Studies, 1996–.

Klan, Tirana, 1995–.

KFOR Chronicle, 1999–2006

Koha, Prishtina,1995–.

Koha Ditore, Prishtina, 1995–.

Kosova Historical Political Review, Prishtina, 1991–.

Labour Focus on Eastern Europe, London, 1996–97.

Mediterranean Quarterly, 1993–.

Monitor, Podgoritsa, 1992–.

National Geographic, Washington, 1995–.

NATO Review, Brussels, 1990–.

Nin, Belgrade, 1991–.
Politika, Belgrade, 1989–.
Revista Ushtarake, Tirana, 1992–.
Serbska, Belgrade, 1992–94.
Serbsko Jedinistvo, Belgrade, 1992–96.
Small Wars and Insurgencies, Colchester, 2000–.
Sudosteuropa Mitteilungen, Munich, 1996–.
Transitions, Prague, 1995–.
Transitions, Prague, 1995–.
Ushtima e Maleve (UCPMB), Gjilan, 2000–2002.
Velika Srbija, Belgrade, 1991–.
VIP News, Belgrade, 1994–.
Vojska, Belgrade, 1992–.
Vreme, Belgrade, 1994.
Western Balkans Policy Review, Prishtina, 2010–.
World Today, London, 1990–.
Zeri, Prishtina 1992–.
Zeri I Kosoves, Aarau 1982–1999, Prishtina, 2000–2004.
Zeri I Kosoves, Lausanne, 1994–2001.
Zeri I Popullitt, Tirana, 1990–.

Websites

Conflict Studies Research Centre/ARAG: www.defac.ac.uk.
International Crisis Group: www.crisisgroup.org, 1997–.

ABBREVIATIONS AND SPELLING CONVENTIONS

In this book the most common names for the different towns and cities of Kosova are used which includes both Serbian and Albanian origin names. In the period since 1999 and international control of Kosova, many Serbian origin names such as *Urosevac* have been effectively replaced by the Albanian name, thus *Ferizaj*. After independence in 2008, this is not the case with all names in daily usage, so Serbian *Podujeve* is still more common than Albanian *Besian* amongst others. I have used the names in most common usage throughout on what I hope is a common sense basis. With independence it is likely that many Serbian origin names will begin to disappear from much usage in daily life, if surviving in official documentation.

I have as far as possible tried to avoid the recurrent use of the many complex abbreviations for organisation names that resulted in a veritable 'alphabet soup' in many international community documents after 1999. I have adopted the convention that the first time that an organisation, political or military movement or non-governmental organisation is mentioned in the text the appropriate abbreviation is given after it, for example Yugoslav People's Army (JNA), or International Crisis Group (ICG). See the list below for some of the most common abbreviations used in the period of the recent conflict.

Basic biographical information on many Kosovar Albanian wartime participants is contained in the International Crisis Group reference document, *Who's Who in the New Kosovo* (2000) www.crisisgroup. org. The Serbian government has also published various material on ethnic Albanian war participants, the largest volume being *Albanian Terrorism and Organised Crime in Kosovo and Metohija*, BIA, Bel-

ABBREVIATIONS AND SPELLING CONVENTIONS

grade, 2003. It contains much material purporting to be objective information that is in fact unsourced and inaccurate speculation and propaganda, although it can be useful in showing family relationships. On the Albanian side, there is a very good biographical record of deceased Kosova Liberation Army members in eleven volumes, to date, *Fenikset e Lirise, Prishtine 2001–*, but no publication on the composition of the army as a whole. The Bush administration's 'banned list' of Kosova Albanians involved in paramilitary activity forbidden to enter the USA that was made in during the Macedonian conflict in 2001 is also available, although it contains many factual inaccuracies. It was never openly published but many photocopied copies are available around Prishtina.

Place name spellings and other geographical coordinates are taken from the excellent *Kosovo Atlas* that was published by the United Nations Humanitarian Community Information Centre (HCIC) in Prishtina in February 2000.

ACRONYMS

AAK	Alliance for the Future of Kosova
AACL	Albanian American Civic League
AKSH	Albanian National Army
ANA	Albanian Army
BBC	British Broadcasting Corporation
CNN	Cable News Network
DAA	Democratic Alliance of Albanians
DPA	Democratic Party of Albanians
DUI	Democratic Union for Integration
EU	European Union
KFOR	Kosovo Force (the NATO peacekeeping mission in Kosova)
KLA	Kosova Liberation Army
LDK	Democratic League of Kosova
LKCK	National Movement for the Liberation of Kosova
LPK	Kosova People's Movement
NAAC	National Albanian-American Council
NATO	North Atlantic Treaty Organisation
NLA	National Liberation Army of Albanians (in Macedonia)
OSCE	Organisation for Security and Cooperation in Europe
PDD	Party for Democratic Action
PDK	Democratic Party of Kosova
PDP	Party of Democratic Prosperity
SHIK	Albanian Intelligence Service
SPS	Socialist Party of Serbia
UCPMB	Liberation Army of Preshevo, Medvedja and Bujanovac
UN	United Nations

INDEX

Aarau: 263

Aaronovitch, David: 3–4

Ademaj, Remzi: death of (1998), 154; founder of KLA, 154

Afghanistan: Operation Enduring Freedom, 253

Agani, Fehmi: 117, 137, 179, 196

Ahmeti, Ali: 50, 90, 129, 133, 169, 245, 250; co-founder of LPK, 236; exile of, 245; family of, 240; leader of LPK, 115; logistics chief of KLA, 168; role in NLA, 238–9, 243

Al Qaeda: 75

Albania: 1, 15–16, 21, 26–7, 31, 33–5, 37, 43–4, 51–2, 55, 62, 66, 69, 83, 102, 105, 110, 115, 122–3, 135, 159, 162, 211, 213, 216, 240, 248; Albanian Defence Academy for Kosovars, 66; Albanian Intelligence Service (SHIK), 75; Albanian Military Academy, 62, 84; Bajram Curri, 131, 170, 180, 228; Black Drin valley, 34, 39; borders of, 19, 34–5, 38, 91, 122, 129, 135, 137, 139–40, 148, 154, 239; cultural revolution, 63; Diber, 39; Dibra, 40; Dukagjini, 130; Durres, 99, 129, 134–5; German Diaspora in, 153; Gjirokastra, 63, 74; government

of, 61, 221; Has, 39, 91, 181; Kukes, 129, 160, 175, 228; LPK network, 90; military of, 63, 74, 141, 182, 220; Mukje, 21; Mulleti, 129; Sigurimi, 39, 61, 74, 91; Tirana, 17, 19, 21, 33–6, 38–9, 48, 54–5, 60–63, 68, 73–76, 81–2, 84, 96–7, 99, 110–11, 113, 115, 117, 123–4, 126–7, 129, 134–6, 141, 146, 157, 159, 168, 170, 180, 192; Tropoja, 39–40, 122, 124, 129–30, 163, 180, 217

Albanian-American Civic League: lobbying activities of, 159

Albanian Communist Party: formation of, 22

Albanian Party of Labour: 39

Albanian Question: 97

Albright, Madeline: 192, 198, 203; memoirs of, 191; US Secretary of State, 146, 157, 179, 191, 196

Alliance for Kosova: 173

Alia, Ramiz: 60, 66; background of, 54; President of Albania, 61

Amnesty International: 66

Aradhen Clirimitare te Pejes: founding of (1991), 62

Austria: 111; Albanian Diaspora in, 124; Vienna, 133, 189, 200

Bajrami, Agim: 124–5

INDEX

Bakalli, Mahmut: chairman of Central Committee of Communist Party of Kosova, 48

Balkan Wars (1912–13): 12, 43, 231

Balli Kombëtar: 8, 21, 26, 47, 97, 123, 197; defeat of (1949), 69, 94, 230; members of, 41, 52; supporters of, 44, 56; Tivat massacre (1945), 31

Becker, Sally: imprisonment of (1998), 145

Bektashi sect: influence of, 23

Belgium: 59; Brussels, 49, 62, 98, 138, 178, 194, 206, 244; The Hague, 2, 252

Bereshova, Liri: background of, 35; family of, 35

Berisha, Sali: 72, 74, 82, 92, 97, 102, 117; administration of, 64, 97, 126; overthrow of (1997), 168; President of Democratic Party, 69

Berne, Swiss capital: 116

Besa: formation of (1990), 62

von Bismarck, Otto: 12

Blair, Tony: 152, 157, 190, 227–9; administration of, 157, 253; British Prime Minister, 151; memoirs of, 190, 207

Bonaparte, Napoleon: 11

Boskovski, Lupo: Macedonian Interior Minister, 237

Bosnia: 21, 68; Sarajevo, 29

Bosnian war (1992–5): 89, 107, 126, 170, 244; Dayton Accord (1995), 72, 74, 82, 92, 96, 103, 190–1; Operation Deliberate Force (1995), 151; Operation Storm (1995), 149; Siege of Sarajevo (1992–5), 152

Brovina, Colonel Qamil: 37

Buja, Rame: 197–8

Buja, Shukri: 124–5

Bujapi, Abedin: KLA commander, 175

Bukharin, Nikolai: 46

Bukoshi, Bujar: 67, 89, 163, 216; background of, 66; LDK 'Prime Minister', 134

Bulatovic, Momir: President of Montenegro, 111

Bulgaria: 173; Batak Massacre (1876), 186; military forces of, 17, 21

Bush, George W.: administration of, 233, 235, 240

Byzantine Empire: 13, 15

Caesar, Julius: 11

Campbell, Alistair: 190

Cara, Indrit: 213

Carcani, Adil: 35

CARE International: reconstruction projects, 229

Catholic Church: 23, 65, 96; Vatican, 56, 95, 137, 217

Ceku, Agim: 65, 150, 154, 216, 228; background of, 149; commander of TMK, 250

ceta: 37, 62, 77–8; concept of, 22; Serbian, 24

Chechnya: First Chechen War (1994–6), 102, 114

Chernomyrdin, Viktor: Russian Special Representative for Yugoslavia, 221

Chetniks: 21, 25, 47

China: 37; Long March (1934–5), 77; sphere of political influence, 39

Chirac, Jacques: President of France, 198

Christianity: 171

Churchill, Winston: 150, 222

Chuvakin, Dimitri: Soviet Ambassador to Albania, 33

Clark, Wesley: 180, 202; meeting with Slobodan Milošević (1999),

366

190; Supreme Allied Commander Europe (SACEUR) of NATO, 174, 190, 193, 196, 207–8, 226
von Clausewitz, Carl: 11
Clinton, Bill: 166; administration of, 163, 193, 195, 206, 233; Monica Lewinsky affair (1998), 163
Cold War: 7, 39, 76, 83, 97–8, 100; end of, 251; power blocs of, 51
Communism: 4, 7, 12, 17, 24, 43–4, 46, 56, 61, 81, 94, 96, 173, 230, 251; appeal of, 22, 43; Chinese, 45; imposition of, 46; revisionist, 56, 94; Soviet, 45; Yugoslav model of, 37, 67, 94, 109
Communist International (Cominform): Tito's break from (1948), 33
Communist Party of Kosova: Central Committee, 48
Community of Sant'Egidio: 95; aims of, 95–6; offices of, 95; personnel of, 98
Congress of Berlin (1878): 54, 251, 255
Conference on Security and Cooperation in Europe (1975): Helsinki Final Act, 1, 98, 127
Conrad, Joseph: *Under Western Eyes*, 59
Contact Group: 175, 198; members of, 135; policy positions of, 146
Cook, Robin: 157, 190, 196; British Foreign Secretary, 151, 199
Covic, Nebosja: 'Programme for the Solution of the Crisis in Pcinja District' (2001), 235
Croatia: 31, 34, 64, 68, 73, 96, 149, 215; military of, 149, 191; Stubicka Toplica, 65; Zagreb, 64, 69; Zagreb Military Academy, 65
Croatian War of Independence (1991–5): Siege of Vukovar (1991), 152

Cuba: 61; Revolution (1953–9), 45, 53
Curri, Bajram: 39–40
Cyprus: example of guerrilla warfare in, 145
Czechoslavkia: Prague, 57

Deakin, William: associates of, 39
Demaci, Adem: 46, 49, 53, 89, 97, 145, 158, 160, 178, 192, 202; associates of, 192; background of, 43; co-founder of LCKK, 48; family of, 43; imprisonment of, 44–6, 48; influence of, 97; KLA Political Spokesman, 196; programme for Revolutionary League for the Unification of the Albanians, 77
Demiri, Alajdin: background of, 116; Macedonian Ambassador to Switzerland, 116
Democratic Army of Greece: 155
Democratic Party of Albania (PDSH): 74; members of, 168
Denmark: 70
Deva, Xhafer: pro-German militia led by, 20–1
Dimitrejevic, General Nebosja: 130
Dini, Lamberto: Italian Foreign Minister, 191
Dimitrov, Georgi: 51
Djindic, Zoran: 235
Djukanovic, Milo: leader of Youth League, 48
Drewienkiewicz, General John: 189

Egypt: Cairo, 39
Eisenhower, Dwight D.: 222
Elshani, Garfurr: 100
European Union (EU): 96, 97, 127, 170, 228, 249, 251; personnel of, 200
Everts, Daan: OSCE director, 123, 181

Feith, Peter: chief international community negotiator, 235

First World War (1914–18): 15, 21, 30, 215, 254; Battle of Vimy Ridge (1917), 187; Treaty of Versailles (1919), 7, 13, 16, 18–19, 39, 53

Forcat e Armatosura te Republikes se Kosoves (FARK): 67, 117, 222; founding of (1990), 65; growth of, 116; links to small arms traders, 170; members of, 109, 157

France: 61, 135, 251; *Le Monde*, 42; military of, 107; Paris, 191, 198

Friedrich Naumann Stiftung: analysis of KLA, 223

Galicia, Shote: folklore surrounding, 20

Gazidede, Bashkim: background of, 75; SHIK Intelligence chief, 75

Geci, Halit: funeral of (1997), 101, 107

Georgievski, Lupjo: Macedonian Prime Minister, 241

Germany: 12, 49–50, 52, 56–7, 64, 69, 111, 133, 135, 150, 180, 193, 236, 240, 246; Albanian Diaspora in, 134, 197; Berlin, 17, 57; Heilbron, 52; military of, 77, 243; Munich, 95, 237; RAF Reindahlen, 181; Ramstein Air Base, 192; Untergrupenbach, 52

Gervalla, Bardosh: murder of, 52

Gervalla, Jusuf: 49, 52; co-founder of LCKK, 48; co-founder of LNCKVSJ, 49; murder of, 52; poetry of, 50

Gjilan, Idris: 230

Gjilane, Mullah: leader of Ballist Prevesho revolt, 94

Gladstone, William: 186

Gligorov, Kiro: 97

Gramsci, Antonio: 45, 51

Greece: 2, 7, 39, 64, 244; Athens, 44, 126; borders of, 63, 105; Civil War (1946–9), 8, 51, 63, 82, 94, 155; economy of, 248–9; Karpenisi, 108; New Democracy, 126; Thessaloniki, 14, 230

Greek Communist Party (KKE): 35; criticisms of, 94

Greek People's Liberation Army (ELAS): 65; origins of, 108

Greek Orthodox Church: 23

Hadri, Enver: background of, 62; leader of Brussels *ceta*, 62

Hadrian: 8

Halimi, Riza: Mayor of Preshevo, 235

Haliti, Xhavit: 50, 73, 75, 100, 108, 110, 115, 133–4, 146, 180, 197, 206; KLA representative in Tirana, 168; leader of LPK, 61

Haradinaj, Daut: 107

Haradinaj, Luan: 100; death of, 91; family of, 71

Haradinaj, Ramush: 50, 91, 116, 121, 135, 153, 172–3, 215; *A Narrative of War and Freedom*, 74, 97; family of, 71; trial of, 252–3

Hasani, Nait: imprisonment of, 111

Haxhiu, Ahmet: 42; background of, 134; leader of LPK, 61

Hayduk: 19

Haziri, Xhavit: leader of LPK, 61

Hill, Christopher: 192; US Ambassador to Macedonia, 153, 178, 188, 200, 242

Hitler, Adolf: 17

Holbrooke, Richard: 157–8, 166, 179; meeting with Slobodan Milošević (1998), 160–1, 165, 171, 178, 186–7, 196, 201–202; US envoy to Balkans, 82, 125, 134, 146

Homeland Calling fund: 167; per-

sonnel of, 75, 100, 255; recipients of, 75
Hoti, Musa: shooting of Yugoslav consular official in Brussels (1981), 49
Howard, Michael: British Shadow Foreign Secretary, 157
Hoxha, Edmond: assassination of (1997), 99; background of, 99–100; funeral of (1997), 99
Hoxha, Enver: 27, 33, 36, 38, 51; Communist forces led by, 21, 146; regime of, 76
Hoxha, Fadil: 37, 47
Human Rights Watch: estimation of population movement during Kosova War, 148; research conducted by, 162
Humolli, Fatmir: influence of, 69
Hungary: borders of, 209
Hurd, Douglas: 95
Hussein, Saddam: 163
Hyseni, Hydajet: background of, 197

Ibrahimi, Lahi: role in coordination of military equipment purchases for KLA, 116
Idris, Mullah: associates of, 232
Imeraj, Nexhat: poetry of, 87
International Criminal Court: 2
International Criminal Tribunal for the former Yugoslavia (ICTY): 5, 84, 253; trial of Ramush Hardinaj, 252–3
International Crisis Group: 161, 194; *Kosova Group*, 127
International Macedonian Revolutionary Organisation (IMRO): 2, 6, 93
Iraq: Operation Desert Fox (1998), 163; Operation Iraqi Freedom (2003–11), 253
Islam: 20, 42, 63, 75, 79, 169, 171,

231, 253; Shia, 23; Sunni, 23, 241
Islamic Intellectuals Association of Albania: members of, 75
Israel: 205; Likud Party, 206; Mossad, 36; Tel Aviv, 206
Italy: 21, 32, 41, 135, 180, 217, 251; Aviano Air Base, 192; Bari, 39; Rome, 5, 17, 95, 113, 135

Jackson, General Mike: 180–1, 227–8; criticisms of, 217; timetable for demobilisation, 225
Jashari, Adem: 50, 53, 62–3, 68, 112–14, 124; first commander of KLA, 20; meeting with Ibrahim Rugova (1991), 64
Jashari, Ismet (Commander Kumannovo): 124–5
Jihadism: Egyptian, 75
Jovanovic, Zivadin: Yugoslav Foreign Minister, 184

Kacaks: 18–19, 123; tradition of, 66
Kacanik Constitution: 66
Kadare, Ismail: 13
Karolli, Kostas: background of, 62–3
Katundarija: concept of, 45–6
Kenya: example of guerrilla warfare in, 145
Kingdom of Yugoslavia (Kingdom of Serbs, Croats and Slovenes): 4, 6, 13, 28, 38, 243; occupied by Nazi forces (1941), 14, 17–18
Kissinger, Henry: 171
Klugman, James: background of, 39
Kolarov, Vasil: presence at Pan-Slav Congress (1946), 26
Konushevcsi, Ilir (Commander Megimit): assassination of, 91
Kosova: 1, 7, 18, 21, 28, 31–3, 42–3, 53, 62, 65, 83, 107, 109,

132; Batusche, 122; borders of, 15, 19, 34, 71–2, 83, 99, 109, 122, 124, 137, 139, 154, 162, 165, 169, 198, 230, 235, 237, 250, 254; Bukosaj, 200; Burrell, 47; Carraleve, 147; Catholic population of, 173; Constitution (1991), 158; Decan, 29, 85, 102, 122, 132–3, 137, 172, 188, 196, 217; declaration of independence (1990), 65; Dobratin, 165; Dollova, 136; Dragash, 169; Drenica, 8–9, 16, 19, 24, 29, 34, 40, 48, 55, 69, 71, 82, 84, 101, 106, 110–11, 115, 120, 123, 125, 129, 137, 147, 152, 160, 162, 168, 172, 175, 180, 214, 216, 229, 234, 251; Drenica revolt (1944–9), 24–5, 28, 31–2, 55, 73, 94, 106, 141; Drenoc, 137; Dukagjini, 49, 55, 71–2, 126, 153, 172, 218, 251; ethnic Albanian population of, 2–4, 9, 12–13, 17–18, 22, 31–2, 44, 49, 52, 56, 60, 64, 66, 72, 89, 92, 95, 99, 103, 106–7, 139, 142–3, 158, 178, 180, 192, 203, 207, 211–12, 216, 221, 226–7, 230, 250, 252, 254; ethnic Montenegrin population of, 18; ethnic Serbian population of, 12–13, 18, 54, 68, 95, 102, 108, 138–9, 142, 177, 182, 188, 212, 219, 222–3; Ferizaj (Urosevac), 25, 49, 53, 93, 113, 123, 125, 168, 187, 209, 211–14; Fushe Kosova, 139; Gjakova, 39–40, 47, 96, 122–3, 131, 173, 196, 217; Gjilane, 17, 49, 157, 162, 194, 233; Gllogjan, 71, 127; Gllogoc, 111; Glodjane, 153, 163; Glogovac, 176; Gorazdovac, 136; Grabanica, 136–7; Hani I Elezit, 15; Independence of (2008), 10, 248, 252–3; Izniq, 89, 154–5; Junik, 29, 89,

99, 122–3, 129, 132–3, 152, 163, 172; Kacanik, 17, 93, 125, 139; Kamenitsa, 157; Kepuze, 137; Kline, 86, 89, 113, 136–7; Koshare, 122–3, 131–2; Koshare Pass, 62, 181, 217; Lake Battlaves, 162, 166; Lapusnik, 147; Lipjan: 125, 189; Llap, 41, 71–3, 77–8, 85, 88, 90, 134, 157, 182–3, 187, 194–5, 198; Luzhan, 89; Maleshevo, 113, 137, 141, 153, 167; Mazhiq, 167; Medenic, 167; Metohija, 33; Mitrovica, 13–14, 16, 24, 41, 46, 56, 73, 104, 123, 141–2, 160, 165, 167, 183, 187, 209, 229; Molliq, 122; Nivikaz, 122; Novo Berde, 15–16, 162; *opstinas*, 225, 229; Pashtrik, 172; Pec/Peja, 14, 40, 44, 62, 85, 96, 122, 124, 131–4, 136–7, 147, 149, 153, 163, 170; Podujevo (Besian), 29, 41, 71, 77, 85, 88–9, 92, 113, 142, 181, 188, 214; Ponoshec (Ponosevac), 131–2; Prekaz, 55, 62, 100, 111–13, 115, 121, 123, 127; Prekaz I Eperme (Gornja Obrinje), 176; Prishtina, 15, 17, 28–9, 40–1, 43, 45, 48–9, 51, 53–4, 56, 60, 68–9, 92, 94, 99, 101, 105, 113, 120, 125, 131, 133, 136–7, 139, 141, 147, 149, 162, 167, 171, 175–6, 185, 187–8, 192, 195–9, 209–11, 214, 217, 228–9, 232, 236, 240, 253; Prizren, 15, 23, 39, 104, 139–41, 147, 153–4, 156–7, 160, 163, 168, 176, 182–3, 186, 194, 196, 212, 232; Quaf e Morina pass, 157, 176; Racak, 153, 159, 185–6, 189–90, 194–5, 198; Rahavec, 72, 125, 132, 137, 139–40, 143–6, 148, 153, 157, 182, 187; Roma population of, 212, 223; Rrashan, 167; Rugova Pass, 14, 170; Sar, 172;

Scutari, 15; Serbian conquest of
(1912), 12; Shala, 156; Shkodra,
15; Shtime: 125, 187, 189; Stari
Trg, 14; Suva Reka, 138–9, 147,
154, 186, 188, 210; Theranda,
15; Trepca, 14, 25, 56; Turkish population of, 23; Vushtrri,
37, 41, 71, 73, 88, 93, 104, 125,
141, 160, 200, 209; Vranje, 206;
Zajm, 136, 165; Zvecan Castle,
13–14
Kosova Committee: 267; aims of,
19
Kosova Democratic League (LDK):
42, 46, 59–60, 82, 98, 109, 134,
172–3, 237; founding of (1989),
56; members of, 38, 60, 68, 96,
109, 117, 120–1, 137, 158, 179,
197, 232; model of, 65; recipient
of 'Homeland Calling' fund, 75
Kosovo Diplomatic Observer Mission (KDOM): 189, 215; change
to KVM 147, 196; staff of, 147,
158, 166
Kosova Liberation Army (KLA): 3,
6–7, 12–13, 16, 18–19, 27, 30,
36, 40, 50–2, 63, 65, 69–70, 73,
76, 83, 85, 88, 92, 94, 100, 117,
119, 125, 140, 144, 149, 156,
161, 166, 172, 178, 184–5, 190,
209, 218, 230–1, 237, 246, 251–
2, 254; commanders of, 3, 20,
47, 97, 107, 167, 172, 175, 197,
200–1, 213, 235; defeat at Rahovec (1998), 125, 143, 147, 152–
3, 157, 182; formal demobilisation of (1999), 10, 227; founding
of (1990), 59; funding of, 116;
General Staff, 130, 133–4, 141,
144, 150, 154, 158, 174, 176,
192, 195, 197, 200, 202, 215;
growth of, 121; ideology of, 77;
merger agreement with LKCK
(1998), 133; memorials, 254; military assets of, 148; Operative

Zones, 233; records produced
by, 5; Serbian view of, 1; soldiers
of, 112, 141–2, 180, 201, 218,
225, 253; supporters of, 149; territory controlled by, 20, 137–8;
territory seizure tactics of, 141;
volunteers, 79; war identity of,
155–6
Kosova People's Movement (LPK):
42, 52, 56, 69, 75, 78, 83, 86,
90, 93, 98, 119–20, 125, 154,
167, 191; formerly LPRK, 62;
ideology of, 109, 148, 156; members of, 47, 54, 61, 67, 100,
108, 112, 115, 197, 231, 235,
238; structure of, 46, 99; *Zeri I
Kosoves*, 111, 149
Kosova Red Front: formation of
(1979), 77
Kosova Security Force: proposal for
creation of, 249
Kosova Verification Mission
(KVM): 160–2, 173–4, 186,
189, 191, 206, 215; deployment
agreement, 163, 171; formerly
KDOM, 147, 196; shortcom-
ings of, 161, 178–9, 181; staff of,
174, 183–4, 188–9, 199
Kosova War (1998–9): 2, 5, 8, 15,
29, 65, 105, 186; Krusche Massacre (1999), 186; NATO entry
into (1999), 5–6, 142, 215; Operation Allied Force (1999), 9–10,
115, 124, 171, 193, 210–2, 214;
Operation Horn, 145, 180, 220;
Operation Horseshoe, 90, 92,
106, 137, 207, 211–12; Operation Nimble Lion, 192–3; Prekaz
Massacre (1998), 115, 123, 217;
Racak Massacre (1999), 153,
159, 185–6, 189–90, 194–5;
Rambouillet Agreement (1999),
191, 198, 200, 202, 215–16, 227,
255
Kosovo Protection Corps (KPC):

227, 249; members of, 234; pro-
posal for demobilisation of, 249
Kostunica, Vojislav: President of
Federal Republic of Yugoslavia,
249
Kosumi, Bajram: 197
Kouchner, Bernard: 226; UN Repre-
sentative, 222
Krasniqi, Ahmet: 153; murder of
(1998), 111, 157
Krasniqi, Florin: arms imported by,
159
Krasniqi, Jakup: 197; KLA press
spokesman, 158, 188
Krasniqi, Metush: co-founder of
LNCKVSJ, 49
Krasniqi-Rexha, Ardian: 91; leader
of Besa, 62
Kurti, Albin: arrest of (1999), 210;
associates of, 192; background
of, 158–9
Kusovac, Zoran: writings of, 191

Lama, General Kudusi: 40, 130
Lawrence, T.E.: 70–1, 86
League of Yugoslav Communists:
banning of opposition to, 26
Lebanon: Syrian Invasion of (1976),
205
Leka, King: supporters of, 127
Lenin, Vladimir: 46
Levizja per Republiken Socialiste
Sqiptare ne Jugosllavi (LRSSHJ):
merger with OMLK and
PKMLSHJ (1982), 50
Levizje e Shqiptareve ne Maqedoni:
founding of (1968), 236
Levizjen Popullore per Republiken
e Kosoves (LPRK): 52–3, 69;
change to LPK (1990), 62; forma-
tion of (1982), 50; ideology of,
109; members of, 62
Levizjes per Clirimin Kombetar te
Kosoves (LCKK): 48
Levizja Nacional-Climitare e Koso-

voes dhe Viseve Shqiptare ne
Jugosllavi (LNCKVSJ): 49
Lidhja Demokratike e Shqiptare te
Kroacise (LDSHK): structure of,
65
Limaj, Fatmir: 90, 115, 124–5, 144;
military activity of, 133
Livy: 2
Lladrovci, Fehmi: background of,
64
Lushtaku, Sami: KLA senior com-
mander, 175

Macedonian Orthodox Church: 23
Macedonian Question: re-emer-
gence of, 7
Mackinlay, John: *The Insurgent
Archipelago: from Mao to Bin
Laden*, 251
Maclean, Fitzroy: associates of, 39;
sponsorship of Josip Broz Tito,
150; writings of, 150–1
Mahmuti, Bardhyl: 84, 99, 225;
background of, 146; imprison-
ment of, 47; local spokesman for
KLA, 146, 167
Majko, Pandeli: Albanian Prime
Minister, 157, 168
Malaya: example of guerrilla war-
fare in, 145
Maloku, Naim: 65
Maoism: 37; views of insurgency,
251
Marjanovic, Mirko: Serbian Prime
Minister, 166
Markiste-Leniniste e Kosoves
(MLK) members of, 47
Markovic, Mira: family of, 47
Marovic, Svetozar: Montenegrin
Parliament Speaker, 175
Marxism: 19–20, 37, 42–3, 68, 70,
84, 155; Balkan, 51; classical, 52;
historical and political traditions
of, 108; insurgency theory, 149;

personal variants of, 45; Yugoslav, 51

Marxist-Leninism: 22, 42, 46, 64, 70, 98, 148; orthodox, 52; theory of guerrilla warfare, 70; view of political consciousness, 37

Mashirovka: concept of, 7

Mazower, Mark: 6, 51

Meksi, Alexander: Albanian Prime Minister, 82

Mihajlovic, Draza: 24; royalist forces led by, 21

Military and Professional Resources Inc. (MPRI): personnel of, 151

Milo, Pascal: Albanian Foreign Minister, 137

Milošević, Slobodan: 2, 8–9, 54, 61, 68, 83, 87–9, 91, 95–6, 98, 102, 104, 106, 115, 121, 126, 136, 142–3, 145, 148, 157, 166, 171, 174, 176–7, 180, 191, 200, 206, 222; alliances formed by, 134; chairman of National Defence Council, 92; family of, 47; leader of SPS, 110, 134, 145; meeting with General Wesley Clark and General Klaus Neumann (1999), 190; meeting with Richard Holbrooke (1998), 160–1, 165, 171, 178, 186–7, 196, 201–202; overthrow of (2000), 235, 253; preference for verbal communication, 5; prevention of OSCE's entry into Kosova, 96; regime of, 4–6, 17, 46, 59, 72, 83, 103, 127, 132, 149, 207, 226, 252, 254; view of KLA, 105

Milutinovic, Milan: President of Serbia, 203

Mitsotakis, Constantine: Greek Prime Minister, 126

Mladic, Ratko: 177

Montenegro: 14, 21, 23–4, 39, 65, 162, 211; borders of, 110; Durmintor, 6; military of, 30; Podgoritsa (Titograd), 48; Tivat, 31, 44

Mugosa, Dusan: 22

Musliu, Shafket: role in founding UCPMB, 231

Mussolini, Benito: 17; death of (1945), 222

Mustafa, Rrustem (Commander Remi): 67, 135, 171, 195–6; meeting with William Walker (1998), 183; writings of, 78

Nano, Fatos: Albanian Prime Minister, 115, 126, 157, 163, 168, 218

National Democratic Party (NDA): 239

National Liberation Army (NLA): 240, 242–3; members of, 237–9; territory held by, 244–5

National Movement for the Liberation of Kosova (LKCK): 69, 73, 84, 154, 191; *Climiri*, 83; creation of (1993), 68; ideology of, 148; members of, 197; merger agreement with KLA General Staff (1998), 133; view of NATO, 194

Nationalism: 7, 21, 25, 79, 97, 158; Albanian, 6, 8, 40, 48, 140, 227; cultural, 41; extremist, 72; fundamentalist, 146; Greek, 54; Marxist, 90; Serbian, 92, 207, 249; ultra, 72, 134

Netherlands: Holland, 180

Neumann, General Klaus: meeting with Slobodan Milošević (1999), 190

Nixon, Richard: Watergate Scandal (1972–4), 2

North Atlantic Treaty Organization (NATO): 56, 68, 96, 124, 126, 135, 138, 145, 149, 152–3, 157–8, 160, 166, 177, 185, 192, 199, 205, 218, 220, 228, 233, 236, 248, 251, 254–5; Concept Operation Plan (CONOPLAN) 10601, 193; entry into Kosova War

(1999), 5–6, 215; Kosovo Force (KFOR), 10, 15, 84, 216, 222, 226, 228–30, 240, 250; LKCK view of, 194; members of, 180, 193, 203, 249; Operation Allied Force (1999), 9–10, 115, 124, 171, 193, 210–12, 214; personnel of, 98, 174, 178, 183, 190, 193, 241–3, 246
Northern Ireland: Good Friday Agreement (1998), 55

Odalovic, Veljko: call for UN to designate KLA as terrorist organisation (1998), 183
Ojdanic, Dragi: 176–7; spokesman of Serbian Ministry of Defence, 145
Organisation for Security and Cooperation in Europe (OSCE): 198, 211; personnel of, 123, 181, 183, 186, 200; prevention of entry into Kosova by Slobodan Milosevic, 96
Organizata Marksiste-Leniniste e Kosoves (OMLK): founding of (1976), 48; merger with PKMLSHJ and LRSSHJ (1982), 50
Organizata per Bashkimin e Trojeve Shqiptare: 44
Ostremi, General Gezim: 250; leader of NLA, 238
Ottoman Empire: 4, 6–7, 13, 15, 19, 22, 28, 35, 71, 230–1, 239; Constantinople, 15; culture of, 45; military of, 12, 14, 160, 177; *vilayet* system, 24, 39
Oxfam International: reconstruction projects, 229

Pajaziti, Zahir: 71, 73; background of, 84; killing of, 90
Pan-Slav Congress (1946): attendees of, 26

Papovic, Radovan: assassination of (1997), 73
Partia Komuniste Marksiste-Leniniste e Shqiptare nen Yugoslavi (PKMLSHJ): merger with OMLK and LRSSHJ (1982), 50
Partisans: 21, 63, 86, 109–10; commanders of, 22; ethnic Albanian members of, 24, 35; mechanised troops of, 28
Patten, Christopher: 95
Pavkovic, General Nebosja: 145, 199–200, 214
People's Liberation Army: 21
Perisic, General Momcilo: 175; Chief of General Staff of VJ, 145; removed from post (1998), 102, 146, 176–7; Yugoslav Chief of Staff, 123
Perritt, Henry: *Kosovo Liberation Army: The Inside Story of an Insurgency*, 3
Peter II, King: 24; exile of (1941), 18
Petritsch, Wolfgang: EU Special Envoy, 200
Philby, Kim: *My Secret War*, 3
Poland: 187; Warsaw, 57
Polluzha, Shaban: attack on Trepca mine complex (1944), 25
Prishtina, Hasan: 40, 52
Prizren League: 140
Procopius: *History of the Wars*, 1; *Secret History*, 1
Provisional Government of Kosova: destruction of, 222, 226–7, 250; personnel of, 227; significance of, 216
Provisional Irish Republican Army (IRA): model of, 55, 60, 75
Pushkolli, Dr Fehmi: writings of, 85

Qerimi, Ramiz: 64
Qira, Zijadin: 37, 109; arrest of (1951), 36; associates of, 38; background of, 34–5; cover story of, 36; political views of 35–6

Qosja, Rexhep: 99, 197

Radek, Karl: 46
Radio Free Kosova: 211; establishment of, 162
Radosalijevic, Goran: role in Racak Massacre (1999), 189
Ramadani, Agim: 217
Ramadani, Hasan: background of, 77; imprisonment of, 77; murder of (1994), 77
Ramet, Sabrina P.: 4
Rankin, Sir Reginald: *The Inner History of the Balkan Wars* (1931), 2
Rankovic, Alexander Leka: 32, 42, 44
Raznatovic, Zeljko (Arkan): 68, 123; head of Serb Volunteer Guard, 88; paramilitary units (Tigers) commanded by, 105, 112, 211, 219, 231; visit to Kosova, 88
Republic of Ireland: Easter Uprising (1916), 113
Republic of Macedonia (FYROM): 4, 24, 54, 62, 65, 110, 135, 138, 181, 187, 190, 195, 211, 237, 253; Aracinovo, 243; Bitola, 245; borders of, 34–5, 40, 71, 110, 136, 139, 154, 237; ethnic Albanian population of, 35, 167–8, 170, 244–6; Gostivar, 169, 238, 241, 245; Haracinje, 237; Independence of (1991), 237; Insurgency (2001) 7–8, 10, 69, 169, 234–5, 239; Kicevo, 244; Kumanovo, 243; LPK presence in, 84; Mavrovo, 245; military of, 237, 237, 243–4; Mt. Grammos, 155; Mt. Vitsi, 155; Ohrid, 35, 241, 245; Ohrid Accords (2001), 245–6, 252; Oslomej: 240; Plav, 170; Podgorica, 111; Popova Shapka incident (2001),

242; River Ibar, 142; Selce, 239; Shipkovica, 234, 239; Skopje, 14, 16, 24, 170, 175, 232, 236, 240–5; Struga, 17, 34–5, 241, 245; Tanusche, 237, 239; Tearce, 237, 239; Tetovo, 47–8, 97, 116, 160, 168–70, 236–9, 242, 245; Vardar River, 14; Veleshte, 34–5
Revolutionary League for the Unification of the Albanians (LRBSH): 44; founding of (1964), 42; members of, 42
Roberts, Ivor: British Ambassador to Yugoslavia (1993–6), 95, 151
Robertson, George: NATO General Secretary, 242
Roman Empire: 15, 28, 105; fall of, 8; Rome, 247, 254
Romania: 173
Ruehe, Volker: German Defence Minister, 159
Rugova, Ibrahim: 80, 83, 89, 127, 133, 145, 161, 172, 191, 206, 215–16, 222, 226, 238; leader of LDK, 38, 46, 56, 60, 65, 68, 75, 94, 96, 108, 116, 120–1, 158, 197, 218; meeting with Adem Jashari (1991), 64; strategy of pacifism, 98, 101; supporters of, 154, 199
Russian Empire: military of, 214–15
Russian Federation: 135, 205; initial support for Slobodan Milošević, 221; Moscow, 5

Salihu, Jashar: 99
Sallust: 2
Sandjak: 31; Novi Sad, 209
Second Balkan War (1913): 35
Second World War (1939–45): 6–7, 13, 21, 23, 35, 43, 45, 47–8, 52, 54, 59, 61–2, 71, 83, 87, 97, 100, 110, 123; Auschwitz concentration camp, 187; Battle of Berlin

(1945), 140; Communist movements during, 109; Drenica revolt (1944–9), 24–5, 28, 31–2, 55, 73, 94, 106; popular resistance movements during, 108; resistance effort guidance literature, 85; theatres of, 156, 222

Selimi, Rexhep: 71, 73, 75, 107; KLA General Staff commander, 144

Selimi, Suleyman: 200; KLA commander, 84

Serbia: 6, 14, 24, 29, 39, 75, 103, 136, 183, 205, 248; Belgrade, 5, 8–9, 16, 19, 26–9, 32–5, 38, 41–4, 47–9, 54, 56, 60, 85, 87–8, 91, 93, 95–6, 104, 106, 110, 119, 122–4, 126–7, 130–1, 133–4, 137, 139–45, 154, 156, 158, 160–1, 165–6, 171, 176, 178, 199–200, 217–18, 221, 230, 233, 235, 240–1, 247–50, 253; Bor, 32; *Borba*, 42; borders of, 99, 162, 165, 235; government of, 179; 'Greater Serbia' project, 248; Leskovac, 104; Ministry of Defence, 145; Ministry of Interior Affairs (MUP), 86–7, 101–2, 106, 122, 127–9, 131, 133, 135, 138, 144, 152, 161, 173, 175, 181, 187, 195, 199, 201, 207, 207, 212, 214–15, 218; National Defence Council, 92; Nis, 53, 71, 96, 102, 104–5, 117, 124, 129, 140, 162, 211, 230, 232; Preshevo, 65–6, 230–33, 236, 239, 242, 252; Preshevo Valley, 4, 65, 241, 250; River Danube, 32; River Ibar, 142; Special Counter-Terrorist Unit (SAJ), 215; Special Operations Unit (JSO), 131, 133, 136, 190, 237; Vranje, 71

Serbian-Montenegrin Federation: separation of (2006), 9

Serbian Orthodox Church: 14, 18, 23, 249–50

Serbian Radical Party (SRP): 177; coalition formed with SPS (1998), 134; paramilitary units ('White Tigers') of, 212, 219

Serbs: 9, 12, 43, 68, 121, 127; population of Kosova, 12–13, 18, 54, 68, 95, 102, 108; view of KLA, 1, 3

Sesejl, Vojislav: leader of SRP, 134, 177, 212

Shala, Shaban: KLA commander, 167

Shaqiri, Xhezair (Commander Hoxha): 243; role in Insurgency in Republic of Macedonia (2001), 239

Sheholli, Maliq: execution of (1997), 100

Shehu, Mehmet: 22, 34, 146; communication with Josef Stalin, 33; Communist forces led by, 25

Short, General Mike: 206, 220; head of KFOR, 222

Simatovic, Frenki: JSO units commanded by, 137, 190

Simnica, Drita: memoirs of, 156

Sinn Fein: ideology of, 75

Skanderberg, George Kastrioti: grave of, 99

Slovenia: 34

Socialist Federal Republic of Yugoslavia: 3–4, 7, 47, 65; State Security Administration (UDBA), 3, 29, 41, 62, 77, 127, 135, 215

Socialist Party of Serbia (SPS): 89; coalition with SRP (1998), 134; members of, 110, 145

Solana, Javier: Secretary General of NATO, 98, 183, 206

South Africa: Second Boer War (1899–1902), 11, 87

Soviet Union (USSR): 27, 36; Ministry of Foreign Affairs (MFA), 33; Moscow, 6, 27, 33–4; Red Army, 22, 24; sphere of political influence, 39

Spain: 193, 251; Civil War (1936–9), 22, 25, 33, 59, 70, 86, 132, 218

Spanish Popular Front: influence of, 22

Stalin, Josef: 31, 33, 35–6; communication with Mehmet Shehu, 33; ideology of, 41

Stambuk, Vladimir: Vice President of Serbia, 211

Stanisic, Jovan: Serbian security chief, 106

Starinov, Anna: background of, 70–1

Stojicic, Radovan: Serbian Police Minister, 106

Sullivan, Sean: chief international community negotiator, 235

Sweden: 70

Switzerland: 50, 52, 54–6, 69–70, 76, 107, 109–10, 236, 245–6; Albanian Diaspora in, 124, 153, 155, 197, 229; Basel, 67; Berne, 67, 116; Geneva, 54, 66, 85, 136; KLA presence in, 225; LDK presence in, 67; LPK Exterior presence in, 64–5, 75, 98, 107, 112, 125, 131, 167–8, 197, 238; Perparimi club, 75; Zofingen, 66; Zurich, 54, 59, 65–7, 69, 75, 121, 133, 174, 180

Syla, Azem: 197–8

Syria: Occupation of Lebanon (1976–2006), 205

Tartt, Donna: *The Secret History*, 2

Teresa, Mother: 95; death of (1997), 89

Thaçi, Hashim: 2, 50, 53, 75, 90, 110, 115, 120, 124, 127–8, 135, 158, 180, 191–92, 197, 199, 201, 206, 215, 218, 222, 250; attempted assassination of (1998), 111; background of, 121; family of, 69; head of Provisional

Government of Kosova, 227; KLA Political Spokesman, 72, 144; Kosova Prime Minister, 67, 185, 252; member of LPRK, 67

Thaci, Menduh: 97, 168; background of, 169

Tito, Josip Broz: 4, 7, 16, 24, 26, 31–2, 37, 39, 44, 46–7, 51, 56, 62, 86, 94, 109, 176, 184, 207, 230; associates of, 39; break from Cominform (1948), 33; Communist forces led by, 19, 21; criticisms of, 43; death of (1980), 9; forced emigration of Albanians to Turkey under, 28; ideology of, 41; reform policies of, 37; repression of Albanian nationalism under, 8; sponsors of, 150; view of Albanians, 26–7

Tolaj, Agron: imprisonment of, 111

Tolbukhin, Marshal Fedor: presence at Pan-Slav Congress (1946), 26

Trajkovski, Boris: 242; President of Republic of Macedonia, 241

Trotsky, Leon: 46

Tudjman, Franjo: 67; President of Croatia, 64

Turkey: 15–16, 35, 43, 45, 194, 251; forced emigration of Albanians to, 28, 43–4, 168; Istanbul, 44, 168

Ukraine: 244

United Kingdom (UK): 6, 93, 135, 145, 150, 250; Conservative Party, 95, 157; Defence Intelligence Service (DIS), 151; Foreign and Commonwealth Office, 98, 150–1; government of, 95; Greenham Common Peace Camp, 135; Hereford, 180; London, 18, 98, 133, 145, 150, 181, 202, 227, 229; military of, 77, 107, 180, 217, 227–8, 238; Ministry of Defence, 206; Navy of,

207; Royal Air Force (RAF), 192;
Secret Intelligence Service (MI6),
150; Special Air Service (SAS),
107, 180–1, 220–1; *The Times*,
42; Whitehall, 226
United Nations (UN): 17, 95, 163;
Geneva Conventions, 114; High
Commissioner for Refugees
(UNHCR), 136; Interim Administration Mission in Kosovo
(UNMIK), 95, 210, 226, 228–30,
240, 252–3; international arms
embargo, 103, 237; Peacekeepers, 243; personnel of, 217, 222;
recognition of Kosovan Independence by members of, 248; Resolution 1199, 166; Resolution
1244, 222, 226; Security Council, 220, 226
United States of America (USA): 2,
31–2, 36, 38–9, 56, 70, 75, 89,
105, 126, 130, 142, 145, 150,
171, 205, 218, 250; 9/11 attacks,
75, 235; Air Force (USAF), 171,
174, 192, 221; Albanian Diaspora in, 76, 127, 159, 197, 218,
232, 241; Central Intelligence
Agency (CIA), 75–6, 174, 179–
80, 193, 220; Congress, 193;
Constitution of, 44; Defence
Intelligence Agency (DIA), 151,
174; Department of Defence,
249; Federal Bureau of Investigation (FBI), 159; 'Grand Strategy' of, 248; House of Representatives, 163; military of, 77,
207, 238; Navy of, 194; New
York, 36; Pentagon, 147, 151,
180, 182, 191–92, 194, 198, 206;
State Department, 82, 146, 157,
179, 202, 206; student movements in, 47; Washington DC, 5,
31, 61, 134, 147, 151, 179, 202–
3, 229, 233, 249
Ushtria Climitare e Presheves Med-

vegjes dhe Bujanocit (UCPMB):
234; formation of (1999), 231–
2; lack of initial military identity,
233; military assets of, 233; personnel of, 234, 239, 241; supporters of, 232; surrender of
(2001), 234

Védrine, Hubert: French Foreign
Minister, 199
Veliu, Fazli: 50, 84, 168, 238,
250; arrest and imprisonment of
(1999), 236, 240; background
of, 240; co-founder of LPK, 236;
family of, 240; supporters of, 69
Velouchiotis, Aris: 108
Veseli, Kadri: 71
Vickers, Miranda: *The Albanian
Question—Reshaping the Bal-
kans*, 1
Vieria de Mello, Sergio: 216
Vietnam: 45
Volleback, Kurt: 200
Vukamonovic, Svetozar (General
Tempo): criticisms of KKE, 94

Walker, William: 186, 188–90;
KVM chief, 189; meeting with
Rrustem Mustafa (1998), 183
War on Terror: 2
West, Nigel: *The Secret War for the
Falklands* (1931), 2
Wilson, Woodrow: 38–9

Xhaferi, Arben: 47–8, 97, 245, 250;
background of, 244; influence of,
168–9
Xhemali, Emrush: 99; background
of, 90; founder of LPK, 90

Young Pioneers: 43
Youth League: members of, 48
Yugoslav National Army (VJ): 7,
11, 86, 88, 92, 102–4, 119–
20, 124, 130, 135–6, 136, 152,

155, 157, 161, 171–2, 174, 176, 182, 186, 195, 201–202, 207, 212, 217, 234, 246, 252; bases of, 117; commanders of, 122, 146, 183; doctrine of, 9; General Staff, 145; infantry shortages, 160, 178; military assets of, 132–3, 144, 148, 153, 162–3, 167, 175, 199, 206, 214–15, 219, 228, 231, 233; permanent presence in Kosovo, 104, 211; regiments of, 129; shelling of villages by, 155; use of anti-personnel mines by, 132

Yugoslav People's Army (JNA): 7, 41, 53, 60, 74, 104, 128, 152, 246; doctrine of, 9; former personnel of, 149, 238; Kosovar conscripts, 41; Prishtina Corps, 9, 40, 53, 89, 96, 102, 123, 192, 200

Yugoslavia: 30, 34; collapse of, 8

Zeka, Kadri: murder of, 52
Zemaj, Tahir: background of, 117;
Zervas, Napoleon: leader of EDES, 109
Zimmerman, Warren: US Ambassador to Serbia, 60
Zog, King: 19, 39
Zurapi, Bismil: KLA General Staff commander, 144
Zurich, city: 69, 75, 121, 174, 260, 261
Zurich Kosova Democratic League: Kosova Solidarity Fund, 66